HD 6079 .W56 1984

S0-BSS-617

Women and trade unions in
eleven industrialized

WOMEN AND TRADE UNIONS

IN ELEVEN INDUSTRIALIZED

COUNTRIES

Women in the Political Economy,
a series edited by Ronnie J. Steinberg

WOMEN
AND
TRADE UNIONS

IN ELEVEN INDUSTRIALIZED

COUNTRIES

Edited by
Alice H. Cook,
Val R. Lorwin,
and
Arlene Kaplan Daniels

 Temple University Press
Philadelphia

Temple University Press, Philadelphia 19122
© 1984 by Temple University. All rights reserved
Published 1984
Printed in the United States of America

Library of Congress Cataloging in Publication Data

Main entry under title:

Women and trade unions in eleven industrialized countries.

(Women in the political economy)
Bibliography: p.
Includes index.
1. Women in trade-unions—Case studies. I. Cook,
Alice Hanson. II. Lorwin, Val R. (Val Rogin),
1907–   . III. Daniels, Arlene Kaplan, 1930–
IV. Series.
HD6079.W56 1983   331.4   83-17946
ISBN 0-87722-319-X

To Madge

CONTENTS

FIGURES

TABLES

Women and Trade Unions
in eleven industrialized
countries

1 INTRODUCTION

Alice H. Cook

This book is about the variety of women's experiences with trade union organization in developed countries with market economies. The overwhelming common experience, I believe, was that of industrialization and the accompanying rise and persistence of strong labor organizations. Recent history has seen women moving massively into the world of work, and their numbers in the unions too are growing rapidly.

Here I want to give an overview of women's common experience and to note some of the modifications that have arisen through special circumstances in individual nations. Differences from country to country stem in part from the uniqueness of each national economy, its traditional views on women's roles, its educational system, and to some degree the structures and ideologies of its labor unions. Thus, history and tradition are important factors in the analysis; similarly, the rate and scope of change modify history differentially. Our ultimate question is how much the unions as powerful social institutions have come to recognize, influence, and integrate into their organizations changes in women's status. First, however, I offer some general considerations about our two major variables—women and unions—as background to the problems they both must face.

WOMEN IN THE LABORFORCE

During both world wars women were actively recruited into the workforces of their countries—even the neutral ones—only to be summarily sent home when armies of men were demobilized and returned to claim "their" jobs. The post–World War II boom soon brought women back, partly because they were needed to fill the places of men who were killed or wounded or imprisoned, but mainly because the shifts in life styles on the one hand and in production methods on the other, plus the growth of the service and white-collar sectors, caused employers to seek out women to

3

fill jobs on assembly lines and in offices, supermarkets, schools, hospitals and clinics, banks, insurance companies, restaurants, and hotels.

Whereas in 1950 the female participation rate in the countries we present here ranged from 35 percent in Sweden to 60 percent in Finland, with France and Denmark at 50 percent and Ireland, Italy, Norway, and the United States in the range between 32 and 40 percent, by 1977 the figures for all countries except Ireland and Italy had moved to or above the 50 percent range, Sweden—with 70 percent of its women working—being at the top.

The female share of the labor force is highest in Finland, Sweden, and Denmark (46, 44, and 42 percent respectively). The United States and Japan follow closely (40 percent), and Germany, the United Kingdom, Italy, and France are just behind (38 percent). Only Ireland (27.5 percent) still remains in the range typical of the fifties.[1]

An experience common to most industrialized countries is the rapid increase in participation in the labor force by married women and mothers, including mothers of preschool children, many of whom are single parents. Characteristic of these developments are new demands on the national infrastructure, unanticipated when social policies were first worked out in the postwar years, for transportation, training institutions, and agencies caring for children and the elderly. Characteristic too are the halting and piecemeal adjustments most countries have made in their labor market policy to accommodate women's enlarged role as wage earners. Segregation of jobs into "men's" and "women's" work greatly exacerbates this lack of accommodation to the overarching problem of equality as a social issue. The problems that most women face in entering the labor market, traceable as they are to gender differentiation in job assignment, become personal rather than social.

The tardy and disjointed adjustment of labor market institutions to women's new economic role is evidence of the failure to attack continuing job segregation as a central element in women's disadvantagement. Moreover, segregation is aggravated by the almost total feminization of the occupations in which women work: in offices, banks, and communications, in health services, education, social work, and the assembly of manufactured articles. Nor is segregation limited to selected occupations; it pervades whole industries and branches of the national economies. These sectors tend to fall outside the purview of established unions and remain largely unorganized (and are considered unorganizable). Job segregation, by isolating women in a limited number of crowded—even overcrowded—occupations, promotes low pay and low mobility. And these elements in turn produce a kind of stalemate in women's occupations, making them unattractive for men to enter and difficult for women to escape.

As a consequence, the advocates of equal opportunity have sought to open "men's" jobs to women. The measures they have advanced include

subsidies to employers and training institutions, equal opportunity legislation, educational programs for young women and their parents, and special
vocational counseling for women of all ages. The efficacy of such programs
over the few years that they have been available has not yet been marked, as
Table 1-1 shows. It indicates more severe segregation by occupation than by
industry or manufacturing subdivisions: there are few industries where
women are not employed to some degree, but within industries women and
men are typically widely separated by occupation. As a study by the Organisation for Economic Cooperation and Development points out, "There
appears to be a tendency for countries with high female participation rates
and well developed tertiary sectors to show the highest degree of concentration, while those with lower female employment show less concentration."[2]
Thus, Norway, Sweden, and the United States show the highest indexes of
sex segregation by occupation; Norway, Sweden, and the United Kingdom
the highest by industry; and Norway, Finland, and Japan the highest by
manufacturing subdivision.

EQUAL EMPLOYMENT:
POLICY AND REALITY

When the United States and Britain first introduced antidiscrimination legislation,[3] the lawmakers certainly assumed that once legal
barriers to job training and entry were removed, women would enter work
in any occupation and at any workplace on their own merits. It is evident
that women's choice of occupations in countries with equal opportunity
legislation or explicit labor market policies has broadened, and the proportions of women entering many of the male occupations have doubled and
even redoubled. Yet the actual numbers and proportions of female participants in these occupations still remain very low. As we shall see, the slow
rate of progress in this regard has resulted, in Scandinavia, Germany, and
the United States, in a re-evaluation of the worth of women's work in order
decently to remunerate it.

At the same time that women's employment was rapidly increasing, the
recession of the 1970s had the effect of creating higher rates of unemployment among women than among men in most countries. A reason that in
part explains this anomaly is that women's employment rose mainly in the
marginal, depressed occupations that are in any case low-paid; they had not
acquired the skills that would enable them to enter the more stable trades.
Where women had found places in the better-paid occupations, they were
often in the group most recently hired. Thus, the application of a seniority
principle in layoffs affected them more severely than it did men. In a number
of countries, as our authors point out, unemployment rates for women far
exceed those of men. The OECD's report for 1979 showed this pattern in

TABLE 1-1
Indexes of Sex Segregation*

Country	Year	Index	Year	Index
By Occupation†				
Finland	1975	39.5	1976	36.7
France	1968	50.9	1975	48.3
Germany	1970	44.6	1978	45.7
Japan	1970	29.8	1977	29.2
Norway	1973	61.3	1977	58.2
Sweden	1970	51.6	1977	50.4
United States	1970	51.4	1977	51.1
By Industry				
Denmark	1970	45.6	1977	40.1
Finland	1967	38.9	1977	34.1
Germany	1967	35.1	1977	35.5
Japan	1967	22.1	1977	23.4
Norway	1967	58.4	1977	47.0
Sweden	1970	50.5	1977	45.1
United Kingdom	1967	39.6	1977	40.9
United States	1973	34.6	1977	33.1
By Subdivision of Manufacturing				
Finland	1973	40.5	1977	38.4
Germany	1973	32.5	1977	33.0
Japan	1973	27.9	1978	38.1
Norway	1973	48.5	1977	44.7
Sweden	1973	43.0	1977	33.8
United Kingdom	1973	35.2	1977	36.5
United States	1973	35.1	1978	32.7

*Indexes for the first year: the sum of absolute differences from one of the coefficients of female representation in each category, weighted by the percentages of total employment in the second year in the corresponding categories. Indexes for the second year: the sum of absolute differences from one of the coefficients of female representation in each category, weighted by the percentages of total employment in the second year in the corresponding categories.

†"Workers not classifiable by occupation" are excluded from the calculation of the indexes.

Source: OECD, *Women and Employment: Policies for Equal Opportunity* (Paris: OECD, 1980), p. 46. This study defines segregation as "a difference between the female share of a category and the female share of total employment, or, equivalently, as a difference between the percentages of male and female labor force in any category" (p. 39). Note that Germany, that is the Federal Republic of Germany (FRG), is generally labeled here and throughout this volume by the simpler term, or with the addition of the acronym.

Denmark, France, Germany, Italy, Norway, Sweden, and the United States, though not in Finland, Ireland, or Britain. In Japan, the unemployment rate remained substantially the same for both sexes at 2.2 percent for men and 2.0 percent for women.[4]

Table 1-2 looks at trends in both employment and unemployment to show that, except in Great Britain, women have contributed significantly to employment over the last half of the seventies, with Sweden, Italy, and Denmark showing the greatest percentage of growth during this period. Yet women's share of the increase in unemployment is 100 percent in Denmark and Finland, 66 percent in Italy, and 52 percent in the United Kingdom. In this depression, unlike earlier ones, women tend to drop out of the labor market to a lesser degree and instead continue to look for work, report to

TABLE 1-2
Trends in Employment and Unemployment of
Women Workers in Developed Countries, 1976–1980

Country	No. of Women Workers (in thousands)		Female Share of Net Increase (%)	% Change, 1976–1980	
	1976	1980		Male	Female
Employment					
Denmark	1,000.3	1,091.2	82.9	1.3	9.1
Finland	1,008.0	1,038.0	75.0	0.9	3.0
Germany (FRG)	9,276.0	9,679.0	56.8	2.0	4.3
Italy	5,902.0	6,606.0	86.8	0.8	11.9
Japan	19,760.9	21,420.0	62.4	3.0	8.4
Norway	697.0	786.0	71.8	3.2	12.8
Sweden	1,751.0	1,906.0	100.0	−0.5	8.9
United Kingdom	9,524.0	9,773.0	n.a.	−1.9	2.6
United States	35,095.0	41,283.0	63.2	6.9	17.6
Unemployment					
Denmark	51.8	88.7	100.00	−5.3	63.5
Finland	32.0	53.0	100.0	0.0	65.6
Germany (FRG)	493.8	462.5	n.a.	24.7	−6.3
Italy	802.0	982.9	66.2	14.7	22.4
Japan	340.0	430.0	37.7	4.1	26.5
Norway	16.0	18.0	n.a.	−12.5	12.5
Sweden	36.0	45.0	47.4	33.3	25.0
United Kingdom	341.7	564.2	51.9	19.7	65.1
United States	3,320.0	3,291.0	0.0	4.8	−0.9

Source: ILO Year Book of Labour Statistics, 1981, tables 3A and 9A, as cited in *Women at Work* (Geneva, ILO), no. 1 (1982): 15.

employment offices for insurance, and re-enter employment, whatever its conditions and pay, as rapidly as they can.

The economic crisis has been a major test of how fully unions and other labor market institutions have accepted women in all areas of the labor force. The evidence as it accrues in country after country is not heartening.

The old slogan "equal pay for equal work," although it is still the basis for judging sex equity in compensation in Japan, France, Denmark, the United States, and Finland, has largely outlived whatever usefulness it may once have had. The phrase was coined to attack the special women's pay scales that assumed that women should earn less than men because their labor was inherently worth less. Although the demand originated relatively early in labor history, it achieved special significance during the world wars, when women moved into male jobs and men feared that women's low rates would endanger men's hardwon standards. (Even so, few agencies regulating wages during the wars, whatever their pronouncements, were quite willing or able to enforce equal pay.) When women retreated from these occupations at the end of the war, the sharp divisions between men's and women's work again became the rule. Despite the operation of equal opportunity statutes and orders in the United States in the 1970s, only about 18 to 20 percent of women were doing the same work as men in the same establishments and under the same or closely similar conditions. For the few women who do the same work as men, equal pay in most countries has been substantially achieved. But the continuing widespread job segregation by sex limits further application of the principle so long as it is confined to equal or closely similar work for the same employer.

The question of women's wages continues therefore to cry for attention, for women's segregated work is universally paid at lower rates than men's work. Nor can the differences in earnings between men and women be accounted for, as many economists had expected to do, by finding significant differences in experience, training, and full-time employment. A growing number of scholars conclude that the differential that remains after these factors are taken into account must be attributed to discrimination. Yet even where job evaluation systems have established serious discrepancies between men's and women's wage scales, both public and private employers have often been unwilling to implement the results (see Table 1-3).[5] Our authors, on the whole, report little improvement in women's relative wages over the entire postwar period. (The exceptions are in Norway, Denmark, and Sweden, among manual workers, where the operation of "solidary wage" policies have favorably affected all low-paid workers' wages, including women's.)

Related to the issue of job segregation—at least as a rationale for its continuance—is working women's "double burden." The phrase is used to designate women's continuing responsibility for home and children, even

TABLE 1-3
Female Earnings as a Percentage of Male Earnings
in Selected OECD Countries (averages, 1968 and 1977)

Country*	Year	
	1968	1977
Denmark	74	85
France	86	86
Germany	69	73
Ireland	55 (1969)	61 (1973)
Japan	43 (1960)	56 (1975)
Norway	75	80
Sweden	78	87
United Kingdom	60	72
United States	55 (1973)	66

*The ILO does not include a figure for Italy. *EEG Social Statistics*, however, shows a figure of 80 percent for 1975, cited in OECD, *Equal Opportunities for Women* (Paris: OECD, 1979), p. 78.
Source: Women at Work, no. 1 (1982): 8.

when they take on full-time work. Presumably because women bear this double burden, they are not expected to have the primary commitment to work that characterizes men's attachment to their jobs. They are therefore given unskilled work—frequently synonymous with monotonous, repetitive, small-muscle work—with little responsibility for productivity and little opportunity for upward mobility.

So burdensome is the double load that women typically carry that its weight has already made part-time work largely women's province. The widespread unwillingness of unions to deal with part-time work and its problems as negotiable issues only underscores the inferior status of this whole cohort of women workers. The adjustments that have been made have come mainly from unions organizing service workers rather than from those in the manufacturing and office jurisdictions. Some few have bargained to improve the wages and working conditions of part-time workers; some have provided that part-time workers shall have first opportunity to fill vacant full-time jobs; some stipulate that all fringe benefits and wage scales apply to all workers in proportion to the hours worked. Still, unions' concern for part-time workers is at best marginal and spotty, and the woman who must work part time cannot be sure of union understanding for her plight or support for its amelioration.

Indeed, only Sweden has treated part-time work as an acceptable element of labor market policy. Forty-five percent of working women there are employed part time, a substantial proportion of them in government posts and in the retail trades, where strong unions have integrated the special problems of part-time work into their training, promotion, and wage agendas. Indeed, as our Swedish chapter amply demonstrates, labor market policies in that country have confronted the part-time issue, as they have dealt with most women's problems, directly and imaginatively.

The Swedes approached the achievement of equal job opportunity by a variety of routes: a series of collective agreements between unions and management associations, a wide range of initiatives on the part of the national labor market board, and the establishment in the prime minister's office of an equal opportunity commission. Yet despite their early and many-faceted undertakings, they were the first to discover—and with some alarm—that their best efforts to move women into what had previously been men's jobs were making only slow progress. Rita Liljeström in her study, *Roles in Transition*, called attention to the ways how men's and women's radically different familial roles meant that most household tasks fell to wage-earning wives, much as they did to the unpaid wife working full time at home. The hurdles these working women have to surmount just in finding enough hours in the day to engage in paid work—not to mention training or union activity or the women's movement or political struggles—are too high.

Moreover, the social pressures that parents, relatives, and husbands exert on working women to maintain their wifely roles and their place in traditional work add to their difficulties in moving into men's jobs. Liljeström particularly notes the burden on young workers, many of whom are still adolescent boys and girls. At the very point in their lives when they are establishing their gender identity, young people are asked to make unorthodox occupational choices in a society that still attaches traditional gender symbols to occupations. Substantial changes in the present patterns of job segregation by sex will probably take much longer than the early advocates of equal opportunity assumed. However, an alternative prospect is that radical innovations in work processes themselves may produce rapid attitudinal changes. For example, office work and health care, where women now predominate, are among the areas where work processes will change radically through automation and computerization. Workers will have to learn new skills, and jobs will have to be re-evaluated. The result may be that men will enter these occupations in greater numbers than they have done in the past, and organization rates may increase and wages improve.

Maternity and child care leave, as well as child care support, have been seen nearly everywhere as women's issues. Within the last decade, however, "parental leave" in the months of infancy has become a legal right in several countries and the subject of keen political debate in several others. Some countries that have introduced "parental leaves" have extended them to include a number of days each year for either parent to take paid leave to care for sick children or infirm family members. While the right has been extended to men as well as to women, men have been slow—though their numbers have continuously increased—to take advantage of it. In fact, employers tend to discourage men from taking such leave, and thus women are still most of those people who interrupt work for family needs.

No country, not even the most progressive and generous in providing child care, has adequately met the needs for it. Some countries—notably the richest of them all, the United States—have not even adopted a maternity leave policy. The result is that unions' collective bargaining agendas have come increasingly to include demands for employers to support or supplement publicly subsidized child care and maternity benefits and to provide additional days of parental or family leave. These demands and provisions underscore the relation of equality in the home to equality at work. The weight of the evidence in all the countries represented in this book is that job equality will not be achieved without an attack upon the double burden. The battle will have to be waged both in the home and through the provision of social support systems, of which child care is the chief one.

UNIONS AS AGENTS OF CHANGE

Historically, unions have been seen as engines of change and have presented themselves in that way. Many of them owe this image to their creation by socialist or, later, communist parties and their association with the parties' political goals of revolutionary social change in which the working class would play the decisive role. So strong were these ideological views in most of continental Europe, at least up to World War I, that the "woman question" was subordinated to the goal of revolution in the belief that the special problems of women workers were irremediable under capitalism and women could hope for equity only in a new society. But as unions became accepted institutions and their right to organize and bargain collectively was often statutorily or even constitutionally recognized, they began to build their positions solidly into the market economies. Similarly, their associated labor parties became accepted, working elements of parliaments and immediately before and after World War II came to govern in many of these countries.

In the early nineteenth century, unions greatly modified capitalism through achieving—not without bloody struggles—contractual relations with employers that tended to secure workers against arbitrary dismissal and to give them more and more areas of what later came to be called co-determination: the rights to have grievances heard, to bargain for fringe benefits, in some cases to participate in limited ways in management, or at least to veto certain management decisions. Labor parties—usually strongly supported by their associated unions—sponsored legislation on education, social welfare, and, later, sex equality,[6] with the result that modern capitalist nations are all characterized by a tightly knit welfare infrastructure that no modern conservative party would seriously consider dismantling.

Today, whether leftists, liberals, or conservatives are in office, the unions represent an irremovable power in all the market economies, and a power exercised not only in behalf of their members but in behalf of working people generally. In each of the countries with which we deal, the national labor confederation wields considerable social and political influence. First, the confederation is the acknowledged representative of a very substantial special interest group; second, labor influences economic and social policy through its customary or statutory presence in many public agencies: labor market boards, vocational training institutions, social security agencies, and even in many cases the economic councils advising the heads of state. Moreover, union conditions tend to become the norm for all working people, especially in countries where unions organize a large part of the manual and white-collar working class. In all cases, union workers are better off in terms of wages, working conditions, and security than are all but a very few of the unorganized. In short, the unions are an established labor market institution, and as advocates of the interests of wage and salaried workers, they have powers not given to any other.

For all these reasons, exclusion or discouragement from union membership or second-class citizenship within unions is an insupportable inequity. While women have long been union members (although even today they are not members of all unions), they have historically played a relatively minor role, in terms of both numbers and influence, within them. With the massive inflow of women to the labor forces in all these countries, their place within the unions takes on a new significance. Because no other institution is prepared or authorized to represent workers in collective bargaining for wages and working conditions, the unions' fulfillment of this responsibility to women as well as men is of primary importance.

Unions have ranged from exclusionary to ambivalent in their treatment of women. Laura Blankertz has analyzed the causes of these attitudes. Unions in the 19th century were first, she says, established mainly to protect the privileged positions male workers held under patriarchy, and these early unions exerted exclusionary pressures upon women. In this period women developed considerable ability to organize themselves. As capitalism developed, units of production enlarged and were widely dispersed, and national unions came into existence. As mechanization reduced the need for skilled labor, unskilled men and women competed with each other for jobs. Exclusion no longer served a purpose, and the unions reluctantly began to include women. They made demands on employers for equal pay for equal work in the expectation that under these circumstances employers would prefer to hire men and therefore women would be employed less and less. At this stage, Blankertz notes, "The main method that male workers used to control this competition became discriminatory policies within the union itself."[7]

Underlying social policy, both inside and outside the unions, was the expectation that employers could and probably would impose full exploitation in terms of hours, compensation, and conditions of work on all workers, both men and women, a practice that would serve to weed out the "unfit." Union men who had fought hard to achieve their minimal work standards saw women as unstable and therefore unreliable members of the labor force, with neither sufficient fortitude nor sufficient reserves to withdraw their labor in a strike, and too expendable to succeed if they should strike. In this regard male unionists reflected the general social view of women as workers. Although women—including married women—had been part of the labor force since the begining of industrialization, society still viewed female workers as almost exclusively young and single or, alternatively, as widowed and poverty-stricken and working only until dire need was met. At the same time, all working women were regarded as mothers, or potential mothers, who needed protection against assaults upon their chastity and excessive strains on their health. From these perspectives and from the public debates on the treatment of working women, a consensus arose that women as future mothers should be protected against long working hours in the factory. Later, attention turned to outlawing night work and, later still, to providing seats for rest and limiting the weight that women might lift.

Homework was the ultimate in exploitation. It saved employers factory space and machines; it dispersed workers so as to avoid collective action; and although it was acceptable to many women with young children who had little opportunity to gain factory employment, it earned them even lower wages than women received in factories. Reformers and trade unionists thus set out to prohibit or regulate homework.[8] To the extent that they were successful in some countries, it was because the issue was presented to legislators as a way of protecting consumers against contamination from the foul tenements where work was fabricated rather than out of consideration for the homeworkers.

The view developed that women made up a different kind of work force from the male one. This belief rested on the conviction that women's God-ordained and natural roles were those of wife and mother; men were their breadwinners. This notion determined how society and governments regarded working men and how the institutions of the labor market—not least among them unions and the working-class organizations with which they were allied—regarded, and disregarded, working women.

The inevitable effect of all these preconceptions—women's temporary attachment to the labor force, separate gender roles at work as well as at home, and women's need for protection—was that women's problems as workers did in fact differ from those of men. Women, as a result, became members of a secondary labor force, performing marginal tasks, receiving lower wages, occupying a narrower range of jobs, even serving as a reserve army of labor. Indeed, they constituted so different, so other, a category of labor that, like slaves in colonial economies, they were scarcely regarded as part of the labor force. They became—and remained for more than a century—invisible. Union men rarely saw them as colleagues eligible for union membership; and if admitted to unions at all, women entered as something less than full members, often lumped with apprentices and other male minors.

In consequence, women who worked and suffered special exploitation in segregated occupations formed their own unions. These were usually short-lived, either because they could not sustain themselves against employer opposition or because the general unions of unskilled men that were beginning to form absorbed women into their organizations in order to increase their numbers and thus their base of power. Even when unions of unskilled as well as skilled workers began to accept women generally into membership, however, they often sequestered them in a special women's division, where they were tolerated but rarely consulted and never selected for leadership.

Nearly every modern union with a sustained history shows traces of this kind of development. As unions have become powerful, male-dominated institutions in modern industrial and postindustrial economies, they have found it as difficult as other social institutions to realize that for all their democratic structures and procedures, they still see women as inferiors. Women's growing demands in the seventies and eighties for equal access to training and jobs, equal pay for work of equal value, and opportunities for a full political role in the unions are all unsettling to the men who run them because they call for fundamental changes in attitudes and structures. Customs rooted in historical reasoning and behavior are modern barriers to change. Unions have come late, partially, and reluctantly to an acceptance of the goal of equality for women.

To what degree has ideology in the European socialist or Christian unions or the pragmatic, "nonideological" stance of the American unions— affected their willingness to accept women and respond to women's demands? In the nineteenth century, in Europe, ideological differences inspired by Marxist and counterbalancing Christian principles resulted in the creation of political parties that were avowedly working class or adhered to some extent to programs aimed at improving the conditions of wage and salaried workers. From these emerged unions and union confederations dedicated to the achievement of these programs in the workplace.

Many women of national or international fame in working-class history emerged in this period, usually in the left-wing organizations: Clara Zetkin, Emma Goldman, Rosa Luxemburg. But less radical women also played important roles in establishing the early unions in every country. While some rose to important positions in the political sphere, almost none achieved leading posts in the unions. Union rhetoric, once women were accepted into membership, was more supportive and egalitarian than was union practice.

For the countries we consider, our authors for the most part record the permeability of unions of all kinds to the ideas and goals of sex equality, largely germinated within the women's movement, taken up by liberal and reformist political parties, propagated by international governmental agencies, and implanted in the unions mainly by outside liberal sources. For even though socialist- and communist-affiliated unions have insisted that equality is a major goal, there is little evidence that sex equality has been more readily expressed in their programs than in those of Christian and nonpartisan unions. Indeed, in several countries with multiple centers, including the Low Countries, Italy, and France, the evidence suggests that the Christian unions, perhaps under the influence of radical elements within the Catholic church, have turned their attention to these disadvantaged members while the older, better-established socialist unions have focused on other issues. Of the countries examined in this volume, probably Ireland and Japan are the most resistant to sex equality. In both countries a long tradition, bolstered in the one case by the Catholic church and in the other by Confucianism, has produced strongly established antiegalitarian customs that unions have not seriously challenged.

I believe, in short, that the progress women have made in their organizations is a consequence not so much of the ideological foundations of the individual centers, as of the women's own efforts within the organizations to state their needs and to insist upon responses. Even this forward momentum probably owes more to influences outside the union, and specifically to the new women's movement, than to those within.

Unions are complex structures performing many functions internally and externally, the chief of which is probably collective bargaining with employers. They also function, as already noted, as a major governing institution of the labor market and, through their links with labor parties of various denominations, play a significant role in national political life, both in parliaments and as representatives of a major interest group. They operate internally by their own political rules, which are typically modeled on a democratic system of governance. These sometimes, though not invariably, provide for the representation of such special interest groups as women, youth, skilled workers, and others. They conduct vast educational programs for rank-and-file members and for officers of all grades, both volunteer and full-time. They often operate a wide range of subsidiary institutions that may include banks, construction and mortgage companies, vocational schools, travel bureaus, vacation homes, and cultural organizations. They send representatives by law or custom to a great variety of governmental bodies and educational boards. When we look to unions as agents of change historically or in the present, we must also consider the array of agencies within and outside the labor movement through which trade union influence can be exerted. Each national report included here notes the methods and programs that unions have used to respond to women's demands for change. The question is, to what degree do the unions' internal structure and political life permit women to move into the decision-making bodies where policy and program are constructed?

UNION STRUCTURE AND POLICY AND EQUAL OPPORTUNITY

Most national unions share a pyramidal structure, with local unions at the base, regional bodies at the middle level, and national executives and congresses as the top governing agencies. National unions in turn form a confederation that often has regional and local central bodies.

Training for Leadership

Union leaders typically rise from local or workplace office to regional and then national responsibility. In the European unions, and particularly in Germany and Scandinavia, officers of every grade are encouraged to take union courses of study in their localities and later to attend union residential schools to learn about labor law, organizing and bargaining techniques, economics, labor history, and public speaking. As leaders attain higher posts, they are expected to take specialized courses in such subjects as administration, the economics of their industries, bookkeeping, and accountancy. Few national union leaders come from academic life, though a number of trade union academies have come to offer courses that in duration and substance are comparable to academic studies. This ladder to leadership invites the young in at its lower rungs. Unions in some countries organize apprentices and other young workers, both boys and girls, into a youth section and use that stage to begin their career training within the union. The success rate among boys is fairly high, but young women, once they marry, find the demands of home and children too heavy for them to continue volunteer union work.

Studies conducted in trade union schools show that the women attending these institutions are considerably older than the men—on average, about ten years older.[9] Thus, late starts and the need for extra efforts to overcome the disadvantages caused by dropping out handicap women who might be union leaders, just as the same circumstances handicap them vocationally. Some unions now try to reduce this handicap by providing child care at union meetings and union classes and schools, or by holding union meetings near or at the worksite and scheduling them on company time. (In Japan, however, such an arrangement would be considered illegal aid to union activity on the part of the employer.) Some unions also have plans to restructure their schooling so as to call for less residential time away from home and to hold courses evenings and weekends with perhaps short programs at intervals during the training, in order to make these opportunities more accessible to young parents and particularly to young mothers. Such changes are not universal, however. Until union officials are more sensitive about the problems young women have in this regard and remedies are devised and tried, women will continue to be handicapped in their climb up the leadership ladder.

Women and Union Representation

To the extent that unions are responding to women's special needs and demands within the organization, they are often doing so not out of any abstract sense of equity, but in response to women's sheer numbers and organized strength. Union growth, or even maintenance of membership strength, during the seventies was in most countries attributable entirely to women; male membership often declined. Table 1-4 shows the degree to which women during that decade achieved a representation in union membership comparable to their representation in the labor force.

Do women's special needs, problems, and demands call for a special place within the union structure where they can meet to formulate and work out their programs? Or do such special sections given over to their interests, isolate them from the mainstream of union activity? These questions have found sharply contradictory responses in various countries and among the various unions within national confederations. In Japanese unions and a number of European ones, a women's division is a standard part of union structure. In some cases these divisions were created when unions first admitted women. Some union women's groups, as in the United States and Ireland, are late additions, not located inside national unions but bridging them both nationally and locally in an autonomous women's organization.

Historically the women's divisions within national unions had little independence and almost certainly no budget of their own; given the poverty of the early labor movement, the latter was hardly possible. The resulting dependence contributed to the second-class status of these divisions within the unions' line and staff departments. Moreover, although the women's sections were intended to be a home base, they often became

TABLE 1-4
Percentage of Women in Unions and in the Labor Force
(various years after 1975)

Country	% in Unions	% in Labor Force
Denmark	40.0	42.0
Finland	42.0	46.0
France*		37.0
Germany	20	37.0
Great Britain	33.0	38.0
Ireland	32.0	27.5
Japan	31.0	40.0
Norway	27.0	40.0
Sweden†	36.0 (LO) 50.0 (TCO)	43.7
United States	20.0	43.0

*France has poor or no statistical information on union members since membership is neither well-defined nor sustained.

†LO: Confederation of Labor; TCO: Central Organization of Salaried Employees. These categories reflect the existence of two federations: LO-blue collar; TCO-white collar.

Source: Derived from Organisation for Economic Cooperation and Development, *OECD Labour Force Statistics: Demographic Trends 1950–1990* (Paris: OECD, 1979) and reports from individual countries as cited in the essays that follow.

ghettos walled off from the main center of union politics and functioning. Their programs had little to do with women's work problems but focused instead on assistance to male-determined projects. Frequently they became simply women's clubs, the products of benign neglect.

Some of these sections died a natural death. Some were abolished by the father union on the grounds that they contributed nothing to the union's strength or life. Some were replaced over time by other structures, as when the Scandinavian unions abolished their women's divisions in the mid-sixties in favor of Councils on Family Problems. It is important to note, however, in several of those countries, informal, spontaneous women's committees formed at the grass roots within a few years, dedicated to doing what the abandoned women's divisions had hoped to do: prepare and support women for positions of leadership within the unions.

In the United States, where women's sections were the exception, a new interest in them developed, as it did in Ireland. The interest in the U.S. developed in the mid-seventies, spurred by efforts of the Coalition of Labor Women (CLUW) to gain representation for women on the national executive boards of the major unions. CLUW developed a program on empowerment of women through education, training, and united action. The Irish women took CLUW in the U.S. as their model. Labor education institutions in these as well as in other countries began to offer special training courses for women. In Britain, the annual conference of unions "catering for women workers" had been established after the merger of the Women's Trade Union League (WTUL) with the Trades Union Council (TUC) in the twenties. Although the need for its further existence has repeatedly been challenged, it survives and year after year calls the attention of the TUC and its affiliated unions to women's grievances and demands. In Germany, the women's divisions have had a consistent history over many decades, interrupted only between 1933 and 1946 by Hitler's Thousand Year Reich. Organized at each level of union structure, and in each industrial union as well as at the confederation, these divisions have no power distinct from that of the trade union itself. Their chief officers have seats, voice, and vote in the appropriate executive bodies, and they have a staff employed by the union of which they are a part. The Japanese have a similar structure, though the women there have not yet developed the power and influence enjoyed by women in the German unions.

However slow, halting, and partial the progress on women's issues has been, there is little evidence that unions would have taken up or pursued them without the propelling force of women's internal union organizations. It seems clear from the experience recorded here that where women of this generation have an organizational home within the unions—formal or informal, existing by union statute or by custom, independent or dependent— they eventually seek ways to gain political skills, educate their male colleagues, and claim their representational rights.

Collective Bargaining for Equal Opportunity

If unions were to state their function in one term, it would be collective bargaining. Yet unions bargain in very different ways, over very different issues—once wages are out of the way—and with varying mixtures of centralized and decentralized control over the bargaining agenda. These differences are largely products of the different labor relations systems that have developed, some of them with deep historical roots. Some but not all collective bargaining behavior is limited, defined, and enforced by law. In this collection each author calls attention to such historic and legal factors as they are reflected in union structure, functioning, and locus of power. Here I will attempt only to give an overview of the development of the collective bargaining process.

In the early days of unionism, small groups of laborers working for the same employer sought to force wage agreements. Soon skilled workers in a

locality banded together to establish a minimum rate for the job and some
control over hours and conditions common to all employers in the trade.
When product markets expanded, labor markets also grew, and the national
unions that then developed sought broader and broader areas of bargaining,
a circumstance that affected other union functions as well. By the twentieth
century, with the full development of national—and international—product
markets for many goods, unions organized in these markets sought more
and more centralization of their bargaining, particularly with the big firms
and the basic industries. The move to amalgamate small unions with large
ones followed inevitably.

In several Scandinavian countries, these developments have led to
national bargaining by the trade union center (or centers) with national
employers' associations over hours, wages, holidays, vacations, and the
definition of the rights of each of the bargaining partners. The national
agreements then tend to be fleshed out and extended by bargaining at
regional levels and at the firm and plant level. In Germany, the seventeen
industrial unions bargain by regions and industrial branches with employers'
associations. Even in Britain, where national unions play a comparatively
minor role, the large unions tend to bargain in broader and broader units, as
is the case in the United States as well. In Japan, annual national "spring
struggles" determine at least the normative rate of pay increases, although
the actual bargaining goes on between individual companies and local
unions.

Because few local product markets exist today even in the service and
construction trades, their former seats of power, and because many unions
now have hundreds of thousands and even millions of members, trends
toward centralization are common. The result is that responsibility for union
policy, bargaining, and decision making rests with a relatively small group of
professional office holders. Although the members concerned with a particular contract typically receive a certain amount of information about the
bargaining process and its results, they have little opportunity to influence it
except by yea or nay votes on the final agreement.

By and large, centralization of bargaining has removed decision making
about these important—indeed, critical—union functions far beyond the
reach of local groups of workers, both men and women. For newer union
members, including thousands of women, an opportunity that was historically open to rank-and-filers is now absent from their union experience, and
its absence hampers their potential for growth as future leaders. Centralization is thus an obstacle to the full representation of women among union
leaders. And yet where leaders are at all progressive, a centralized system
has the advantage that agreements can more readily and speedily include
improvements for disadvantaged blocks of members. The solidary wage
policy in Scandinavian countries, for example, has been successful in part

because it was developed at the national level and made uniformly and nationally applicable.

Women universally complain that while convention resolutions may support their demands, at the bargaining table these demands are all too often dropped or traded off for gains that only tangentially, if at all, address their needs. The union leadership—if it responds to such complaints—notes that child care, for instance, is of little interest to the bulk of its male or older membership, yet it may cost so much that its adoption would palpably affect the wage package. Perhaps no example is more telling than the disappearance in the late 70's of the "light-wage" categories from the German unions' agendas on the grounds that the time was not ripe for a radical adjustment in wage rates, however justified it might be.

Would women be better off if they participated more visibly and actively in the bargaining teams of their unions? A definite answer is hard to find, so few and scattered are women in these positions. Yet women union leaders firmly believe that general change will not take place until they are represented not just in the large bargaining commissions that act as consultative bodies to the negotiators, but among the negotiators themselves. The experience of the few women's unions might be expected to offer positive evidence, but their general weakness in numbers, their largely unskilled constituencies, and their general lack of militancy on bargaining issues have resulted in their following rather than leading the male-dominated unions. Where white-collar and academic unions are strong, women are more apt to appear in leadership roles—though still by no means in proportion to their membership numbers—and such unions by and large are more responsive to women's demands. Nevertheless, collective bargaining remains an area extremely resistant to women's influential participation. The same can be said for the more dramatic activity of strikes, the extreme action to which unions resort when collective bargaining breaks down.

For many years labor relations literature was concerned with the incidence and duration of strikes as a measure of labor militancy and union vitality. Strikes were certainly characteristic of the early history of labor organization, when union workers often had to withdraw their labor if they were to gain even grudging admission to collective bargaining. The early days of the labor movement's struggle for legitimacy produced heroines as well as heroes. Matchworkers in Oslo and London conducted strikes in the 1890s; the latter was led by Eleanor Marx. Elizabeth Gurley Flynn joined Carlo Tresca and "Big Bill" Haywood in galvanizing women and children in the 1912 strikes at Lawrence, Massachusetts, memories of which are still stirred by the battle song "Bread and Roses." Women textile workers joined the men in the long battle for their rights at Crimmitschau in Saxony.

National unions acquired the power to make strikes "legal" by gaining control over the building and disbursement of strike funds. The success of a local struggle might well depend upon the national union's stamp of approval. Did women's unions have the resources to finance strikes, and did issues that local women's groups might raise in the shops succeed in winning union approval? Similarly, when collective bargaining breaks down and a strike ensues, women are often not included in the strike committees. Margaret Maruani, in her essay in this volume, records the exceptional circumstances of a number of women's strikes in France. Maruani suggests that many such episodes must remain in the shadows: for every women's strike that gained union attention, many have gone unrecorded. She herself has a particular interest in certain strikes that women have conducted in France, not so much because they were fought for specifically women's issues (such as protecting women's jobs in a period of layoffs when men were prepared to sacrifice them) as because these actions illustrate the introduction of a "feminine dimension" into the struggle—the fact that the strikers combined their family and work responsibilities by including husbands and children in the strike and evolved informal ways of reaching decisions by consensus.

Similarly, Harriet Holter and Bjørg Aase Sørenson, reporting on four women's strikes in Norway, see them as critical and immediate learning experiences for the participants, which allowed them to achieve some power and to attain leadership. A number of British unions, including TASS, the white-collar section of the Amalgamated Union of Engineering Workers, has sanctioned and even encouraged local strikes of women—and other union members who elect to join them—to achieve equal pay for work of equal value. In Germany, a series of strikes by women "guest workers" (i.e. foreign workers) in the early seventies were first disregarded and discouraged by the national union and then, after outside radical groups showed their support, gathered under the union wing as national union leaders became convinced, in several cases over the opposition of local leaders, that the women's cause had merit.[10]

Control of strikes has come to be a function of national offices; it has passed from the hands of the persons most concerned—those who will strike—to those who supply strike support. From women's point of view, it has passed from their control to that of men far removed from their local grievances and needs. All the more urgent, then, is the need for women in these national executive posts.

Affirmative Action to Provide Female Leaders

Our authors point universally to the scarcity of women in the unions' executive bodies. It may be useful to note how and when some of the few women who have achieved those positions were selected.

British unions, more than those of any other country, have been willing to reserve seats for women. This practice began, as we have seen, when the WTUL united with the TUC in the twenties. At that time the TUC set aside two seats for women, a number that was increased only in the 1980s. Nevertheless, by 1983 three women have been president of the TUC, a position that changes annually. Several British unions have introduced reserved seats for women in the unions' executive and legislative bodies and will maintain them at least until their constituents gain confidence in women's abilities and elect them as they do men, on their essential fitness for office, however defined.

The practice has advocates outside Britain as well. Some Scandinavian women raise the issue of quotas for women with each new frustration in the results of union elections. The German women too have brought the issue before the Congress of the German Trade Union Federation (DGB), specifically in regard to the election of delegates to that body from the affiliated unions. So far, they have been able to move the Congress only so far as to "urge" its affiliates to devise methods for the proportional representation of women, but no operating models have emerged.

The term "affirmative action" originated in the United States to apply to employment practices rather than to the election of either paid or volunteer officers. The union as employer is as subject to antidiscrimination rules as any other institution; indeed, a number of former union staff members have brought charges of sex discrimination against unions under the Equal Employment Opportunity law. But relatively few unions fall under the legal requirement to prepare affirmative action plans for their own hiring, training, and promotions, although all employers are encouraged to do so. If unions are to achieve equality within their organizations, their own law, as laid down in their constitutions and bylaws, must allow for measures that will promote it.

Our Scandinavian authors point to a special circumstance that has a negative effect on women's lives within the unions. The close interrelationship of the political and economic branches of the labor movement—the labor party and the trade union—means that union leaders often serve in parliament and local government office. At the same time, party activists are expected to be union activists as well. In short, a good unionist qualifies for a high post when he also plays an influential role in party affairs. For women this dual range of activity creates a formidable barrier to candidacy for office, particularly if they are married and carrying the major responsibility for homemaking and child care. But, as already noted, women's active lives within the union begin considerably later than men's, and the period during which they are available for the slow accession up local and regional office ladders to national leadership is short. For those who aspire to these positions, the unwritten expectation of dual activity in party and union makes things much more difficult.

And yet in France, Germany, Great Britain and the United States some exceptional women have become members of the top executive bodies of their unions. In Britain, as noted above, their membership was the result of the amalgamation of a women's union organization with the TUC and women waited sixty years before more places were found for them. In Germany, a woman has not only been a member of the governing board for a decade but was first vice-president of the DGB. Her accession to that post came during the Year of the Working Woman (1972), when the DGB committed itself to the recognition of women. In 1981 she was joined, just before her retirement, by two other women. In the United States, the executive council of the AFL-CIO was persuaded by its new president to accept his appointment to that body of the president of the Coalition of Labor Union Women; she was joined at the next convention by another woman, who had been elected to a newly created vacancy. Jeannette Laot of the French Confederation of Democratic Labor has written that as the lone woman member of her executive, where she held a "reserved seat," she was "listened to but not heard." Nevertheless, in the end she was able to win the executive over to her views on women's rights to birth control and abortion, topics most unions have sedulously avoided facing.

INFLUENCES FROM WITHOUT:
INTERNATIONAL ORGANIZATIONS AND
THE WOMEN'S MOVEMENT

Recognition that change is both required and inevitable is more prevalent among top union leaders, exposed as they are to political debates, policy papers, and influences outside the labor movement. National and international governmental bodies and the women's movement have brought pressure upon unions to modify their policies, programs, and procedures in respect to their female members. A number of experiments and pilot projects have resulted, and they provide an encouraging study.

Two categories of international organizations bear upon trade union policy affecting women. One consists of the international organizations of labor itself, to which most of the national confederations reported on here are affiliated: the International Confederation of Free Trade Unions (ICFTU) with headquarters in Brussels; the World Federation of Trade Unions (WFTU), its communist counterpart, with headquarters in Prague and affiliates in both communist and noncommunist countries; the European Trade Union Confederation, made up of national confederations from most of the European countries, with its core among the confederations in the Common Market (EEC) countries; and the trade secretariats of associated national unions within various employment sectors—metal, white-collar, chemical, public service, food—many, though by no means all, of them located in Geneva.

The trade unions have addressed the equality issue most recently and notably in the ICFTU Täljoviken Report, "The Integration of Women into Trade Union Organizations" (1977), adopted by the affiliated confederations and distributed widely among them. In addition, a number of the more important trade secretariats have held international women's meetings and issued reports and resolutions on women's role in the trade unions, calling particular attention to their absence from positions of leadership and policy making and reporting on successful experiments conducted by some of their national bodies.

In addition, unions and unionists are represented in the delegations to the chief international governmental bodies, and all of these have spoken out forcefully on the need for sex equality in the labor market. These intergovernmental organizations include the International Labour Organisation (ILO); the Organisation for Economic Cooperation and Development (OECD); the European Economic Community (EEC), with its European Parliament, High Court, Social Fund, vocational training center (CEDEFOP),[11] bureau for dealing with questions concerning the employment and equal treatment of women, and the wages, income, and social welfare division; and the Nordic Union of the Scandinavian countries.

Of these, the ILO led historically with its carefully fashioned conventions and recommendations, first on protective and maternity legislation in the twenties and thirties, then on equal pay for work of equal value (1952), and most recently on the outlawing of discrimination and the conditions of workers with family responsibilities. In the tripartite bodies of the ILO, many of these have been adopted with the joint votes of labor and government against the opposition or abstention of employer delegates. Once adopted in an ILO meeting, the Conventions are open to ratification by member states, an act that makes them part of the respective national legal code. These Conventions have come to represent normative labor standards even in nonsignatory nations.

The founding charter of the EEC—the Treaty of Rome—included as Article 119 an agreement that the member nations would adopt legislation requiring equal pay for equal work. By 1975 the EEC had required its member nations to institute equal pay for work of equal value, nondiscrimination in employment, and equal gender rights to social security. At first six nations were involved; now the number has grown to ten and may soon include twelve.[12] The EEC in the intervening period has several times warned tardy or delinquent members that failure to meet these requirements will result in charges before the Community's High Court. The Court itself has decided a number of individual cases, mainly from Great Britain, each of which has pointed to some shortcoming in the British statute on equal pay.

All the intergovernmental bodies concerned with labor matters have, during the past decade, established bureaus or advisory bodies on women's issues. The Nordic Council issued a statement on sex equality in the labor market; the OECD called a High-Level Conference of Labor Ministers on the Employment of Women as well as numerous other meetings touching on various aspects of the same subject; similarly, the International Institute of Labour Studies, associated with the ILO, has undertaken studies and conferences on issues affecting women at work.

Many of these projects stemmed from the International Women's Year (IWY) conference, called by the United Nations and held in 1975 in Mexico City, whose program was eventually extended into the International Women's Decade. An interim meeting took place in 1980 at Copenhagen, and another is planned for the decade's end in 1985. Each meeting included important agreements on matters affecting working women. The trade unions of most countries were represented at all these events, and, inevitably, these discussions and reports have had a powerful influence on national union agendas.

Much of the activity of the intergovernmental bodies is directed to improving labor market practices affecting women, usually by proposing drafts of legislation. Equal opportunity in training, placement, and promotion, pay equity and shorter hours, and the creation and maintenance of support systems for transportation, child care, and education on released time have been some of the subjects of these policy recommendations.

These same issues figured prominently in the programs of the women's movement. During the sixties and seventies, when women moved massively into the labor markets of their countries, the movement grew strong. These were, however, unrelated phenomena, although they came to interact significantly. Women joined the paid labor force because rising costs and rising aspirations demanded a second earner in many families. They could find work in ever larger numbers because of the increase in jobs in the white-collar and service sectors. The measure of independence and self-consciousness they won as wage and salary earners made them receptive to the ideas floated into public debate by the women's movement. These ideas embraced political, economic, and personal aspects of women's role and place in an egalitarian society, raised questions about their representation in parliaments and unions, and spoke to their growing disillusionment with monotonous, low-status, low-paid work and to their demands for equal employment opportunities. They called attention to job segregation and women's endemic low pay and raised the issue of comparable worth: equal pay for work of equal value. They lifted the issue of women's traditional homemaking role and its imposition of the "double burden" to the level of a social problem demanding social solutions.

The women's movement was not new. In many countries organizations had been in continuous existence since the first struggles for enfranchisement began in the nineteenth century. The Fawcett Society in Britain, the Frederika Bremer Association in Sweden, and the League of Women Voters in the United States are all examples of the movement's deep roots and longevity. Many of these societies were made up of professional and other middle-class women with few enduring connections to women manual and white-collar workers. These latter women had their own organizations in the women's sections of the labor, social democratic, and communist parties and in the women's divisions of the trade unions. Historically the two women's movements had often confronted each other as representing very different groups of women, differing both in goals and in immediate interests. Accordingly, they had refused to enter cooperative activities or coalitions.

The women's movement of the sixties deeply influenced both types of organization. The "new wave" of the movement was concerned that women discover their own female identity, establish control over their own bodies, and change the laws that oppressed them as women, in and out of marriage; in a word, it put forward the goals of equality between the sexes in every area—social, political, and economic—and a redefinition of the most intimate interpersonal relationships.

They could only have such an effect if women workers were ready to hear and if what they heard fitted their situation. Bianca Beccalli shows how unified and intimate these ties were in Italy. Irmgard Ruhnke, as I note in the chapter on Germany, traced the growth of feminist ideas in the German labor movement, noting changes in the official utterances of the DGB, and not only of its women activists. From denoting women in the 1950s as "double earners," the confederation had advanced to calling them "co-workers" a decade later. The question of child care, at first treated as a necessary aid for mothers forced through widowhood or other economic necessity to work, was later seen as a desirable contribution to childhood development; thus, the DGB moved from mere support for child minding, where that was necessary, to advocacy of peer socialization and preschool education.

During this period the long-standing women's divisions of the German and Austrian unions took on a new life and purpose; spontaneous women's groups formed in Swedish and British workplaces; and unions that had never seriously considered forming women's sections began to hold women's conferences and to make structural changes within their organizations to accommodate women. Thus, the Coalition of Labor Union Women was formed in the United States, and the Trade Union Women's Forum followed its example in Ireland. In Norway and Denmark, the "new women's movement" sought contacts with trade union women. In the United States, the National Organization for Women (NOW) formed an alliance with the AFL-CIO and other progressive groups to resist the encroachments of the "new right" and to forward the joint interests of women, minorities, consumers, and labor.

Modern communications technology, with its instantaneous reproduction in words and pictures of events like the IWY meetings in 1975 and 1980, served to unite women around the world on many of the same issues. The attraction was not so much that the ideas were new as that their time had come, and not just for educated and professional women, but for wage earners and would-be wage earners as well.

In short, international agencies, both governmental and volunteer, have come to include working women's issues on their agendas for change. They are exerting an influence that in some cases is admonitory and in others mandatory upon governments and labor market institutions. The new women's movement can claim credit for formulating many elements of the programs these agencies have adopted, and it has been mainly responsible for propelling them with force and speed into the international arena.

UNIONS AND NATIONAL POLICY

Unions have two main tools for bringing about changes in the lives of working women. Through their political programs they can strongly influence social policy; and through collective bargaining they can shape procedures and conditions within the workplaces.

As noted above, unions in many countries were the creatures of the early socialist or labor parties. The relationship in the Scandinavian countries has remained close, particularly in the case of the blue-collar unions and their confederations. In some countries the formal separation of party and unions did not come until after the turn of the twentieth century, and it is still possible to speak of the labor movement as having two arms, one political and the other economic. In Great Britain, where unions and party are also closely related, it was the unions that formed the Labour party and not the reverse. In the United States, no such relationship ever existed, nor has it been strong in Ireland, though for quite different reasons. In Germany, until Hitler abolished both unions and labor parties, and in the Netherlands, Belgium, Italy, and France, a multiple trade union movement was allied with one or more left-of-center parties or with a Christian party that was seeking to counteract the influence of marxism among its working-class members. Postwar Japan's modern labor movement took the course of establishing four differently aligned trade union centers, two of them closely allied to political parties, while the German labor movement dropped all formal ties to political parties in order to establish a unitary trade union center that would be nonpartisan, though not nonpolitical.[13]

Examining countries with labor party–union alliances, our authors note that working women's issues have been frequently treated there as political matters and thus become the responsibility of the party rather than of the unions. As a result, the perceived need to protect women against special conditions of the working environment or to provide support systems for them has been the subject of legislation rather than collective bargaining. By politicizing women's issues, in other words, unions can write them off their bargaining agendas. To be sure, in countries where women constitute only a fraction of union members, they may be more effectively served by statutory regulation than by collective bargaining. The fact is, however, that the existence of legislation should by no means limit collective bargaining, which may, when the negotiators will, raise standards above the legal norms, as when a union contract provides for longer maternity leave than the law allows, adds parental leave for child care before national policy has been determined, or agrees to wage systems based on comparable worth while the law still requires only equal pay for equal work.

Moreover, unions that use the existence of legislation to excuse themselves from dealing with women's issues at the bargaining table, may also offer less than wholehearted support to members appealing to the law for relief from discrimination. The equal opportunity commissions charged with enforcement of the antidiscrimination laws in Britain and the United States have seen many women going before court or tribunal without the aid of their unions.[14]

Although collective bargaining and legislation seem desirable supplements to each other in working out national policy on equal employment issues, unions in several countries have insisted that these matters be left entirely to collective bargaining. In Sweden, for example, when the Socialist party was defeated by a liberal-conservative coalition in 1976, the latter came into office promising equal opportunity legislation. The unions opposed it, demanding autonomy of the "social partners." As a result, the bill that was finally adopted called for implementation either by law or by collective agreement. In practice, as our Swedish authors show, the unions are left with a free hand to deal with issues of sex equality or discrimination arising in the shops, but they have made little use of the law, whereas a substantial number of individuals have brought their problems to the Equality Ombud, the state's enforcement officer. In early 1982 the German unions opposed similar legislation in their country on the same grounds, though with somewhat less reason: German unions represent less than 40 percent of working women, while Swedish unions include more than 70 percent. On the other hand, contract terms in Germany can be and usually are extended to cover nonorganized firms, making union agreements more widely effective than union membership figures would suggest.

The unions' widespread devotion to voluntarism in dealing with issues of equal employment opportunity at the very least places upon them the burden of dealing positively and wholeheartedly with issues of sex equality in employment. Their performance falls considerably short of this expectation. Indeed, one is tempted to ask whether, if governments and organizations outside the unions had not sought legislation, the unions on their own initiative would have worked toward achieving equal opportunity and equal pay, however defined. One recognizes that the history of all these undertakings, whether government- or union-initiated, is very short and that information so far is fragmentary, but it seems clear that further progress, particularly in a period of worldwide economic recession, will depend upon the unremitting commitment and united action of all the groups that have so far defined the issues and espoused the goal of equality for working women.

This view necessarily places major responsibility on organizations of working women and their close allies. These women have been the objects of governmental and union attention. They now face the problem of taking the initiative in changing both union and, eventually, governmental approaches to women's problems—of being actors rather than objects.

"WOMEN'S WAY"

Several of our authors believe that women will approach this task in "women's way," a way of approaching and solving problems significantly different from the ones men have developed. Moreover, they see its use as offering more hope of success than the procedures men have devised. In their view, women's way is nonbureaucratic and egalitarian, direct and nonhierarchical, dealing immediately, flexibly, and humanly with problems without the constraints of set procedures. Parliamentary procedure, chains of command, and bureaucratic routines involving successive steps are unfamiliar, disconcerting, misleading, and ineffective. Responsible individuals meeting face to face and dealing in good faith can achieve much more.

The suggestion that women's way is a way out of women's inferior position assumes, first, that women's problems and experiences are entirely different from those of men and, second, that women have uniformly experienced the standard organizational processes as repressive rather than as an encouragement to participation. These assumptions also guide the development of the new scholarship on women.

Many women scholars have concerned themselves in recent years with opening up the history, the prehistory, and the anthropology of women's unique and separate experience. They are mapping its geography and geology, the accretion of layers of custom that have hardened into tradition and the tectonic movements of these rocky plates, as they undergo social upheavals, so that we can more accurately recognize women's world and place ourselves in it. Sociologists are tracing the "line of fault"—the point of rupture in women's experience within the social forms of consciousness.[15]

Women's world, as Jessie Bernard argues, is so different from men's and so segregated from it that it is not surprising that women and men have developed different practices for dealing with problems.[16] As Thelma McCormack contends,

> women's relation to the political process has been very different from that of men . . . [and therefore] generally understood in terms of deviations from a male norm of political behavior . . . [often designated] as "backwardness." . . . [But] women represent a separate political culture from that of men, one that adds up to a female design for political living that is dissimilar from that of the male.[17]

So long as women's experience remains centrally related to children and family and, even at the workplace, is primarily mediatory between managerial policies and ideas and their practical application, working women will inevitably encounter problems with which men are unacquainted and which call for solutions that have hardly been tried and certainly not proven.

Some experiences with women's way are presented in this volume. Essays record the efforts of the women's movement, notably in Norway and Denmark, to restructure unions, particularly women's unions, and reframe their goals. Bianca Beccalli has shown for Italy how working women distinguished between masculine and feminine "worlds" both at work and at home, perceiving the unions essentially as a reflection of the masculine world. They claimed that the workplace reproduces the principles of male dominance found in the family. Women called their uneasiness at trying to imitate the male model of union militancy "laceration," a wounding of their essential beings. They responded by insisting on recognition of women's difference and argued to change the rules of the game for both men and women. These efforts so far have produced more insights and innovations than permanent results. Carefully thought out and ideologically motivated, they were the work of a minority of union members, who met the usual fate of ideological minorities dealing with entrenched bureaucracies. Their failure does not mean that they were misguided or wrong, but merely that in those organizations women's way has not yet been able to mobilize the power to bring about substantial change.

Other experiments with women's way occurred in some recent women's strikes in France. There, in critical, isolated settings, women spontaneously improvised adequate and workable solutions to the problem of maintaining resistance. They occupied the factory, bringing their children and their husbands as visitors or co-residents into the striking community.

Fragile and unclear as this evidence is, the Swedish experience with bringing about change through national policy intervention by government agencies is not clearly persuasive either. "Very basic changes at all levels of society and culture are required to liberate women," says Heidi Hartmann.[18] The short run of a few years is not long enough to provide solutions; generations may be required to create attitudes as well as policies conducive to achieving gender equality.

If circumstances change attitudes more thoroughly than education can, as many practitioners in this field believe, the question arises whether women who shared the male experience at work and in organizations would still find male methods of operation inefficient and stultifying and continue to insist upon women's way. Not all trade union women are committed to finding and demonstrating a new way of dealing with union issues and managing union affairs. The German and Austrian women's divisions, for example, have accepted the existing union structures and thereby committed themselves to matching and working through every level of union hierarchy as laid out in the constitutional blueprint.[19] While their success has not been revolutionary, they have had notable and consistent influence on policies and programs in their confederations and unions. The question therefore is: how is efficiency in policy making and management to be achieved, and can sex equality exist on the job without also being attacked in the home.

The first challenge of efficiency is to find a better way than bureaucracy to manage large organizations and government. Unions, even small ones, are large institutions in the sense that they are national in scope and hierarchical in structure. It is important to remember that women are by no means the only critics of centralization, bureaucracy, and hierarchy. To the degree bureaucracy is associated with buck-passing, avoidance of issues, working by the book, and other variations on delay and evasion, women's way must appeal to many male unionists.

Some unions, among them some of the most highly centralized, have had to recognize that the pendulum must swing toward decentralization for at least some of their activities: educational programs, "quality of worklife," "quality control," health and safety administration, and, yes, even sex equality. As these activities establish a life of their own in the shop and in the local union, women can be expected to find activist roles. The problems are specific, close to home, and in expanding areas, demanding the participation of more people than have previously "manned" these union posts. As the local bodies of the unions go through this reorganization and revitalization, and women find a place in it, women's way can permeate union life at its grass roots. "Appetite," the Germans say, "comes with the eating." Success at the local level can stimulate efforts to use these methods in the regional and national bodies, in large assemblies as in small ones. The critical condition is that women have enough opportunities to demonstrate the uses—and successes—of their way.

The adoption of women's way would mean widespread changes, not just in procedures, but in attitudes toward decision making in unions and in governments. It will be used first mainly in situations that women already dominate—in their own groups, where it is already widely accepted. Then, as women move into mixed groups in significant numbers, they will have the opportunity to demonstrate its usefulness in improving the range and intensity of participation. Robert Lekachman has suggested what may happen:

> As an egalitarian I shall faintly applaud with one hand a victory of the women's movement which consists only of a fairer distribution of the rewards of a highly defective capitalist society. A better, but probably more utopian outcome, implies the triumph and generalization of the values now deprecated as merely feminine. Should the day arrive when "feminine" values are held in higher esteem than various cutrate versions of militantly military virtues, schools will teach, hospitals will heal, advertisers will rival each other in speaking the truth, and politicians will consult the interests of the governed.[20]

NOTES

1. Organisation for Economic Cooperation and Development, *Women and Employment: Policies for Equal Opportunity* (Paris: OECD, 1980), p. 22.

2. Ibid., p. 46. For the methods of computing the "Indexes of Sex segregation" and the interpretation of the index, see note to Table 1-1.

3. The same ends were sought in Sweden and, to a lesser degree, in Germany through changes in the policy and practice of labor market boards, while government offices concerned with women's issues were established in France, Italy, Norway, Denmark, Ireland, and Japan at about the same time.

4. OECD, *Women and Employment* p. 47.

5. See Helen Remick on the state of Washington and Christof Helberger on the German Federal Republic in *Equal Employment Policy for Women: Strategies for Implementation in the United States, Canada, and Western Europe*, ed. Ronnie Steinberg Ratner (Philadelphia: Temple University Press, 1980).

6. Germany is the major exception to this pattern of historical development. Measures for social welfare there mainly originated in the Bismarck government under the Empire and were an attempt to nip the rising force of socialism in the bud. Japan's history shows some similarities to Germany's.

7. Laura Enion Blankertz, "Patriarchal Capitalism: An Application to the Historical and Contemporary Participation of Women in Labor Unions" (Ph.D. diss., Bryn Mawr College, 1980), pp. 18–19.

8. It is an irony of history that in the 1980s, advocates of "quality in work life" tout the "computer cottage" as the ultimately desirable work environment for

women, who can thus do their paid work at home while constantly linked to an overseer and a central printout facility.

9. Unpublished studies by school directors in both Sweden and Germany present these findings. They are reported in Alice H. Cook and Roberta Till-Retz, "Trade Union Education in Europe" in *Labor Education for Women* ed. Barbara Mayer Wertheimer (Philadelphia: Temple University Press, 1981).

10. A similar situation in a long drawn-out legal case that German women employed in a photo company brought finally to the Supreme Labor Court. Although they had the support of their national union, as a friendly reporter noted, local officers in the persons of "male works councillors and union functionaries . . . defended tooth and toenail the 'little difference', not only in pay (men received 1.58 DM per hour as night shift bonus, while women received only 0.19), but in all other respects where discrimination showed itself in the plant."

11. The Common Market funds CEDEFOP to assist member nations in setting up pilot projects in vocational training. The EEC has further authorized the use of its European Social Fund (ESF) to assist target groups within the member nations, including migrant workers, the unemployed and underemployed, the handicapped, and youth, to train and retrain for new occupations. About 30 percent of the people benefiting from such projects are women (*Women of Europe*, Special Supplement no. 7 (1981): 15).

12. Of the countries reported on here, Denmark, Germany, France, Great Britain, Italy, and Ireland are members of the EEC.

13. Val R. Lorwin, "The Red and the Black; Socialist and Christian Labor Organization in Western Europe" XIV International Congress of Historical Sciences, San Francisco, August 22–29, 1975.

14. In the United States, the Equal Employment Opportunity Law (EEOL) requires unions to carry joint responsibility with management for the implementation of equal employment regulations. In addition, the National Labor Relations Board, which administers the Labor Relations Act governing all aspects of collective bargaining, requires unions to fulfill a "duty of fair representation" in matters of discrimination as well as in the processing of other grievances. However, the U.S. Supreme Court has ruled (*Denver-Gardner*) that even where a union has carried such a case through its grievance procedure to final and binding arbitration with a negative result for the claimant, she does not lose her right to go beyond the unions' procedures and may appeal to EEOC and the courts. Unions have consequently been reluctant to invest time and money in cases that may not, after all, be finally settled under the procedures to which they and the employers have agreed in their contract.

15. Dorothy E. Smith, "A Sociology for Women," in *The Prism of Sex: Essays in the Sociology of Knowledge*, ed. Julia A. Sherman and Evelyn Torton Bank (Madison: University of Wisconsin Press, 1979), p. 135. See also Jean Lipman-Blumen, "Toward a Homosocial Theory of Sex Roles: An Explanation of the Sex Segregation of Social Insitutions," and Constantina Safilios-Rothschild, "Dual Linkages Between the Occupational and Family Systems" in *Women and the Workplace: The Implications of Occupational Segregation*, ed. Martha Blaxall and Barbara Reagan (Chicago and London: University of Chicago Press, 1976).

16. Jessie Bernard, *The Female World* (New York: Free Press, 1981).

17. Thelma McCormack, "Towards a Non-Sexist Perspective on Social and Political Change," quoted in Smith, "A Sociology for Women," p. 148.

18. Heidi Hartmann, "Capitalism and Patriarchy," in Blaxall and Reagan, *Women and the Workplace*, p. 168. Hartmann goes on to say: "Because both the sexual division of labor and male domination are so long standing, it will be very difficult to eradicate them and impossible to eradicate the latter without the former. The two are now so inextricably intertwined that it is necessary to eradicate the sexual division of labor itself in order to end male domination."

19. "The rational actor, choosing and calculating is the abstracted model of organization or bureaucratic man, whose motives, methods, and ego structure are organized by the formal rationality structuring his work role. At work, his feelings have no place. Rationality is a normative practice organizing and prescribing determinate modes of action within the bureaucratic or professional form." "A Sociology for Women," p. 150.

20. Robert Lekachman, "On Economic Equality," *Signs* 1 (Autumn 1975): 102.

BIBLIOGRAPHY

Barbash, Jack. *Trade Unions and National Economic Policy*. Baltimore: Johns Hopkins University Press, 1972.

Barkin, Solomon, ed. *Worker Militancy and Its Consequences, 1965–1975*. New York: Praeger, 1975.

Bernard, Jessie. *The Female World*. New York: Free Press, 1981.

Blainpain, Roger, ed. *Women and Labour: A Comparative Study*. Bulletin of Comparative Labour Relations (Netherlands), Kluwer Deventer, Bulletin no. 9, 1978.

Blankertz, Laura Enion. "Patriarchal Capitalism: An Application to the Historical and Contemporary Participation of Women in Labor Unions." Ph.D. dissertation, Bryn Mawr College, 1980.

Commission of the European Communities. "Equal Opportunities Action Programme, 1982–1985." *Women of Europe* (Brussels), Supplement no. 9, December, 1981.

Holter, Harriet, "Women and Democracy in Working Life." *Economic and Industrial Democracy*, Special Issue on Women 3, no. 4 (November 1982).

International Confederation of Free Trade Unions, "Integration of women into Trade Union Organizations: The Täljoviken Report," Brussels: ICFTU, 1977.

International Labour Organisation. *Equality of Opportunity and Treatment for Women Workers*. Report no. 8. Geneva: ILO, 1975.

Kamerman, Sheila, and Alfred Kahn. *Family Policy: Government and Families in Fourteen Countries*. New York: Columbia University Press, 1978.

Liljeström, Rita. *Roles in Transition*. Stockholm: Swedish Institute, 1976.

Lorwin, Val R. "The Red and the Black: Socialist and Christian Labor Organization in Western Europe." International Congress of Historical Sciences, San Francisco, August 22–29, 1975.

Moltke, Konrad von, and N. Schneevoight. *Educational Leaves for Employees*. San Francisco: Jossey-Bass, 1977.

National Commission for Manpower Policy. *European Labor Market Policies*. Special Report no. 27. Washington, D.C.: NCMP, 1978.

Nordic Council and the Council of Ministers. "ILO and Women in Employment and Occupation." NU 1976:6. Stockholm: Gotab, 1976.

Organisation for Economic Cooperation and Development. *Equal Opportunities for Women*. Paris: OECD, 1979.

———. "High Level Conference on the Employment of Women: Women in the Labour Market, Analytical Report." Paris: OECD, 1980.

———. *Women and Employment: Policies for Equal Opportunity*. Paris: OECD, 1980.

OECD Observer. "A Conference at OECD: Women in the Labour Market." May 1980.

Pettman, Barrie, ed. *Equal Pay for Women: Progress and Problems in Seven Countries*. Bradford, England: MCB Books, 1976; Washington, D.C.: Hemisphere Publishing Co., 1977.

Ratner, Ronnie Steinberg, ed. *Equal Employment Policy for Women: Strategies for Implementation in the United States, Canada, and Western Europe*. Philadelphia: Temple University Press, 1980.

Robertson, Priscilla. *An Experience of Women: Pattern and Change in Nineteenth-Century Europe*. Philadelphia: Temple University Press, 1982.

Sloane, Peter T., ed. *Women and Low Pay*. London: Macmillan, 1980.

Statistical Office of the European Community (Eurostat). *Economic and Social Position of Women in the Community*. Luxembourg: Eurostat, 1981.

Sullerot, Evelyne. "Equality of Remuneration for Men and Women in the Member States of the European Economic Community. In *Women and Society: International Perspectives*. Geneva: ILO, 1976. Also in *International Labour Review* 112 (August–September 1975): 2–3.

Szalai, Alexander, ed. *Use of Time: A Multinational Study*. Paris: Mouton, 1972.

Tilly, Louise A., and Joan W. Scott. *Women, Work and Family*. New York: Holt, Rinehart and Winston, 1978.

Treiman, Donald J. *Job Evaluation: An Analytic Review*. Washington, D.C.: National Academy of Sciences, 1979.

Treiman, Donald J., and Heidi I. Hartmann. *Women, Work and Wages: Equal Pay for Jobs of Equal Value*. Washington, D.C.: National Academy Press, 1981.

United Nations, *The Economic Role of Women in the ECE Region*. E/ECE/1013. New York: UN, 1980.

Vogel, Eliane. "Some Suggestions for the Advancement of Women." *International Labour Review* 112 (July 1975): 1.

Windmuller, John, ed. *Collective Bargaining in Industrialized Market Economies*. Geneva: International Labour Organisation, 1974.

2 DENMARK

Brita Foged, Helle Otte, and Anne Olsen

The Danish trade union movement has developed in close connection with the Social Democratic party (SD). The party has always had a monopoly of political power in the trade union movement and has been the largest party in the Danish parliament since 1924. The Social Democrats have traditionally been movers and shakers for equality between the sexes, whether in the trade unions or in society in general. Although disagreements between the unions and the party have arisen from time to time, none of these have concerned policy toward women. The dominance of the SD, together with a highly centralized system of collective bargaining, has sometimes for better, sometimes for worse, been decisive for the position of women in Danish society.

THE DANISH LABOR MARKET

Denmark is a nation of just over 5 million persons, a homogeneous population of whom 1.4 million live and work in greater Copenhagen. Just over 2,578,000 persons are in the labor force, of which women make up about 43 percent. As Table 2-1 makes clear, the number of women in the labor market has, except for one or two years, been increasing steadily since the war; the number of working married women has been growing rapidly since 1965. Table 2-2, which looks at these labor participation rates by age cohorts, shows that by 1979, for the ages thirty-five to forty-four, women's overall participation rate, and interestingly the participation rate of married women, came close to that of men.

The labor market discriminates in assigning occupations to women. Certain branches of business and industry are heavily populated by women. In the branches where both men and women work, women are employed in sections of the production process characterized by routine and monotonous work. Such work is the easiest to rationalize, and the result is that unemployment is higher for women than for men.

TABLE 2-1
Growth of Danish Workforce, by Sex and
Marital Status of Women in Various Years, 1950–1979
(numbers in thousands)

			All Women		Married Women	
Year	Total	Men	No.	% of Workforce	No.	% of Workforce
1950	2,036.0	1,356.4	680.0	33.0	263.0	13.0
1955	2,115.4	1,405.5	710.0	34.0	292.5	14.0
1960	2,060.3	1,425.3	636.0	31.0	245.0	12.0
1965	2,232.7	1,473.9	758.8	34.0	366.2	16.0
1970	2,390.0	1,469.3	920.5	39.0	568.0	24.0
1974	2,478.6	1,464.0	1,014.7	40.0	664.7	27.0
1977	2,578.9	1,489.8	1,089.1	42.0	716.0	28.0
1979	2,627.0	1,478.0	1,148.8	43.0	753.8	28.6

Source: 1950–1965, Danish census; 1967–1979, labor market force data, cited in part in Brita Foged, et al., *Deltid—Kvindetid* (Part-Time—Women's Time) (Aarhus: Modtryk, 1980), p. 60.

In the last ten years a new inequality has developed. Women make up a very substantial portion of part-time workers, while men tend to work full time. This gender distinction is often found even outside the sectors where women predominate and is a product of the kinds of jobs men and women hold. Men's jobs generally demand a certain degree of all-round knowledge, so that the worker's presence is required during the whole of the production process; this is not true of much of women's work.

As in the rest of the world, women's situations are shaped by society's need for them to fill the double role of mothers and workers. The resulting conflict between the demands upon them and the goals they seek is a daily experience for Danish women workers.

Women are thus in many respects marginal to the labor market, and their marginality largely determines the roles they are assigned in both unions and society. The social consequence is patriarchy in work life: men's dominance in the industrial hierarchy and in the skilled and better-paid jobs. These patriarchal attitudes are carried over into unions as well, and there they prevail, reflecting the hierarchical structure and the traditional values of the system with which the unions constantly have to deal.

The "social safety network" functions reasonably well in keeping people above the poverty line, despite the cuts that have been part of the adjustment of social policy to the crisis of the late seventies and early

TABLE 2-2

Percentage in Danish Workforce, by Age Cohort, Sex,
and Marital Status of Women, 1972, 1975, 1979

Age	Men			All Women			Married Women		
	1972	1975	1979	1972	1975	1979	1972	1975	1979
15–19	53	48	45	46	38	34	58	53	78
20–24	81	80	85	71	75	71	67	72	84
25–34	94	94	96	68	74	85	64	70	84
35–44	97	97	98	69	73	83	66	71	82
45–59	92	92	93	58	60	55	56	58	64
60–64	78	79	62	30	32	33	28	31	32
65–74	32	33	25	8	9	8	8	8	0
All ages	81	80	79	54	55	61	54	58	66

Source: Equality Council, *Annual Report 1979* (Copenhagen: Equality Council, 1980), p. 38.

eighties. Nearly all medical care is free. Unemployment insurance, mainly financed by the national treasury, is managed by the unions for their members and pays up to 90 percent of wages up to $270 per week. In the past this amount has been quite sufficient to cover a family's needs, but a sharp rise in food prices and rents has meant that many of the unemployed can no longer maintain their standard of living. Moreover, the government's increasing use during the seventies of indirect taxes on consumer necessities has greatly intensified the pressure on family budgets. By 1980, for example, taxes on butter represented 25 percent of its price.

THE FORMATION OF THE PARTY AND THE UNIONS

The Danish section of the First International was established in 1871 to represent the economic and political interests alike of Danish workers. Unions and party were a single body until 1878, when they divided into two organizations, though close political cooperation has continued to this day. The unions put forward immediate demands for wage increases and improvements in working conditions; the party put forward such long-range political demands as the subordination of the monarchy to parliament, universal male suffrage, and the abolition of capitalism. Once parliamentary authority was established in 1901, the SD fought mainly within the framework of parliament, while the socialist revolution was pushed into the background. Here it intensified its demands for immediate reforms to lessen social inequalities; one such reform was women's suffrage. Danish women gained the vote in 1915 through a campaign supported by the SD.

Reformism reached its peak in the period between the wars. When the SD formed a coalition government in 1933, it abstained from pursuing a class policy in favor of what it called a "democratic policy for the benefit of society as a whole." The party not only initiated programs of class cooperation but acted as intermediary in resolving industrial disputes. It strengthened industrial development, for which it won the workers' support by social reforms that considerably improved their conditions of life. Rising social welfare was also a product of the unions' success in raising wages, the party's implementation of a tax policy that favored the lowest paid, and the introduction of programs to aid workers in periods of illness and unemployment.

Tensions inevitably developed between the two branches of the workers' movement, and the union more than once had to moderate their demands in order to preserve the SD's position in parliament. In 1963, 1975, 1977, and 1979, an act of parliament under SD governmental leadership, instead of a freely bargained collective agreement, determined wages. Ironically, whenever the party has intervened in a collective bargaining impasse, as it has done repeatedly, the unions have had to pay dearly for it.

The domain of the unions has been limited to wages and working conditions. Everything else is seen as a political issue and thus in the domain of the party. For women, this division of labor made a feminist struggle within the unions impossible. All demands related to women's double work at home and in paid employment have been excluded from union consideration. Child care and maternity leave, education and culture, have never been trade union issues. In their avoidance of these issues, the unions' day-to-day work has in effect been more than nonfeminist; it has been antifeminist. Part of the reason for this neglect of social issues generally and women's issues in particular lies in the union structure itself, for workers are not organized industrially. In a Danish machine factory, workers may be organized into four or five unions: one for skilled male metal workers, another for unskilled male workers, one for unskilled female workers, and one or even two for white-collar and administrative workers.

The unions we speak of here are those affiliated to the Danish Confederation of Trade Unions (Landesorganisation—LO), whose long history and close ties to the powerful SD make it the dominant factor in Danish trade unionism. We draw on our work with LO for an explanation of the situation of women in trade unions. Here we deal with two LO affiliates, the Danish Women Workers' Union (Kvindelig Arbejderforbund i Danmark— KAD) and the Commercial and Office Employees Union (Handels og Kontorfunktionaerernes Forbund—HK), which together include 60 percent of the women members of LO. Another 200,000 women are organized in two other national federations, one primarily for civil servants and public employees, the Office and Civil Servants' Union (Funktionaer og Tjeneste-madsforbundet—FTF), and the National Association of University-Trained-Employees (Akademikernes Centralorganisation—AC).

The organization of working women was a slow and difficult process. The majority of working women around 1900 was employed at laundry and cleaning or in textiles, clothing, tobacco, agriculture, and domestic service. These were all traditional women's trades whose products or services can be seen as extensions of women's work in the home. Until late in this century, very poorly paid industrial homework (or outwork) was a common feature of many working women's lives: it enabled them to take care of their children and to work between household chores. Unintentionally, such women were a threat to wage standards.

The Danish unions—including some all-women unions—established themselves in the twenty-year period between 1880 and 1900. By 1900–1920, 45 percent of the women in Copenhagen worked for wages, mostly doing unskilled work in the traditional women's trades. Their wages amounted to about 50 percent of the skilled, and about 60 percent of the unskilled, male worker's wage. In 1901 only 22 percent of working women were organized, as opposed to 76 percent of working men. The women's organization rate increased, however, and by 1925, 65 percent of the female industrial workforce (or 23 percent of the entire workforce) was organized. By 1935 the figure was over 26 percent.

The first attempts to organize women were undertaken by skilled male workers to prevent the possibility of wage cutting and strikebreaking by women. These early efforts all followed strikes. Union men very early began to pressure women to give up their own unions and to organize alongside the men. Most of the twenty-eight women's unions did; only KAD survived the nineteenth century as a women's union. Founded in 1885 as a "Union of Washing and Cleaning Women," KAD was renamed in 1886 and thereafter accepted all unskilled women. Inger Düback notes that it also took in women who belonged to other organizations in an early attempt to establish itself as a federation in its own right, an effort that accounts for the jurisdictional disputes and charges of splitting the labor movement in which it has been involved from the very beginning.

It is possible to trace a continuous development from the male handicraft and artisans' guilds to the modern Danish trade unions, a continuity that has significantly influenced their concentration on men and men's issues. From the beginning they organized male workers and fought primarily for better wages for them. As a result, the skilled worker dominated the Danish working-class movement, and his wages could normally cover the needs of a family. This followed the accepted nineteenth-century idea of the man as breadwinner and the woman as the center of family life in the home, a concept that was largely myth. For the unskilled worker was unable to sustain a family on his wages, and his wife had to work both in the home and outside it. Yet because much of women's work was invisible except to their families, it was invisible to the unions as well. Household work was not within their focus. Moreover, women worked mainly in the traditional women's trades, and their participation in the industrial labor force outside the food, textile, and clothing sectors was very small.

Further, many women could not work full time. They could turn to homework or to other kinds of loosely structured part-time work like cleaning, laundry, or paper delivery. The casual and often seasonal character of many women's unskilled jobs made KAD's attempt to organize and bargain so difficult that, in the end, it accepted the norms of the male unions in order to survive. Like them, it rejected part-time workers as legitimate objects of union efforts; and it bargained for women's wages, as they did for men's, as the earnings of single breadwinners. Indeed, the bulk of women workers in the factories and services were single. Like the male-dominated unions, KAD left issues not directly related to wages and working conditions to the SD.

WOMEN WORKERS IN THE SIXTIES AND SEVENTIES

Since World War II women have become a more permanent part of the workforce, and many more women are working. Most women now working came into the labor market in the boom years of the sixties, when the number of women working grew by nearly 300,000 or 45 percent. This resulted in a higher degree of organization and in a raising of women's consciousness about problems at work and at home.

Blue-Collar Workers

Technically advanced industry has pulled many women out of their traditional trades and into the "mixed" branches, although the new forms of women's work did not alter the labor market's general segregation by sex and women's relatively low pay. In electronics, women worked on assembly lines; men were charge hands, inspectors, and skilled technicians. Although women's work in these new industries calls for dexterity and accuracy in monotonous work on small elements, it is as low-paid as work in the traditional women's industries was.

In 1970 three-quarters of the women in industry were in ten branches. Among the older industries textiles, clothing, and footwear, which employed 42 percent of all women in industry in 1955, employed only 30 percent by 1970. Food, beverages, and tobacco increased slightly, from 21 to 23 percent. But metal working employed twice as many women as before and accounted for 21 percent of women's industrial employment (up from 15 percent in 1955). In electronics assembly, women were more numerous than men.

White-Collar Workers

The greatest increase in women's work, in Denmark as elsewhere, has taken place in distribution, office work, and public administration and services. By 1972 nearly 480,000 women worked in these branches, about twice as many as were employed there in 1950.

Here, as in production, the sexual division of the labor market is obvious. Certain nonindustrial workplaces, such as stores, banks, insurance companies, and offices, have gone through a process of rationalization and intensification that has resulted in their feminization. Women's jobs are more routine and monotonous, and they are lower-paid than men's. In public services, women's work is an extension of housewifely tasks. They work in nurseries and schools, social work, old people's homes, and health services. But they are teachers, not principals; nurses, not doctors; social workers, not social work executives. Most of them have the lowest pay and the poorest working conditions in their branches.

The public sector, however, has responded more directly to women's changed employment status than has the private sector. Unlike the trade unions, which traditionally have ignored women's special problems, the SD has been willing to take up this task. Beginning in the mid-fifties, it moved from an emphasis on cultural activities for women to a deep concern for the problems of married women potentially or actually in the labor market. The party saw the necessity of making women's entrance into the labor market possible not only by building sufficient day care facilities, but also by emphasizing public responsibility for the maintenance of the entire labor force, including its women.

Child Care

The need for public child care was the most obvious expression of the family's changing situation. Up to 1960 only about 30 percent of married women worked for wages. By 1973, 55 percent did. In this period the number of day care centers built and supported by public funds more than tripled. Although the number of places remains insufficient, the proportion of children under seven who can be provided for has increased from 7 percent to 20 percent.[1]

Apart from child minding, public authorities also took over other responsibilites that had traditionally belonged to the family. A rapid development in social, health, and family policies was joined with the labor market policy as early as the sixties. Among the measures introduced were family consultation centers, maternity aid programs, improved child allowances, and a variety of programs to aid single mothers. All these programs required extensions of public education to train staffs, and there were new vocational training schemes and higher education courses for nursery staffs, social workers, family consultants, and persons working with the handicapped. These educational opportunities particularly attracted women.

Part-Time Work

From 1967 to 1978 the number of working women increased by 204,000, or 24 percent. The number of those engaged in part-time work, however, increased by about 90,000 in the shorter, six-year period from 1973 to 1979, and at about the same percentage rate. Table 2-3 shows this development.

Before the sixties boom, part-time work, although poorly paid and not covered by unemployment insurance or many other social benefits, was nevertheless common. During the boom, and following certain developments in the retail trades, such as the change from small, independent shopkeepers to supermarkets, employers were glad to find part-time workers to deal with peak and slack periods and created many such openings. But the great increase in the proportion of part-time work also came about in part because many women were forced to go from full-time to part-time work. During the economic crisis that succeeded the boom, employers tended to force the type of work that suited them onto their employees. In the public as well as the private sectors, women—and not men—were offered part-time work. Part-time employment was used not only to rationalize work hours but as a means of intensifying work: people can work harder for four hours than they can continuously for eight.

TABLE 2-3
Part-Time Workers, by Sex, in Denmark
(various years, 1973–1979)

| | No. of Workers (in thousands) | | | | |
	1973	1975	1977	1978	1979
Men	56.2	59.8	61.3	63.6	57.6
Women	398.0	425.5	459.6	480.0	487.8
Total	454.2	485.3	520.9	543.6	545.4

Source: *Investigation of Employment*, 1973, 1975, 1977, 1978, and 1979 (Copenhagen: Danish Statistical Department).

This increase in the tempo of work among part-timers is, of course, one reason why the trade union movement has always opposed the introduction of part-time work. Indeed, in industry, where the unions are strongest, they managed to keep the number of part-timers to a minimum until very recently. Full-time work has generally been a condition for membership in the unemployment insurance system that the unions operate. The one exception has been the retail trades, where, because organization was low, the unions were powerless to limit the expansion of part-time work even had they wished to do so. In 1970 HK, the union having jurisdiction in this area, faced the reality of the high proportion of part-timers in its sector and took the initiative in changing the unemployment insurance law so that persons working twenty hours or more a week (later the limit was lowered to fifteen hours) would be covered. Disagreements on this issue, many still unresolved, divided other unions, with the result that each was left to decide for itself whether or not it would insure the part-time workers in its trade. Of the fifty-nine unemployment schemes covering all kinds of wage workers in 1979, twenty-three—all among unions covering areas traditionally considered men's work—still do not insure part-timers.

In May 1979, 41 percent of those insured against unemployment were women, and of these 28 percent were part-timers. Most women who work part time are around twenty-five years of age, when the pressure of family responsibilities begins to tell; others are women who began their working careers late and cannot or do not wish to manage full-time jobs. Among these groups, relatively few are organized, a fact that helps explain the low insurance rate for part-timers.

Unemployment

The percentage of women working and seeking work continued to increase during the seventies while, paradoxically, the number of unemployed women also rose. Indeed, the female exceeds the male unemployment rate and has done so since 1974. Counting part-timers and noninsured workers as well as the insured, in 1979 an average of 84,711 women were unemployed, as compared with 77,134 men. When one considers the higher number of "discouraged workers" among women, it is clear that female unemployment is far greater than that among men. This pattern of high unemployment is directly linked to the structure of women's jobs. It is the industries where women predominate that have gone out of business during the crisis or have greatly cut their workforces as a result of mechanization.

Unlike earlier depressions, when women in large numbers simply dropped out of the workforce, unemployed women now tend more frequently to stay in it and register for insurance and jobs. The drastic increase in the cost of living has made it imperative that a family have two incomes, even if one comes from unemployment insurance, if it is to keep up the standard it achieved in the sixties. A 1970 law allows part-timers to pay full contributions to unemployment compensation and thus to supplement their part-time wages with part-time unemployment pay. New provisions, however, greatly limit the conditions under which this is possible: right-wing critics insisted that women who were not at all interested in working were drawing unemployment insurance simply to stay home with their children. These new regulations and others will clearly affect some women's ability to remain in the labor market. A 1978 Child Care Circular, for example, provided that unemployed women or those returning from maternity leave are ineligible for unemployment insurance unless they are able to prove that they have provided for nursery care for their children. The irony is that these attacks on women continue while women's legal rights are extended.

Initiatives for Equal Rights

The activities of the women's movement have been of the greatest importance in the development of equal job rights in the seventies. The movement worked for equal pay with certain groups within the unions notably female brewery workers in Copenhagen. The metal workers, the book and paper workers, several unions under left wing influence, and HK. It has also penetrated the SD. Beginning in 1974, the party began a campaign against sex discrimination. The campaign stressed women's double burden but directed its efforts mainly to what individual women could do for themselves; it had little to say about men's role in occupational changes and the reform of family life and made no reference to collective action through unions. Slogans urging women to enter "men's occupations" reminded them that "women can do anything" and that "women's skills and gifts, their love and care, are needed." But as the crisis deepened and unemployment became a long-term, widespread reality, the SD offensive faded away.

Equal pay for equal work had already been won in 1970 through collective bargaining. Following Denmark's admission to the European Economic Community (EEC) in 1973, the government had to draw up equal rights laws. The result was the establishment of an Equal Rights Commission and the passage in 1976 of an Equal Pay Act that provided for equal pay for equal work and "work to which equal value is ascribed." In 1978 the SD government introduced a nondiscrimination bill, subsequently adopted by parliament, that sought to outlaw sexism in work life. Want-ads may no longer specify the worker's sex; they can only describe the job. Persons claiming sex discrimination may take their cases to court for adjudication. The act has also led to a debate over allocating quotas for each sex in political life. The debate was initiated by the Socialist People's party (Socialistisk Folke-parti—SF) and specifically by the women's group within the party. It is the largest party to the left of the SD in parliament, and it has implemented a quota system internally with the result that a majority of its parliamentary group today is made up of women. The debate now affects wider areas of society, including the labor market and education, to name two of the most important.

Women and the Economic Crisis

These positive beginnings soon had to confront the crisis of the mid-seventies. First came cuts in day care appropriations. In 1974 a 4 percent cut in staffs was ordered. Since professionals could not be fired under the union agreement, kitchen staffs were let go and nurses and teachers asked to take over that work in addition to their own. In the end cooked meals were canceled in nurseries and kindergartens. Then, in 1975, 15 to 18 percent of the trained staffs were fired despite their contracts. Altogether about five thousand employees were let go. In 1976 the national government handed over the responsibility for child care to the local authorities at the same time that it cut the funding of these programs. The local authorities in turn became less and less willing to build new nurseries and kindergartens. While the number of children waiting for places increased, the number who could be accepted shrank, and their mothers could not take jobs.

Maternity Leave

For many years statutory maternity leave has been fourteen weeks, which can be taken either before or after childbirth. The major part of this leave is paid for directly from the state treasury. In the late seventies demands for extended leave were put forward, and in 1979 the socialist parties and the women's movement launched a campaign for six months' maternity and three months' paternity leave, all to be paid for by the employers. A Children's Commission, set up jointly by the government and the Equal Rights Council, proposed a postnatal leave of seventeen weeks to be shared between the parents and, where necessary, eight weeks' pregnancy leave before birth. The response from the government was meager: a proposal to retain the fourteen-week maternity leave and to add, where necessary, an eight-week pregnancy leave and a one-week paternity leave following childbirth.

Nontraditional Jobs

The SD effort of the seventies to attract women to men's occupations may become a reality in the eighties. Employers are in support of such a policy, as is evidenced by a campaign they launched through the Danish

Employers' Association (DA) against a sex-divided labor market. The motivation behind this offensive derives neither from the women's movement nor from the trade unions, but from the shortage of skilled workers in the export industries. Women are taking up many jobs in these branches that were earlier reserved for men: welding in the shipyards is one example. The employers' prognosis for the late seventies and eighties is that 300,000 women will join the labor market while the intake of men will remain constant. The employers' change in attitude toward women is based on their observation that women no longer withdraw from the labor market when they have children, as well as on their own interest in drawing labor from the public sector into production. The present 20–25 percent female share of private sector employment they hope to increase to the 40–45 share now characteristic of the public sector. We cannot avoid the suspicion that this interest in employing women is tied to certain expectations: further division of labor in the former male skilled sectors, the employment of women to do the work at semiskilled rates, and the introduction of part-time work into these trades to increase their productivity.

HOW THE TRADE UNION MOVEMENT FUNCTIONS

LO, with just over a million members, is, as we noted above, the dominant factor in Danish trade unionism. The central problems concerning women in unions are thus related to LO. Over 482,000 women are organized under LO, making up roughly 40 percent of the total membership. Of these, 95,000 are in KAD; 67,000 in the Municipal Workers' Union (Dansk Kommunalarbejder Forbund—DKA); and 188,000 in HK. That is, just under 75 percent of all LO's women members are in these three unions. LO is overwhelmingly a blue-collar federation. HK, essentially a union of office workers, affiliated to it in 1932, joining with a few small office employees' unions to make up LO's white-collar component. Table 2-4 gives an overview of the numbers of blue- and white-collar workers organized in Denmark.

Trade union structure is hierarchical, and decision-making power resides in the executive committees at the upper levels of the institutions. The Danish trade unions have become steadily more centralized throughout this century as they have gained power and become accepted by and integrated into society. To an ever increasing degree, National Agreements are negotiated between LO and the employers' group, DA. More and more issues are centrally decided, with the result that the bargaining power of the individual trades and of local unions is increasingly limited. The National Agreement is renewed every second year, and DA and LO traditionally manage these negotiations themselves, enlisting the help of an official mediator only when necessary.

TABLE 2-4
Number and Percentage of Organized Workers in Denmark,
by Type of Employment, 1950–1976

	No. Organized		% Organized	
Year	Blue-Collar	White-Collar	Blue-Collar	White-Collar
1950	583,978	130,555	64.5	30.2
1960	668,382	286,795	68.9	50.8
1970	726,225	420,362	71.2	50.3
1976	841,024	642,472	84.0	58.2

Source: Peder J. Pedersen, *Aspekter af Fagbevaegelses vaekst i Danmark, 1911–1976* (Aspects of the Growth of Trade Unions in Denmark, 1911–1976), Memo 1979-5 (Aarhus: Økonomisk Institut, Aarhus Universitet, 1976), cited in Johannes Due, *Lønudviklingen for arbejdere efter 1950* (Wage Developments for Workers After 1950) (Copenhagen: Lavinkomstkommissionens Sekretariat, 1979).

In recent years the system has begun to disintegrate as a result of repeated government intervention in the negotiations. If this trend continues, it could mean the end of free bargaining. In 1981, however, unions and employers succeeded in many branches in making their own agreements without government aid, and even though their bargaining powers have been somewhat restricted, both DA and LO have nevertheless gained in influence over the government's economic policy.

Wage Systems

Union wage systems in Denmark allow for two kinds of wage setting, one for skilled and one for unskilled workers. The first, or minimum, rate in the biennial agreements allows skilled workers to negotiate locally for rates above those won nationally and thus permits a substantial amount of wage drift. The second is a standard rate set nationally for unskilled workers and only very rarely modified upward in local agreements.

This difference in wage systems has, of course, increased the inequality between skilled and unskilled earnings and has created divisions between the two categories. It has further had the effect of creating strong and weak unions and wage categories. The General Workers' Union (Specialarbejderforbundet i Danmark—SID) has responded, with the support of KAD, by fighting hard and successfully for an LO "wage policy based on solidarity"—that is, an understanding that the strong unions of the skilled will hold back on their demands while the standard rate for the unskilled rises. In 1977 the bargaining partners introduced a guaranteed wage of 29 kronor for the unskilled, and by 1981 this had been raised to 39 kronor. One result of this policy has been to raise women's earnings to the point that their registered wages for unskilled labor average 90 percent of men's.[2] Although it is in a sense short-sighted to raise women's wages on their unskilled jobs without attempting to improve their access to skilled work, the fact is that the solidary wage principle, coupled with centralized bargaining, has proved extremely effective. It is worth noting that the 90 percent of male earnings unskilled women receive is a higher proportion than exists in other countries.

Equal Pay

Equal pay has been one of LO's "general demands" in collective bargaining since 1957. Although Denmark ratified the ILO Convention 100 on equal pay in 1960, LO and the employers reached agreement in principle on the subject only with the National Agreement of 1971. The first steps toward realizing equal pay for equal work came with the 1973 National Agreement. After 1973 the standard rate of wages for men and women became the same, including cost-of-living adjustments and other increments detailed in the National Agreement. Minimum rates also became the same, and the regulation of wages above the minimum was to follow the same lines for men and women. Piecework rates and bonuses were to be set without regard to sex. Furthermore, all restrictions on women's access to certain kinds of work were to be abolished.

These agreements were all of a formal character. In reality, wage differentials based on sex have proved difficult to eradicate. Defining equal work is the crux of the problem. Employers all too frequently make men's and women's work just sufficiently different to legitimize different pay scales, with women always getting the lower wage. Only where jobs are identical are men and women sure of getting the same rates of pay. Nevertheless, the National Agreements are important to women because raises for men tend to mean raises for women too. When skilled workers get an increase, the unskilled—both men and women—usually succeed in at least maintaining the old relationship between skilled and unskilled wages, though this dependence on the raising of the skilled male wage for improvement in their own status is not an ideal situation.

UNIONS AND WOMEN

Trade union leaders often distance themselves from the people who have elected them and pursue policies that may not always have the support of us workers on the shop floor. Moreover, they show no enthusiasm about delegating any of their responsibility to us; sometimes it feels as if they have simply gone over to the other side of the negotiating table and look at us, as so many others do, as workers who are only hands with heads. . . . Much too often women who have become leaders have turned ladylike and refined—a pity, for we have no place for that kind of thing. What we need are women who will fight.

The above observations were made by Dagmar Andreasen, a sixty-year-old member of KAD who expresses a problem that affects women in all organizations. Women's inferior status in the labor market is, of course, due to their weak position—even weaker than that of unskilled men—vis-à-vis their employers, and no common struggle of men and women against the oppression of women as women has developed. That oppression consists chiefly in their assignment to low-paid tasks without access to skill training or promotional opportunities. Male trade unions have in effect accepted women's role in the labor market as unskilled and casual labor and as a consequence have often fought women instead of fighting their labor market function. They have not promoted, either among their members or in their official programs, an awareness that women in production are exploited not only as labor, but specifically as women.

KAD: An Independent Women's Union

For all its weaknesses and difficulties, KAD has shown steady growth throughout its existence. Founded in the late nineteenth century with about 800 members, its membership had grown by 1926 to 11,000 and by 1960 to a respectable 52,000. In 1979 it stood at 95,000.

Membership is spread all over the country, but the union, like many others, has its center of strength in Copenhagen. Because KAD members represent many occupations and come from many industries, they are organized in Copenhagen in industrial and occupational divisions. (Thus, division 5 is for women in the metal industry.) Elsewhere, however, where members are more scattered, each area has its own division to which all women in the locality, regardless of occupation, belong.

Altogether KAD has fifty-seven divisions. Local divisions bargain with all local employers of union members, while in Copenhagen each division bargains within its respective industry or trade. The major items of negotiation for KAD, as for all LO affiliates, are handled at the central office of LO. Centralized bargaining between LO and DA cover such issues as hours, holidays, and minimum or standard pay, leaving little room for the unskilled to carry on meaningful local bargaining.

Part of KAD's weakness lies in its structure. It organizes workers in widely different trades and therefore runs repeatedly into demarcation disputes with other unions, a fact that contributes to its marginal position in the labor movement. In addition, KAD, like the rest of the Danish union movement, has had internal problems with democracy and membership participation. Like other unions, KAD operates as a centralized, representative democracy. Each of its fifty-seven sections sends delegates to a general assembly that meets every six months; the highest authority is the convention that meets every third year to elect officers and write a program. As is also true of other LO unions, KAD's central executive committee has been headed consistently by social democrats, frequently right-wingers, who have never been interested in a less centralized or more democratic structure. Various opposition groups that have sprung up over the years within KAD have endeavored unsuccessfully to change its bylaws and structure. One of their goals has been to establish some procedure for calling interim meetings of the assembly and providing for membership referenda on issues before the executive.

The problems of its women members: double work, inadequate child care, and lack of educational and training opportunities, have never been on the KAD agenda, although it has a long history of fighting for better wages through collective bargaining. In short, it has followed the model of the male unions in structure and choice of issues. It has done so partly in response to its generally weak and marginal position among the male-dominated unions, which to this day continue to accuse KAD of splitting the working class by remaining independent. Unfortunately, KAD gives substance to these accusations by its failure to win support for a women's program that would justify its independent existence and it has consistently fought rank-and-file activists seeking to develop the unions independent strength.

KAD's leadership for its part maintains that it has difficulty in mobilizing the members to any kind of activity, whether it is militancy in collective bargaining or candidacy for positions as shop stewards or higher-level posts. Three factors seem to us to account for the members' apathy: restricted democracy within the union; the fact that it has never achieved a high rate of organization among women and hence lacks collective power; and its failure to deal with working women's unique situation in the shop and in the family.

Union leaders simply do not see the problem in these terms. They attribute the low percentage of organization to the low level of trade union consciousness among women: that is, a failure of appropriate personal commitment. KAD's official solution to its lack of influence in the trade union movement is to bring more women into the LO hierarchy and to teach women to concentrate on improving their wages and working conditions, ignoring, if they can, or managing as individuals, their family obligations.

In view of this concentration on wages, it is ironic that it was not until the 1950s that KAD added a demand for equal pay to its program, and then only in the restricted sense of equal pay for equal work. On this point, the union has been formally successful, though woman still get lower wages than men because they work at segregated, low-paid jobs. Women's failure to rise into skilled jobs or win promotions KAD regards as a problem of the individual: it has never raised the issue with employers or other institutions in the labor market. Thus, women themselves are seen as responsible for unequal pay, and the union avoids the central problem. KAD was not even the active initiator of the solidary wage policy; SID led the way, and KAD followed.

The first efforts to introduce what became the solidary wage policy in the sixties were not successful. It was early in the seventies that a general movement toward wage equalization began, as LO raised the standard minimum rates at each successive bargaining session. Continued success throughout the deepening recession has perhaps been due to the fact that further large-scale increases for the strong groups have become harder and harder to attain.

The result of the solidary wage policy, as noted above, has been a steady increase in women's wages. In 1970, 25 percent of KAD members were earning wages within 5 percent of the average union worker's wage; in 1978, 43 percent were. When the range around the average is broadened to 15 percent, then 71 percent of KAD members fell within it in 1970 and 94 percent in 1978. During the same period minimum rates also rose. The effect has been that more and more KAD members are earning the minimum wage: in 1960, 77 percent were; in 1970, 83 percent; and in 1978, 86 percent. Figure 2-1 illustrates the relationship of the unskilled male and female wages to the skilled male average wage over the period from 1920 to 1973: note the sharp rise in women's wages in relations to men's that followed the National Agreement of 1973.

Even before the 1971 National Agreement, activist groups within KAD were pressuring it to pursue its stated goal of equal pay. (These efforts were the first real cooperative undertaking of women unionists and women's liberation groups.) Despite the strong pressure that developed within KAD during this period, the 1973 National Agreement and the later agreements to equalize cost-of-living and other increments had the effect of diminishing union interest in further action to improve women's access to higher wages.

Recently several skilled workers' unions, notably those in the strong metal trades, have endeavored to build up affiliations with both unions of the unskilled, SID and KAD, in the hope of forming broad industrial unions. KAD insists, however, on its independence and particularly opposes any affiliation with SID. So long as women's wages continue to rise under the solidary wage policy implemented through the National Agreement, KAD has no great need for amalgamation, for it will not gain any more collective bargaining power for wage negotiations by joining with

Figure 2-1
Percentage of Skilled Worker's Average Wage Earned by
Unskilled and Female Workers in Denmark, 1920–1973

Percentage of Skilled Worker's Average Wage

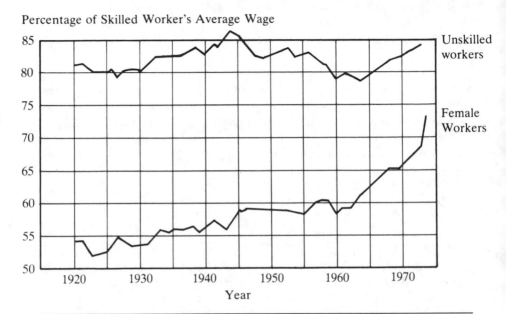

Source: Due, *Lønudviklingen for arbejdere*, p. 39, and information from statistical material of the Danish Employers' Association.

another union. It is further discouraged by the knowledge that the usual experience of women's unions that have merged with male ones has been subordination at all levels of union functioning.

HK: A White-Collar Union

All employees in commercial, office, and retail sales work are organized in HK. Although it was first formed in 1900, no employer recognized it until 1916, when a cooperative store signed a contract with it. Its first major organizational success, for both men and women, came in 1917–1920, record years for most Danish unions, when its membership doubled and it entered into agreements with a large number of employers. It affiliated with LO in 1932, mainly in order to keep its members from being used as strikebreakers.

Up until the 1960s, HK put most of its efforts into attempting to regulate working conditions by parliamentary statute. It obtained an act regulating the opening hours of shops but gave relatively little attention to improving conditions in the shops where members and potential members worked. Although HK made great advances in the sixties it has failed to organize a high proportion of its jurisdiction.

Occupational differences among its members make it difficult to carry through effective solidaristic politics. HK's diverse membership includes unskilled workers in libraries and laboratories as well as shop and office workers, and it is organized in both the public and the private sector. About 30 percent of HK's members are in the public sector, mainly in offices, while the 70 percent in the private sector are divided about equally between offices and stores. In the private sector it deals with a few large firms and many small ones. In the small firms the bond between worker and employer is frequently strong, and in such cases the unwritten law is "We don't discuss wages with each other."

Although the preponderance of the workers in HK's jurisdiction have always been women, it did not have a female majority until 1965. Table 2-5 gives the number and percentage of women working full and part time at white-collar jobs in Denmark.[3]

Women make up 75 percent of the union's membership, which passed 250,000 in 1980. Most of these women accept their secondary roles in the workforce, as in the larger society, although the women's movement is helping to change this attitude. Women's work in service and office jobs is typically thought of as particularly adapted to women's nature, whereas in fact the work, the wages, and the attitudes of supervisors are repressive of women as people. Nor have the employers alone been guilty of this contradiction; men in the union, on the whole, share these views.

The highest body of the union is an elected national executive commit-

TABLE 2-5

Number and Percentage of Women in Three White-Collar Sectors in Denmark, by Marital Status and Hours Worked; 1970

Sector	No. (thousands)		%	
	Total	Part Time	Total	Married
Distribution (private sector)	113	37	33	53
Office work (private sector)	47	14	31	46
Public administration	30	6	20	31
Total	190	57	30	48

Source: Foged, *Deltid-Kvindetid*, p. 104.

tee, of whom about 10 percent are now women. Their representation on this committee has risen slowly over a number of years. The chairperson is a man. The paid staff in local branches and head offices are appointed, not elected, and their positions are divided rather sharply into male and female ones. Women do secretarial work for both staff and elected officials, and many deal with internal matters mainly related to the unemployment compensation system. The vast majority of the staff are male; they deal mainly with the employers and are the union's external representatives.

The union's journal provides further clues to its attitude toward women members. By the seventies the references to "lovely ladies" had disappeared from the paper, and there tended to be more articles about workplaces numerically dominated by women. These articles, however, do not make it clear that the work they describe is still women's work done in female ghettos. Officially, the union does not recognize the occupational segregation between women and men.

Nevertheless, in 1965—long before any of the other mixed unions came out for equal pay—HK included a demand for it in its negotiations. It still treats equal pay primarily as a wage issue that women must fight for. As for other aspects of equality, the National Committee has placed them in the hands of a national Women's Equality Committee with both men and women members. (The men come mainly from important positions on the full-time staff, while the women are from local branches.) The committee's aim is to define women's problems and commission studies on how to achieve equality. It produced a discussion paper for the union's 1977 convention.

Although the debate on equality at this convention was scheduled for a single day, women delegates brought up related issues throughout the meeting. Women made up only about one-third of the delegates, but the opportunity to discuss their problems made them vocal, and a spontaneous enthusiasm spread among them. They were, of course, concerned about equal pay, but they argued that equality must be sought also through a reduction in working hours and the provision of free day care facilities. A lively discussion of internal union democracy led to the adoption of the referendum method for ratifying centrally negotiated collective agreements; previously they had been ratified by committees composed mainly of men. This change was carried by the votes of both men and women.

Specific women's demands, however, were rejected, the union's male president citing "the little difference between the sexes that we are all so glad about." The convention recommended, but did not require, that local branches set up equality committees. For all the women's activity at the meeting, the number of women on the National Executive Committee did not increase. As usual, candidates were elected who were already well known and well placed in the union hierarchy.

In contrast, in spite of the precedent created by the appointment of both men and women to HK's national Equality Committee, many local committees consist entirely of women. This is the case, for example, in the book and paper branch in Copenhagen. Many women who would not otherwise have had the time or confidence to seek official union positions have taken an active part in these committees. During the last half of the seventies, as a consequence of their work, local branches have given a higher priority to issues of sex equality. One important demand is for union-sponsored child-minding facilities for all those attending union study groups.[4] The demand has been met in at least one HK branch to the extent that child care is grudgingly offered on a trial basis. A demand for reimbursement for the child care costs of parents attending union meetings and courses has also been partly met. Not only do women activists benefit from these improvements, but other women are able to begin to become active.

Women's groups have not been as successful in other areas, however. The demand raised by a number of activists for a women's meeting to discuss an agenda for collective bargaining was blocked by the national leadership on the grounds that equality is a question for both men and women and therefore to limit such a meeting to women would be undemocratic. The problems of women, the executive seems to assume, will be solved by equality, but the way to achieve equality is for women to learn in union courses to behave more like men.

WOMEN'S FUTURE IN THE UNIONS

The experience of the last decade would seem to indicate at least two facts about women's situation in the unions. First, women are no longer passive, either at home or on the job; they have responded to a wide range of women's issues. As a result of the growth in the number of women union members and the penetration of the unions by women's organizations, women are more and more aware of their condition and prepared to work for change. Second, women's groups within the unions and the women's movement alike are insisting that their struggle for equal rights can furnish a new basis for the whole trade union movement. The traditional structure of many labor organizations has discouraged or even barred discussions of women's double work and life. In women's groups, by contrast, it has been possible to make the common features of women's lives visible. Such groups have exposed the occupational inequality and hierarchical structure of work life, in which women are at the bottom: the divisions that persist between full-and part-time workers, the unions' almost exclusive concentration on men's conditions and problems, the dominance of men in the unions, and the general acceptance of the myths of man as breadwinner and woman as a passive element in family and social life.

Bringing women's problems before the unions should contribute not just to raising women's consciousness, but also to opening men's eyes to the relation between work and family and the need for their participation in both. Were the double burden, for example, to become a central theme of this struggle, men as well as women would be involved and benefited, for men also have family lives, though their roles are sometimes marginal, whatever their wishes in the matter. For the present, though, the question of shorter hours provides one example of how far apart the sexes are and how disparately they view a major union demand in collective bargaining.

Shorter Hours and Parental Leave

Many Danish unions advanced the demand for shorter hours in their 1979 negotiations, mainly in the form of a proposal for a thirty-five-hour week with forty hours' pay. What they got instead was a small increase in the number of paid holidays. Such a solution, while not objectionable in itself, does nothing to increase equality between the sexes. On the contrary: holidays often mean extra work for women at home. For men as for women, it is of decisive importance that the reduction of total working time take the form of fewer hours per day and not fewer days per week or year. The latter alternatives will only increase the pressure on family life—already intense when both parents work—and make the contrast between work and leisure even greater than it is today. Men may refuse to take a greater share of family responsibility on days they consider set aside for leisure, and thus longer weekends may end up increasing women's work at home. A reduction in daily hours, on the other hand, improves the possibilities of getting men to share daily housework and parenting. It may in addition enable more women to work full time.

Paternity leave is a closely related issue. Men, as well as women, can be parents and should be able to obtain paternity leave. It is a fundamental condition for equality in the labor market that both men and women be eligible for leave after childbirth or when a sick child needs care.

Quality of Work Life

Danish unions have not yet fully directed their attention to restructuring jobs and improving the job environment; they have traditionally only bargained for more pay for difficult work and poor conditions. Now they are beginning to focus on the job and not just on the persons doing it. There is also a need to consider the social uses and purposes of the products of work and to analyze how each workplace can best be used to produce goods that people need.

Working Class Unity

The structure of work and of the unions themselves has resulted in severe cleavages between workers, even organized workers. In Denmark these are visible between part-time and full-time workers, skilled and unskilled ones, and the men and women who have come to play particular gender roles in both categories.

The distinction between skilled and unskilled workers has led the unskilled to claim that the skilled feather their own nests in wage negotiations at the expense of less advantaged workers. It is a sign of hope that the two unions of the unskilled, SID and KAD, have succeeded in promoting the solidary wage policy. SID's proposal to amalgamate with KAD also shows a new sense of solidarity. But the continuing job differentiation between men and women is the real root of women's inequality. It is the nature of women's jobs—not the fact that many working women are mothers—that traps women in part-time work. The structural and sectoral divisions in the labor market further support and profit from the part-time work of women.

Even though unskilled women have their own union, KAD has not dealt with these problems because it is at bottom no different, either structurally or politically, from the other unions. Constricted by the structure and power of the male labor movement with which it is affiliated, it accepts the dominant myths, viewpoints, and priorities of the unions that men dominate in their own interests.

Alliances

Today unions and other groups work together in a way that was not possible a generation ago. The relationship of today's women's movement to the trade unions, for example, is different from that of the fundamentally middle-class feminist movement of the twenties and thirties. At that time the SD rejected the issues raised by middle-class women as irrelevant to the party's working-class constituency. Now, in order to maintain its electoral supremacy, the SD has extended its base far beyond the working class. The party must inevitably adopt a stance that will reflect the demands of these new voters—including feminists—and integrate them into its politics. The SD has demonstrated repeatedly that it is responsive to such pressures and indeed must be responsive to them to ensure its hegemony.

Opposition groups within the unions have historically been unsuccessful because of the unions' high degree of centralization and the extensive overlapping of party and union leaderships. Now, however, such groups can look forward to alliances with autonomous forces like feminist and consumer groups and can co-opt their demands and even their programs. An alliance between the women's movement and the labor movement in "equal pay groups" helped achieve the equal pay breakthrough of 1973. The prospect of a similar alliance is raised by the affiliation of KAD to the Danish Women's National Council (Danske Kvinders Nationalräd—DKN).

Changes in the nature of work brought about by technology, changes in the concept of women's role stemming from the women's movement, changes in attitudes toward work and wages arising from the restructuring of the labor market and the participation in it of more and more women, and changes in the scope and goals of SD politics all must have their effect. It is doubtful that they will quickly and radically change women's place in the unions, but inevitably they will change traditional bureaucratic views and policies.

GLOSSARY

AC	Akademikernes Centralorganisation: National Association of University-Trained Employees
DA	Danish Employers' Association
DKA	Dansk Kommunalarbejder Forbund: Danish Municipal Workers' Union
DKN	Danske Kvinders Nationalräd: Danish Women's National Council
EEC	European Economic Community
FTF	Funktionaer og Tjenestemadsforbundet: Office and Civil Servants' Union
HK	Handels og Kontorfunktionaerernes Forbund: Commercial and Office Employees' Union
ILO	International Labour Organisation
KAD	Kvindelig Arbejderforbund i Danmark: Danish Women Workers' Union
LO	Landesorganisation: Danish Confederation of Trade Unions
SD	Social Democratic party
SF	Socialistisk Folkeparti: Socialist People's party
SFAH	Selskabet til Forskning i Arbejdervaegelsens Historie: Society for the Study of Labour History
SID	Specialarbejderforbundet i Danmark: General Workers' Union

NOTES

1. Some of the improvement is unquestionably a product of the constant decline in the birth rate that followed the introduction of the pill in the sixties and the right to free abortion in 1973.

2. Not all wages are registered in the statistics provided by employers or state authorities. Only one-third of employers are organized in DA, and the statistics DA compiles are based on research carried out among its members. It is essential to keep

in mind that a large part of the female labor force works for unorganized employers outside the registered and controlled labor market.

3. HK's jurisdiction includes some "pink-collar" workers not counted in Table 2-5, while some of the academics in public administration included here are actually not HK members.

4. The Architects' Union, outside LO, has a plan similar to this.

BIBLIOGRAPHY

Aarbog fra Selskabet til Forkning i Arbejderveaegelsens Historie, 1978 (Society for the Study of Labor History Yearbook, 1978). Copenhagen: SFAH, 1979. (Hereafter *SFAH Yearbook.*)

Borchorst, Annette, et al. *Hvor gik kvinderne hen, da de gik ud?* (Where Did the Women Go When They Left Home?). Aarhus: Modtryk, 1976.

Borchorst, Annette, and Randi Markussen. *Kvindegruppetekster* (Women's Groups Texts), no. 24. Aarhus: Fagtryk, 1975.

Broch, Birthe. "Kvinder i konfektionsindustrien, 1890–1914" (Women in the Clothing Industry, 1890–1914). Copenhagen: SFAH, 1977.

Christensen, Margit, et al. *Kvinder i elektronikindustrien* (Women in Electronics). Aarhus: Modtryk, 1976.

Dahlsgard, Inga. "Women in Denmark Yesterday and Today." In *Det danske Selskab.* Copenhagen, 1980.

Dübeck, Inger. "Female Trade Unions in Denmark." *Scandinavian Journal of History* 5 (1980).

Due, Johannes. *Lønudviklingen for arbejdere efter 1950* (Wage Developments for Workers After 1950). Copenhagen: Lavinkomstkommissionens Sekretariat, 1979.

Emerek, Ruth, and Birte Siim. *Kvinder i tobaksindustrien* (Women in the Tobacco Industry). Aarhus: Modtryk, 1976.

Equality Council. *Annual Report 1979.* Copenhagen: 1980.

Foged, Brita. *Kvindearbejde, 1950–1971* (Women's Work, 1950–1971). Aarhus: Modtryk, 1975.

———. "HK's Kvindeopfattelse" (HK's Concept of Women). In *SFAH Yearbook, 1978.* Copenhagen: SFAH. 1979.

Foged, Brita, et al. *Deltid—Kvindetid* (Part-Time—Women's Time). Aarhus: Modtryk, 1980.

Walter Galenson. *The Danish System of Labour Relations.* Cambridge: Harvard University Press, 1952.

Knudsen, Knud, and Jan Kaare Knudsen. *Arbejdere, arbejderbevaegelse Danmark, 1920–1939* (Workers, Workers' Movements in Denmark, 1920–1939). Aarhus: Fagtryk, 1979.

Knudsen, Knud, and Jørgen Bloch Poulsen. *"Arbejdskamp, Arbejdsret"* (Workers' Struggles, Workers' Rights). *Politisk Revy,* 1979.

Markussen, Randi. *Lavindkomstproblemer blandt underordnede butiksfunktionaerer* (Low-Income Problems Among Subordinate Shop Workers). Copenhagen: Lavinkomstkomissionens Sekretariat, 1980.

————. "Socialdemokratiet, Veldaerdsstaten og Kvinderne" (Social-Democratic Party, the Welfare State and Women). *DJH #18*. Aarhus: Modtryk, 1980.

Possing, Birgitte. "Arbejderkvinder og kvindearbejde i Københaven ca. 1870–1906" (Women Workers and Women's Work in Copenhagen around 1870–1906). Aalborg: AUC, 1980.

Sandvad, Karin. "Den kvindelige fagbevaegelse i København 1870–1900" (The Women's Trade Union Movement in Copenhagen 1870–1900). In *SFAH Yearbook, 1972*. Copenhagen: SFAH, 1973.

Stiegl, Lars and Helle Otte. "Socialpōlitik i Danmark 1891–1977" (Social Policy in Denmark 1891–1977). *DJH 10*. Aarhus: Modtryk, 1977.

3 FEDERAL REPUBLIC OF GERMANY

Alice H. Cook

HISTORY

German unions have a long history: more than a hundred years under four very different systems of government—the Empire until 1918, the Weimar Republic until 1933, the Thousand Year Reich until 1945, and the present Federal Republic. Each of these changes has involved a radical readjustment, and three have required a new beginning. While the unions inevitably carry with them relics of their varied history, including certain continuing problems, the circumstances surrounding these problems have changed decidedly over time. One of them is where and how to deal with women in the unions—"die Frauenfrage"—an issue that has produced eloquent rhetoric and attracted the attention of important theoreticians.

At every stage, official trade union views have reflected accepted social attitudes on women's role in society. At the very time when the classical socialist writers were drawing from history and Marxist doctrine the lesson that the emancipation of women will come with the emancipation of the working class,[1] the unions were debating whether women should be permitted to work outside the home; or, if they were, whether they should be allowed to join men's organizations. Although the socialist principle of equality early dictated that they should be admitted to unions, and union policy after 1892 called for their inclusion, they were received for the most part into a women's segregated division that remained understaffed and underbudgeted.[2] The small number of women who joined unions and the even smaller number who rose to prominence became an excuse for union leaders to neglect the organization of women and to blame women themselves for an inherent lack of interest, initiative, and stability. Resolutions on equal pay floated ephemerally on a sea of special women's pay rates, set by collective bargaining at 70 to 75 percent of the male rate even when the work was the same.[3]

Attitudes toward women as workers and as union members changed with the changing social climate, but it took until the 1970s to revise women's legal status. Till then, the male worker was legally the breadwinner and head of the family. His spouse was assigned by law to her position as wife and mother and could work only with her husband's permission. Women were judged to need special protection in working life, not because they were unduly exploited as workers, as indeed they were, but because their exploitation might endanger their procreative function and thus damage the future of the race. Protective laws limited daily and weekly working hours, forbade night work, and closed underground construction and work at heights to women. Indubitably, these laws, strongly supported by the unions and their women members, had the effect of strengthening the other factors that confined women in a narrow range of segregated jobs— "women's work"—presumably fitted to their weaker physical and mental powers and commanding lower wages.

Unions, originally creatures of the Social Democratic party (Sozialdemokratische Partei Deutschlands— SPD),[4] continued to be closely allied to it up to 1933, although after the turn of the century they moved further and further away from the party's presumably revolutionary purpose.[5] Indeed, it was the unions that, as their power increased and as the party rose to visibility and influence in parliament, moved the party in the direction of social democracy and away from social revolution.[6] One effect of this shift was to place the achievement of women's equality in the very distant future and to commit the unions only to gradual movement and spasmodic attention to women's issues. Before the end of World War I, the party and the unions, like the bourgeois women's movement, believed that when women won the suffrage most of their problems would be solved by political means. (Women gained the vote with the founding of the Weimar Republic in 1919.)

Women were actively recruited into men's jobs during World War I, and all protective legislation was set aside to enable them to take on men's work in the war industries. After demobilization, however, only a few women remained in the jobs that had been traditionally men's, and the old pattern of female employment almost immediately reasserted itself. Indeed, the social-democrats who took over the government in 1918 issued decrees removing women from their jobs as men returned from the front.[7]

The 1920s produced few advances for women. Central issues for the unions at the beginning of the decade were the establishment of the system of works councils and the problems engendered by inflation and unemployment. Unemployment engulfed them at the end of the twenties, and thereafter they were almost exclusively engaged in defensive actions against both communists and the growing Nazi movement.

The Hitler period from 1933 until the end of World War II was, in contrast to the nominal egalitarianism of the Weimar Republic, unabashedly antifeminist; Hitler aimed to push women out of the labor market. An executive order of August 1933 directed employers to discharge all married women whose husbands earned above 125 DM per month. Exceptions, however, were allowed for reasons of business necessity or if no unemployed male could be found to fill the woman's job. Although Nazi purists espoused the view that no women should work outside the home, the vast majority recognized that economic necessity and the surplus of women over men made this an impossible dream. "Womanly work" in agriculture, social work, domestic service, nursing, education, and any profession concerned with women or children was readily acceptable. "As the need for women in areas outside the realm of 'womanly work' increased, Nazi ideology labeled such employment 'a woman's sacrifice for her people.'"[8] Social programs available to working women included greatly extended and enriched maternity protection, a benefit not diminished in the postwar years.[9] During the Nazi period the women's organization, Die Frauenschaft, systematically brainwashed women about their social role with a thoroughness that left its mark, even when women became heads of families through widowhood or the imprisonment of their husbands.

By 1939, 52.8 percent of all women able to work and between fifteen and sixty years of age were employed. Of these, almost half were married. Officially, female unemployment had fallen to 18,500 in 1939 from 940,000 at the beginning of the Nazi regime. During the war years, 1939–1944, women's employment grew slowly from 14,626,000 to 14,897,000.[10]

When the present trade union organization, the DGB (Deutscher Gewerkschaftsbund), was established in 1949, it was headed almost entirely by leaders whose experience had been gained in the 1920s and whose ideas of reform were largely a reaction to the Weimar and Nazi experiences. They would correct the weaknesses that had led to their defeat. They insisted upon a unified, nonpartisan, industrial union structure to avoid the dangers of rival unionism, craft organization, and divisive ties to political parties.[11] Lest there be any misunderstanding, they early made clear their loyalty to the state.[12]

Women were included, of course, in the new union structure. As in the prewar years, a women's division was established as their home base, and for the first time its head, a woman, would be ex officio a member of the DGB executive. The federation's president, Hans Böckler, insisted, however that this post be filled by a Catholic, a member of the Christian-Democratic Union party. Thus, the one woman on the executive was a member of a small political minority within the unions, although her party made up the majority in parliament and formed the government.

As Germany rebuilt under a series of conservative governments, economic and business leaders, having absorbed several million German refugees from the East, adopted the policy of importing millions of foreign workers. Mobilizing the potential resource represented by housewives was not discussed. The result was a stagnation in women's entry into the labor market: during the entire postwar period, they have made up somewhat less than 37 percent of the workforce.

International organizations have had a significant influence on German policies on working women. The European Economic Community (EEC), the International Labour Organisation (ILO), and the Office for Economic Cooperation and Development (OECD) have all set forth norms on employment to which member countries are expected or (in the case of the EEC) required to conform.[13] Several ministries of the German government and parliament itself have called for a replication of the studies produced by these agencies to serve as a base of information and guidance on the development of national policies for working women.[14]

The unions' program on women, adopted at the DGB's founding convention in 1949, contained three major points: women's right to work, the extension of protective legislation, and equal pay for equal work. In 1963 and again in 1969, the program was considerably rewritten. The three major points became the right to work, the advancement of equal opportunity, and the achievement of equal rights. These general goals were specified in sixty-five demands, grouped under ten headings and addressed to various age groups; young women, married and single women, women at re-entry, and retirees.[15] At the 1980 celebration of the seventy-fifth anniversary of women's work in the trade unions, special emphasis was given, in addition, to reform of the pension system and to improvement of maternity protection.[16]

In the thirty years since the founding of the DGB, its approach to women's problems has undergone important changes as a result of both internal and external pressures. In 1950, for example, the unions referred to working women as "double earners." After Maria Weber became the second head of the DGB Women's Division in the mid-sixties, it initiated an educational program on the status and problems of women directed at both trade union women and their male colleagues. It commissioned a number of studies on working women, one of which showed that married women worked mainly out of economic necessity and in doing so contributed significantly to family earnings and to the economy. The official union position shortly shifted to positive support for women combining work and marriage. Concern that women with small children should not work outside the home became an interest in increasing the number of places in nursery schools and kindergartens. The attitude toward these centers then changed too: once seen as necessary but undesirable substitutes for mothers' care, they are now valued for their contribution to preparing children for formal education and social life with peers.[17]

These efforts had their immediate culmination in the DGB's designation of 1972 as the Year of Working Women. All unions focussed on women's problems that year, and Weber herself became first vice-president of the federation. When International Women's Year (IWY) followed in 1975, the Women's Division took advantage of the circumstances to re-mobilize its members and reiterate their demands and views within the federation. The recession of the late 1970s, however, has unquestionably diminished the momentum that these efforts had developed.

LEGISLATION AND POLITICS

Postwar German unions were founded on the principle that they would be nonpartisan but by no means nonpolitical. They use their close contacts in the parties to initiate proposals and lobby for support, including on women's issues. Representatives of all parties speak at the national women's conferences and often remain to listen to the debates and decisions.

Although German women have little political interest, according to the DGB's own studies and independent investigations,[18] much trade union activity is devoted to improving protective legislation for working women. The present major emphasis, however, is on reforming pension laws in the interest of sex equality; the Supreme Court has ruled that present legislation is unconstitutional and must be rewritten by 1984.[19] This ruling follows an EEC directive on equality in pension rights.

A review of legislative activities during the first half of the seventies indicates the range of successes achieved by the trade union and women's organizations despite the rank-and-file women's generally low commitment to political activity:

- 1971—extension of the vocational training act to support training for housewives who wish to go to work;
- 1972—reform of pension insurance to permit the self-employed and housewives to participate;
- 1973—governmental support for family day care as an aid to both working mothers and mothers of small children who wish to earn an income by caring for others' children;
- 1974—provision for the health insurance program to pay for parental leaves up to five days a year to care for sick children;
- 1975—a new marriage and divorce law permitting women to choose to work irrespective of husbands permission and providing for equal responsibility between the spouses for the maintenance of the marriage and household responsibilities.[20]

German working women may be apathetic about electoral politics, but they—and their allies in other women's groups—are ready and able to act as a pressure group to improve women's status and working conditions.

The majority of trade union women and men who are party members belong to the SPD. This political predominance became clear during the campaign for the right to abortion in the 1970s. Although not all unions came out in favor of the reform bill, out of consideration for their Catholic members, yet in city after city, sometimes under SPD leadership, sometimes under union banners, women demonstrated, signed petitions, and lobbied members of parliament in behalf of a new law.

On such matters, as well as on issues of wages and working conditions, the trade union women's alliance with the German Women's Council (der Deutsche Frauenrat) has brought them support far beyond labor's ranks and, on such issues as parental leave for the first year of a child's life, far more support than they have gained from their male union colleagues. The council speaks for broad band of German women—nearly all those involved in women's organizations. While Maria Weber was head of the DGB Women's Division and first vice-president of that organization, she served two separate terms as president of the council. Alliances with nonpartisan women's organizations represent an important source of strength for union women.

WOMEN IN THE LABOR MARKET

German women in 1980 made up 52.4 percent of the nation's population. They were 37 percent of its 23 million wage and salary earners. Projections of both employment numbers and ratios of men to women up to the year 2000 indicate slight changes.[21] Fifty-nine percent of working women in 1979 were in white-collar work, 36 percent in production, and 5 percent in the civil service. Of the 8.5 million employed women in Germany, about 600,000 are foreign "guest workers," somewhat more than one-fourth of all the foreign workers still in Germany in 1980.

Since 1972 the number of unemployed women has increased steadily, and since 1977 women have made up more than half of the unemployed.[22] The Federal Employment Institute Bundesanstalt für Arbeit—BfA—Germany's labor market board—finds three main reasons for women's high rate of unemployment: lack of qualification for skilled work; preference for part-time work at a time when such openings are sharply diminishing; and the age of many women seeking to enter the labor force.

A growing number of working women are married and have children. in 1950, 36.4 percent of women wage and salary earners were married; in 1977, 60.6 percent were, and about 3 million of these women had children under fifteen years of age.[23] The fact that most German schools close at 1 P.M. and provide no lunch service means that many mothers must seek part-time employment. In 1977, 27 percent of all working women held part-time jobs.[24] In the ensuing recession, part-time workers were among the first eliminated from industry and, to a lesser degree, from offices. Despite the cuts in part-time job openings, however, the number of women seeking part-time employment is increasing steadily along with the number of married women in the labor force. The unions, led in this instance by their women's divisions, for the most part oppose the extension of part-time work, seeing it "not as leading to full-time work but only to its fractionalization and serving to encourage rationalization and the increase of labor intensification."[25]

Women find work predominantly in about seventeen occupations out of a total of several hundred.[26] The BfA established in 1969 under the Employment Promotion Act, is responsible for the national labor market policy and program. In addition to administering the unemployment insurance system, its overall task is to "maintain a quantitative and qualitative equilibrium of supply and demand on the labor market that has priority over other activities."[27] It is also charged with improving the integration of women into the world of work and an increasing number of occupations. The law specifically calls for special attention to "women whose placement is made difficult under the normal conditions of the labor market because they are or were married or for other reasons tied down by household duties" (Par. 2 [5]). In carrying out this mandate, the BfA supports many voluntary and proprietary agencies in offering vocational programs deemed to meet labor market needs; it also subsidizes employers to conduct on-the-job training and provides counseling and placement services at the several hundred employment offices.[28] The BfA's policy is set at every level of its operation by tripartite boards to which the unions send about one-third of the members. The law calls for women to serve on these boards, and the unions have named 30 of the 32 women who serve at the regional level, out of a total of 861 members, 215 of whom are named by the unions. The unions take credit for having influenced both the adoption of the law and the policies of the BfA, although they are well aware of the inadequacy of its measures and their own contribution to its policy and program.[29] The Women's Division report on women's work for 1977–1981, presented to the 1982 DGB Congress, for example, details the difficulties unemployed women face in meeting the eligibility requirements for assistance with vocational training grants.[30]

A central determinant of how well such programs meet women's needs is the BfA view of women's role in the labor market. How has the BfA, in particular, responded to women's special problems during the recession? On the negative side, considerable anecdotal evidence gathered by the unions substantiates charges of bias and male chauvinism, particularly on the part of local labor office staffs. Maria Weber points to the existence of separate departments and staff for men and women and to the fact that women have been directed consistently toward less secure occupations with less opportunity for upward mobility than men.[31] A decided trend has developed since 1976 of making conditions for training more stringent and less available to women.[32] The BfA points to falling numbers of women applying for training exactly when unemployment became critical.[33] Although these numbers showed a considerable increase in following years, women are far underrepresented among trainees.[34]

A great variety of training projects for young women in both traditional and nontraditional occupations is supported by federal and provincial ministries with a wide range of sponsors, including private industry, vocational training centers under public and private auspices, the trade unions, and adult education agencies.[35] On the whole, however, the picture is of a society and a powerful labor movement only marginally concerned with the fate of female workers, whether young or mature. It is difficult to conclude that the BfA places equal opportunity high on its agenda, nor is there evidence that the unions have insisted that it do so.

WOMEN IN THE UNIONS

Women's membership in the unions has increased steadily since the major drive to enroll them in 1972, the Year of Working Women. Over the period from 1967–1977, the number of unionized women grew from 976,793 to 1,402,643, or from 15.3 percent of total union membership to 18.8 percent.[36] At the end of 1978, this figure had increased to 19.1 percent. In 1979 it was 19.6, and by 1980 it had passed 20 percent.

In 1972 and in several years thereafter, women represented more than half of all new members enrolled. In 1975 women made up 75 percent of new members; in 1979 they were 63 percent. In 1976 and 1977 men's membership fell while women's continuously rose, and this trend persisted through 1980.[37]

White-collar workers have been the main source of growth in DGB unions. Women increased their proportion of white-collar union membership from 30.1 percent to 35 percent between 1967 and 1977. Women's membership in the independent white-collar union DAG also increased in that period, although total membership was falling.[38]

In both the DAG and the DGB, women's interests are represented by a special women's division with a female staff.[39] In the DGB this is one of several functional departments replicated in each industrial union's structure.

Only a few unions have reported the number of foreign women in their membership, and still fewer have kept track of their election to union office. The DGB and some but not all of its affiliates have established departments concerned with foreign workers, but the largest of these, the IG Metall, the Metal Workers' Union, has made no attempts to reach its women members through education programs, largely because tradition and custom forbid many of these women to join mixed groups with men or to participate in public affairs. The IG Chemie, the Chemical Workers, have been able to report that 14.4 percent of the foreign workers elected as works councillors were women in a union where 15.4 percent of the membership is female.

At its 1949 founding convention, the DGB adopted guidelines for its work with women. Although a change in these was considered at a special DGB Congress in 1971, they remain unchanged. They prescribe the structure of the Women's Division, call for its close cooperation with the federation and "with democratic women's organizations that recognize and support trade union demands," and draw special attention to international relationships through government and trade union bodies.[40] Despite the lack of structural and administrative change, the division's program, as noted above, has been considerably revised over the years. In administering this program, the division has taken on a substantial life of its own as an active political entity within the DGB. A spokeswoman evaluating this program in 1976 could see changes for the better in respect to equal pay for work of equal value and some improvement in women's social security rights, but she was dissatisfied with the very slow movement in achieving changes in women's education, in the retrogression of labor market policy as evidenced by high female unemployment rates, and in the inadequacy of the five days' annual leave allowed women to care for sick family members.[41] Small wonder that delegates to the 1977 National Conference petitioned the DGB to work out an "action program that would set timetables for the realization of the federation's policy statement on women."[42]

The Year of the Working Women in 1972 represented both a climax of many years of the division's work and a leap forward. The unions emphasized the evaluation of women's work in the "light-wage" groups in union scales for production workers (discussed in more detail below in the section on collective bargaining) and the campaign to increase the number of women members. The DGB journal devoted its entire November issue that year to a discussion of women's problems.[43] Externally, the division brought its program to public attention by advertising in twenty-nine journals and magazines a questionnaire on women's work and home life addressed to organized and unorganized women and their husbands. The report that emerged was based on nine thousand replies; many respondents had attached letters containing details of family discussions on the issues raised. The report commanded wide attention. Several institutions, among them the BfA, distributed copies to their entire staffs.[44]

To what degree has this activity resulted in integrating women into union structure at its various levels? Women's participation rate in union meetings and honorary (unpaid) positions at the shop and local level is illustrated in Table 3-1. As the table shows, these rates are not drastically below women's proportion of total membership. It is when we look at full-time trade union offices that the participation of women in every leadership post except that of secretarial employee plummets, as Table 3-2 makes clear.

Although Table 3-1 shows consistent, if slow, improvement over the years in women's participation in union office, a decided decline in their representation on bargaining committees has occurred at the district level. The offsetting gain in their appearance on national bargaining committees has to be evaluated with the knowledge that most bargaining goes on at the regional or district level with the appropriate associations of employers, industry by industry. Without detailed knowledge about the unions con-

TABLE 3-1

Participation of Women in Honorary Functions
of the Trade Unions of the DGB, 1974 and 1979

Position	No. of Officials 1979	No. of Men 1979	No. of Women 1979	Women as Percentage of Participants 1979	1974
*Local office**					
Executive Board	20,186	18,099	2,087	10.3	9.6
Shop Steward	190,171	160,270	29,892	15.7	10.6
Other	33,818	30,728	3,090	9.1	7.5
*District Office**					
Executive Board	1,324	1,191	133	10.0	8.9
Bargaining Commissions	3,113	2,785	328	10.5	12.8
Other	3,861	3,293	568	14.7	4.2
National Executive†					
Executive Committee	337	311	26	7.7	7.5
Bargaining Commissions	1,179	1,045	134	11.4	6.1
Other	573	499	54	9.8	6.5

*Figures for local and district office do not include the Printing and Paper; Railroad; Education and Science; Distributive, Banking, and Insurance; Art; Leather; and police unions. The figures for shop stewards also do not include the Chemical Workers, and the figures for bargaining commissions do not include the Foodworkers' Union.

†National executive figures do not include the Printing; Paper and Education and Science; Distributive, Banking and Insurance; Leather; and Police unions.

Source: DGB Geschäftsbericht (Quadrennial Report), Women's Section, "Women's Work, 1977–1981" (Düsseldorf: DGB, 1981), p. 96.

cerned, one can only speculate about the overall loss or gain in women's influence at critical points of bargaining. A few unions have reported on women's participation in bargaining. The Candy and Confectionery section of the NGG, the Foodworkers, called attention in 1980 to the increase from four to six women in their twelve negotiating bodies; the Metal Workers in 1979 reported that there were 60 women delegates to their negotiating bodies, 5 percent of the total number.[45] As we shall see in the discussion of collective bargaining, however, the nature of all bargaining systems is such that the real influentials in the process are the professionals who conduct the "hard bargaining" that is crucial to a settlement. Women seldom appear

TABLE 3-2

Representation of Women on the DGB, 1974 and 1979

	No. of Staff Members				Women as % of Total Staff	
	Total	Men	Women			
Position	1979	1979	1979	1974	1979	1974
County						
County chair	210	206	4	4	1.9	1.7
Business mgrs. and assistants	305	264	41	23	13.4	11.0
Business agents	170	158	12	8	7.1	5.0
Youth and education directors	32	30	2		6.3	
State Districts						
Full-time members of exec. committees	27	26	1	1	3.7	3.7
Business agents	92	66	26	24	28.3	15.3
Secretaries, admin. aides, and other employees	837	25	812	723	97.0	97.7
National Executive						
Full-time members of exec. committees	9	8	1	1	11.1*	11.1
Department heads	130	110	20	20	15.4	15.9
Secretaries, admin. aides, and other employees	195	46	149	124	76.4	76.5

*In 1981, a second woman was named to the National Executive Committee of the DGB, thus bringing the female participation rate to 22.2 percent.
Source: DGB, *Geschäftsbericht, 1977–81* (Quadrennial Report), Women's Section, "Women's Work, 1977–1981," p. 97.

among this group. The honorary members of the bargaining commissions in fact play little role in deciding agendas and are mostly called in to approve or disapprove accomplished agreements.

Among full-time staff, as Table 3-2 makes clear, women are in an overwhelming majority as secretaries and administrative aides. Most of the women holding full-time staff positions are in the women's divisions, although some unions have been making efforts to recruit them for positions as business managers and business agents. The four women who are heads of county offices are particularly noteworthy, as are the twenty women department heads at national DGB headquarters. This table does not detail the appearance of women in comparable offices in the individual industrial unions. It is important to note, however, that the second-largest union in Germany, Öffentliche Transport und Verkehr, the Public Transport and Traffic Workers (ÖTV), in 1981 selected a woman to be national president, the first such occurrence in German labor history.

Interviews conducted with women staff members in four industrial unions suggested that many who wished to advance in union careers avoided, if they could, work in their union's women's division because they saw it as a backwater where they would stagnate. "Women are treated as though they are women by profession" is the way Claudia Pinl puts it.[46]

An important campaign begun during the Year of Working Women was aimed at increasing the number of women works councillors. These are not necessarily union members, but they are elected triennially under federal law by the entire body of employees in all but the very smallest concerns. About 85 percent are in fact union members. Several, but not all, unions have a second—and fully union—body of stewards (Vertrauensmänner) in the shop whose job is to carry on union administrative business: organizing, dues collection, propaganda, communications. The Metal Workers' and the Chemical Workers' unions give them equal status with the works councillors in terms of schooling and support by union staff. In such unions the office of shop steward would be an equally likely springboard to full-time or honorary union leadership.[47] Table 3-3 shows what has been achieved in getting women elected to positions on work councils, particularly since 1972, when the women began their campaign to increase their representation on them. Comparable figures on shop steward elections, which are conducted according to union bylaws with varying terms of office, rules for eligibility, duties, powers, and perquisites, have not been assembled.

Among the women elected to works councils in 1981, 4,731 were chairpersons. Table 3-4 shows the increase in these numbers, as compared with those for 1978, in four unions. It also shows some part of the DGB statistics on women chairpersons. Significantly, the number of women chosen as chairs for works councils has increased in these last two elections not only in HBV and Textil where women predominate in the workforce, but in the male-dominated jurisdiction where IG Chemie and IG Metall organize.

TABLE 3-3

Number of Women Elected to Works Councils
in Four Trade Unions and the DGB (various years, 1959–1981)

Union	1959	1961	1963	1965	1968	1972	1975	1978	1981
IG Chemie	1,440	1,458	1,484	1,479	1,416	2,094	2,418	2,602	2,973
HBV	1,539	1,827	2,169	1,990	1,839	3,629	6,373	8,237	10,668
IG Metall	3,188	2,631	3,900	4,221	3,918	5,767	6,872	6,984	7,562
Textil-									
Bekleidung	4,949	5,238	5,271	5,019	5,535	7,199	7,441	7,722	7,738
Total in DGB	15,281	15,469	16,707	16,175	16,246	23,409	30,006	33,319	38,356
Women as % of total council membership	NA	NA	NA	NA	11.4	13.5	15.7	17.1	19.3

NA = not available
Source: DGB, *Geschäftsbericht, 1977–81*, Women's Section.

TABLE 3-4

Participation of Women as Works Council Chairpersons, 1978 and 1981

	1978			1981		
	No.	Female W.C. chairs		No.	Female W.C. chairs	
Union	of firms	No.	%	of firms	No.	%
IG Chemie	2,489	217	8.7	2,573	276	10.7
HBV	5,054	1,117	22.1	6,107	1,565	25.6
IG Metall	10,528	361	3.4	10,168	442	4.3
Textil-						
Bekleidung	2,762	1,384	50.1	2,699	1,458	54.0
DGB*	35,294	3,803	10.7	36,307	4,731	13.0
DGB (1975)†	17,509	1,831	10.5			

*Fourteen of the seventeen affiliated unions reporting.
†"Only a part of the unions reporting."
Source: DGB *Geschäftsbericht, 1977–81*, Women's Section.

In the textile unions, just over half the councils are headed by women, and in Distribution, Banking, and Insurance (HBV) 22 percent are. DAG reports a similar increase among women councillors, but only in the private sector; in the public sector, women in the DAG's jurisdiction lost positions between 1975 and 1978.[48]

A recent study of the DGB documents women's inferior position from top to bottom.[49] Individual interviews with women activists and their letters to their own publication further illustrate widespread problems in dealing with their male colleagues, even for women in official positions.[50] In shops, women councillors usually speak only or mainly for the female minority whom the male majority can overlook without penalty to itself. Reports abound of women on the councils being given responsibility for what are regarded as women's concerns: the canteen, sanitation, retirees. Thus, they gain little of the experience with compensation, job assignment, overtime, layoffs, or grievances necessary if they are to move up the ladder of union officership,[51] nor do they have an opportunity to influence the decisions of the works councils, much less win appointments to bargaining committees. Manfred Wilke has analyzed trade union structure to show that these committees are mainly made up of works council chairpersons in the large firms of the region covered by the collective agreement. Full-time union staffs in turn tend to be selected from those with collective bargaining experience. Such staff members are then in a position to sit with the major influentials and decision-makers within the unions.[52]

A further indicator of women's second-class position is the small number who have been elected as delegates to the national union and confederation congresses, although a recent figure suggests improvement. Only 7.5 percent of delegates to the DGB Congress in 1978 were women; in 1982, 11.4 percent were.[53]

At the instigation of the International Confederation of Free Trade Unions (ICFTU), which at a recent meeting had examined exactly this problem, the DGB 1978 Congress urged unions to use trained women systematically in areas other than the typical women's fields of women's problems or social policy.[54] Various women's groups in the unions have advocated a quota system as a means of enlarging the number of women participating at congresses or on executive bodies, but these proposals have been repeatedly modified in favor of simply "asking" unions "to find appropriate means for the election of women as delegates or officers."[55]

Unions are beginning to appoint women to the many public and quasi-public agencies where trade union representatives are mandated, as well as to the boards of companies that are required under the co-determination law to have trade union representation. But their numbers make up only a tiny fraction of the whole.[56]

TRADE UNION EDUCATION

Systematic training in the trade union schools is a general requirement for office, even for works councillors and shop representatives. These courses usually begin with evening programs in the area where the shop or office is located; they progress through advanced programs offered under regional union sponsorship, often involving some short (weekend or week-long) full-time residence; and they culminate in longer residential programs at well-equipped and well-staffed trade union schools. Crowning the system are three academies offering six- to nine-month programs usually considered to be of university grade.[57]

Union members are selected for such training by local education staff. Works councillors are entitled by law to three weeks' paid released time for training during their term of office. Unions normally bear the costs of travel, materials, tuition, and room and board. The issue of released time for further education has been extended to other areas of the education system and been entered on the agendas for union negotiation.[58] Its extension would be of significant aid to women who are often marginal earners with few reserves and little persuasive power with their employers for securing paid leave.

As things stand, women tend to be found in local evening courses about in proportion to their union membership, but their attendance falls off in residential programs. Again, home duties and low income appear to interfere seriously with their training for union office.

The DGB's Women's Division leaders take the view that even when women attend such courses, they are apt to be seriously handicapped in participation and learning by their inadequate preparation and by the overwhelming predominance of male students. As a result, a substantial number of introductory residential courses especially for women have been set up in the DGB and industrial union schools. Experience on the whole supports this approach. Some 600 women a year went through DGB residential programs over the nine-year period between 1968 and 1976.[59]

Although women's attendance at the standard mixed courses in residential schools had reached 14 percent by 1976 (from 4.6 percent in 1965), the percentage of women attending all such programs reached 20.2 percent by that year, a substantial contribution to women's training. It means that two or three women participate in each mixed program and one to four enroll in each class at the residential academies.

The IG Metall who do not hold segregated courses for women, report that about 8 percent of their school enrollees, including those in regional short-term programs are women.[60] The IG Chemie students are only about 7 percent female, and they enroll six times as many women in women's courses as in the standard program. This union arranges for child care in connection with several of its schools.[61] The Chemical Workers have also been particularly diligent in preparing materials for general courses that introduce men as well as women to women's problems.[62]

Important questions remain. The German unions, unlike the Swedish, have so far not considered a reorganization of their schools to decentralize the residential programs and set up regional or even local classes that women might more readily attend. Very little has been done to provide child care at either residential or evening courses. Although women seem to prefer all-women classes to mixed ones, the unions have not undertaken to evaluate their relative success in improving women's skills as union leaders.

COLLECTIVE BARGAINING AND WOMEN

Bargaining is unrestrictedly in the hands of the "social partners," employers' associations and unions.[63] It is the responsibility not of the DGB but of each industrial union, and except for part of the public sector, it takes place at the regional level and by branches of industry, following the pattern of organization of the employers' associations. Women seeking improvements in wages, working conditions, or employee benefits must rely upon their union bargaining commission (Tarifkommission) to achieve these changes.

Among the issues most discussed in the early eighties are: changes in wage scales to abolish the "light-work" categories instituted in 1955 after the Supreme Labor Court declared "women's wages," as such, unconstitutional; the thirty-five hour week; the integration of blue-collar and white-collar rates into a single scale; and the inequities arising from wage drift. Lesser bargaining issues involve maternity leave and parental child care leave.

The works councils play a significant role in some of these matters because although they are not agents of the unions, they are responsible for the administration of union contracts within the workplace and may negotiate certain additions to the contract, including wage incentives, bonuses, and premiums on payments above the minimums laid down in the agreements.[64] Women complain that many works councils have interpreted the law's requirement that they use "social considerations" as one of the criteria in layoff decisions[65] as permitting the dismissal of married women whose husbands work; thus, the councils have actually contributed to the high rate of women's unemployment.

The overriding issue for women over the past fifteen years has been the light-wage categories. These were introduced after 1955 into the normal six-step wage scale and became the bottom three steps, mainly applied to women's work. The women's divisions of the unions began systematically to dispute the equity of this assessment of women's work and to insist upon a re-evaluation of the pay grades in the late sixties. They enlisted the aid of the Minister of Labor when the SPD came to power in 1969, and in 1973 he commissioned a study of the problem. This report, issued in 1975,[66] was advised to test "whether it would be scientifically justifiable to characterize a job as 'heavy' if it involved high muscular exertion, but to classify it as 'light' if it merely led to nervous stress and strain with slight physical exertion." Clearer definitions of "stress," "demand," and "burden" were sought, on the grounds that the constitutional requirement for equal pay makes these elements "of prime importance as orientation data for classifying corresponding wage brackets."

The report gave the social partners the responsibility for relating the scientific study of stress and demand to specific wage scales. After an extended period of study, the DGB and the IG Metall both issued statements of acceptance of the report. The employers, some months later, rejected the report, claiming that the light-wage groups were not specifically a women's concern, since some men were included in them, and that present scales reflected appropriate values for this type of work.[67]

The recession dampened both government and union interest in revising the job evaluation systems underlying wage scales. Even the women appeared to have been discouraged.[68] And yet over the intervening years, groups of women in at least three large concerns have undertaken the long, weary task of dealing with their colleagues, their works councils, their trade unions, and finally the labor courts to persuade them all in turn that the "light work" they were doing in, respectively, a honey packing plant, a photographic enterprise, and an electrical wire-spooling establishment was stressful, heavy, deafening, and altogether work that "no man would take on, even if it were paid higher than the second wage group."[69] The women in the photographic establishment won their case in 1982, and there is reason to hope that the other labor courts will look with similar understanding on the cases before them. The hard fact is that the matter of women's equal pay for work of equal value must still be fought out case by case; one now finds neither general understanding nor the possiblity of a general solution.

Individual unions have undertaken other attacks on the inequities of women's wages. The NGG, for example, have had some success in restructuring job descriptions to bring women into category III or IV instead of I or II.[70] Further, they have integrated blue-collar and white-collar pay rates into one scale. The Printing and Paper Union has added to the job description for grade IIIB, the phrase "work with hand or machine characterized by physical or nervous stress"; this description, when put into practice, can advance workers from grades I and II to grades III or IV. The I G Metall, notably in its Hamburg district, has shaped wage demands to benefit the lowest-paid groups by demanding raises.[71] Other women have achieved higher rating by bringing charges of categorical inequities to the labor courts.[72] But even

where courts and collective agreements take such matters into consideration, the equality effect may be nullified if works councils agree to above-
minimum payments for workers whom the employer particularly wishes to
retain or reward, usually skilled men, and it would be extremely difficult
politically for a council to sustain itself should it decline to agree to such a
proposal.

Some unions are bargaining for extensions of support systems for
women. The HBV reported that in 1978 it had signed agreements providing
for women's right to return to their jobs up to eighteen months after the
birth of a child. At the same time it pressed for extensions of paid maternity
and even parental leave.[73]

The fact is that many of the problems of German working women are
embedded in the dual bargaining system,[74] where decisions made by works
councils can outflank both regional agreements and national legislation,
particularly on such matters as layoffs and wage drift. For many councillors
share employers' beliefs that protective laws affecting women's employment
add enough to costs and personnel officers' workloads to create a bias
against women's employment in positions above the lowest wage levels.
Hence the appeals for more women in the bargaining commissions, as well
as in the works councils.[75]

TRENDS AND ISSUES OF THE 1980S

The most serious questions facing German unions in the eighties are those embedded in the economic recession: unemployment, technological change, part-time and short-time work, training, and retraining.

Labor market projections show a continuing movement of women—
married and unmarried—into the labor market. The period during which
married women leave the labor market to care for children probably will
shorten. But on the whole, women's participation rate will continue to hold
at its present moderate level of about 36 percent of the labor force, and
women's unemployment rate will continue to exceed men's, mainly as a
consequence of ongoing low levels of qualification for skilled jobs.[76] What
indications have we of how unions will deal with these circumstances in the
next decade? Will they move further to integrate women into their structure
and functioning?

The mounting rate of technological change in both production and
service sectors, with its tendency to rationalize routine jobs, has a dispropor-
tionate effect on women. The unions acceded to putting the light-wage issue
on the back burner in part because they recognized that improvements in
wages for assembly and other routine, unskilled jobs might only motivate
employers to accelerate the elimination of these jobs.

The unions' chief response to problems of both structural and cyclical unemployment is to demand spreading the work over a shorter week. The goal they set is thirty-two to thirty-five hours of work for forty hours' pay, and their tactics prescribe a gradual adjustment of hours downward until the goal is reached.[77] Women very much want shorter hours, but they want a shorter day, adjusted to children's school schedules, rather than a shorter week. Union proposals for a shorter week, even should they be realized, will only indirectly, partially, and incidentially respond to women's needs. A four-day week will not meet their needs as well as a six-hour day.[78] Fully a quarter of all persons seeking work want part-time work, and nearly all of these are women. Moreover, in the service sector, where women predominate in many enterprises, including retail trade, banking, restaurants, and hotels, work is often already organized to be part-time.[79]

While recognizing that part-time work has certain advantages for young mothers who must work, the unions would rather support full-time work opportunities and child care than respond to the needs of workers in these fragile positions, many of which have in any case disappeared as the recession has deepened.[80] The problem, however, will not go away. Until the unions find ways to reach these workers, raise their standards, and protect their interests—whether by legislation or collective bargaining or both—part-time work will remain threatening to them and exploitative of the women in these jobs.

Recognizing that women's continuing educational disadvantages lies more in vocational training than in basic schooling, the unions have put great emphasis on programs directed toward structural and curricular school reform, particularly the full-day, uniform school (Gesamtschule), in which academic programs, as well as early and middle terminal ones, are offered side by side. The unions have, however, been less consistent in cooperating with labor market and school authorities when they seek to open up wider occupational opportunities for girls and women.[81] Recent increases in the number of women receiving vocational training give some faint hope for a turn in this direction.[82] A study for the Economic Commission for Europe notes that the proportion of girls in secondary education and above has risen considerably, and as a result, "a greater number of women with good qualifications can be expected in future."[83]

The same report, while calling attention to a campaign aimed at promoting "a readiness for a more flexible and equitable distribution of tasks in family and working life," sees no rapid change in the dual burden that working women carry as housewives and mothers. Women will continue to interrupt their working lives just when men are consolidating theirs. These circumstances must continue, then, to have a negative effect on women's availability for training.

Availability is only half the problem: The training offered is the other half. The courses women usually take, and into which they are regularly counseled, generally differ in quality from those of men, are designed to bring women into the traditional female occupations, and are shorter in duration than the usual three to four years of apprenticeship required for skilled work. These matters all lead back to the sterotyped division of work in the labor market. The Germans still customarily list job openings by sex, and while the labor offices say that they are increasingly endeavoring to make jobs available to all workers in line with their qualifications, they also add that the ultimate decision rests with the employer.

A continuing social problem for all Germans, and not least for the unions, is the large number of foreign workers, particularly in production and the blue-collar trades. A high percentage of foreign workers have lived in Germany for more than ten years. Their children were born there and fill the inner city schools. The unions have been late and slow in trying to deal with their problems. The women suffer double discrimination as women and as foreigners. Most of them received little schooling in their own countries, and they work in Germany at unskilled jobs at the lowest levels of the pay scale. Unemployment is a double crisis for them because once unemployed, they are liable to expulsion from the country. Ignorance of the language isolates them from their German neighbors and fellow workers; the customs of their homeland do not prepare them for public life; and both conditions limit their availability for union work and labor education. Most of them come from village backgrounds. And yet a higher percentage of them work than of native German women. In the early seventies some carried through more or less successful strikes against various aspects of their exploitation, and in several cases the unions came to their defense, however tardily. The problems of reaching them across the barriers of language and custom and of dealing with their problems in the face of growing unemployment among native Germans have so far deterred the unions from building staffs, programs, and procedures directed at their critical needs.

Germany has been struggling with the question of equal jobs opportunity for about ten years. Indeed, as early as 1966 the federal parliament instructed the government to report every two years on "objections" raised by the federal and provincial governments on the application of Article 119 (equal treatment of men and women) of the Treaty of Rome, the basic document for the Common Market. In 1974 the parliament set up an Inquiry Commission on the "Rights and Social Conditions of Women in Society," covering a much broader range of equality considerations than employment. That commission made an interim report in December 1976.

Beginning, however, in 1975, the EEC Council issued three mandatory directives covering different aspects of equality of work and workers: on equal pay; equal access to employment, vocational training, promotion, and working conditions; and equal treatment in matters of social security.[84] The first two were to find legislative implementation in each member state by 1978. Most states, including Germany, were dilatory, and most were granted postponements. Germany passed a law on equal pay and opportunity in 1980, but in January 1982 the EEC issued a formal warning to the Bonn government that it was opening legal action against Germany in the High Court at Strasbourg. Should the alleged shortcomings of the law become evident, Germany would be charged, probably by the late fall of 1982, with failure to meet its legal obligation. The law was defective, the EEC said, because it covered only cases where a worker was already employed and thus did not apply to recruitment or hiring. The burden of proof did not require the employer to show that he had not discriminated, but rather required the complainant to show that she had suffered discrimination. The Brussels Commission found this "antidiscrimination law" too lightly conceived.[85]

When the final report of the Inquiry Commission appeared in 1980, it evoked a heated, though delayed, parliamentary debate. The commission's recommendations covered a wide range of social, familial, educational, and economic concerns, but it did not hold that a law was necessarily the best way to realize reforms in these many fields. The chancellor saw the decisive issue as providing opportunity for good vocational and skill training for women, and his party members stated that there was a need for quotas in training facilities in both the public and private sectors. The Free Democrats favored a broad and inclusive law against discrimination. The Christian parties wanted more attention given to the housewife and her possible re-entry problems and favored more opportunities for part-time work; they doubted the value of law in dealing with inequalities in the family.[86] All these views were repeated in a January 1982 public hearing that brought all the leaders of women's organizations to Bonn. The trade unions on this occasion declared a broad anti-discrimination law unnecessary and viewed the whole matter as one to be dealt with by the social partners at the level of the firm.[87] These spokespersons held that the state and its laws cannot be depended upon to bring about sex equality; only the unions can speak and act dependably for working women. For the present, then, trade union women are opponents of the feminists, many of whom have turned to the Free Democratic party to represent them in behalf of an antidiscrimination law.

Union women are, however, hard at work on a new pension law, since the Supreme Court has ruled that the present law must be revised by 1984. The eventual outcome will be a test of both union and women's influence within the government and parliament.

Within the unions, the triennial election campaigns to bring more women into the works councils will unquestionably continue. The crucial question is how these increasing numbers of women will make themselves felt in improving women's conditions in the workplace. Will they be able to intervene in a broad range of issues and so gain the experience that will enable them to move up in union offices and careers? Will union educators directly tackle the problem of women's attendance and performance at their own training schools? Will they include material on women's issues in the standard curriculum?

The small number of women nominated for union office will not rise without special measures. It is doubtful that the unions in the near future will adopt any kind of quota system, but they have made some provision for the representation of other constituencies, such as youth and white-collar workers. Why not women?

The women's divisions will surely remain. As long as they do, they are at once a sign of women's continuing inferiority and a medium for doing something about it. A number of unions are conscious of the need to name women to staff positions. A beginning has been made in sending a few of them to corporation boards and public bodies. The DGB Women's Division in committed to full support of this trend and through its member unions is probably responsible for what has been done so far to bring more women into union leadership. Pressures from international agencies, both governmental and trade union, that are concerned with equity for working women have had a demonstrable effect on government policy and union behavior. These unquestionably will continue.

A visiting American scholar who carried out his research at DGB headquarters in Düsseldorf encapsulated women's current status in the German union movement:

> I must say . . . that I was surprised by the crass sexism apparent in all areas of the German trade unions. . . . I saw women almost exclusively in positions where they served men, whether in the offices, the library, or the canteen. But [sexism] was also evident in the consciousness of the men, who took these circumstances as a matter of course. . . . Even the young college graduates, from whose otherwise open attitudes I would have expected something else, could hardly be distinguished in this regard from their older colleagues. The discrimination is not stated or discussed and continues therefore to be an ongoing reality. . . . I would like to think that the DGB and its affiliated unions possess sufficient sociopolitical influence that they could mobilize to do away with this most critical of inequities in the Federal Republic. I could imagine as a first concrete step that they could undertake a systematically planned mass campaign inside and outside the unions to discredit sexism morally. In the last analysis the issue is one of fundamental democratic rights, not just formally, but in all its substance.[88]

GLOSSARY

BfA	Bundesanstalt für Arbeit: The Federal Employment Institute
BDA	Bundesvereinigung der deutschen Arbeitgeberverbände: Federal Union of German Employers' Associations
DAG	Deutscher Angestellten Gewerkschaft: German White-Collar Workers' Union (independent)
DGB	Deutscher Gewerkschaftsbund: German Trade Union Federation
HBV	Handel, Banken, und Versicherung: Union of Distributive, Bank and Insurance Workers
ICFTU	International Confederation of Free Trade Unions
IG Metall	Industriegewerkschaft Metall: Metal Workers' Union
IG Chemie-Papier-Keramik	Union of Chemical, Paper and Ceramic Workers
ILO	International Labour Organisation
NGG	Nahrung, Genuss and Gaststätten: Food, Confectionery and Restaurant Union
OECD	Organisation for Economic Cooperation and Development
ÖTV	Öffentliche Dienste, Transport und Verkehr: Union of Public, Transportation and Traffic Workers
SPD	Sozialdemokratische Partei Deutschlands: German Social-democratic Party
Textil	Leder und Bekleidung: Textile, Leather and Clothing Union
WSI	Wirtschafts- und Sozialwissenschaftliches Institut des DGB: Economic and Social Science Institute of the DGB

NOTES

1. See, for discussion of this question, Friedrich Engels, *Die Ursprung der Familie, Privateigentums und des Staats* (The Origin of the Family, Private Property, and the State), 1902; August Bebel, *Die Frau und der Sozialismus* (Women and Socialism), 1878; Klara Zetkin, *Zur Geschichte der proletarischen Frauenbewegung Deutschlands* (Toward a History of the Proletarian Women's Movement in Germany), 1912.

2. Gisela Losseff-Tillmans, *Frauenemanzipation und Gewerkschaften* (Women's Emancipation and Trade Unions) (Wuppertal: Hammer, 1978).

3. Heide M. Pfarr and Klaus Bertlesmann, *Lohngleichheit: zur Rechtsprechung bei geschlechtsspezifischer Entgeltsdiskriminierung* (Wage Equality: The Courts' Decision on Sex Discrimination in Remuneration), Band 100, Schriftenreihe des Bundesministers für Jugend, Familie und Gesundheit, 1981 (Stuttgart: W. Kohlhammer), especially chap. 2.

4. In addition to the socialist unions, there existed also a Federation of Christian Trade Unionists, allied with the Catholic-oriented Center party and based on the pope's 1891 encyclical *Rerum Novarum*, and the Hirsch-Duncker Federation of liberal origins and sponsorship. Of these the "free" (socialist) trade unions were "by

far the most powerful." Gerard Braunthal, *Socialist Labor and Politics in Weimar Germany* (Hamden, Conn.: Archon Books, 1978), p. 112.

5. "The labor officials discreetly switched from an ideological to a pragmatic commitment. They made the shift in order to gain maximum benefits for the workers under the entrenched capitalist system, but did little to weaken the system, is evident in their opposition to the socialization of industry. In pursuit of this pragmatic course, they were influential in swaying party leaders to take a more moderate ideological stance." Ibid., p. 172.

6. Dieter Schuster, *Die deutsche Gewerkschaftsbewegung* (The German Trade Union Movement) (Bonn: Vorwärts Druck, 1976), pp. 27–34.

7. Jean H. Quataert, *Reluctant Feminists in Germany Social Democracy, 1885– 1917* (Princeton: Princeton University Press, 1979).

8. Dörte Winkler, *Frauenarbeit im "Dritten Reich"* (Women's Work in the "Third Reich") (Hamburg: Hoffman und Campe, 1977), pp. 44–45. See also Leila J. Rupp. *Mobilizing Women for War: German and American Propaganda, 1939–1945* (Princeton: Princeton University Press, 1978).

9. Losseff-Tillmans, *Frauenemanzipation*, p. 643.

10. Winkler, *Frauenarbeit*, pp. 33–55 and tables on pp. 198–99, 201.

11. Hans Böckler and his lieutenants in the leadership of the postwar unions had planned for a single trade union in which the industrial unions would be subdivisions. The plan was abandoned in the face of the industrial egotism of several powerful groups that took an early lead in reorganization, among them chiefly the IG Metall. By the time of the founding convention, "Einheitsgewerkschaft"—Unit (or Unity) Trade Union—the term used today to describe the trade union federation, had come to mean an industrial organization of sixteen unions, each of which would include all ranks of workers—blue-collar, white-collar, and civil service (if applicable)—within the industrial jurisdiction. See Manfred Wilke, *Die Funktionäre* (The Functionaries) (Munich and Zurich: R. Piper & Co., 1979), pp. 114–16, and Theo Pirker, *Die Blinde Macht* (Blind Power) (Munich: Verlag Olle and Wotter, 1960). Defections from this plan began when the white-collar workers insisted on their own industrial union (one had existed during the Weimar period). Substantial numbers of them withdrew to form their own independent union (the DAG), which has ever since fought hard to maintain its jurisdiction outside the DGB. At present, the DGB unions, taken together, have more than twice as many white-collar workers as the DAG, and rumors rise spasmodically that the DAG is coming home to the DGB or, alternatively, forming an alliance with some other organization.

12. Walter Freitag, the second DGB president, said at its Third Congress in 1954: "We say 'Yes' to the State . . . . The State which is freely elected, freely constructed from the will of the people. We are not stupid enough to identify ourselves with the opposition to the State [even though] it is perhaps not yet fashioned in the way we want it to be." DGB *Protokoll* (Proceedings), p. 77.

13. Germany's progress in conforming to the equal rights provisions of Article 119 of the Treaty of Rome, charter of the EEC, was so dilatory that the EEC commission warned the Federal Republic in 1979 that it would be brought before the European High Court if it did not at once move to adopt legislation consistent with the charter. "EG Kommission droht Bundesrepublik Klage in Sachen Lohngleichheit an" (The European Commission Warns the Federal Republic That It May Be

Charged in the Matter of Equal Pay), *Frauen und Arbeit*, no. 8 (1979): 16. The government, which for some time had had a draft of appropriate legislation ready to lay before a badly divided parliament, was able on June 25, 1980, to announce that it had been rather quickly adopted. The DGB Women's Committee immediately expressed disappointment that its proposals for improvement of the draft had been completely disregarded. It expressed the concern that "discrimination on the basis of sex will be treated cavalierly." "Arbeitsrechtliches EG-Anpassungsgesetz" (Labor Legislation Conforming to the European Commission Norm), *Frauen und Arbeit*, no. 8/9 (1980): 13–15. The parliament required the government to present it with a report on the outcome of the law by December 31, 1982, but no report had issued by that date.

14. German studies on the interests and needs of working women include: *Bericht der Bundesregierung über die Situation der Frauen in Beruf, Familie und Gesellschaft* (Report of the Federal Government on the Situation of Women at Work, in the Family, and in Society), Bundestag Drucksache V/909, Bonn, 1966; two reports on the state of the family in 1968 and 1975 (*Familien Berichte*) Bundesminister für Jugend, Familie und Gesundheit, Bonn; sections in the annual reports, beginning in 1970, on the state of the nation (*Bericht der Bundesregierung und Materialien zur Lage der Nation*) Bundesministerium für Innerdeutsche Beziehungen, Kassel: AG Wenderoth; and the ongoing work of a commission on women originally appointed by the chancellor to issue progress reports on the recommendations of the 1966 study (*Bericht der Bundesregierung über die Massnahmen zur Verbesserung der Situation der Frau, Bundestag Drucksache VI/3689, Bonn, 1972*), followed by the report of a parliamentary inquiry commission (Enquête Kommission) set up after the publication of the 1972 report "to prepare proposals that would lead to the realization of full legal and social equality for women in society" (*Zwischenbericht der Enquête Kommission Frau und Gesellschaft) Bundestag Drucksache 7/5866, p. 4*). This inquiry commission was reorganized in 1977 to include among its nonparliamentary members a trade union woman. Its final report to parliament, *Schlussbericht der Enquête-Kommission Verfassungreform*, was submitted August 29, 1980.

15. "Programme of the German Trade Union Federation, DGB, for Women Workers: Principles and Demands" (Düsseldorf: DGB, 1969); *Women and Work* (*Frauen und Arbeit*) 1969.

16. Irmgard Blättel, "75 Jahre hauptamtlich gewerkschaftliche Frauenarbeit" (75 Years of Full-Time Trade Union Women's Work), *Frauen und Arbeit*, no. 110/11 (1980): 14–16.

17. Irmgard Rhunke, "Zur Ideologie gewerkschaftlicher Frauenarbeit" (Toward an Ideology of Trade Union Women's Work), Diplomarbeit, Freie Universitaet, Berlin, 1973, pp. 66–70.

18. Carola Stern, ed., *Was Haben die Parteien für die Frauen getan?* (What Have the Parties Done for Women?), citing Margarete Heinz, *Politisiches Bewusstsein der Frau* (Women's Political Consciousness) (Hamburg: Rowohlt, Ro-ro-ro 4006, 1976), p. 10.

19. "Gleichbehandlung von Mann und Frau in Rentenversicherungsrecht" (Equal Treatment of Men and Women in the Pension Insurance Law), *Frauen und Arbeit*, no. 8/9 (1980): 2–13.

20. Luc Jochimsen, "Wie Haltet Ihr es mit den Frauen in Beruf und Politik?" (How Do You Stand on Women in Work and Politics?), in Stern, *Was Haben die Parteien.*

21. Gunter Buttler and B. Hof, *Bevölkerung und Arbeitsmarkt bis zum Jahr 2000* (Population and Labor Market to the Year 2000) (Deutscher Institutsverlag, 1977), pp. 59–61.

22. For a detailed analysis of women's unemployment by age, training, seniority, education, marital status, part- or full-time employment, occupational sector, geographic region, and duration of unemployment, see Brigitte Nauhaus, *Probleme der Frauenarbeitslosigkeit in der gegenwärtigen Krise* (Problems of Women's Unemployment in the Current Crisis) (Cologne: Pahl-Rugenstein, 1979).

23. Cited in Herta Däubler-Gmelin, *Frauenarbeitslosigkeit, oder Reserve zurück an den Herd?* (Women's Unemployment; or, Reservists, Back to the Kitchen?) (Hamburg: Rowohlt, Taschenbuch, 1977).

24. See tables 19 and 20 in Nauhaus, *Probleme der Frauenarbeitslosigkeit*, pp. 40, 41.

25. "IG Metall für Kommunalwahlrecht und gegen Teilzeitrabeit" (Metal Workers' Union Favors Right of Local Suffrage [for foreign workers] and Opposes Part-Time Work), *Frankfurter Rundschau*, September 29, 1980.

26. Institute für Arbeitsmarkt und Berufsforschung der Bundesanstalt für Arbeit, *Frauen und Arbeitsmarkt: Quintessenzen*. (Women and the Labor Market: Quintessence) (Nuremberg:, 1976).

27. BfA, *The Federal Employment Institute of the Federal Republic of Germany*, 1971/72 (Nuremberg, BfA), pp. 6–11.

28. For a full discussion of policy and practice, see Gunther Schmid, "Selective Employment Policy in West Germany: Some Evidence of Its Development and Impact," in National Commission for Manpower Policy, *European Labor Market Policies*, Special Report no. 27, GPO (Washington, D.C.: 1978), pp. 167–222; and Monika Langkau-Hermann and Jochem Langkau, *Der Berufliche Aufstieg der Frau* (Upward Mobility for Women) (Opladen: Westdeutscher Verlag, 1972); the same authors have focused on the training—and other problems—of reentry women in their paper "The Federal Republic of Germany," in *Women Returning to Work: Policies and Programs in Five Countries*, ed. Alice M. Yohalem (Montclair, N.J.: Allanheld, Osmun, 1980). That these pilot programs are carried out only with the greatest difficulty and accompanied by considerable discrimination is attested in a newspaper account of a conference held in Bremen to report on and evaluate them. It speaks of "opposition from employers and male trainers and bureaucratic frustrations." The drop-out rate of girls is considerably above that of boys, in part because the labor office pays women only 860 DM per month, in contrast to the male rate of 1150 DM, but "the particular difficulty is the bias of firms against taking women and girls into 'men's trades.'" *Frankfurter Rundschau*, October 10, 1980.

29. Ursula Engelen-Kefer, director of the DGB Section on International Social Policy, at the Ninth National Women's Trade Union Conference, June 2, 1977, *Protokoll* (Proceedings), pp. 124–26.

30. "Geschäftsbericht der Abteilung Frauen . . . 1977–80" (Report of the Women's Division . . . 1977–80), National Women's Conference, DGB, *Protokoll* (Proceedings), 1981, pp. 33–43.

31. *Frauen und Arbeit*, no. 7/8 (1977): 11.

32. "Geschäftsbericht der Abteilung Frauen"; Däubler-Gmelin, *Frauenarbeitslosigkeit*, pp. 112–16; Nauhaus, *Probleme der Frauenarbeitslosigkeit*, pp. 157–60.

33. *Quintessenzen*, p. 24.

34. BfA, Statistik, "Förderung der beruflichen Bildung" (Advancement of Vocational Training) (Nuremberg: BfA; 1978). In 1979 women made up 31 percent of enrollees in all BfA programs.

35. Barbara Hegelheimer, *Bildungs und Arbeitsmarktpolitische Massnahmen zur beruflichen Förderung von Frauen in der Bundesrepublik Deutschlands* (Training and Labor Market Policy Measures for the Vocational Advancement of Women in the German Federal Republic) (Berlin: CEDEFOP, 1979). This report, issued by the European Center for Advancement and Vocational Training (CEDEFOP), details all measures undertaken within Germany up to the date of its publication. For a trade union evaluation of the programs, see Helge Tölle, "Förderprogramme zur Berufsausbildung der Mädchen," (Programs for the Vocational Training of Girls), *Gewerkschaftliche Bildungspolitik* 12 (1978): 271–73.

36. DGB, "Gewerkschaftsmitgliederentwicklung, 1967–1977" (Trade Union Membership Growth, 1967–1977), (Dusseldorf: DGB, Duplicated n.d.).

37. *Frauen und Arbeit*, no. 3(1976), 4(1977), 4(1978), 4(1979), and 8/9(1980).

38. DAG, "Innenrevision und Statistik" (Internal Audit and Statistics) (Hamburg: DAG, 1978).

39. DAG, "Familienpolitisches Programm der DAG" (Family Policy Program of the DAG) (Hamburg: DAG, 1976). The DAG downgraded its Department of Women's Affairs to a section of the Department of Economic Policy in 1972 and abandoned its monthly journal, *Frauenstimme* (Women's Voice), at the same time. At its next convention it substituted for its policy statement on women a family-oriented policy program. The DGB equivalent is "Richtlinien für die Frauenarbeit im deutschen Gewerksschaftsbund" (Guidelines for Women's Work in the DGB) (Munich: Gründungkongress, DGB, October, 1949).

40. DGB, "Richtlinien."

41. Irmgard Blättel, "Gewerkschaftliche Politik für Frauen" (Trade Union Policy for Women), *Gewerkschaftliche Monatshefte* Vol. 27 (1976): 612–15.

42. 9. Bundesfrauenkonferenz des DGB, 2–3 June, 1977, *Protokoll* (Proceedings) p. 244.

43. *Gewerkschaftliche Monatshefte* 23: no. 11 (1972).

44. "Jahr der Arbeitnehmerinnen: Erfolge, Erfahrungen, Konsequenzen" (Year of Working Women: Successes, Experiences, Results), *Frauen und Arbeit*, no. (1973): 1–12.

45. IG Metall, *Fakten, Daten, Hinweise* (Facts, Data, Suggestions) (Frankfort: IG Metall, 1979), p. 36.

46. Claudia Pinl, *Das Arbeitnehmerpatriarchat* (Male Chauvinism Among Workers) (Cologne: Kiepenheuer & Witsch, 1977), pp. 94–98.

47. For an in-depth discussion of the functions of these two groups and the unions' relationships with them, see Wilke, *Die Funktionäre*, pp. 28–46.

48. DAG, Accounting and Statistics, "Betriebsratswahlen 1978, vorläufiges Ergebnis" (Preliminary Results, Works Council Elections, 1978, Count of Women,) Duplicated (Hamburg: DAG 1978).

49. Pinl, *Das Arbeitnehmerpatriarchat*.

50. "Eine Personalrätin Schreibt," *Frauen und Arbeit*, no. 1 (1977): 9; Annemarie Renger, *Gleiche Chancen für Frauen? Berichte und Erfahrungen in Briefen an die Präsidentin des deutschen Bundestages* (Equal Opportunity for Women? Reports and Experiences Gathered in Letters to the President of the German Parliament) (Heidelberg and Karlsruhe: C. F. Müller, Juristischer Verlag, 1977).

51. Sabine Rosengladt and Claudia Pinl, "Mehr Frauen in die Betriebsräte!" (More Women in the Works Councils!), *Emma* (March 1978): 28–29; Johanna Hund and Christine Preiss, *Die Unbescheidenen: Betriebsrätinnen Erzählen* (The Assertive Ones: Women on Works Councils Tell Their Story) (Köln: Pahl-Rugenstein, 1979).

52. Wilke, *Die Funktionäre*, pp. 185–200.

53. Pinl, *Das Arbeitnehmerpatriarchat*, pp. 87–93; *Frauen und Arbeit*, no. 6/7(1982): centerfold, p. 1.

54. "DGB Kongress unterstützt IBFG Aktionsprogram" (DGB Supports the International Confederation's Action Program) *Frauen und Arbeit*, no. 6/7(1978): p. 24.

55. 9. Bundesfrauenkonferenz des DGB, 2–3 June, 1977, *Protokoll* (Proceedings), p. 59.

56. IG Metall notes an increase of women serving as labor representatives in the labor courts, from 45 in 1972 to 73 in 1975; in the social courts, an increase from 35 to 37; in the advisory bodies to the social insurance programs, from 313 to 324; and in the board rooms of companies, from 3 to 10. *Fakten, Daten, Hinweise* (Facts, Data, Insights) (Frankfurt: IG Metall, 1975). The 1979 edition gave no information on this point.

57. See Alice H. Cook and Roberta Till-Retz, "Trade Union Education in Europe," in *Working Women and Trade Union Education*, ed. Barbara M. Wertheimer (Philadelphia: Temple University Press, 1981).

58. Dieter Goers, *Zur politischen Kontroverse um den Bildungsurlaub* (Contribution to the Political Controversy About Educational Leave), Wirtschafts-und Sozialwissenschaftliches Institut des DGB Studien (WSI) (Düsseldorf: Bund Verlag, 1978). For general background see Konrad von Motlke and Norbert Schneevoigt, *Educational Leaves for Employees* (San Francisco: Jossey-Bass, 1977).

59. DGB, Frauenabteilung, *Geschäftsbericht* (Officers' Report), 1968–1970, pp. 39–40; 1974–1976, p. 49.

60. I.G. Metall, Frauenkonferenz, *Geschäftsbericht* (Officers' Report), 1979, p. 120.

61. IG Chemie-Papier-Keramik, *Tätigkeitsbericht der Hauptabteilung Frauen* (Activity Report of the Headquarters Women's Division), presented to the Eighth Bundeskonferenz, 1976, p. 89.

62. These include such titles as "Role and Influence of Women in the Political Life of the Republic," "Proper Job Evaluation—Healthy Working Conditions," "The Educational Situation of Women in Industrial Society," and "Partnership of Man and Woman."

63. See Schuster, "Die deutsche Gewerkschafts bewegung"; Hans Reichel, "Recent Trends in Collective Bargaining in the Federal Republic of Germany," in *Collective Bargaining in Industrialized Market Economies*, ed. John Windmuller (Geneva: International Labour Organisation Publications, 1974); and Wilke, *Die Funktionäre*, pp. 66–81.

64. See Joachim Bergmann and Waltner Muller-Jentsch, "The Federal Republic of Germany: Cooperative Unionism and Dual Bargaining System Challenged," in *Worker Militancy and Its Consequences, 1967–75* ed. Solomon Barkin (New York: Praeger, 1975), pp. 235–76.

65. BvG, Betriebsverfassungs Gesetz (Law on Enterprise Labor Relations) 1972 as amended 1974, Bb 1.I 13 and 469, pp. 52–55.

66. Walter Rohmert and Josef Rutenfranz, *Arbeitswissenschaftliche Beurteilung der Belastung und Beanspruchung an unterschiedlichen industriellen Arbeitsplätzen* (Scientific Determination of Stress and Demand in Varying Industrial Workplaces) Bonn: Bundesminister für Arbeit und Sozialordnung, 1975). Discussions of this report and its impact are included in Alice H. Cook, "Collective Bargaining as a Strategy for Achieving Equal Opportunity and Equal Pay: Sweden and West Germany," and Christof Hellberger, "Work Analysis as a Means to Achieve Equal Pay for Working Women: The Federal Republic of Germany," in *Equal Employment Policy for Women: Strategies for Implementation in the United States, Canada and Western Europe*, ed. Ronnie Steinberg Ratner (Philadelphia: Temple University Press, 1980).

67. "Comment Given on February 28, 1977, by the Federal Union of Employers' Associations on the Research Report and Expert Comment on the Subject of Occupational Science Assessment of Burden and Stress and Different Industrial Workplaces," and "Comment Given on September 18, 1976, by the German Federation of Trade Unions on the Research Report and the Expert Comment on the Subject of Occupational Science Assessment of Burden and Stress and Different Industrial Workplaces," Duplicated (Bonn: German Federal Diet Printed Matter, 8/547 Ministry of Labor and Social Order, March, 1977).

68. At the 1977 National Women's Conference, only two resolutions on wages, both very general in wording, were introduced. Although both passed unanimously, neither brought forth a word of discussion from the floor. 9. Bundesfrauenkonferenz des DGB, *Protokoll* (Proceedings), 2–3 June, 1977.

69. Viola Roggenkamp, "Was Männer nicht können—machen Frauen oft für wenig Geld: der ungleiche Kampf um gleichen Lohn für gleiche Arbeit" (What Men Can't Do—Women Often Do for Little Money: The Unequal Struggle for Equal Pay for Equal Work), *Die Zeit*, no. 41, October 10, 1980.

70. "NGG Aktion: Gerechte Eingruppierung—gerechter Lohn" (NGG Action: Proper Categories—Proper Wage), *Frauen und Arbeit*, no. 8/9 (1980: 18–19.

71. *Fakten, Daten, Hinweise*, 1979, 36.

72. "Nach 18 Jahren Lohnstreit Höhergruppierung" (After 18 Years, Wage Struggle for Higher Work Category), *Frauen und Arbeit*, no. 8/9 (1980): 20; "HBV Frauen gewannen Eingruppierungsklage" (HBV Women Won Their Grievance on Job Group), ibid., p. 19.

73. *Info für die Frau*, (HBV) no. 1 (1978): 12.

74. The phrase is coined by Bergmann and Muller-Jentsch, "The Federal Republic of Germany," pp. 248–52.

75. Irmgard Tiemann, "Mehr Frauen in die Tarifkommisionen" (More Women in the Negotiating Committees), *Frauen und Arbeit*, no. 2 (1977): 6–8.

76. Nauhaus notes that most discussions about lowering women's rates of unemployment take refuge in setting goals of full employment for everyone. She sees a diminution in present rates as likely only if a widespread attack on discrimination

against women in the workforce takes place. *Probleme der Frauen Arbeitslosigkeit*, p. 150.

77. Long strikes by IG Metall in 1979 over a shorter work week ended inconclusively, with a compromise calling for more holidays per year but no change in the basic forty-hour week.

78. "Arbeitsmaterial für die gewerkschaftliche Frauenarbeit zur Durchsetzung der gleichen Rechte und Chancen der Frauen" (Working Materials for the Trade Union Women's Work Toward Achieving Equal Rights and Opportunities for Women), *Frauen und Arbeit*, no. 7 (1980): 3.

79. The major study of part-time work is *Zur Struktur der Teilzeitbeschäftigung* (On the Structure of Part-Time Employment) (Nuremberg: BfA für 1976).

80. "IG Metall . . . gegen Teilzeitarbeit." the union's position, with which the women agree, is that part-time workers tend to undercut hard-won union standards; that such workers are for the most part unskilled and unable to make effective demands on their employers; that their commitment to work is questionable; and that part-time jobs are dead-end ones, leading neither to promotion nor to training.

81. WSI has given great attention to these problems and to union demands for more paid leave from work for education and training. See the DGB's *Gewerkschaftliche Monatshefte* for a variety of reports on studies and policies over the past decade.

82. Nauhaus notes a few exceptions in measures taken by national and state governments and projects sponsored by educational and social agencies, on all of which a few unions participate. *Probleme der Frauenarbeitslosigkeit*, pp. 147, 160. Hegelheimer, *Bildungs und Arbeitsmarkt politische Massnahmen*, reports on these projects in detail.

83. Economic Commission for Europe "Report on the Participation of Women in the Economic Evolution of the Federal Republic of Germany," Seminar on the Participation of Women in the Economic Evolution of the ECE Region, Paris, July, 9–12, 1979, p. 7.

84. Commission of the European Communities, "Women at Work in the European Communities: 50 Questions, 50 Answers," *Women of Europe*, Supplement no. 7 (1981).

85. Rolf Seeland, "Gleichberechtigung am Arbeitsplatz" (Equal Treatment at the Workplace), *Parlament*, August 4, 1979, pp. 43–52.

86. "Mit Hilfe von Gesetzen zur Gleichstellung der Frau?" (Equality for Women with the Help of Law?) *Frankfurter Allgemeine Zeitung*, March 20, 1981.

87. Ingrid Hoffman, "Sex Discrimination Is a Public Issue," *Informationen für die Frau*, 31 no. 2 (1982): 3–4.

88. Andrei S. Markovits, "Das Alltagsleben in deutschen Gewerkschaftszentralen: Eindrücke eines amerikanischen Sozialwissenschaftlers" (Everyday Life in the German Trade Union Headquarters: Impressions of an American Social Scientist), *Gewerkschaftliche Monatshefte*, December 1979, pp. 793–4.

BIBLIOGRAPHY

Bebel, August. *Die Frau und der Sozialismus* (Women and Socialism). 1878.
Braunthal Gerard. *Socialist Labor and Politics in Weimar Germany*. Hamden, Conn.: Archon Books, 1978.

Cook, Alice H., "Collective Bargaining as a Strategy for Achieving Equal Opportunity and Equal Pay: Sweden and West Germany." In *Equal Employment Policy for Women: Strategies for Implementation in the United States, Canada and Western Europe*, edited by Ronnie Steinberg Ratner. Philadelphia: Temple University Press, 1980.

————. "Vocational Training, the Labor Market, and the Unions." In *Equal Employment Policy for Women: Strategies for Implementation in the United States, Canada and Western Europe*, edited by Ronnie Steinberg Ratner. Philadelphia: Temple University Press, 1980.

Engelen-Kefer, Ursula. "Beschäftigung und Qualität des Arbeitslebens, Auswirkungen für Frauen, am Beispiel der Bundesrepublik Deutschlands" (Employment and Quality of Working Life, Their Effect on Women, Using the Example of the Federal Republic of Germany), in *Women, Work, and Society*, research series no. 57, part 2. Geneva: International Institute for Labour Studies, 1980.

Hegelheimer, Barbara. *Bildungs und Arbeitsmarktpolitische Massnahmen zur beruflichen Förderung von Frauen in der Bundesrepublik Deutschlands* (Training and Labor Market Policy Measures for the Vocational Advancement of Women in the German Federal Republic). Berlin: CEDEFOP, 1979.

Kutsch, Marlies. *Die Frau im Berufsleben: Der Weg zur Chancengleichheit am Arbeitsplatz*. (The Working Woman: The Way to Equal Opportunity at the Workplace). Herderbucherei, 1979.

Losseff-Tillmans, Gisela. *Frauenemanzipation und Gewerkschaften* (Women's Emancipation and Trade Unions). Wuppertal: Hammer, 1978.

Menschik, Jutta. *Gleichberechtigung oder Emanzipation: Die Frau im Erwerbsleben in der BDR* (Equal Rights or Emancipation: Woman in Paid Employment in the German Federal Republic). Frankfurt: Fischer, 1971.

Nauhaus, Brigitte. *Probleme der Frauenarbeitslosigkeit in der gegenwärtigen Krise* (Problems of Women's Unemployment in the Current Crisis). Cologne: Pahl-Rugenstein, 1979.

Pfarr, Heide M., and Klaus Bertelsmann. *Lohngleichheit: Zur Rechtssprechung bei geschlechtsspezifischer Entgeltdiskriminierung* (Equal Pay: The Courts' Decisions on Sex Discrimination in Remuneration). Schriftenreihe des Bundesministers für Jugend, Familie und Gesundheit, vol. 100. Stuttgart: Verlag W. Kohlhammer, 1981.

Pinl, Claudia. *Das Arbeitnehmerpatriarchat* (Male Chauvinism Among Workers). Cologne: Kiepenheuer and Witsch, 1977.

Pirker, Theo. *Die Blinde Macht* (Blind Power). Munich: Verlag Olle and Wolter, 1960.

Quataert, Jean H. *Reluctant Feminists in German Social Democracy, 1885–1917*. Princeton: Princeton University Press, 1979.

Reichel, Hans. "Recent Trends in Collective Bargaining in the Federal Republic of Germany." In *Collective Bargaining in Industrialized Market Economies*, edited by John Windmuller. Geneva: International Labour Organisation Publications, 1974.

Rupp, Leila J. *Mobilizing Women For War: German and American Propaganda, 1939–1945*. Princeton: Princeton University Press, 1978.

Schmid, Gunther. "Selective Employment Policy in West Germany: Some Evidence of Its Development and Impact." In National Commission for Manpower Policy, *European Labor Market Policies*. Special Report no. 27. Washington, D.C.: GPO, 1978.

Schuster, Dieter, *Die Deutsche Gewerkschaftsbewegung* (The German Trade Union Movement). Bonn: Vorwärts Druck, 1976.

Wilke, Manfred. *Die Funktionäre* (The Functionaries). Munich and Zurich: R. Piper & Co. 1979.

Periodicals

Frauen und Arbeit (Women and Work) Dusseldorf, DGB, Women's Division.

Gewerkschaftliche Monatshefte, (Trade Union Monthly), Dusseldorf DGB.

Emma, Zeitschrift für Frauen von Frauen (Magazine for Women by Women) Cologne.

Informationen für die Frau (Information for Women) Bonn-Bad Godesberg, Deutscher Frauenrat (German Women's Council).

Die Zeit (The Times) Political Weekly, Hamburg.

4 FINLAND

Elina Haavio-Mannila

WOMEN'S WORK IN FINLAND

Since the beginning of the industrialization process, the participation of Finnish women in paid work has been influenced by two factors: the varying growth rates of different industrial branches and the mechanization of the factories. The first determined the development of the sex ratio among industrial workers; the second increased the participation of women—and children—in industrial work at a time when traditionally male-dominated handwork (whose mechanized procedures no longer demanded muscular strength) was first being channeled into industry.[1]

Modern manufacturing was established in Finland in the 1840s, when the first cotton, wool, and clothing factories were founded. From that time until the 1870s, industrial growth was greatest in the textile and metal industries, the former dominated by women, the latter by men. In the period immediately thereafter, industrial growth occurred mainly in the sawmill and paper industries, where women were rarely employed. Thus, the proportion of women among all industrial workers increased from 16 percent in 1845 to 24 percent in 1865, since textiles were growing more rapidly than other industries, but it had declined to 19 percent by 1885, while the male-dominated industries expanded. The proportion of women in the workforce, however, soon began to increase again as more and more mechanization was introduced into production, creating the routine jobs that were often assigned to women. By 1913 they made up 19 percent of the labor force.[2]

When the service sector began to be significant, the participation of women in paid work increased still further. Table 4-1 shows this development in men's and women's labor force participation rates (LFPR) both in industry and construction and in the services and further shows how the female labor force over the years has been divided between these two sectors.

TABLE 4-1

Proportion of People Aged Fifteen and Over Employed in Agriculture, Industry, and Services, by Sex, and Proportion of Women in Agriculture, Industry, and Services in Finland, 1910–1975

| | % of Population Over 15 in | | | | | | % of Women in | | | |
| | Agriculture and Forestry | | Industry and Construction | | Services | | Agriculture and Forestry | Industry | Services | Industry and Service |
Year	Men	Women	Men	Women	Men	Women				
1910	56	32	10	3	6	5	37	25	45	36
1920	54	36	13	8	8	6	42	27	46	39
1930	49	35	15	5	9	8	43	26	49	38
1940	49	37	21	8	13	13	46	29	52	39
1950	42	24	29	11	18	17	41	31	53	41
1960	32	16	32	11	24	23	35	28	55	42
1970	17	8	31	12	24	29	33	29	57	44
1975	10	6	29	12	26	33	42	31	58	46

Source: Elina Haavio-Mannila and Kyllikki Kari, "Changes in the Life Patterns of Families in the Nordic Countries," in *Yearbook of Population Research in Finland*, 17 (1980), pp. 9 and 11.

The percentage of men in industry has always been low in Finland. In 1910, 10 percent of men over fifteen years of age worked in industry, and this figure had grown only to 29 percent by 1975, a low rate compared with other countries. While men's industrial LFPR increased 290 percent in these sixty-five years, women's rate advanced from 3 to 12 percent, a 400 percent increase. As high as this growth rate was, the service sector demonstrated an even more rapid rise for both men and women. In 1910 only 6 percent of men and 5 percent of women worked in services; by 1975 these proportions had grown to 26 and 33 respectively, increases of 433 percent for men and 660 percent for women. Throughout the century the proportion of women working in services has exceeded that for industry, and this proportion has risen steadily with each decade.

Yet from the beginning of this century, more women have worked in industry in Finland than in any of the other Nordic countries—Denmark, Norway, and Sweden.[3] In 1975 women made up 46 percent of the nonagricultural labor force. This high proportion of women among those working for pay is partly due to the relatively low participation rates of men.[4] Altogether, a higher proportion of women work for wages in Finland than in any other noncommunist country.[5]

PUBLIC POLICIES AND WOMEN'S ISSUES:
THE UNION ROLE

Because so many women work for pay in Finland, one would expect them to exert strong pressures to improve their position in the workforce, either by getting their unions and the Labor party to write appropriate legislation or by adding women's issues to the bargaining agendas that shape collective agreements. Let us see whether this is true.

In general, public policies may be initiated by any of several bodies—women's organizations, political parties, government, and parliament—and be carried out through legislation. Women members of the Finnish parliament have been more active than men in putting forward policies concerning women and have thus functioned to some degree as representatives of their special electorate, primarily consisting of women.[6] Similarly, one might assume that in trade unions women would articulate the special needs of women members. For this to occur, however, four conditions need to be fulfilled:

- Women must join unions, participate in their meetings, and state their demands there.
- They must have access to the various levels of decision making in order to be influential. Specifically, they must be elected to serve as official delegates, board members, or officers.

- Male members of decision-making bodies must acknowledge the legitimacy and importance of women's demands—a condition particularly difficult to achieve in unions where women are in a minority—and put these items on the collective bargaining agenda.
- Employers also must agree to these proposals if they are to become part of the collective agreement.

Let us examine the situation of Finnish women trade unionists to see to what degree and under what circumstances these four conditions are fulfilled.

Women as Union Members

Although the first trade unions were not formed until the 1880s, workers had started their own cultural and relief activities as early as the 1850s. When unions were founded in 1887, they first functioned as subdivisions of these early workers' organizations. Thus, the political labor movement and the trade union movement developed side by side within the same associations. Not until after 1907, when the Finnish Trade Union Association (Suomen Ammattijärjestö—SAJ) was founded, did the functions of political party and labor union begin to separate.[7]

According to David Matheson, the radicalization of the Finnish industrial trade union movement was probably aided by the fact that the mobilization of the working class in general began through a mass political organization springing from a political party.[8] Up until the Civil War (1917), the revolutionary Social Democratic party (SDP) played a key role in defining strategy for the relatively weak SAJ. After the war the Finnish Communist party was able to assert control over SAJ and continued to do so until the union was disbanded in the 1930s.

When the Central Organization of Finnish Trade Unions (first called Suomen Ammattiyhdistysten Keskusliitto, but since 1960 Suomen Ammattiliittojen Keskusjärjestö—SAK) was formed in 1930, it was dominated by Social Democrats, establishing a pattern that has lasted down to the present day. After the wars with the Soviet Union, the Finnish Communist party and the People's Democrats began to compete with the SDP for influence in the Central Organization. However, this phenomenon brought with it the paradox that has seemed to dominate the history of the trade union movement: the mass movement would be weaker without the communists, who have continuously represented a sizable constituency within the working class, but their presence has invariably divided the movement, and particularly the leadership.[9]

The Finnish trade union movement has from the start been part of the national and international labor movement. It constantly emphasizes its independence of the political parties,[10] though parties are in the SAK leadership: at its 1976 convention, about 63 percent of the representatives were Social Democrats and 37 percent People's Democrats (communists). In the 1975 elections for parliament, by comparison, the SDP won 54 seats and the People's Democratic League[11] 40 out of the total of 200. Thus, power relations between Social Democrats and communists in the SAK roughly correspond to those in parliament.

This close relationship between trade unions and socialists generally is also evident at the grass roots level. In a 1975 survey of the urban population, trade union membership correlated strongly with support for the SDP. In addition, socialist support was considerably higher among persons inclined to attend union meetings than among persons who are just union members.[12]

Women first organized in separate trade unions in the 1890s under the wings of the workers' organizations in Helsinki. The first organized women were seamstresses, washerwomen, domestic servants, and women working outdoors. The first strike organized by women workers took place in 1899 at a skirt factory in Turku, where 150 newly organized seamstresses struck against an attempt to cut their wages. The strike, which lasted seven weeks, ended in a partial victory for the workers. They received financial and moral support from the organized workers in Turku.[13] In general, though, trade unionism started in the traditionally handwork-dominated, highly skilled areas of work. Factory workers (about 25 percent of them women), whose working conditions were much worse than those of the skilled workers, began to organize only after the general strike of 1905 had led to the general awakening of union consciousness among the working class.

The general strike was more political than economic. It aimed at enlarging the recently restricted autonomy of Finland as a grand duchy of Russia, and ultimately at total national independence. Other strike goals included general and equal suffrage, a one-chamber parliament, and freedom of organization, speech, and assembly. The most significant results were the granting in 1906 of general suffrage to all citizens, including women, and parliamentary reform; both had been central demands of the labor movement since its establishment.[14] (The bourgeois feminist movement had joined in the socialist demand for general adult suffrage in 1904.) As a result, Finnish women were the first in Europe to get voting rights in national elections and the first in the world to become eligible to sit in parliament. In the first elections in 1907, 19 women were elected to the 200-member parliament. Nine of them represented the SDP, which won 80 seats altogether. Thus, the SDP elected a higher proportion of women than the bourgeois parties.

In these early years, women joined unions at a much lower rate than men. By about 1910, only 11 percent of female industrial workers belonged to trade unions, while 31 percent of men were members.[15] In 1906, 1,836 women were in unions, 12 percent of the country's 15,355 union members. Of the unionized women, 75 percent worked in textiles, paper, and tobacco or as seamstresses; only 25 percent came from all other branches of industry or trade. Commercial workers had hardly begun to organize, and among food workers, only bakers had formed unions.[16]

The proportion of women in labor unions has steadily increased, and in 1979 they represented 42 percent of the 900,000 members (both blue- and white-collar) of the SAK,[17] very close to their representation in the labor force, now totaling about 1.7 million wage earners. Figure 4-1 shows the rapid growth in SAK membership in the latter part of the 1940s and again at the beginning of the 1970s.

FIGURE 4-1

Growth of Membership and Proportion of Women Members in SAK, 1907–1977

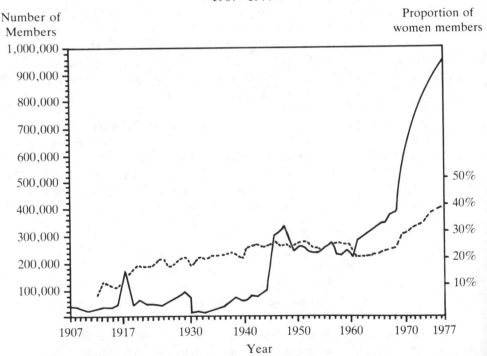

Number of Members

Proportion of women members

Source: Pirko Alakapee and Marjaana Valkonen, "Naiset ammattiyhdistysliikkees-sä" (Women in the Trade Union Movement), in *Nainen SAK: laisessa ammattiysliik-keesä* (Women in the SAK Trade Union Movement) (Jyväskylä: Gummerus, 1979), p. 136.

The membership increase of the 1940s followed the signing of the so-called January Declaration in 1940 and a General Agreement between employers and unions in 1944. These opened the way to collective bargaining by establishing the unions' right to represent the workers, although the war postponed the consummation of the first collective agreements until 1945. The General Agreement was reformed in 1946 and is still the basis for collective bargaining on labor contracts and such aspects of working relations as wages and working hours.[18]

The General Agreement not only benefited blue-collar workers and their unions but called for the organization of white-collar workers as well. The Finnish unions have since formed three more specialized confederations analogous to the SAK. In 1944 the Central Union of Intellectual Workers (Henkisen Työn Keskusliitto—HTK) replaced an earlier organization in which only civil servants had had bargaining rights. In 1956 this organization changed its name to the Confederation of Salaried Employees (Toimihenkilöja Virkamiesjärjestöjen Keskusliitto—TVK). With the change in name came a change in policy that moved the organization closer to functioning as a modern trade union. A second confederation is that of technical employees, STTK, set up in 1946; a third, the Cooperative Committee for Academically trained Employees (AKAVA), was founded in 1950. Altogether, the organization rate of workers in Finland is among the highest in Western Europe, standing at about 80 percent.

After the Civil War the number and proportion of women industrial workers increased. First, the war made many women sole providers for their families; second, industry was developing rapidly in the now independent Finland. The proportion of women union members rose from 12 percent in the prewar period (1916) to 22 percent in 1920. By 1924 the unionization of women was more advanced than that of men, even though organizing in the 1920s demanded great courage, and union activists sometimes lost their jobs. The rapid progress of organizing among women was partly a result of the activity of the Women's Council in the SAK, which in many locations had its own staff devoted to the education of women workers.[19]

A major advance in the number and proportion of women union members came in the 1970s. It followed a slack period during the 1960s, when a split in the SDP was replicated in the trade union centers. The power struggle between factions in the SAK during that time used up most of its energy; cooperation to attain common goals—including improvements in the position of women—was impossible. Even during this decade, however, trade unions achieved important gains that benefited many women workers: maternity daily allowances, workers' pensions, and reform in working hours. The greatest victory in principle was the ratification of the International Labour Organisation's (ILO) Convention 100 on equal pay. Yet many problems, not least of them women's wages, were left as challenges to the reunified trade union movement in the 1970s.[20]

Employment of women, particularly married women, increased in the 1960s and 1970s. Increases in the unionization of women followed, and in the seventies women reached organization rates equal to men's. This was partly a consequence of changes in women's attitudes toward work lives. The prevailing belief of the 1950s that there was no necessity for working wives to organize was finally outdated. Working for pay was no longer a short-term experience for women, and union activity to improve the position and rights of workers was no longer considered only a concern of men. These changes in attitudes were influenced by discussions of sex roles in the mass media, which were particularly lively in Finland in the late 1960s. By 1976, 86 percent of male and 84 percent of female wage earners were union members.[21] Three years earlier the percentages were about nine points lower; 77 and 75 respectively.[22]

Among white-collar workers, the TVK reports that 76 percent of its members are women. In fact, more than half of all women union members are in this central white-collar organization with jurisdiction over a number of sectors where women dominate, such as nursing and banks. Of all union members in Finland in 1978, 47 percent were women, as Table 4-2 shows.

Women as Union Leaders

Table 4-3 and Figure 4-2 offer evidence on women's leadership roles in Finnish unions. The former displays their participation in leadership posi-

TABLE 4-2
Proportion of Women Members in Four Finnish Confederations, 1978

Confederation	Total membership	% of women
SAK	980,643	41.9
TVK	303,679	76.0
AKAVA	156,657	40.0
STTK	98,253	13.1
Total	1,539,232	46.6

Source: Juha Saarinen, "Naisten osuus työmarkkinajärjestöjen, puolueiden, maatalousuottajien ja osuustoimintaliikkeiden päättävistä elimistävuoden 1978 lopussa" (Proportion of Women in the Decision-Making Organs of Labor Market Organizations, Parties, Agricultural Producers and Cooperatives in 1978), manuscript (Helsinki: Council of Equality, 1976).

TABLE 4-3
Proportion of Women in Leadership Posts in Local Unions
and Local Central Bodies of Unions in the SAK, 1977

Level and Position	% of women
11 National Unions	
Local unions: officers	
Chairpersons	18.0
Secretaries	42.7
Treasurers	37.5
Members	53.5
14 National Unions	
Local central bodies: officers	
Chairpersons	1.2
Secretaries	32.5
Treasurers	26.5
Education secretaries	20.5
Shop stewards	21.7
Members	50.3

Source: Alakapee and Valkonen, "Naiset ammattiyhdistysliikkeessä," pp. 149–151.

tions in the local unions and local central bodies; the latter, their rate of participation on the boards of the various central confederations of blue- and white-collar workers.

Table 4-3 makes it clear that even at the local level women are in a decided minority among union leaders. The positions they hold are mainly those of secretary and treasurer, while chairpersons are much more often men. Among the manual workers' unions of the SAK, only 22 percent of shop stewards are women, although women make up 50 percent of the membership. In contrast, in the white-collar unions of the TVK, the proportion of women shop stewards is the same as that of women members.

As Figure 4-2 shows, in all the confederations women's representation union boards is well below their representation in the union membership. Figure 4-3 displays the proportion of women among delegates to the unions' conventions, and these figures fall below the rate of their membership in the various organizations. The best representation of women among board members and delegates is in the AKAVA unions, where women are academically trained and belong to professional associations. TVK unions make a much better showing than those in the SAK in Figure 4-3, though this is not the case for Figure 4-2.

Two explanations for these differences in leadership participation by academic, white-collar, and blue-collar women can be suggested: the higher

Figure 4-2
Proportion of Women on the Boards of Finnish National Unions in Designated Central Organizations, Compared with the Proportion of Women Members, 1978

Percentage of Women on Boards

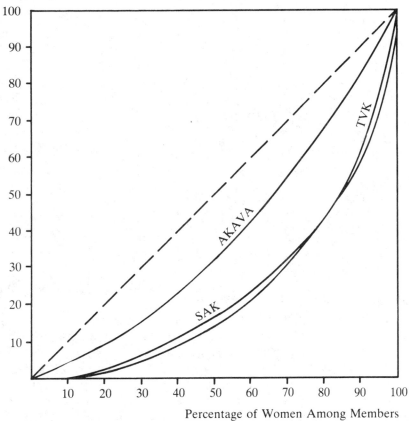

Percentage of Women Among Members

Source: Saarinen, "Naisten osuus työmarkkinajärjestöjen."

educational level of women in the AKAVA and TVK, a characteristic that presumably makes them more competent and more available for union leadership; and the small size of these unions, which lessens the competition for positions of responsibility. Studies carried out by the governmental Council of Equality[23] suggest that the pattern exhibited in Figure 4-4 holds for the Finnish trade union movement in general: the correlation between the proportion of women members and that of women board members is considerably more favorable in small than in large national unions. The

Figure 4-3
Proportion of Women Among the Delegates to Conventions of
Finnish National Unions, Compared with the Proportion of Women
Members, 1978

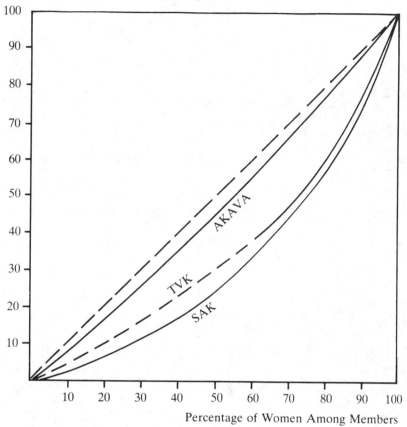

Percentage of Women Among Delegates

Percentage of Women Among Members

Source: Saarinen, "Naisten osuus työmarkkinajärjestöjen."

board members of the larger unions are, of course, more powerful and influential than those of the smaller ones.

The four central organizations (SAK, TVK, AKAVA, and STTK) hold their conventions every two to five years. Recent years have seen a considerable increase in the proportion of women serving as delegates to these bodies from the national unions and as elected members of the governing councils and executive boards, although they remain underrepresented in terms of total female union membership. At the SAK's 1976 convention, for

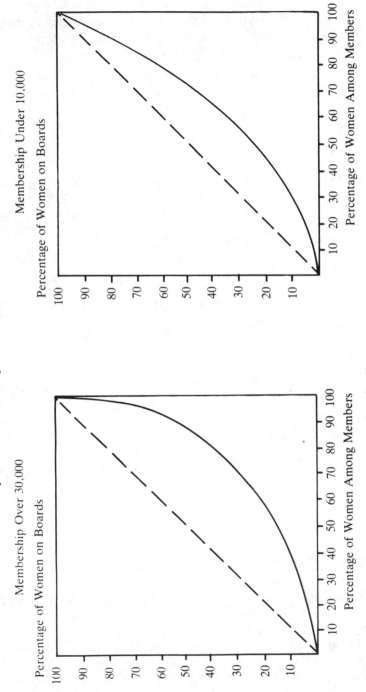

Figure 4-4

Proportion of women on the Boards of Large (Over 30,000 members) and Small (Under 10,000 Members) National Unions of the SAK and TVK, Compared with the Proportion of Women Members, 1978

Source: Saarinen, "Naisten osuus työmarkkinajärjestöjen."

example, (109 of the 473) delegates from the national unions were women (23 percent); 37 of the 171 elected to the national council (22 percent); and 2 of the 22 elected to the executive board (9 percent). At this time women made up 42 percent of the union's membership. These figures represent a dramatic advance in female representation since the previous convention in 1971 (Table 4-4).

The TVK reports that in the councils of delegates of its various affiliated unions, there has until recently been a male majority, although a majority of the members these men represent are women. In the 1960s women made up about 20 percent of the councils of natioal unions. This proportion improved through the 1970s and had reached 46 percent by 1978. Similarly, the proportion of women on the national board of the TVK increased during the 1970s, and in 1981 six of its twelve members were women. No comparable data are available from the AKAVA and STTK.

As for the paid officers of the national unions and central organizations,

TABLE 4-4
Female Representation at SAK Conventions and on the SAK Council (various Years, 1930–1981)

Year	% of Women Delegates	% of National Unions Sending Women delegates	% of Women on SAK Council	% of National Unions electing women to SAK Council
1930	2.6	12.5	0.0	0.0
1934	4.3	12.5	0.0	0.0
1937	4.1	17.5	0.0	0.0
1940	9.2	25.5	0.0	0.0
1943	9.7	36.4	4.8	9.1
1947	6.3	28.9	3.9	7.9
1951	10.4	31.6	7.7	15.8
1956	6.9	28.2	6.8	12.8
1961	6.7	29.2	6.1	16.7
1966	7.6	37.5	7.4	16.7
1969	9.1	24.4	7.9	15.6
1971	10.8	44.8	12.8	34.5
1976	23.0	67.9	21.6	53.6
1981	30.3		34.9	

Source: Alakapee and Valkonen, "Naiset ammattiyhdistysliikkeessä," p. 155, and information from SAK.

TABLE 4-5

Proportion of Women Among Paid Officers in Three Finnish
Confederations, 1978

Confederation	No. of paid officers	% of Women among Paid Officers
SAK	648	10.5
TVK	158	50.0
AKAVA	80	36.2

Source: Saarinen, "Naisten osuus työmarkkinajarjestöjen."

here again men are overrepresented in relation to their membership numbers (Table 4-5). This disproportion is most obvious in the manual workers'
trade unions (SAK), where only 10.5 percent of paid officers are women.
One reason may be that for the SAK's blue-collar members, becoming a
union officer represents greater upward mobility than it would for a white-
collar worker. Thus, blue-collar men can be expected to be more interested
in these positions and to offer more competition to women candidates.
Women in blue-collar trades, moreover, for the most part hold isolated,
low-status jobs and are largely unknown to their male colleagues. This too
puts them at a disadvantage in seeking union office.

The TVK also has a higher proportion of male functionaries than of
male members, but the difference is not so great as in the SAK. Only in the
AKAVA, the professionals' organization, is proportion of women paid
officers almost equal to that of women members. Perhaps because union
officership does not represent upward mobility for these workers, posts are
more accessible to women.

In light of these facts, what possibilities are there for women workers to
articulate and press for a greater role in trade unions? We see that women
have taken the first of the four steps outlined above: they have joined unions
to almost the same extent as men. Thus, they have opportunities to express
their demands, including matters of special concern to women, at union
meetings, where all members have the right to speak and vote.

They must also be elected to positions of influence and power, however, either as delegates or as council and board members or as paid officers.
While the data presented here show an increase in women's participation in
the decision-making bodies of the unions, particularly over the last decade,
they also suggest that women will find it easier to rise to positions of power in
small organizations than in large ones. We see further that the relative
rewards for individuals moving into positions of power and particularly into
paid office, seem to have some influence on the sex ratio among office

holders. Women have relatively easy access to positions that call for practical work without much status or pay, such as that of secretary or treasurer of a local union, whereas men seek posts carrying rewards in money or status, such as that of chairperson or paid officer. I do not, of course, suggest that union secretaries and treasurers are without influence. Women have made considerable progress. I believe, however, that they still have a long way to go.

Women's Divisions and Councils for Equality

The chief structural adaptation that blue-collar unions in Finland have made to address the special needs of women was the establishment of special women's divisions or secretariats. These were also established in the other Scandinavian countries, but there they have ceased to exist. In Norway's Landsorganisajon a special women's division functioned from 1940 until 1975. In Sweden a similar unit, established in 1947, was abandoned in 1967, and in Denmark the women's division set up in 1949 was replaced in 1960. In Finland, by contrast, the Women's Council (later Council on Women's Questions) of the SAK was established as early as 1937 and is still active. (Even before 1937, in 1923–1929, a special division of the SAK was dedicated to increasing unionization among women workers and developing women's trade union consciousness.)

The Council of Women's Questions in the SAK is an expert body of twelve members representing important national unions with large numbers of women workers. It can make statements on matters related to the position of women in the unions and bring them to the executive board. It can also make proposals to the SAK social policy council. Its special work, however, directed by the secretariat in the main office, is that of education, research, and organization for and with women members. It has encouraged women to speak up at meetings, and one of its important achievements has been the rapid rise in the proportion of women at the conventions and in the council of the SAK. One of the results of the Council's activity may have been the relatively high participation of women in union education in the 1950s and 1960s, when the proportion of women at union educational courses was higher than the proportion of women union members. In the 1970s their participation was lower, the result of an increased emphasis on education for shop stewards, of whom women are a minority.[24]

The council in 1971 drew up a program stating the ideal of total equality of men and women in work life and in the whole of society. The Nordic Trade Unions (Nordens Fackliga Samorganisation) adopted a similar program in 1976. (Close cooperation and similar interests characterize the trade union bodies within the Nordic countries: both the Swedish and the Finnish trade unions, for example, have recently achieved longer parental leave from work with full pay following the birth or adoption of a child.) Finnish trade union women revised their program in 1976 to include many more aspects of working life: the position of women at work; discrimination and equality; wages; social security; shift work; part-time work; vocational, continuing, and trade union education; and the role of women not only in the trade unions, but in international cooperation.

The SAK's women's division has branches in many of the SAK central bodies, and their popularity seems to be growing: in 1972 local central unions reported sixty women's divisions, and by 1978 the number had grown to seventy-one. They form a connecting link among women from different occupations and unions, and they can initiate proposals not only within the unions, but also before local authorities, whom they press for improvements in public services in their communities.

Women's Issues in Collective Bargaining

In satisfying the special needs of women trade union members, the fourth condition to be fulfilled is that employers must agree to the proposals made by women or their representatives so that they can become part of collective agreements. What results have been achieved by collective bargaining on the issues of women's wages and social policies related to women workers?

Whether women's groups have had an influence on the wages of men and women in industry is unclear. What is unmistakable is that women's position in the labor market has advanced during this century. The reasons are, of course, manifold. Women's level of education has greatly improved, and they have gained experience as workers. It is probable that as a consequence they have more precise knowledge about their rights and are more assertive about fighting for them both together with men and on their own.

Women's annual wages in industry in 1903–1913 were only about half those of men. In the bakery, tobacco, and textile industries, where women predominated, their wages were about 60 percent of men's; in the printing and paper industries, 50 percent; and in the glass industry about 39 percent. Although both women and men were paid best in the printing industry, whose workers pioneered—in Finland as in many other countries—in forming trade unions, the wage difference between the sexes was no smaller than it was elsewhere in industry.[25]

Table 4-6 shows the development of women's wages for the years 1936–1977. The figures show that women's hourly earnings in industry as a proportion of men's increased from around 57 percent in 1936–1944 to 68 percent in 1945. The next step upward started in the late 1960s, and by 1977 women were earning 75 percent of the male wage. The increase in the relative wage level of women in 1945 was related to the first collective

TABLE 4-6

Women's Hourly Earnings in Finnish Industry as a Percentage of Men's (Separately Paid Weekday Holiday Compensation Excluded), 1936–1977

Year	%	Year	%	Year	%	Year	%	Year	%
		1940		1950	65.1	1960	66.4	1970	70.4
		1941		1951	67.4	1961	66.0	1971	70.8
		1942	56.6	1952	66.3	1962	65.7	1972	71.3
		1943	57.0	1953	68.3	1963	66.7	1973	71.7
		1944	57.9	1954	67.3	1964	67.7	1974	72.4
		1945	67.7	1955	67.6	1965	68.1	1975	72.5
1936	56.8	1946	67.3	1956	68.9	1966	68.9	1976	73.4
1937	57.4	1947	65.4	1957	68.4	1967	69.1	1977	74.6
1938	58.4	1948	66.1	1958	67.7	1968	69.3		
1939	55.9	1949	66.6	1959	67.2	1969	69.8		

Source: Pirkko Österberg, "Naiset ansiot" (Earnings of Women), in *Nainen SAK: laisessa ammattiyhdistysliikkeessä* (Jyväskylä: Gummerus, 1979), pp. 30–31.

agreements between several national unions and their employers. The relative decrease that began in 1957 was halted in 1962 by Finland's ratification of the ILO's equal pay convention. Thereafter, separate wage scales for men and women were gradually abandoned. Yet even though the same wage is now paid for the same work, a difference between the wages of men and women prevails in Finnish industry. As Marja Kavonius has demonstrated, employers have many devices for avoiding the equal pay rule.[26] Finnish blue-collar women have good reason to continue their struggle for equality in financial compensation.

In the TVK, as I have pointed out, women form a decided majority, making up 76 percent of the membership. A large proportion of them are working in low-salaried jobs. Thus, the improvement of the position of women in working life has become a central issue in the TVK. In 1974 the confederation set up a Council on Equality to study questions related to women's low and unequal wages and to propose measures to solve these problems. A questionnaire went out to a sample of 1,500 members of unions belonging to TVK. The results were published in 1976 under the title *Matalapalkkaisuuden ongelma TVK:ssa* (The Problem of Low Salaries in the TVK).[27] Marja-Liisa Anttalainen brought the study up to date in 1979.[28] Both reports demonstrate that women are paid much less than men for their work, even when a wide variety of background variables are controlled. Moreover, the situation deteriorated between 1975, when women earned on average 79 percent as much as men, and 1979, when the ratio had dropped to 76 percent.[29]

On the basis of the first report, the TVK adopted in 1978 a program for achieving equality in several areas: (1) security in work life—a just division of income, full employment, continuing education, family policy; (2) influence in work life—democracy in the organization, office, and workplace and in personnel policy; (3) terms of employment—recruitment, salaries, evaluation of work, in-service training, working conditions, benefits, and security of employment. The program aims to deal with these issues by legislation and bargaining, as well as by work in union committees, education programs, and attitude training.[30] In 1979 the TVK drew up a program for improving the earnings of low-paid workers that affected precisely those fields where women predominate. It proposed among other things that reserve funds be established through collective bargaining to supplement wages in the sectors where women are clustered. Bargaining under this program began in 1979. It remains to be seen whether such a solution for correcting women's wage inequities will be widely accepted by employers.

THE TRADE UNION MOVEMENT AND SOCIAL POLICY

Until after World War II internal conflicts in Finland and some extreme right-wing political ideologies made it difficult for unions to function effectively. Their activity of necessity was mainly directed toward preserving their right to exist and achieving the right to bargain collectively with employers, but they also endeavored to influence social policies through state and local administrative bureaucracies and, chiefly, government committees set up to assess social conditions and recommend remedies. After the war, when collective bargaining could finally begin on the basis of the General Agreement of 1944, the influence of the unions increased substantially. Collective agreements on the federation level often included social policy clauses as well as understandings on wages. Paid maternity leave began to appear in some agreements. But these benefits varied widely, depending on the national unions involved, with the result that women were often treated very differently under different agreements.

In the period immediately after the war, the focus was on family policy and the care of the invalided. The legislation providing for children's allowances is a symbol of the new turn that made collective bargaining a substantial element in decision making on all forms of social policy. The first law on general children's allowances was passed in 1948, but employers had already been obliged a year earlier, through bargaining, to pay such allowances to their workers. The early achievement of this goal, in fact, was not so much a reflection of the place of this issue on union agendas as a way of circumventing the wage controls that limited the unions' ability to press directly for wage increases.

In the 1950s the unions played almost no role in widening social security. In the 1960s, however, the trade union movement became broadly influential, and labor market organizations participated actively in the development of a workers' pension system.

Since 1972 social policy developments have focused on the active labor force and included measures related to children's day care and workers' health care. The role of labor market organizations in reforming and developing social policy increased throughout the decade. The reforms have frequently taken the form of so-called social packages tied to centralized labor market agreements.[31] Most of the social security measures have been particularly significant for women, who have on the whole more social security problems than men. Quite recently, however, it has become apparent that women's needs and perspectives have not always been considered in developing new policies; for example, a twenty-three-person national committee established by the government in 1980 and composed of representatives of the labor market organizations and some scholars had only one woman named to it. Later, another was named as a substitute for a resigning member.

In other areas it remains to be seen whether women's interests will prevail. Trade union policy in the near future will probably be chiefly concerned with working hours, and this is, of course, an issue of major importance to women, who suffer severely from problems of time allocation. At present union men are more interested in increasing their annual vacations than in shortening their daily working hours, whereas women would much prefer the latter.

Given the Finnish circumstances, the role of trade unions in determining social policy is crucial. But so long as the decision-makers are mainly men, their agendas will be organized around the issues to which they give priority. Women have not yet succeeded in winning sufficient representation and influence at the critical levels of trade union policy making to place their issues prominently on these agendas. Until they do, their needs and problems will be insufficiently addressed and remain largely unsolved.

WOMEN'S TRADE UNION ACTIVITY AND EQUALITY

We have seen that Finnish women's representation declines as one moves upward in the unions' hierarchies and that their wages are lower than men's because of continued sex segregation in the labor market. Yet Finnish women have been quite active in the trade union movement. What accounts for this apparent contradiction?

First, legislation and other public activity aimed at leveling off sex differences or inequalities have made it possible for Finnish women to participate to some extent in decision making about working conditions. According to Kandolin and Uusitalo, who compared welfare indicators among the four Scandinavian countries in terms of social inequality between the sexes, "It seems legitimate to conclude that men and women in Finland are less unequal than in the other [Scandinavian] countries [and that among these] inequality between the sexes is greatest in Norway."[32]

The indicators according to which women fare well in Finland are:

1. *Life expectancy*. The inequality in favor of women is particularly great in Finland, the result not just of their longevity but also of the excess mortality of Finnish men.

2. *Physical health*. In Scandinavia as a whole, inequality in this area is in favor of men; in Finland, however, the sexes are almost equal because of the high incidence of illness among Finnish men.

3. *Anxiety*. Men have higher levels of anxiety in comparison with women in Finland and Sweden than in Denmark and Norway—in Finland because of their absolutely high level of anxiety, in Sweden because of women's low level.

4. *Education*. This is an area of equality in Finland; the largest inequality is in Norway and is in favor of men.

5. *Sex segregation* in education. This is considerable in all four countries but least in Finland.

6. *Employment*. Sex segregation is least in Finland, greatest in Norway.

7. *Occupation status*. Inequality in this area is least in Finland.

8. *Political activity*. The general inequality in favor of men is least in Finland.

9. *Societal activity and organizational memberships*. The general inequality in favor of men is least in Finland and greatest in Denmark.

Thus, the low levels of sexual inequality in Finland in health, education, employment, occupation, politics, and social activity are probably the main factors behind women's high participation in local trade union activity. An additional explanation may be the unions' increasing competition for members during the last decade. Women have been a reserve pool of potential union members. Now this pool has been emptied: almost all working women have become organized. The feminist consciousness of unionized women has also risen in this period, and women are the most vocal supporters of the solidary wage policy, which calls for significant increases to the lowest wage groups.

Reforms in laws and social policy on marriage, the family, divorce, the status of women, and the care of children have been developed through pressures from the trade unions. Clearly, the unions still have a central role in advocating the interests of working women, though, because of their male dominance, they do not always take this responsibility seriously or carry it through consistently. Finnish women, for all the social progress in their country, have not yet achieved economic or political equality with men in the labor market.

GLOSSARY

AKAVA	Cooperative Committee for Academically Trained Employees
HTK	Henkisen Työn Keskusliitoo: Central Union of Nonmanual workers. In 1956 it became the TVK.
ILO	International Labour Organisation
Nordic Trade Union	Nordens Fackliga Samorganisation—council of the major trade union confederations in the Nordic countries
SAJ	Suomen Ammattijärjestö: Finnish Trade Union Association
SAK	Suomen Ammattiliittojen Keskusjärjestö: Central Organisation of Finnish Trade Unions
SDP	Social Democratic party (also referred to as the Labor party)
STTK	Confederation of Technical Employees
TVK	Toimihenkilö-ja Virkamiesjärjestöjen Keskusliito: Confederation of Salaried Employees
VTY	Central Committee of Public Servants

NOTES

1. Pirkko Österberg, "Naisten ansiot" (Earnings of Women), in *Nainen SAK: laisessa ammattiyhdistysliikkeessä* (Women in the SAK Trade Union Movement), (Jyväskylä: Gummerus, 1979), p. 7.

2. Riitta Hjerppe and Per Schybergson, *Kvinnoarbete i Finlands industri ca. 1840–1912* (Women's Work in Finnish Industry, ca. 1840–1912), Communications, no. 5 (Helsinki: University of Helsinki Institute of Economic and Social History, 1977), p. 4; Österberg, "Naisten ansiot," p. 7.

3. Hjerppe and Schybergson, *Kvinnoarbete i Finlands industri*, pp. 38–39.

4. Irja Kandolin and Hannu Uusitalo, *Scandinavian Men and Women: A Welfare Comparison*, Research Reports, no. 28 (Helsinki: University of Helsinki Research Group for Comparative Sociology, 1980), pp. 26–27.

5. Elina Haavio-Mannila and Kyllikki Kari, "Changes in the Life Patterns of Families in the Nordic Countries," in *Yearbook of Population Research in Finland*, 17 (1980); and Kandolin and Uusitalo, *Scandinavian Men and Women*.

6. Sirkka Sinkkonen and Elina Haavio-Mannila, "Impact of Women MPs and the Women's Movement on Agenda Building," paper presented at the Eleventh IPSA World Congress, Moscow, August 12–18, 1979; Elina Haavio-Mannila, "How Women Become Political Actors: Female Candidates in Finnish Elections" *Scandinavian Political Studies* 2 (1979): 366.

7. Pirko Alakapee and Marjaana Valkonen, "Naiset ammattiyhdistysliikkeessä" (Women in the Trade Union Movement), in *Nainen SAK: laisessa ammattiysliikkeessä*, pp. 33–35.

8. David K. Matheson, *Ideology, Political Action and the Finnish Working Class: A Survey Study of Political Behavior*, Commentationes Scientarum Socialium, no. 10 (Helsinki: Societas Scientiarum Fennica, 1979), pp. 34–35.

9. Ibid.

10. *SAK Today* (1976): 9.

11. Democratic League of the People of Finland—an umbrella political party representing the Communist party in parliament and including communists, members of the People's Democrats, and some Socialists.

12. Matheson, *Ideology, Political Action and the Finnish Working Class*, pp. 92–95.

13. Alakapee and Valkonen, "Naiset ammattiyhdistysliikkeessä," p. 35.

14. Sylvi Kyllikki Kilpi, *Suomen työläisnaisliikkeen historia* (History of the Finnish Working Women's Movement) (Pori: Kansankulttuuri, 1953), pp. 64–81.

15. Hjerppe and Schybergson, *Kvinnoarbete i Finlands industri*, pp. 24, 51.

16. Alakapee and Valkonen, "Naiset ammattiyhdistysliikkeessä," pp. 36–38.

17. The SAK comprises twenty-seven unions and the Central Committee of Public Servants (VTY), a federation of ten unions in the public service.

18. Heikki Waris, *Suomalaisen yhteiskunnan sosiaalipolitiikka* (Social Policy in Finnish Society) (Porvoo: WSOY, 1966), p. 60.

19. Alakapee and Valkonen, "Naiset ammattiyhdistysliikkeessä," p. 52.

20. Ibid., p. 135.

21. Juha Saarinen, "Naisten osuus työmarkkinajärjestöjen, puolueiden, maataloustuottajien ja osuustoimintaliikkeiden päättävistä elimistävuoden 1978 lopussa" (Proportion of Women in the Decision-Making Organs of Labor market Organizations, Parties, Agricultural Procedures and Cooperative in 1978), manuscrip (Helsinki: Council of Equality, 1979), p. 37.

22. Leila Räsänen, "Naisten osuus työmarkkinajärjestöjen, puolueiden, maataloustuottajien ja osuustoimintaliikkeiden päättävistä elimistävuoden 1975 lopussa" (Proportion of Women in the Decision-Making Organs of Labor Market Organizations, Parties, Agricultural Producers and Cooperatives in 1975), manuscript (Helsinki: council of Equality, 1976), p. 4. The figures given include not just full-time and part-time workers but also temporary workers, such as students, who were employed at the time of the labor force survey. If the organization rate were based only on full-time workers, it would be considerably higher.

23. Ibid., Saarinen, "Naisten osuus työmarkkinajärjestöjen."

24. Alakapee and Valkonen, "Naiset ammattiyhdistysliikkeessä," p. 152.

25. Hjerppe and Schybergson, *Kvinnoarbete i Finlands industri*, pp. 21–22.

26. Marja Kavonius, "Metalapalkkaisuus—naisten väistämätön kohtalo?" (Low Salaries—The Unavoidable Fate of Women?), in *Naisnäkökulmia* (Feminine Perspective), ed. Katarina Eskola, Elina Haavio-Mannila, and Riitta Jalinoja (Juva: WSOY, 1979); and *Naisten asema työelämässä palkkauksen kannalta* (Position of Women in Working Life from the Wage Perspective), Valtioneuvoston kanslian julkaisuja (Publications of the Prime Minister's Office), no. 4 (Helsinki: Tasa-arvoasiain neuvottelukunta [Council of Equality], 1975).

27. (Jyväskylä: Gummerus, 1976.)

28. Marja-Liisa Anttalainen, "Palkkaseurantatutkimus 1979" (A Follow-Up Study on Salaires, 1979), manuscript (Helsinki: TVK:n tasa-arvoasiain toimikunta [TVK Council of Equality], 1979).

29. Ibid., p. 46.

30. "TVK:n tasa-arvo-ohjelma ja Tasa-arvo-ohjelman liiteosa" (Program of Equality and Appendix of Program of Equality of TVK), appendix 12, Proceedings of the Twenty-First Convention of the TVK, Helsinki, June 5–7, 1978 (Helsinki: TVK, 1978).

31. Jorma Sipilä, *Sosiaalisten ongelmien synty ja lievittamien* (Birth and Relief of Social Problems) (Helsinki: Tammi, 1979).

32. "In our terminology, 'inequality' and 'welfare' are closely related: 'Welfare' defines the content of (in)equality, that is, welfare differences—and only welfare differences—are 'inequalities.'" Kandolin and Uusitalo, *Scandinavian Men and Women*, p. 58.

BIBLIOGRAPHY

Alakapee, Pirko, and Marjaana Valkonen. "Naiset ammattiyhdistysliikkeessä" (Women in the Trade Union Movement), in *Nainen SAK: laisessa ammattiysliikkeessä* (Women in the SAK Trade Union Movement). Jyväskylä: Gummerus, 1979.

Allardt, Erik. *Hyvinvoinnin ulottuvuuksia* (Dimensions of Welfare). Porvoo: WSOY, 1976.

Anttalainen, Marja-Liisa. *"Palkkaseurantatutkimus 1979"* (A Follow-up Study on Salaries, 1979 Manuscript). Helsinki: TVK:n tasa-arvoasiain toimikunta (TVK Council of Equality), 1979.

Boulding, Elise, et al. *Handbook of International Data on Women*. New York: John Wiley and Sage Publications, 1976.

Haavio-Mannila, Elina. "How Women Become Political Actors: Female Candidates in Finnish Elections." *Scandinavian Political Studies* 2 (1979): 351–71.

Haavio-Mannila, Elina, and Riitta Jallinoja. *Changes in the Life Patterns of Families in Finland*. Working Papers, no. 13. Helsinki: University of Helsinki Department of Sociology, 1980.

Haavio-Mannila, Elina, and Kyllikki Kari. "Changes in the Life Patterns of Families in the Nordic Countries." In *Yearbook of Population Research in Finland*, vol. 17. 1980.

Haavio-Mannila, Elina, and Magdalena Sokolowska. "Position of Women." In *Social Structure and Change: Finland and Poland—Comparative Perspective*, edited by Erik Allardt and Wlodzimierz Wesolowski. Warsaw: Polish Scientific Publishers, 1978.

Hjerppe, Riitta, and Per Schybergson, *Kvinnoarbete i Finlands industri ca. 1840–1912* (Women's Work in Finnish Industry, ca. 1840–1912). Communications, no. 5. Helsinki: University of Helsinki Institute of Economic and Social History, 1977.

Kandolin, Irja, and Hannu Uusitalo. *Scandinavian Men and Women: A Welfare*

Comparison. Research Report, no. 28. Helsinki: Univeristy of Helsinki ResearchGroup for Comparative Sociology, 1980.

Kavonius, Marja. "Metalapalkkaisuus—naisten väistämätön kohtalo?" (Low Salaries—The Unavoidable Fate of Women?). In Naisnäkökulmia (Feminine Perspective), edited by Katarina Eskola, Elina Haavio-Mannila, and Riitta Jallinoja. Juva: WSOY, 1979.

————. Naisten asema työelämässa palkkaukesn kannalta (Position of Women in Working Life from the Wage Perspective). Valtioneuvoston kanslian julkaisuja (Publications of the Prime Minister's Office), no. 4. Helsinki: Tasa-arvoasiain neuvottelukunta (Council of Equality), 1975.

Kilpi, Sylvi Kyllikii. Suomen työläisnaisliikkeen historia (History of the Finnish Working Women's Movement). Pori: Kansankulttuuri, 1953.

Määttänen, Rauha. Naisten osuus TVK:laisessa päätöksenteossa (Proportion of Women in the Decision-Making bodies of TVK). Manuscript. Helsinki: Helsingin teollisuustoimihenkilöt ry:n tasa-arvoseminaari (Seminar on Equality Organized by Industrial Functionaries), 1974.

Matheson, David K. Ideology, Political Action and the Finnish Working Class: A Survey Study of Political Behavior. Commentationes Scientiarum Socialium, no. 10. Helsinki: Societas Scientarum Fennica, 1979.

Nordens Fackliga Samorganisation, Pohjolan Ammatillinen Yh teisjärjestö (Common Organization of the Nordic Trade Unions). Perhepoliittinen ohjelma (Program on Family Policy). Tukholma: 1976.

Österberg, Pirkko. "Naisten ansiot" (Earnings of Women). In Nainen SAK:laisessa ammattiyhdistysliikkeessä (Women in the SAK Trade Union Movement). Jyväskylä: Gummerus, 1979.

Räsänen, Leila. "Naisten osuus työmarkkinajärjestöjen, puolueiden, maataloustuottajien ja osuustoimintaliikkeiden päättävistä elimistävuoden 1975 lopussa" (Proportion of Women in the Decision-Making Organs of Labor Market Organizations, Parties, Agricultural Producers and Cooperatives in 1975). Manuscript. Helsinki: Council of Equality, 1976.

Saarinen, Juha. "Naisten osuus työmarkkinajärjestöjen, puolueiden, maataloustuottajien ja osuustoimintaltiikkeiden päättävistä elimistävuoden 1978 lopussa" (Proportion of Women . . . 1978). Manuscript. Helsinki: Council of Equality, 1979.

Sinkkonen, Sirkka, and Elina Haavio-Mannila. "Impact of Women MPs and the Women's Movement on Agenda Building." Paper presented at the Eleventh IPSA World Congress, Moscow, August 12–18, 1979.

Sipilä, Jorma. Sosiaalisten ongelmien synty ja lievittamien (Birth and Relief of Social Problems). Helsinki: Tammi, 1979.

Suomen Ammattiliittojen Keskusjärjestö SAK r.y. Ammattiyhdistysnaisten ohjelma (Program of Trade Union Women). Adopted at the Eleventh Convention of SAK, Helsinki, June 17–20, 1976. Helsinki: SAK, 1976.

Toimihenkilö-ja Virkamiesjärjestöjen Keskusliitto (TVK) r.y. Matalapalkkaisuuden ongelma TVK:ssa (The Problem of Low Salaries in TVK). Jyväskylä: Gummerus, 1976.

————. "Naisten palkkauksellisen aseman parantaminen" (Improving the Salaries of Women). Draft. September 20, 1979.

————. "TVK:n tasa-arvo-ohjelma ja Tasa-arvo-ohjelman liiteosa" (Program of Equality and Appendix of Program of Equality of the TVK). Appendix 12. Proceedings of the Twenty-First Convention of the TVK, Helsinki, June 5–7, 1978. Helsinki: TVK, 1978.

Uusitalo, Hannu. *Income and Welfare*. Research Reports, no. 8. Helsinki: University of Helsinki Research Group for Comparative Sociology, 1975.

Waris, Heikki. *Suomalaisen yhteiskunnan sosiaalipolitiikka* (Social Policy in Finnish Society). Porvoo: WSOY, 1966.

5   FRANCE

Margaret Maruani

Women's employment, unionism, and feminism in France are at a turning point today, marked by the economic crisis and the success of the Socialist party in the presidential and legislative elections of 1981. I shall focus on the development of these forces in the years since 1968, but we must first look briefly at the history of the unions with regard to women's participation and women's issues, at trends in women's employment, and at the relations between feminism and unionism. The latter I shall consider in the light of several recent, essentially women's strikes.[1]

I shall not discuss all the French unions, but only the manual workers' unions of the two largest and most dynamic national union confederations, which include the majority of those manual workers who are organized. The General Confederation of Labor (Confédération Générale du Travail—CGT) and the French Democratic Confederation of Labor (Confédération Française Démocratique du Travail—CFDT) consider themselves organizations of class struggle. Like unions in other Western countries that so describe themselves, they participate in collective bargaining and in the work of consultative and administrative agencies of governmental and quasi-governmental nature.

WOMEN AND UNIONS IN FRANCE

The old CGT, founded in 1895, the first major trade union center and still the largest, was in large part hostile to the presence in the workforce of women, especially married women, and therefore to their unionization. It was much under the influence of the mid-nineteenth-century anarchist Proudhon, who had proclaimed that woman was either "housewife or courtesan."

At that time only Jules Guesde and his wing of the socialist movement defended women's right to work. Guesde did so in terms that are still relevant:

Less than anyone else should workers, whose civil and political emancipation has permitted them to see all noneconomic emancipation for the lie it is, wish to see the subordination of one sex by another continue forever. . . . Woman's place is no more in the home than elsewhere. Alongside man, her place is everywhere that her energy can be used and she wishes to use it. Why, on what grounds, should one lock her up and pen her within her gender, transforming it—whether or not one seeks to do that—into an occupation, even a craft? . . . Assure women, just like men, the full development and the free use of their faculties. Assure all workers, without distinction of sex, the product of their labor. There lies the solution—and only there![2]

At the turn of the century, France had a much larger percentage of its female population working than did most other European countries, including a large number in agriculture. In 1900 women made up 34.5 percent of the working population, but only some 6 percent of the small number of union members. Their absence from the unions was not necessarily a sign of indifference on their part. They were prevented from working in some industries by men and men's unions, sometimes in natural reaction against employers' use of women at 40 to 50 percent lower wages for the same work, sometimes in ideological reaction against women's working instead of tending the home. Sometimes women took male strikers' jobs, especially where unions had refused to admit them. Working women were seen as competitors with men, and their lower wages threatened to put men out of work or lower the general wage scale. Competition was increased by mechanization, with women replacing men as machines were introduced that simplified or lightened the work process. Women thus formed a reserve workforce of manual laborers, lacking skills, underpaid, easily replaceable, and particularly vulnerable to employer authority and economic fluctuations.

Some unions wanted their men to walk off the job as soon as a woman was hired. The printers and the leather workers were on record to this effect. Madeleine Guilbert has discovered fifty-six strikes by men between 1890 and 1910 to prevent women from working in their shops.[3]

Between 1866 and 1911, 2.5 million women joined the labor force. Clearly now women were in the labor force to stay, and one by one men's unions grudgingly admitted women to membership.

One reason for this was the participation of women in a series of major strikes alongside men; some of the strikes of the pre–World War I generation were, in fact, essentially women's strikes. Women's own attitudes toward work and toward unions also changed with their participation in strikes, and in men's eyes they were no longer competitors or even strikebreakers, but allies or potential allies.

It took until 1913 and the "Couriau affair," however, to start a national debate on the subject of women's membership in unions. Emma Couriau, a printer paid a union wage, was refused membership in the printers' union in

Lyon. Her husband, a union activist of long standing, was expelled from that union for having permitted his wife to work at the trade. Feminist organizations, notably the women teachers of the University Women's Feminist Federation, took up the issue vigorously, and for the next year there was a lively debate in the union press on the issues raised by the affair.[4]

Just before World War I, the CGT launched a campaign for the unionization of women. The war put a stop to it, but the campaign was pursued again afterward, with both setbacks (the economic crisis of the 1930s, World War II, and the Vichy regime of 1940–1944) and great strides forward (the Popular Front of 1936 and the Liberation in 1944–1945).

WOMEN'S EMPLOYMENT

In France as in other countries, women's participation in paid work is not new. In 1906 as in 1975, they made up more than a third of the working population. Between these two dates there were significant fluctuations. In periods of economic crisis, employed women were sent home in order to "create" jobs for men; in periods of war, they replaced men, only to be sent home again after the war.

In 1962, for the first time after World War II, the proportion of women in the workforce ceased to decrease. It grew slowly from 33.4 percent in 1962 to 34.2 percent in 1968, and then rapidly to 38.1 percent in 1975.[5] In those years, the net increase in the number of women in the labor force was 1,384,000; that of men, a mere 159,000.[6]

This rapid rise in labor force participation involved a number of changes in the structure of women's employment. First, there was a growing percentage of wage and salary earners among working women (as opposed to the self-employed, including those in agriculture). This change occurred among men too, but to a lesser extent, as Table 5-1 shows. For the first time, a higher percentage of women than of men in the labor force were wage or salary earners.

A second change was the increase in women's employment in the

TABLE 5-1

Wage and Salary Earners as Percentages of the French Working Population of Each Sex, 1968 and 1975

Year	Women	Men
1968	75.2	77.3
1975	84.1	81.8

Source: Laurent Thévenot, "Les catégories sociales en 1975: l'extension du salariat," *Economie et Statistique*, no. 91 (July–August 1977): 7.

clerical and service sectors. Women accounted for three-fourths of the growth in the number of clerical employees and three-fifths of the growth in the services and middle management. But they also accounted for half of the growth in manual laborers, mostly unskilled or semiskilled, although they had made up only one-fifth of all manual laborers in 1968.[7]

Third, there was a greater continuity in women's, especially young women's, employment, as Table 5-2 shows. Until 1968 a considerable number of women in the 25–35 age group retired from the workforce to bear and rear children. Between 1968 and 1975 the greatest proportionate increase in labor force participation took place in this age bracket, although the highest percentage of employment continued to be in the 20–24 bracket. Although France provides more extensive child care services than most countries, many mothers of young children suffer from what the French call the "double work day" ("la double journée"). Their situation helps to explain women's increasing demands for equality.

Women made some gains in training, skills, and responsibilities in the professional and management groups in the 1968–1975 period. The percentages of women classified as in the "liberal professions and upper management" rose by 8.6 percent, as compared to 5.6 percent for men. In "middle management" the increase was 6.3 percent for women and 4.7 percent for men.[8] Among manual workers, however, the situation evolved differently. The decline in women's classifications by skill levels is shown in Table 5-3.

TABLE 5-2

Women's Labor Force Participation in France, by Age Groups,
as Percentages of All Women of Each Age Group,
1962–1975

Age	1962	1968	1975
17–19	48.7	36.5	35.4
20–24	61.8	62.4	66.0
25–29	45.6	50.2	62.7
30–34	39.2	42.4	54.6
35–39	40.0	41.3	50.6
40–44	41.8	43.4	49.4
45–49	45.1	45.3	49.9
50–54	45.6	45.1	48.1
55–59	31.8	42.3	41.9
60–64	34.2	32.3	27.8

Source: Institute National de la Statistique et des Etudes Economiques (National Institute of Statistics and Economic Studies—INSEE), 1975 census.

TABLE 5-3
Percentage of Women in Manual Labor in France,
by Skill Levels, 1968 and 1975

Skill Level	1968	1975
Foreman	7.2	5.9
Skilled workers	16.3	13.5
Semiskilled workers	23.0	26.8
Unskilled workers	30.1	38.1
All levels	21.3	22.9

Source: Thévenot, "Les categories sociales," p. 16, table 11.

Unemployment figures showed a worsening of the situation of women as the economic crisis of the mid-1970s deepened. A minority of the work-force, women became a majority (55.6 percent) of the unemployed by 1975. Thereafter, the proportion of women among the unemployed increased steadily to reach the record figure of 60.6 percent in early 1980.[9] They experienced three times the male rate of unemployment in 1970 and about twice the male rate from 1975 on, as Table 5-4 shows.

Yet women's employment continued to increase as well, and women held on to their jobs or sought other jobs if they lost them. The continued search of jobless women for work helped to swell the unemployment figures as well as the figures for labor force participation. By the end of 1979, there

TABLE 5-4
Rates of Unemployment in France by Sex in Percentages
of Labor Force of Each Sex (various years, 1970–1979)

Year	Male	Female
1970	1.4	4.2
1974	1.6	4.8
1975	2.7	5.4
1976	3.0	6.7
1977	3.3	7.2
1978	3.4	7.0
1979	4.1	7.9

Source: Organisation for Economic Cooperation and Development (OECD), *Women and Employment* (Paris: OECD, 1980),p. 47, citing OECD labor statistics; for 1979, INSEE, *Enquête sur l'emploi*, March 1979.

were 9,350,000 women working—40.7 percent of the total labor force, as
against 38.1 percent in 1975.[10]

The tie between work and unionism is close for women. Because
women are working in larger numbers, their fighting spirit has grown; and
because their capacities for struggle have grown, they can work. The recent
growth of women's labor force participation may be analyzed in terms of an
internal dynamic: the desire to work has grown with feminine and feminist
struggles of recent years, and the growth in women's employment is one of
the driving forces in women's struggles.

By 1975, when women were 38 percent of the labor force, they
accounted for a more or less comparable percentage of union membership.
French trade union figures, for men as well as women, are characterized by
uncertainty and by sharp fluctuations over time, the latter often corresponding to political developments.[11] The unreliability of union figures reflects the
pluralism, rivalry, and minority status of French unionism (France has a
ratio of union membership to eligible employees as low as that of the United
States). Both the CGT and the CFDT early in the 1970s estimated that
women made up about 30 percent of total union membership; later in the
1970s the CGT offered a figure of 25 percent and the CFDT a figure between
35 and 40 percent.[12]

THE RADICALIZATION OF WOMEN'S PROTEST
AND THE UNION RESPONSE

The increase in women's employment, as I have noted, is both
cause and effect of the expansion and radicalization of the women's protest
movement. The curve of women's employment began to rise in 1968, and
the revitalization of the feminist movement began in 1968–1970. The massive entry of young women into the labor market became apparent in 1975,
and a number of changes in the CGT and CFDT burst into the open around
the same time. The coincidence is striking. These developments may be the
most visible signs of a profound change that I shall discuss along two main
lines: the evolution of the union movement on women's issues and feminism, and the evolution of working women's demands and protests within the
union movement. In the unions, working women's activism appears as a
kind of feminism different from that of the women's movement. This protest
by women workers, now an important element of the social base of the
union movement, is reflected in the general evolution of unionism. I shall try
to show how French unions were jostled, challenged, and penetrated by
feminism—a feminism that came to them from both inside and outside. First
I consider feminism from the inside, analyzing the evolution of union
positions at the peak (confederal) level and women's action in several
strikes. Then I consider the relationship between feminism and unionism.

The Unions and Women's Issues

Although the CGT and the CFDT were in agreement around 1975 on some major issues, their paths to that agreement were very different. On women's right to work and the right to better wages and working conditions, the CGT was the first to take a stand and fight. After World War II "women's collectives" were formed at different levels of the organization. To its general demands involving both women and men, the CGT rapidly added some "women's demands," notably maternity benefits, nurseries, and other collective social infrastructures.

The CFDT (orginally the Confédération Française des Travailleurs Chrétiens: the French Confederation of Christian Workers) from the turn of the century had many women members who did manual work in textile mills and white-collar work in offices. Its dominant outlook was the traditional one: women's place was, if possible, in the home as wives and mothers. But it evolved rapidly with the emergence of liberal and radical Catholic currents during the depression and particularly with the experiences of the Resistance and the Liberation. By 1964 the vast majority of its members dropped the specifically Christian (that is to say, chiefly Catholic) reference to become the CFDT and one of the most innovative social forces in France. The CFDT changed its attitude toward women's issues rapidly. From a 1964 declaration of nondiscrimination between men and women workers, it moved to a declaration in favor of women's liberation in 1970. At this point its position on the exploitation of women as workers and specifically as women converged with that of the CGT.

When the two organizations diverged again, it was the CFDT, more open to the ideas of the burgeoning women's movement, that in 1971 affirmed, however timidly, the fight against predetermined social roles based on male domination. The CFDT was one of the few mass organizations to take part in the formation of the Movement for the Liberalization of Abortion and Contraception, which in 1973 and 1974 was prominent in the last stages of the fight for the repeal of the 1920 antiabortion law.

In 1974 the CGT and CFDT again drew nearer with a joint statement linking the "subordinate position of women at work, in the family, and in society" to a general "reactionary attitude toward the role of women." The statement blamed the "greater exploitation of women than of men in work life" and "the centuries-old inferior social status" of women for their "maintenance in the sole traditional role of mother and wife." The interunion accord then focused on the goal of "real equality between the sexes in work life and in all areas of social life" and on changes that required "transformations of society."[13] Its specific demands covered equality in work, notably in vocational training, employment, wages, and promotion opportunities; changes in the social roles of women and men, including reform of family allowances and services, paid parental leaves, elimination of the sexist content of schoolbooks, and more equal access to community facilities; and greater self-determination in certain specifically feminine areas; including pregnancy, birth, maternity, contraception, and abortion. It was no longer women's work life alone that was at issue, but their entire life situation—not only capitalist exploitation, but also patriarchal domination. In this statement we see the penetration of feminist ideas in the unions.

Enlarging the Scope of Union Action

At late as 1973 the CGT was still opposed to what it called "integral egalitarianism."[14] Soon, however, it went through a profound and sudden change that was difficult for many to accept. In 1977 it organized a conference on "working women today." The debates among women activists, like the statements of confederation officials, showed something of the changes occurring within the largest French labor confederation. "We must clearly state that it is not acceptable, in the life of a couple, that a woman should be the servant of the man," asserted Jean Louis Moynot. Another member of the confederation executive, Joannès Galland summed up the conclusions of the conference in declaring that "the CGT has no reason to have complexes about such problems as sexuality, the sharing of domestic tasks, abortion, and relations beteen husband and wife, even if these questions are controversial."[15] This conference seemed to bestow the CGT's official recognition on changes under way for several years.

In 1978 the CFDT organized a conference that debated many of the same questions. How does one integrate class struggle and women's liberation? How does one link action in the world of paid work with action in the family and society? For the CFDT as for the CGT, topics that had previously been defined as "personal problems"—in particular abortion, contraception, rape, task sharing within the family, and the "ordinary sexism"[16] of daily life—were now seen as collective and social problems and thus appropriate for union action.

The official confederation positions were not arrived at smoothly or by consensus. On the contrary, there was real debate, between the two confederations, between the rank and file and the leadership within confederations, among unions, and among regions. It was a debate among activists, both men and women, who did not always agree on methods, priorities, or even objectives. And in spite of reconciliations and convergences of views, a basic difference persisted between the CGT and the CFDT. The CGT, dominated though not controlled by the Communists, stressed the capitalist exploitation of women. The CFDT, whose leadership is mainly socialist but which has no direct party ties and a more generally eclectic outlook, stressed patriarchal domination as well as that of capitalist institutions. Short excerpts from two interviews with confederation officials in 1978 help make clear this difference:

> CGT official: The principal conflict is between capital and labor. But capitalists take advantage of traditional roles to exploit women. As a union organization, we cannot keep silent about these ideas of domination, which permit the greater exploitation of women than of men.

> CFDT official: In our organization, there has been a debate about which is more important, patriarchal domination or capitalist exploitation. We refuse to say that exploitation is more important. I myself put domination first, but the organization has refused to take a stand.

In the 1980s the CGT and the CFDT seem to be parting ways again. The CFDT continues along the path it has pursued, now focusing on the debate over quotas. It has demonstrated its commitment to getting women into the executive bodies of the confederation and in 1982 acted formally to create substantial quotas for women at all three levels of confederal executive power.

The CGT seems to be moving in the opposite direction, returning to positions that are perhaps more "classical" and, in any case, less feminist. The departure of several leading women officials is an indicator of the change. Christiane Gilles, director of the women's section of the CGT and member of the executive bureau, resigned to take a post in the Ministry of Women's Rights in the new Socialist government. In 1982 a conflict between the CGT leadership and the editorial staff of *Antoinette*, the CGT's monthly feminine/feminist journal, ended with the dismissal of its editor-in-chief, Chantal Rogerat, and most of its writers.

WOMEN ON STRIKE

Official union positions had swung to the side of change because of both internal and external pressures on union officials. The feminist movement reminded the unions that female oppression was not limited to exploitation in the workplace, but feminists' statements and actions had an effect only because they found echoes within the union organizations themselves. It was the emergence of feminist practices, demands, and analyses in the ranks of women unionists that changed the confederation positions.

An analysis of several women's strikes will illuminate the extent of this phenomenon. Starting with the maintenance of employment, working conditions, or wages, women strikers went on to a public and collective consideration of the sexual division of household tasks, women's double burden, abortion, contraception, and so on. In many cases strikes served to reveal the whole condition of women as women reflected, spoke, or wrote about it. An awareness of a feminine identity was being grafted onto class solidarities without supplanting them.

Strikes by women are not necessarily strikes for specifically feminine or feminist demands, but it is interesting to observe, in strikes without such demands, at least at the outset, how a "feminine dimension" develops and challenges traditional trade unionism. Four strikes of which I made case studies in 1977 and 1978 are illustrative. They suggest three main themes: (1) women are able to develop their own form of strike organization; (2) women's strike action brings out their oppression outside the workplace as well as in it; and (3) the strikes reveal cleavages within the unions and between the unions and women's movement.

A Feminist Approach to Strike Organization

The Confection Industrielle du Pas-de-Calais (CIP), a shirt manufacturing firm in northern France, was the target of one of the major strikes over job security in the mid-1970s. It was actually a series of strikes of three years' duration, July 1975 to July 1978. A sitdown strike in which the workers themselves resumed production, it was launched, energized, and sustained from beginning to end by women.

CIP was a small business mainly employing women. In 1975, when the managers decided to go out of business and proposed to dismiss all personnel, a general assembly of women workers decided to occupy the factory and resume production. The managerial and technical staff, the foremen, and the skilled workers—that is, all the men in the factory—abandoned the fight. The women of CIP lived by selling the shirts they made for three years, until they were all hired by a Belgian industrialist.

At first glance this strike has nothing to do with specifically women's issues. It was a response to mass layoffs, like a number of other strikes in France at the time. It was not a community of women who occupied their factory; it was a community of wage earners who had been fired. Certain aspects of the conflict, however, can be understood only by taking into account the feminine dimension. The first was the union mobilization. For women, the decision to strike often involves a family choice as well as a union one. When the CIP workers occupied their factory day and night for more than three years, it was an action by militant members of the CFDT who had lost their jobs, but it was also an action by women who saw that such a strike would upset the traditional pattern of family life and the precarious equilibrium between two people's workdays. Some had to choose between their families and their union action; others tried to reconcile the two. Many occupied the factory with their children, some with their husbands, and others against their husbands' wishes. The strike thus threw into question women's relationships of dependence, authority, and submission outside the workplace—in the family and in society.

Women organized their strikes in accordance with their family needs. The general factory meetings, the rhythms of work, and the strike meetings corresponded to children's school schedules and husbands' work hours. At CIP these constraints led to the development of a system of strike management that was collective, egalitarian, and noncoercive. The general meetings, where all decisions were taken, took place during working hours because women had to attend to domestic tasks after work. No leader arose from the union community because no one could take power by investing much more time than others in union activism: as a consequence of their subordination in family life, the women strikers did not have the means, open to most men, to become bureaucrats and petty bosses in union life. The rotation of functions and the sharing of tasks among the strikers were almost inevitable. The strike's methods were a democratic answer to the general social problem of women's lack of free time.

Strikes and the Revelation of Oppression

For many women a strike evokes an acute and conflict-laden awareness of the constraints of family life. At CIP, as elsewhere, the strike revealed the domination of women in (and by) their families. More and more frequently in recent years, women have spoken out collectively and publicly on these questions. With a strike as a starting point in all of the four cases I have analyzed, the women discussed first among themselves and then in public all aspects of their condition as workers and women: inequalities in pay and skills, working conditions, the right to work, and also the double burden of jobs and domestic tasks, abortion and contraception, the relationship between men and women in the union movement, and relationships of authority and domination within the family. Obviously, these were not new problems for women, but their emergence in the union field was a double breakthrough—out of both the "women's problems" ghetto and the classical union approach. Although women's problems remained the same, the way of addressing them began to change. These traditional concerns of private life were lived, presented, and anaylzed as collective phenomena.

That is the chief significance of the strike of the women at the LIP watchmaking plant in Besançon. It was one of the most spectacular industrial actions of the 1970s, and many unionists have called it a model strike. It was the first French strike over the maintenance of employment in which the plant was occupied, production resumed under worker control, and the product sold by the workers themselves. About half of the strikers were women.

The first strike at LIP began in 1973. As soon as it ended, some women workers formed a women's group, which produced a brochure entitled "LIP au féminin" (The Women's Side of LIP). To their surprise, it was a great success. It was soon translated into a number of languages and issued as a book in 1977, when a second strike was under way at LIP.[17] In the book, the women spoke of how they had lived the conflict—as strikers, as women workers, as union activists, but also, most of them, as wives and mothers of families. They analyzed the repercussions of the conflict, with its attendant changes and tensions, on their lives outside work. They described the division of family tasks according to sex, which, little by little, was recreated within the community of strikers. In short, they refused any longer to separate public life and private life, paid work and domestic work. "Almost everywhere," they wrote, "people still separate social and collective action from private life. People defend revolutionary ideas in the workplace, but at home they conduct their lives along conservative lines. Of course, some are making individual efforts. But we must arrive at collective consideration and collective solutions."[18]

The same themes appear in the strike of the clothing workers of the Confection Industrielle de l'Atlantique in La Rochelle. This was the action of an independent-minded CGT local, composed almost entirely of semi-skilled or unskilled women, with a history of ten years of conflict with management over working conditions. The local organized discussions on family planning, abortion, sexuality, family power relations, and task sharing. As private questions, these had no place in the field of social struggle. "Deprivatized," they acquired a social existence and could be dealt with through the unions and politically. But they called classical union practices into questions because they went far beyond the framework of the factory and the employment relationship. How does one integrate the issue of abortion into union action? What demands can change the division of labor in the home or the domination of men over women?

Strikes and the Revelation of Union Cleavages

These recent changes should not lead us to forget the barriers that persist and the weight of resistance to change. The inequalities between men and women in employment are in some ways reproduced in the union movement. In addition to the inequalities in pay, skills, job security, and unemployment benefits, there are also inequalities in union offices and responsibilites and in the relative importance accorded the demands of men and women. The Rhône-Poulenc-Textile (RPT) strike exposed many of these inequalities. It received much attention because of its central issue: blatant discrimination between men and women.

Early in 1976 the RPT management announced the reduction to half-time employment of married women in three of its units, its headquarters and two factories, Péage-de-Roussillon and La Voulte. Only women were affected, and it was therefore unmistakably clear that what was at issue was not simply a general problem of job security. At headquarters there was a general outcry. Faced with the spontaneous protest of the women concerned, management backed down before a strike could be called. With the agreement of the unions concerned, it imposed a solution that penalized all employees equally but in small measure—a work-sharing arrangement that cut everyone from forty hours a week to thirty-eight.

The first reaction at Péage-de-Roussillon was similar—work stoppages, demonstrations, and the occupation of management offices by the women. These spontaneous actions were rapidly taken over by the CGT and CFDT local unions, which involved all the workers through brief but repeated work stoppages. Six weeks later management abandoned its initial plan and re-established full-time work for all women workers.

At first, however, it had seemed as if the owners held all the trumps: the workers knew of a plan to close their factory, and putting the women on half-time was presented as a way to stave off a general shutdown. Management counted on competition between male and female workers and instead witnessed the massive support of the men for their eighty-four women co-workers.

At La Voulte the management strategy was the same—to pit men against women—but the result was the reverse. Amidst the almost total indifference of the male workers, forty-two women were reduced to half-time work. Although the overall unemployment problem was not as serious at La Voulte as at Péage, the La Voulte management explicitly stated, orally and in writing, that half-time employment for women would forestall transfers of men to the company's other plants. The male workers at La Voulte (both union and nonunion) evidently accepted this reasoning; in a difficult period, seeing the reduction to half-time work for women as a lesser evil, they let it occur.

The Rhône-Poulenc affair was not the only case of its kind. It became well known in France because the press (and not the union press alone) called attention to it, and because Rhône-Poulenc is one of France's largest firms; but how many similar cases have remained in the shadows? The story reveals some of the contradictions in French unionism's response to women's issues, a series of leaps forward and moves backward. Two Rhône-Poulenc units mustered a unanimous and solid defense by all the workers of women's right to employment that would have been impossible only ten or fifteen years before. At La Voulte, on the other hand, the most hackneyed stereotypes about women's role in the workforce prevailed.

In spite of many changes, the union movement is still marked by a double cleavage that separates women from men and unskilled from skilled workers. French unionism is still strongly influenced by its earlier history as a movement of skilled male craft workers.

FEMINISM AND UNIONISM: CONVERGENCE AND CONFLICT

The most striking development in unionism today is the existence of a current of feminism within the working class and within unionism. It is a workers' feminism, different from but deriving some of its vigor from the women's movement.

For the activists of the Women's Liberation Movement (Mouvement de Libération des Femmes—MLF), the contemporary version of French feminism, women's employment was only one concern among many in the 1970s. Abortion, contraception, rape, wife beating, family structure, housework, women's image in the media, the social conditioning of women, the "ordinary sexism" of daily life—the MLF forced society to consider all these issues. The feminists did not invent problems; they gave "rights of citizenship" to old problems. If we now speak openly of them and consider them serious social issues, it is because a tiny minority of women fought to make this happen.

The birthdate of the MLF is the summer of 1970, when a group of women placed at the Arc de Triomphe in Paris, before the Monument to the Unknown Soldier of 1914–1918, a wreath in honor of "the unknown wife of the unknown soldier." The movement expressed itself as such for the first time in a special number (July–October 1970) of the review *Partisans*, "Libération des femmes, année zero" (Women's Liberation: Year Zero). (In fact, 1970 was not the "year zero": French feminism has an earlier, if unrecognized history.)[19] The MLF was a spark plug, an illuminator, a catalyst. In France, as elsewhere, the movement is made up of a multitude of tendencies, opinions, and sensitivities. At first the MLF paid little attention to the issue of vocations and jobs for women. After 1975, however, some segments of the movement found their way into business and workplaces under the simple label of "women's groups." They demanded the right to work, equal pay, and better working conditions. They fought against the "double burden" and, more recently, against part-time work. Feminist activists became members of the women's committees of unions.

One of the goals of feminism was to get the problems of daily life— "simple women's problems"—into politics, to bring out the social aspects of matters traditionally considered personal and private, to denounce what Elena Belotti calls "the scandal of the private realm."[20] What can this same process in unionism be called? The protest against the fatalistic view of the feminine condition, the struggle for equal rights and against male domination, the refutation of so-called biological evidence of female inferiority, the refusal to consider women as subhuman or as deviate copies of the male model—all this is now undeniably at the center of union debate. One of the essential developments in labor organizations is also characteristic of contemporary feminist movements: the determination to expand the social struggle to encompass all that makes up the feminine condition. This determination appears at all levels, among national union and confederation officials and rank-and-file activists alike.

The renewal of unionism in these recent years is, then, the product of several different but converging practices. The new orientation of the CGT and CFDT, the presence in the workplace of women's committees, the involvement of union members in feminist groups, the protests of women workers arising from industrial conflicts—all are signs of a developing feminism. It does not always call itself that, but one would have to be blind not to see it. There is a convergence of two movements that have historically been adversaries, but the relationship remains tense. Why?

First there is history: we saw at the beginning of the century the confrontation between a misogynous unionism and a bourgeois and reformist feminism. But the present tensions between unionism and feminism stem equally from their recent rapprochement. The paradox is only apparent. It is because they are so close, because they struggle over the same issues and sometimes on the same terrain, that frictions arise. Proximity accentuates and contrasts as national union organizations defending women workers encounter a feminist movement fighting for all women. Encounters between feminism and unionism are often conflict-laden because they reciprocally illuminate each other's internal contradictions. Each sends the other back to examine its own inconsistencies and to question its own logic.

EQUAL PAY, EQUAL OPPORTUNITY, AND PART-TIME WORK

It is impossible to say whether we have reached a real turning point for women in trade unions. Let us return to the change in the political situation with which I began. For two decades the CGT and the CFDT were in opposition to most of the policies of the center-right governments headed by Presidents De Gaulle, Pompidou, and Giscard d'Estaing. Yet certain laws passed in this period might have meant progress toward the equality of the sexes. France banned discrimination in wages between men and women in 1946 and reaffirmed equal pay for equal work in the collective bargaining law of 1950. It was at the French government's insistence that the Treaty of Rome, establishing the European Economic Community, included Article 119, which required equal pay for equal work—not, in fact, in the interest of sex equality, but to avoid allowing a competitive advantage to manufacturers (chiefly in textiles) in other EEC countries, which were even farther in practice from equal pay than France.

This EEC principle was embodied in a law of December 22, 1972. It was followed by the law of July 11, 1975, forbidding discrimination because of sex or family situation in hiring or employment, with, however, an undefined and therefore ominous exemption "for legitimate motive." The CGT and the CFDT supported the principles behind these laws. But, as these two labor confederations claim, the laws have been totally ineffective.

A law regarding part-time work was passed on January 28, 1981, over the opposition of labor and feminist organizations. It permits employers to institute part-time work at will. (Although they are required to seek the advice of the labor inspectorate and the plant enterprise committee—corresponding somewhat to the works council in some other European nations—they are not obliged to follow it.) The law may be considered a symbolic attack on women's right to work, since, in all countries, most part-time employees are women.

Since France until recently discriminated against married women in civil service employment, it is noteworthy that a more liberal part-time law, that of December 23, 1980, instituted an experimental period of two years during which civil servants of either sex could opt for part-time work so long as they worked at least half-time. This alternative was to be treated the same as full-time employment for the purpose of determining rights to training or promotion. Families whose children had priority access to public or private child care facilities kept these rights during the part-time experience.

France's rate of part-time employment is far below that of Britain, the United States, Denmark, and Sweden, although above that of Ireland and Italy. Part-time workers made up 13.6 percent of the female labor force in 1975 and 15.2 percent five years later. Male part-timers then accounted for only 2.0 percent of the male labor force. For women, the picture by age groups in 1980 is shown in Table 5-5. The figures included both voluntary and involuntary part-time work.

Conclusion: A Real Turning Point?

The 1981 elections produced a Socialist presidency for the first time in the history of the Fifth Republic (established by de Gaulle in 1958) and a Socialist majority in parliament for the first time in French history. The Socialist party invited the Communist party, a heavy loser in the elections, to share in cabinet responsibilities, but in a minor role; the latter accepted. Despite a history of conflict, both parties have succeeded till now in maintaining the necessary cohesion for government.

The CFDT and the CGT were now in the novel position of having access to government and sympathy with many of its declared aims and policies, although in these hardtimes this relative closeness to power created constraints on union action as well as opportunities. One cannot predict the

TABLE 5-5

Women in the Labor Force Part Time in France, by Age Group, 1980

Age	Part-Time Workers
15–24	8.6
25–39	13.2
40–49	19.2
50–59	18.4
60 and over	25.4
All ages	15.2

Source: Pierre Laulhé, "L'enquête sur l'emploi de Mars 1980: la montée du chômage féminin" (An Inquiry into Unemployment in March 1980: The Rise in Women's Strikes), *Economie et Statistique*, no. 126 (October 1980): 3–13.

consequences of this situation for the unions or women; in a period of economic crisis, conciliatory speeches on equality and women's emancipation tend to give way to appeals for women to return to the home, attempts to limit their employment, and efforts to make their continued employment marginal and precarious. Proposals for part-time work and the proliferation of fixed-period and temporary work contracts bear witness to the variety of ingenious strategies devised by employers to exploit labor's more vulnerable points. In one place we find appeals to the old competitive reflex of men against women workers; at another place there is argument over the crucial problem of hours of work and their adjustment. All these problems remain after the political changes of 1981, even though the possibility of solutions other than those of recession and depression now exists.

More than ever, women's right to work is a burning issue. History reminds us that union responses to women's demands and women's needs are closely linked to women's place in the labor market. At the same time, whether the threats to women's right to work are realized or not depends, in significant part, on the nature and the strength of union responses.

GLOSSARY

CFDT	Confédération Française Démocratique du Travail: French Democratic Confederation of Labor
CFTC	Confédération Française des Travailleurs Chrétiens: French Confederation of Christian Workers
CGT	Confédération Generale du Travail: General Confederation of Labor
INSEE	Institut National de la Statistique et des Etudes Economiques: National Institute of Statistics and Economic Studies

MLF   Mouvement de Libération des Femmes: Women's Liberation Movement

NOTES

1. The research for this chapter was done originally as part of the work for a doctoral thesis in sociology, written under the direction of Prof. Jean-Daniel Reynaud of the Conservatoire National des Arts et Metiers in Paris and published as *Les syndicats à l'epreuve du féminisme* (Unions and the Challenge of Feminism) (Paris: Syros, 1979). In this chapter I lean heavily on that research, done between 1976 and 1978.

2. Jules Guesde, "La femme et son droit au travail," *Le Socialiste*, October 9, 1898.

3. Madeleine Guilbert, *Le femmes et l'organisation syndicale avant 1914* (Women and Union Organization Before 1914) (Paris: Centre National de la Recherche Scientifique, 1966).

4. Ibid.; Madeleine Colin, *Ce n'est pas d'aujourd'hui . . . femmes, syndicats, lutte de classes* (It Is Not Just from Today . . . Women, Unions, Class Struggle) (Paris: Editions Sociales, 1975); Marie-Hélène Zylberberg-Hocquart, *Féminisme et syndicalisme en France* (Feminism and Unionism in France) (Paris: Editions Anthropos, 1978).

5. Institute National de la Statistique et des Etudes Economiques 1968 Census, Employment Inquiry, March 1975.

6. Jean-Daniel Reynaud, *Les syndicats, les patrons, et l'état* (Unions, Employers, and the State) (Paris: Editions Ouvrières, 1978), p. 82, n. 1.

7. Laurent Thévenot, "Les catégories sociales en 1975: l'extension du salariat," *Economie et Statistique*, no. 91 (July–August 1977): 3–31.

8. INSEE, *Données sociales*, 1978; *Le Monde: Dossiers et Documents*, no. 75 (November 1980). For deeper analysis, see Daniéle Kergoat, "Ouvriers: ouvrières?" (Workers: Women Workers?) in *Critiques de l'Economie Politique*, no. 5 (October–November 1978); and Anne-Françoise Molinié and Serge Volkoff, "Les conditions de travail des ouvriers . . . et des ouvrières" (The Conditions of Work of Male Workers . . . and of Women Workers), *Economie et Statistique*, no. 118 (January 1980): 25–39.

9. Pierre Laulhé, "L'enquête sur l'emploi de Mars 1980: la montée du chômage féminin" (An Inquiry into Employment in March 1980: The Rise in Women's Strikes), *Economie et Statistique*, no. 126 (October 1980): 3–13.

10. *Le Monde, Dossiers et Documents*, no. 75 (November 1980), and "Women in the Labor Market," *OECD Observer*, no. 104 (May 1980): 6.

11. For early figures on union membership, see Guilbert, *Les femmes*. For a recent discussion of membership estimates and other measures of union influence, but without a breakdown by sex, see Reynaud, *Les syndicats en France*, 1: 139–46.

12. For the 30 percent estimate by the unions, see Madeleine Guilbert, "Femmes et syndicats en France" (Women and Unions in France), *Sociologie et Sociétés* 6 (1974): 164. The slightly later figures come from Madeleine Colin of the CGT and Jeannette Laot of the CFDT, each for her own organization.

13. The complete text of the statement is in the CFDT's *Syndicalisme hebdo*,

no. 1 (December 26, 1974): 528, and in Jeannette Laot, *Stratégie pour les femmes* (Strategy for Women) (Paris: Stock, 1977), pp. 235–43.

14. See the statement of Christiane Gilles at the CGT's Fifth National Conference on Working Women, reprinted in Confédération Generale du Travail, *Les femmes salariées* (Women Wage Workers) (Paris: Editions Sociales, 1973).

15. Full texts of these statements as well as most of the conference debates are in Confédération Generale du Travail, *Les questions qui font bouger* (Questions That Stir People) (Paris:, 1978).

16. "Le Sexisme Ordinaire" was originally the sardonic title of the department of sexist citations in the Paris magazine *Les Temps Modernes* and then a collective book (no editor was named) with a preface by Simone de Beauvoir (Paris: Seuil, 1979).

17. "Lip au féminin" was issued as a brochure in 1974 by the Collectif de femmes. It was republished as a book by Syros in 1977.

18. *Lip au féminin*, p. 102.

19. On the history of feminism in France, see Leon Abensour, *La femme et le féminisme avant la Revolution* (Woman and Feminism Before the Revolution) (Paris, 1923; reprint ed., Geneva: Slatkine-Megariotis, 1977); Huguett Bouchardeau, *Pas d'histoire, les femmes* (No History, Women) (Paris: Syros, 1977), Maîté Albistur and Daniel Armogathe, *Histoire du féminisme français du Moyen-Age à nos jours* (History of French Feminism from the Middle Ages to Our Time) (Paris: Editions des Femmes, 1977); Jean Rabaut, *Histoire des féminisme français* (History of French Feminism) (Paris: Stock, 1978).

20. Elena Ginini Belotti, "Le scandale du privé," in *Ecrits: voix d'Italie* (Paris: Editions des Femmes, 1977).

21. See published reports of the Committee on Women's Work in the Ministry of Labor, in particular Bilan de L'application de la Loi du 22 décembre 1972 sur L'égalité de Rémuneration entre Hommes et Femmes (Appraisal of the Law of December 22, 1972 on Equality of Remuneration Between Men and Women) (1976), and *Droit au travail des femmes: un bilan critique* (The Right of Women to Work: A Critical Appraisal) (1981). See also Marguerite J. Loree, "Equal Pay and Equal Opportunity Law in France," in *Equal Employment Policy for Women: Strategies for Implementation in the United States, Canada, and Western Europe*, ed. Ronnie Steinberg Ratner (Philadelphia: Temple University Press, 1980).

BIBLIOGRAPHY

Albistur, Maîté, and Daniel Armogathe. *Histoire du féminisme français du Moyen-Age á nos jours* (History of French Feminism from the Middle Ages to Our Time). Paris: Editions des Femmes, 1977.

Bouchardeau, Huguette. *Pas d'histoire, les femmes . . .* (No History, Women . . .). Paris: Syros, 1977.

Centre d'Etudes et de Recherches Marxistes. *La condition féminine* (The Feminine Condition). Paris: Editions Sociales, 1978.

Collectif de femmes. *Lip au féminin* (The Women's Side of LIP). Paris: Syros 1977.
———. *Dix-huit millions de bonnes-à-tout-faire* (Eighteen Million Maids of All Work). Paris: Syros, 1977.

Confédération Française Démocratique du Travail Information. *Travailleuses, combat pour une libération* (Women Workers, Struggle for Liberation). Paris: CFDT, 1979.

Confédération Generale du Travail. *Les femmes salariées*. (Women Wage Workers). Paris: Editions Sociales, 1973.

————. *Les questions qui font bouger* (The Questions That Stir People). Paris: 1978.

Colin, Madeleine. *Ce n'est pas d'aujourd'hui . . . femmes, syndicats, lutte de classes* (It Is Not Just from Today . . . Women, Unions, Class Struggle). Paris: Editions Sociales, 1975.

Guilbert, Madeleine. *Les femmes et l'organisation syndicale avant 1914* (Women and Union Organization Before 1914). Paris: Centre National de la Recherche Scientifique, 1966.

————. "Femmes et syndicats en France" (Women and Unions in France). *Sociologie et Sociétés* 6 (1974).

Guilbert, Madeleine, et al. *Travail et condition féminine: Bibliographie commentée* (Work and the Feminine Condition: Annotated Bibliography). Paris: Editions de la Courtille, 1977.

Kergoat, Danièle. *Les Ouvrières* (The Woman Workers). Paris: Editions Sycomore, 1982.

————. "Ouvriers: ouvrières?" (Male Workers: Female Workers?). *Critiques de l'Economie Politique*, no. 5 (October–November 1978).

Laot, Jeannette. *Stratégie pour les femmes* (Strategy for Women). Paris: Stock, 1977.

Legarrec, Evelyne. *Les messagères* (The Women Messengers). Paris: Editions des Femmes, 1976.

Maruani, Margaret. *Les syndicats à l'épreuve du féminisme* (Unions and the Challenge of Feminism). Paris: Syros, 1979.

Maruani, Margaret, and Anni Borzeix. *Le temps des chemises: la grève qu'elles gardent au coeur* (The Time of the Shirts: The Strike That They Keep in Their Hearts). Paris: Syros, 1982.

Mossuz-Lavau, Janine, and Mariette Sineau. "France." In *The Politics of the Second Electorate: Women and Public Participation*, Joni Lovenduski and Jill Hills. London: Routledge and Kegan Paul, 1981.

Partisans, no. 54–55 (July–October 1970). "Libération des femmes, année zero" (Women's Liberation, Year Zero).

Rabaut, Jean. *Histoire des féminisme français* (History of French Feminism). Paris: Stock, 1978.

Reynaud, Jean-Daniel. "France." In *Worker Militancy and Its Consequences, 1967–75*, edited by Solomon Barkin. New York: Praeget, 1975.

————. *Sociologie des conflits du travail* (The Sociology of Labor Conflicts). Paris: Collection Que Sais-Je? 1982.

————. *Les syndicats en France* (Unions in France). Paris: Seuil, 1975.

————. "Trade Unions and Political Parties in France: Some Recent Trends." *Industrial and Labor Relations Review* 28 (1975): 208–25.

Simon, Catherine. "Syndicalisme au féminin" (Women's Trade Unionism). *Questions Clef*, no. 1 (1982).

Zylbergerg-Hocquart, Marie Hélène. *Féminisme et syndicalisme en France* (Feminism and Unionism in France). Paris: Editions Athropos, 1978.

6 GREAT BRITAIN

Val R. Lorwin and Sarah Boston

The British trade union movement in the 1980s is far from being a homogeneous body with agreed policies and practices relating to women. While the Trade Union Congress (TUC), the organization to which most trade unions are affiliated, has developed a body of policy relating to women workers and women members, a study of individual unions reveals great disparity of attitudes, practices, policies, and structures.[1] This disparity has its roots in the piecemeal development of British unions over nearly two centuries.

As pioneers of trade unionism, the British had no models. They developed in reaction both to their employers and to the experience of their forebears in a variety of organizations, so that today the British union movement contains craft unions, general labor unions, semi-industrial unions, and white-collar unions. However, despite the disparity of structures—and policies—women union members have much in common in the problems they share as women, as workers, and as trade unionists. These problems have their roots in the entry of women into the wage labor market created by the Industrial Revolution, where they began work already as second-class laborers, a reflection of their position in society at that time. The position was not challenged at the time, and it continues to obtain even now, despite the fact that the policies of the trade union movement, backed by legislation, proclaim the rights of women to equality.

WORKING WOMEN'S HISTORY

The Industrial Revolution in Britain was forged on the labor of women and children. In 1838 only 23 percent of textile workers were adult males.[2] But for all their numerical dominance, women textile workers soon found they neither occupied the higher-paid skilled jobs in the industry nor held positions of power and influence in the unions that developed to negotiate wage rates. These textile unions in the early nineteenth century were unique in many respects: they were the first trade unions to organize women, and, indeed, some in the heavy woollen branch were founded mainly by women; they alone organized women in mixed unions—an example not followed by any other unions until the end of that century. Some unions, in fact, maintained their male-only membership rule until the mid twentieth century. The last major union to accept women into membership was the Amalgmated Engineering Union (AEU), which finally in 1942 changed its rule book under pressure from the women who were introduced into their jobs during World War II.

Even more unique than their organization of mixed unions was the textile unions' policy, from the outset, of collective bargaining: negotiating a rate for the job, not the sex of the worker on the job. Its first collective bargaining agreement, signed in 1853 and known as the Blackburn List, embodied that principle, one that remained the basis of all subsequent agreements in the industry. Thus, although a sexual division of labor quickly grew up in the textile industry—albeit one that had great variation from area to area, so that in some regions jobs were "male" that in others were "female"—whoever did the job got the standard rate for it. In effect the unions based their agreements on the concept of what much later was called equal pay for equal work, an example not followed by any other unions (wartime agreements excepted) until nearly a century later.

Until the late nineteenth century, outside the textile unions there is no record of any continuous organization of women workers. To be sure, records of demonstrations, protests, strikes, and brief attempts at organization by women exist, but there is no evidence that such actions led to any continuous or effective organization. Throughout the century, however, male trade unionists found themselves frequently concerned with what they referred to as "the problem of female labor." That problem, when it arose in the craft-based jobs, usually took the form of the employment of women to do "male" jobs. The following extract from the records of the Brushmakers Union in 1829 is typical and eloquently sums up the then apparently irresolvable problem of women undercutting men.

> Now there was another matter the Brushmakers had to put up with. Economic matter know as FEMALE LABOUR. This became serious in 1829. Many a man lost his job. The numbers ON THE BOOK were alarming.
>
> The movement initiated by a few employers was to cheapen labour. . . . Certain masters employed women to do men's work at half-price.
>
> So it came to pass that poor women became the enemy of poor men. . . . Say not that it was wrong of them to take men's jobs at half-price; no, they were poor women; the wickedness was in the hand that withheld the other half.[3]

The Brushmakers revealed a sympathy for and understanding of the plight of poor women, but it was an attitude usually absent from other craft unions confronted with the same problems.

PROTECTIVE LEGISLATION

Although there was little development of the organization of women until the late nineteenth century, the beginnings of what has now grown to be a large body of legislation relating to women workers, their hours, wages, conditions, jobs, and rights was early laid down. In 1842 the Mines Act banned women from working underground. That was quickly followed by the Factory Bill of 1844, which limited the hours of work for women in the textile industry to twelve per day. Later there grew up a body of legislation restricting the hours of women's work in certain other industries where dangerous chemicals such as phosphorus and lead were involved and prohibiting employers from knowingly employing a woman for four weeks after childbirth. From the outset, the predominantly male trade union movement supported this legislation, particularly that restricting women's hours and banning them from underground work. Some unions hoped legislation could be used to ban women from other areas of employment. This early reaction of the movement established a long tradition in the unions of looking to legislation to resolve problems relating to women workers rather than using the normal procedures of organizing workers and negotiating the correction of undesirable conditions.

WOMEN'S ORGANIZATION

The growing body of legislation relating to women did not, however, go unchallenged. The Women's Protective and Provident League was founded in 1874 by Emma Paterson to promote the organization of women workers. One of its first actions was to protest the passing of laws that the league saw as inhibiting women's rights freely to compete with men. A century later the argument continues. Protective legislation still bans women from working underground and, in the main, from working night shifts in factories. Many women believe it inhibits their chance for equality at work. In the 1880s the Women's Protective and Provident League, after its early protest, dropped its opposition to protective legislation, realizing that the benefits it offered working women outweighed the theoretical lack of freedom of choice it imposed on them. The league as early as 1888 got the TUC to pass a resolution calling for equal pay, and it encouraged the founding of several small women's unions.

The Women's Protective and Provident League grew until by the turn of the century it had become a body, now renamed the Women's Trades Union League (WTUL), with several unions organizing women workers affiliated to it. It became the lobbyist for women workers with government, particularly supporting legislation to improve conditions. It fought for and won the appointment of women factory inspectors.

The most remarkable of the unions in that period was the National Union of Women Workers, founded by Mary Macarthur in 1906 and affili- ated to the TUC. It was a general labor union for women, modeled on the general labor unions that had come into being at the turn of the century. Its formation was spurred by the strike in 1888 of the Match Girls, who defied the conventional wisdom of the craft-based unions, which up to that time maintained that unskilled workers, male or female, could not successfully be organized, let alone win a strike. Between its foundation in 1906 and its amalgamation in 1920 with a mixed general union, the National Union of Women Workers grew to a membership of 80,000. Its policies were radical and militant for its day. It set low membership fees and established a strike fund, both policies that were reactions against the elitism and conservatism of the crafts.

Mary Macarthur was a remarkable woman whose contribution to the development of the organization of women workers and the struggle for their rights has never been fully recognized. The period during which she was active, 1900–1920 (she died in 1921), was one of growth and political ferment in the trade union movement. For women, the war years, 1914– 1918, were catalytic. Their recruitment into many industries previously closed to them brought about a growth of organization of women and an acceptance by many unions of women members.

By 1920 women found that most of the gains they had made during the war were lost as they were returned, almost forcibly, to their roles as daughters, wives, and mothers. They could mark up a few victories, how- ever. They had won the vote for women over the age of thirty[4] and the right to enter most professions, although in many a rule against married women applied. (In government the marriage bar remained in force until the Second World War, and in some private industries until the early sixties; it was, in some cases, positively supported by trade unions.) In addition to winning political recognition after the First World War, women trade union- ists won a visible position within the TUC. In 1920 the WTUL merged with the TUC on the basis of an agreement that women were to hold two protected seats on the TUC General Council. Those two seats remained for fifty years the only representation women had on the General Council, with one exception, until 1981, when the number of protected seats was increased to five. Then, as now, women realized that in open competition with men women stood little if any chance of winning elections. In the late twenties, soon after the merger, a separate, non-policy-making women's TUC confer- ence was established, and it has met annually ever since. It is a body without power that advises the General Council on issues affecting women and makes the trade union movement conscious of these issues. Servicing this conference and advising the General Council is the Women's Advisory Committee, made up of General Council members and members elected by the Women's Conference. At the time of its creation, women questioned the establishment of a non-policy-making conference for women, arguing that it would only ghettoize and marginalize them. Many women still believe that to be true. Indeed, in recent years this conference of unions catering to women has debated whether to disband itself. Yet it continues to exist because most women there feel that its removal would leave no channel whatever for the expression of their views.

Within individual unions women's place has varied considerably. Although by the twenties the majority of unions accepted women into membership, many did so only into certain sections organizing women's grades or on the basis of a special reduced membership fee, for which women accordingly received reduced benefits. That practice continued in some unions until 1976, when the Sex Discrimination Act made it illegal. It was one reflection of the rigid sexual division of labor that the trade union movement defended not only in theory, but in the practice of designating certain jobs as women's and negotiating a women's rate of pay, almost without exception lower than the male minimum for that industry. In their national structures a few unions copied the TUC and established separate women's committees or conferences, but the vast majority never saw the underrepresentation of women on their national committees as a problem or felt that any special provision was needed to secure their representation there.

THE POST WAR PERIOD

The Second World War brought women into the labor market and the trade union movement on a scale that had been unimagined during the First. By the fifties women were nostalgically recalling the war years as a time when they did skilled work, received something like equal pay, and were active union members. With historical hindsight it is clear that the seeds of a renewed surge of militancy were sown during the war, even though they took a decade to germinate. The first wave of women's demands came in the fifties when women civil servants, supported by their unions, fought a prolonged and ultimately successful campaign for equal pay. Their victory was followed by the concession of equal pay to women teachers, and by the sixties most other professional women were receiving it as well. Equal pay for manual workers was not won until women pressured the reluctant trade union movement into joining a growing lobby to demand legislation to grant equal pay as a right. Nearly a century after the TUC passed its first resolution calling for equal pay, and after nearly half a century of commitment by the Labour party to that principle, the Labour government finally carried the Equal Pay Act in 1970. It was followed by the passing of the Sex Discrimination Act in 1975. Both acts came into force on 1 January 1976, and both, although long overdue, were undoubtedly steps forward in the long struggle for equality for women. They have proved, however, as many predicted, inadequate to deal with their deeply entrenched inequality.

This discussion of legislation brings us to a consideration of the role of the Labour party and Labour governments. Britain has long been a secular state, and therefore the trade unions have never had any direct religious affiliations. Politically, they are affiliated to the Labour party, which they founded at the beginning of the twentieth century out of a realization that if they were to further the cause of working people, they needed a political arm. Trade union members unwilling to belong to the party can opt not to pay a political levy as part of their union dues. Individual unions at their annual conventions can vote to affiliate to the Labour party, which gives them the right to send voting delegates to party conferences. Although the party was founded and is largely funded by the trade union movement, the two are not always in agreement and are sometimes in open conflict. In general, however, when a Labour government has been in power, it has introduced legislation that the TUC has lobbied for. In fact, over the last decade all the major legislation relating to women's rights has been carried through by Labour governments.

WOMEN'S ISSUES

The TUC's support for legislation against sex discrimination was indicative of a significant change in trade union attitude that occurred very quickly, largely as the consequence of pressure from women trade unionists, whose numbers increased considerably during the sixties and seventies. By 1980 women formed 28 percent of the affiliated membership of the TUC. They found a relatively receptive audience in the unions, in part because a leftward swing took place in the late sixties and early seventies in some of the large unions and in the TUC General Council—a swing now reversed in the early eighties. By the mid-seventies it was clear that the TUC had accepted, at least in principle, that if women were to achieve equality the struggle would involve many wider issues than those of the traditional trade union preserves—wages and conditions.

To analyze the position of women workers and trade unionists in the eighties, it is necessary to look in more detail at certain changes since 1970, focusing particularly on issues that highlight the still unresolved central problems in their struggle for full equality.

Wages

Wages have always been a central issue for the unions. The issue has also been central to the uneasy and unequal relationship between male and female workers, both at the workplace and within the unions. The idea that the male as breadwinner has a right to a larger pay packet has been generally discredited. For one thing, in every third household in Britain, a woman is the major or sole breadwinner. Moreover, wages have never been based on the worker's need; indeed, supplemental benefits such as family allowances are not paid to compensate for the extra financial burden of dependents. Finally, it is blatantly inequitable to pay women less then men on the same job. To remedy this last inequality where it occurs, the Equal Pay Act was adopted. Its formulation was in the end a compromise between the TUC's insistence on "equal pay for work of equal value," to be achieved after a two-year implementation period, and the employers' preference for the narrower concept of "equal pay for equal work," with full implementation only after seven years of gradual adjustment. The compromise act gave equal pay to women who do "the same or broadly similar work" or "work rated as equivalent with that of any men, if—and only if—her job and their jobs have been given an equal value."[5] The compromise five-year implementation period gave both employers and trade unions ample time not only to come up to the requirements of the act but also to work out ways of restructuring their workforces by re-evaluating jobs or segregating work on sex lines so as substantially to evade the act. An *Employers' Guide to Equal Pay*, developed and widely circulated during the years prior to 1976, suggested how compliance with the act could be minimal, largely by evasion of its terms; and there is evidence that some employers used such tactics.[6] On the trade union side, their acceptance or tolerance of such tactics very much depended on their commitment to pursuing equal pay. A report published by the TUC on affiliated unions' attitudes to equal pay before the implementation of the act found that "attitudes toward equal pay of unions varied about the appropriate definition, presumably according to whether their main aim was to safeguard the position of their male members or to gain parity for women."[7]

As a matter of fact, the TUC until the late sixties resisted supporting equal pay legislation, preferring to put its own house in order through wage negotiations rather than being forced to change.

In terms of improvement in wages, the equal pay law has given little to women. In 1970, when the law was adopted, their average gross hourly earnings were 63.1 percent of men's. By 1977 they had increased to 75.5 percent, the peak so far, for by 1978 they had fallen back to 73.9 percent. A few groups of women, either through support from their unions in negotiations or through official or unofficial strike action, had won their rights to equal pay, but by the end of the seventies most women still found themselves in women's jobs earning women's rates. The only change has been that the law no longer allows that job designation or permits agreements to call for a women's rate. Britain's entry into the EEC has provided a new initiative to amend the British equal pay legislation and bring it in line with the broader definition of "equal pay for work of equal value" embodied in Article 119 of the Treaty of Rome. Basing its contention on European Community standards of equal pay, the TUC now maintains that Britain's equal pay law infringes the EEC Directive on Equal Pay and the Treaty of Rome. The present Thatcher government argues on the contrary that the British legislation in its present form complies with both and has so far failed to bring in any amendments to the law.

The Abortion Act

In 1967 an act was passed by a free, non-party-aligned vote making abortion legal in Britain on medical and social grounds and available free through the National Health Service. At the time of the passing of the act, the trade union movement expressed no opinion on the issue. Since the adoption of the act, several MPs have made attempts through private members' bills to amend it so as to limit its scope and, in particular, to restrict the grounds on which women can get legal abortions. By the early seventies the TUC, through a resolution of its Annual Conference, committed itself to a policy of supporting women's right to free, legal abortions. When, in 1979, a private member's bill was introduced to amend the act, the TUC mounted a campaign to lobby against it. The campaign culminated in a major TUC-sponsored demonstration supported by trade unionists, men and women, from all over Britain. The bill was defeated.

Maternity Leave

Having accepted the need to fight for wider issues relating to women's rights, the TUC campaigned also for the introduction of statutory maternity leave. Its efforts resulted in a measure of success: the passage of the Employment Protection Act of 1975. It contained a section giving women in Britain, for the first time, statutory protection against loss of a job through pregnancy and childbirth. The provisions of the act were, however, minimal. The protection applied only to women who had worked for the same employer for two years before the eleventh week prior to the expected date of confinement. The act also provided for twenty-nine weeks of leave, of which only six were to be paid. This minimal legislation has already been eroded by the Conservative government, which has amended it further to limit women's eligibility. Claiming maternity leave is now so complicated that many women lose their rights through failure to comply with the procedure within the narrow time limits. As a consequence, Britain in its provision of statutory maternity leave lags far behind many other countries, including most of the other members of the EEC.

When the Employment Protection Bill was introduced in 1975, the TUC lobbied unsuccessfully for a much better statutory provision and drafted a model program in an attempt to encourage its affiliated member unions to negotiate better agreements. Many trade unions therefore have a better record on maternity leave than on other rights for women.[8] Most trades unions negotiating maternity leave for women working in the public sector have improved on the minimum provided by law; many have allowed, for example, a one-year eligibility clause and twelve weeks or more of leave at full pay followed by extended periods at half-pay. In the private sector, unions have negotiated fewer maternity leave agreements, but those negotiated still contain improved terms. Only a handful of agreements have succeeded in gaining paternity leave.

Child Care

The campaign for better maternity leave focused attention on the provision or lack of provision of child care facilities. Clearly, women pointed out, maternity leave was of little benefit to them if they could not return to work at its conclusion because of the lack of child care. As with statutory maternity leave, Britain in this regard lags behind many other European countries and behind France, in particular, which provides free child care and nursery schooling.

State child care in Britain falls into three main categories: day care for babies and toddlers, nursery schools, and the provision for older children of child care after school hours and during holidays. In all three categories only limited state provision is made, and that mostly in urban areas. Even these limited provisions have been reduced since the late seventies by cuts in public expenditure. Although the TUC officially supports the provision of child care facilities and nursery schooling for all children, it has done little to pursue or lobby for this policy. In fact, it supported the raising in the seventies of the minimum school-leaving age from fifteen to sixteen years without considering, as many educationists argued, that the money might have been better spent in providing nursery education for all children.

Some individual unions have negotiated the establishment of creches at factories or workplaces, but otherwise the trade union movement has done little to increase the provision of child care facilities. Women with children who return to work are mainly forced to find their own child care, usually private and often expensive. Much care of preschool children is done by child-minders, some registered and supervised by local authorities, but many unregistered, untrained, and unsupervised and sometimes offering a very questionable level of care.

Part-Time Work

The lack of free or cheap child care facilities means that women who cannot afford the costs of private child care either cannot work or are forced into homework or part-time work. Although the last may suit many, for others it is the only type of work they can do or get. Over three million women work part time in Britain. Part-time work in industry came into being as a major source of employment for women during World War II. It was introduced with the backing of the government, which saw it as a way of encouraging women to work while still allowing them time for their second jobs at home. The employers quickly realized the benefits of employing women part-timers. Two four-hour shifts, each staffed by a different woman, produced higher productivity than one eight-hour shift, with its decline in productivity through increasing fatigue and lack of concentration, a particular problem in the many women's industrial jobs characterized by high repetitiveness and monotony.

Part-time work, initially seen as a wartime necessity, became a major feature in postwar women's employment. Part-timers are not eligible for many of the rights of full-time workers. They usually are disqualified from maternity leave, pension schemes, and company training programs. In times of cutbacks and layoffs part-timers are usually the first to be sacked, and they do not qualify for redundancy pay, a lump-sum payment to laid-off workers, based on the length of employment with a firm. Part-time work has another advantage for the employer: it relieves him of the pressure to do anything about adequate child care facilities.

Part-time work is all too often a ghetto in which women are trapped. Trade union demands for a shorter working week for all have come to be seen as a central demand of benefit to women. A shorter working week would enable many more women workers to take full-time jobs while still managing their second jobs at home with less fatigue and stress. It would also allow time for male workers willing to do so to share the home jobs. A few, but only a few, unions have negotiated a working week of thirty-seven hours. The average still remains at forty.

The Sex Discrimination Act

Women argued that the Equal Pay Act alone would do little for them unless it was supported by legislation to make sex discrimination illegal. In 1975 the Labour government carried the Sex Discrimination Act, making discrimination on the grounds of sex illegal in employment, education, housing, advertising, and the provision of goods, facilities, and services. Like the Equal Pay Act, it was a compromise. It excluded certain key areas of discrimination, such as taxes and pensions, and failed to establish adequate legal machinery to enforce nondiscrimination on any significant scale. The act's main weakness is that the onus lies on the individual woman to take her own case to a tribunal. She may be supported, and some have been, by her trade union. However, many cases of discrimination in employment are at the point of entry, when a woman frequently does not yet have trade union backup.

At the time of the passing of the act, an Equal Opportunities Commission (EOC) was established to advise, educate, investigate, and take up cases of discrimination, but its powers, compared to its counterpart in the United States, are weak, and it has been reluctant even to use the powers it has. Aware of the act's shortcomings, the Women's Advisory Committee of the TUC has begun to draft amendments to it, though with little real expectation that the present Conservative government will consider them.

Like the Equal Pay Act, the Sex Discrimination Act has given women rights in law. Employers, for example, can no longer advertise openly for employees of one sex or the other, nor can apprenticeship schemes, with the approval of trade unions, any longer be open only to men. There is, however, little evidence that these provisions have led to a significant change in the overall pattern of discrimination in employment. The fact that women form such a small percentage of those employed in top jobs or in skilled jobs outside the traditional women's skills reveals the serious lack of opportunity for women. Although the media frequently report "first woman" news—the first woman prime minister, first woman pilot, first camerawoman, and soon—such breakthroughs into male preserves, though important, make little difference in the overall pattern of women's employment.

HOW MUCH EQUALITY?

Despite the fact that women in the 1980s have more legislation protecting their rights as workers than ever before, form both a higher than ever percentage of the workforce (42 percent) and of organized workers (28 percent), and have won in the trade union movement a body of policy proclaiming their rights to full equality, their position within both the trade union movement and the labor market is unequal. We have already noted that although women gained many legal rights in the seventies, their average earnings as a percentage of men's had dropped by the end of the decade, and they had become more unequal rather than less.

Low pay and lack of opportunity are still the major characteristics of women's employment. The Equal Pay Act's failure to make their earnings equal to men's can only partially be accounted for by the weakness of the act and the evasive tactics of some employers and trade unions. Women's average low pay arises from the fact that most work in women's jobs for women's wage rates, historically lower than the minimum male rates in any industry. Although it is now illegal to label jobs and wage rates by sex, the workforce in Britain has been so systematically structured along a sexual division of labor that there still exists a tacit recognition of women's jobs, with a consequent low pricing of them. Even though many women have demanded the right to work at and be trained for men's jobs, men (with the exception of a few who have chosen to become midwives) have shown no desire to enter women's jobs. This is not at all surprising: most men would regard the average woman's wage as derisory. Nor is job segregation simply a matter of history. The twentieth century, contrary to popular belief, has brought about the increasing ghettoization of women into a relatively few occupations. At the turn of the century, women worked in a much greater variety of jobs and in a higher percentage of skilled jobs than they do today: 24 percent of women were skilled workers, as compared to 14 percent sixty years later. Even this latter figure is misleading, for hairdressers account for a large proportion of the skilled 14 percent.

The ghettos of women's employment in Britain, as in so many other countries, are in textiles, food, drink, and tobacco manufacturing, light assembly work, the service industries, and clerical work. Within industry women are further ghettoized mainly into semiskilled light work.

The one major improvement since the turn of the century has been the entry of women into the professions. The barring of women from the professions—and from serving as MPs—was made illegal in 1919 by the Sex Disqualification (Removal) Act. Nevertheless, in sixty years of participation in the professions and the House of Commons, they have made little progress. In 1980 only 7 percent of barristers were women, 11 percent of academics, 14 percent of dentists, 22 percent of doctors, 4 percent of architects, 0.5 percent of engineers, and 0 percent of trade union general secretaries. Most professional women work in three main areas: teaching at the elementary and secondary levels, nursing, and social welfare work, all, but particularly nursing, are areas of low pay for the professions. In 1982 only 20 women were MPs out of a total of 635.

The low average earnings of women are both the cause and the result of their inequality at work. The report that the Women's Advisory Committee presented to the 1981 Women's Conference of the TUC, *Women Workers, 1981*, reminded the delegates that the 1980 report had found "the problem of low pay still unresolved and the high proportion of women workers in low paid occupation militated against the goal of true equality between men and women workers, notwithstanding the Equal Pay Act."[9] Yet the TUC reported little action on the problem, stating only that it was to be tackled from a "number of different angles." Two approaches were identified: an attempt to break down job segregation, and a simultaneous attempt to raise the earnings of the lowest paid. To achieve the latter goal, the TUC has recommended targeting low-paid groups in each industry. The trade union movement has had to recognize that many low-paid areas of employment— precisely those that traditionally employ women—have low levels of organization. These low levels have more to do with the nature of the work than with the sex of the workers. Among these groups are workers in agricultural, clerical, shop, and home work, who in many cases work in near isolation. The low level of organization partially accounts for the low wages.

Minimum Wages

At the beginning of the twentieth century the correlation between low organization and low pay was recognized to the exent that certain areas of work that were not or could not be covered by collective bargaining were brought under the legal protection of a minimum wage. After considerable campaigning, the Trades Board Act was carried in 1910, establishing that legal minimum wages were to be fixed in four industries, all of them based on women's homework. That act formed the basis for the fixing of legal minimum wages by boards called Wages Councils in a number of industries where wage levels were and are regarded as unacceptably low and where the level of trade union organization was and is insufficient for negotiating wages for workers in the industry.

Periodically debated within the trade union movement has been the demand for a national minimum wage, though it has never won majority support, the fear being that a national minimum would for many become the norm. Nevertheless, a national minimum fixed at a rate representing a low minimum for men would still have the effect of raising many women's wages. It would thus offer some protection to workers who had no other protection or bargaining power. For the foreseeable future, however, it is questionable whether a national legal minimum wage could or would be fixed at a level beneficial to any but the very lowest paid.

Homework and the Foreign Worker

The very lowest-paid category consists of homeworkers, almost all women. Although employers are required by law to report on the number of homeworkers they employ, there are in fact no official statistics on homeworking. The only national figures come from a survey done in 1968–1969, which estimated that there were at least a quarter of a million people engaged in homework and an additional 130,000 child-minders.[10]

Recent reports on homework read like the accounts of sweated labor published at the beginning of this century. The women work excessively long hours for derisory pay, and most of them are trapped in the work by their domestic situation. The only substantial difference from the turn-of-the-century conditions is that women from ethnic minorities have become the new group of sweated labor. They are particularly open to exploitation because of their ignorance of the English language and of their rights, a situation frequently exacerbated by the attitudes of their own cultures, particularly in the case of Moslem women.

In 1975 the TUC submitted to the Labour government certain proposals on this subject for inclusion in the Employment Protection Bill. Had they been accepted, these would have brought homework wages within the scope of Wages Councils and made the registering of all homeworkers with local authorities obligatory. The proposals were rejected. The TUC, however, has persisted in considering the problem of homework. A working party drafted a comprehensive statement in the late seventies that admitted trade unions "have in the past adopted a hostile attitude to homeworking."[11] Although the TUC still officially discourages homeworking, it at least now seeks to extend both legal and trade union protection to homeworkers while arguing that the movement should also seek to remove the conditions that force women into homework.

Job Evaluation

Women's work is low-paid primarily because it is women's, and women's skills are unrecognized or, when recognized, undervalued. The undervaluing of women's skills received particular attention in a clause of the Equal Pay Act stating that jobs would be rated as equal if given an equal rating by a job evaluation scheme. In such schemes, women frequently have found that their skills—for instance, manual dexterity—were valued lower than heavy work, or than the "light work" of management. The trade unions' response to job evaluation is varied; some unions question the whole approach, but most accept it provided that they can be party to it. In some cases women, with support from their unions, have argued successfully for a re-evaluation of their skills, but generally trade unions have not challenged the traditional discriminatory evaluations.

The EOC in its annual report for 1980 says that

> what matters is not simply that job evaluation has been undertaken, but that it has been conducted and implemented in a manner free of sex bias. The case of *O'Brien and others v. Sim-Chem Ltd* heard in the House of Lords during 1980 has shown that where a job evaluation scheme has rated women's work as equivalent to that of their male colleagues, they have a right to equal pay, even though the result of the evaluation may not have been put into effect.[12]

Unions' Equality Programs

Although improving minimum wages and re-evaluating women's skills would cause some upward movement in women's average earnings, the TUC has recognized that neither approach is sufficient. It is committed to a program called "Aims for Women at Work,"[13] whose fourteen points cover a wide range of needs, including educating and training girls in non-sex-stereotyped roles and for non-sex-stereotyped jobs; giving women equality of opportunity in employment; and providing adequate maternity leave and child care facilities. While committed to achieving equal opportunity for women in both training and promotion, the trade union movement has in fact done little to encourage equal opportunity, though in the last decade it has done less actively to discourage it than was formerly the case: earlier practices included the refusal of certain unions to accept women into apprenticeships, a rule that stood right up to the passing of the Sex Discrimination Act.

THE EFFECTS OF THE RECESSION

The early seventies marked definite progress in women's struggle for equality, at least in terms of law. Although at the time many women criticized the weakness of the antidiscrimination legislation and the failure of the trade union movement to back it strongly, in fact a historical perspective reveals that women gained during that period. With the exception of maternity leave rights and abortion rights, which have been eroded by the Conservative government, none of the statutory gains have been changed or weakened in the eighties. The strengthening or broadening of the legislation as called for by the TUC has not happened, but such demands themselves are a reflection of a real change in the TUC's attitude. The change is also revealed in the greater seriousness with which issues relating to women are discussed in its congresses and dealt with by its executive bodies. The fact that results have been so meager at the levels of legislation and collective bargaining reflects the economic recession and the more conservative political climate.

Through the late seventies and early eighties, unemployment in Britain steadily grew, reaching in 1982 a record figure of three million. The unemployment and employment profiles of men and women have differed substantially. Female employment began to increase in the sixties and continued to do so until 1979. By 1980 a decided reversal had set in. The total number of women employed fell by 120,000, and that fall has continued. Male employment, by contrast, steadily declined between 1975 and 1980, a decline that then continued and increased into the eighties. While official statistics register higher unemployment figures among men than women, those figures conceal the real extent of women's unemployment, since a far higher number of women do not or cannot register as unemployed. As a consequence, rising unemployment has had a far more serious effect on women than the numbers alone suggest.

In a climate where workers feel daily threatened by the prospect of job loss, few male workers are willing to promote and fight for women's rights to equal opportunity because they feel that such rights might be given to women at their own expense. Nevertheless, trade unionists' attitudes have changed since the Great Depression. At its height fifty years ago, many trade unionists argued for the banning of married women from work on the grounds that men had the first right to any available employment. At least that solution to the problem of unemployment has not recently been put forward by any trade union.

In 1979 the political climate in Britain changed when a Conservative government was elected with a large majority committed to monetarist policies. Although Britain has its first woman prime minister, women can count no tangible gains under her government, but rather many setbacks. At best they are simply holding their own. The savage cuts in public expenditures meant not only jobs losses for large numbers of women in public sector employment, but also a cutback in many of the services that had relieved some of the burden of the double day. Cuts in education services and programs for the young, old, sick, and handicapped have placed the burden of caring for these groups on the shoulders of women, limiting their ability to work or pursue further education and training. The TUC, affiliated to the Labour party, is committed to fighting for its return to government at the next general election. In the meantime it can do little more than protest against Conservative policies.

Although these political trends may be reversed, the full effects of the technological revolution on employment patterns generally, and on women's jobs in particular, remain to be seen. Already the first effects are evident. The great development area of women's employment in the twentieth century in terms of numbers—clerical work—is already on the decline as women's work is more and more superseded by word processors, microchips, and computers. As two trade unionists note:

> Micro processors will revolutionise many areas of work. Work which involves the processing of information (e.g., typing) and its storage (e.g., filing) will be most affected. Telecommunications has already been affected—but the impact on office work could be revolutionary. In larger companies, for example, clerical and typing jobs could be completely re-organised and largely de-skilled resulting in heavy redundancies if there is inadequate trade union control.[14]

WOMEN'S PLACE IN THE UNIONS

Throughout the history of women's fight to organize, they have had to struggle not only to be accepted by the predominantly male trade union movement, but, having been accepted into it, to become equal members. The final formal sign of their acceptance as equal members—paying equal subscriptions and receiving equal benefits—was achieved through the Sex Discrimination Act. By the time the act was passed, in fact most unions had already abandoned their practice of accepting women into membership only on a second-class basis. Having achieved equality of rights to membership, however, women still have to achieve equality of representation within the trade union movement. The number of women organized increased steadily during the sixties and seventies, representing the most significant growth area of trade union organization. In 1980 women made up 28 percent of the total TUC-affiliated membership. Much of that increase comes from the increased organization of white-collar workers and reflects the changing labor market in Britain, where the proportion of nonmanual jobs rose from 38 percent in 1961 to 48 percent in 1978. The growth in women's membership in turn has helped to change the traditional belief of white-collar workers that trade unions were mainly for blue-collar, male workers.

Despite the increase in women's membership, their position within individual unions and within the TUC is one of gross underrepresentation. The only union historically to have ensured representation of women on its national executive committee in numbers proportional to their membership was the Dundee Jute and Flax Workers Union, which in 1906 established a constitution calling for the seating of men and women on the executive in direct proportion to their numbers in the membership. Except in the all-women's unions at the turn of the century and one or two unions founded in the nineteenth century primarily by women, women have played almost no role in the main running and decision making of trade unions or the TUC. Even unions with a higher membership of women than men cannot boast a majority of women on their executives. The Union of Shop, Distributive and Allied Workers is the seventh largest in Britain, with a 60 percent female membership, but only three women are on its sixteen-member national executive; until recently, there was only one.

A few unions have followed the policy of the TUC in creating "protected seats" for women on their national executives. Some others that have no such policy have nevertheless strongly encouraged women to stand for election. These unions, however, are exceptional, for the national trade unions are still overwhelmingly dominated by men. Surveys of the underrepresentation of women reveal that women are much more active at the shop floor level and that their underrepresentation increases at each higher level in the pyramidal structure of most unions.

Trade unions as employers of women have a thoroughly bad record. In many unions women have had to fight for the right to be appointed as national officials or organizers against arguments that women cannot do the job because they will not be authoritative enough to command the respect of members and management. A survey in 1975 of sixty-two unions revealed that only 71 full-time women officials were employed by the unions surveyed, compared with 2,259 males. The Transport and General Workers Union (T & GWV) is the largest union in Britain, with a membership of just over two million, of whom about 342,000 are women. It employs only 7 full-time women national officials out of 500. Like most other organizations, British trade union headquarters employ women chiefly as secretaries and clerical staff.

Women have long been aware of their underrepresentation in the trade union movement. The Women's Advisory Committee has frequently addressed itself to the question. Only recently the TUC committed itself to a program of action to try to improve the situation. In 1980 it drew up a ten-point charter aimed at putting its own house in order. "Equality for Women Within Trades Unions" urges that

1. the National Executive Committee of the union publicly declare to all its members the commitment of the union to involving women members in the activities of the union at all levels;
2. the structure of the union be examined to see whether it prevents women from reaching the decision-making bodies;
3. where women's membership is large but no women are on the decision-making bodies, special provision be made to ensure that women's views are heard either through the creation of additional seats or by co-option of women representatives;
4. the National Executive Committee of each union consider the desirability of setting up within its constitutional machinery advisory committees to ensure that the special interests of women members are protected;
5. similar committees at regional, divisional, and district level also assist to encourage the active involvement of women in the general activities of the union;
6. efforts be made to include in collective agreements provisions wherever practicable for time off without loss of pay to attend branch meetings during working hours;
7. where it is not practicable to hold meetings during working hours, every effort be made to provide child care facilities during meetings for use by either parent;
8. child care facilities, for use by either parent, be provided at all district, divisional, and regional meetings, and particularly at the union's annual conference and at training courses organized by the union;

9. although union training courses may be nominally open to members of either sex, special encouragement be given to women to attend them;
10. the content of journals and other union publications be presented in non sexist terms.[15]

Some unions have already implemented some of the above recommendations. A few run creches at their annual conferences or at other special conferences, but none run them as a matter of course at all major meetings. There is a notable absence of child care facilities at the main TUC annual conference. Recently, some unions have set up special committees at national and branch levels to discuss issues relating to women and to give women a channel through which to express their opinions. However, the trade union movement is still split over the wisdom of creating separate women's committees, conferences, or officers, as existed in the twenties, although recent experience has shown that unions that have established effective committees or employed a national official to deal specifically with women's problems have made more progress than unions lacking these structures. Recently, women have been urging their unions to employ a national official whose full-time job would be to deal with problems relating to women members and who would have the power to negotiate on their behalf. A few such officials have been appointed.

Trade union response to pressure from women has varied. On the whole the craft-based unions have retained their well-entrenched male elitism, but there are exceptions. One such union that has during the past decade made a commitment to fighting for equality for women is the craft-based Association of Cinematograph, Television and Allied Technicians (ACTT). In the early 1970s it produced the most comprehensive study by any trade union in Britain to date on the employment of women in the areas it organizes and its own structure, highlighting the problem of the underrepresentation of its women members.[16] The report made many recommendations, some of which have now been followed up. Recently, after the women members campaigned vociferously for such an appointment, a full-time equality officer was employed.

In general, however, it has been unions such as TASS, the white-collar section of the engineering union, the AUEW, that are most committed to pursuing active equality policies for women. This is partially a reflection of the fact that women white-collar workers are generally more confident and articulate than blue-collar women and more prepared to assert their rights. It is no coincidence that the rise in the organization of white collar workers has also led to a rise in the number of women within the trade union movement who are influenced by the wider women's movement and have pressed for representation in their unions. The public employees' unions, with their high percentage of women members, have begun, in line with the white-collar unions, to make a greater commitment to fighting for a better deal for the women. Lagging behind so far are the general labor unions—unions representing all grades of workers, but particularly production workers—and those organizing such male-dominated areas as mining and train driving.

Although there is no agreement about the best way to achieve the fully equal participation of women in the trade union movement, the TUC charter and some of the actions taken by affiliated unions show a consciousness of the need to move forward. Throughout the last decade (indeed, the last century), women have had to push for, lobby, demand, and sometimes just take the rights they believe they should have. The trade union movement in the last decade has shown itself susceptible to such pressure. Women realize that as a minority in the movement, they need to have the power of the movement with and not against them. History, however, has given them reason to doubt the commitment of these male-dominated organizations, whose first priority has always been to protect the jobs, wages, and opportunities of their male members. Short-term male self-interest has blinded them to the truth that trade union "brotherhood" means not just men, but women as well, and that a movement so united would be infinitely stronger. Inequality, as the Brushmakers noted in 1829, makes "poor women the enemy of poor men." The trade union movement has still a long way to go before inequality is abolished and equality achieved.

GLOSSARY

ACTT	Association of Cinematograph, Television and Allied Technicians
AUEW	Amalgamated Union of Engineering Workers
EEC	European Economic Community
EOC	Equal Opportunities Commission
G&MWU	General and Municipal Workers Union
NFWW	National Federation of Women Workers (merged in 1921 with what became the G&MWU)
TASS	Autonomous white-collar section of the AUEW
T&GWU	Transport and General Workers Union
TUC	Trade Union Congress
WTUL	Women's Trades Union League (merged in 1921 with TUC)

1. For details see Jack Eaton and Colin Gill, *The Trade Union Directory: A Guide to All TUC Unions* (London, Pluto Press, 1981).

2. E. J. Hobsbawn, *Industry and Empire* (London: Penguin Books, 1969), p. 68.

3. William Kiddier, *The Old Trades Unions from Unprinted Records of the Brushmakers* (London: George Allen and Unwin, 1930), pp. 99–100.

4. Women did not win full adult suffrage on the same terms as men until 1928.

5. Equal Pay Act, 1970, Clause 1 (4) and 1 (5).

6. Peter Paterson and Michael Armstrong, *An Employer's Guide to Equal Pay* (London: Kogan Page Associates, 1972), pp. 53–54.

7. *Special Report on Equal Pay to the Fortieth TUC Women's Conference, 1970* (London: TUC Publications, 1970), p. 7.

8. For further details of agreements, see Labour Research Department, Women's Rights at Work (London: LRD Publications, 1979), p. 43.

9. TUC Women's Advisory Committee, *Report 1980/81*, and *Report to the Fifty-first TUC Women's Conference, 1981* (London: TUC Publications, 1981), p. 10.

10. *Homewoming: A TUC Statement* (London: TUC Publications), p. 3.

11. Marie Brown, *Sweated Labour: A Study of Homework* (London: Low Pay Unit, 1974).

12. Equal Opportunities Commission, *Fifth Annual Report, 1980*, p. 9.

13. London: TUC Publications, 1975.

14. Judith Hunt and Shelley Adams, "Women, Work and Trade Union Organisation," *Studies for Trade Unionists* 6, no. 21 (March 1980): 11.

15. "Report for 1980–81," p. 82.

16. "Patterns of Discrimination Against Women in the Film and Television Industry" (London: Association of Cinematograph, Television and Allied Technicians, 1975).

BIBLIOGRAPHY

Allen, Sandra, Lee Sanders, and Jan Wallis, eds. *Conditions of Illusion: Papers from the Women's Movement*. Leeds: Feminist Book, 1974.

Boston, Sarah. *Women Workers and the Trade Union Movement*. London: Davis-Poynter, 1980.

Clegg, H. A. *The Changing System of Industrial Relations in Great Britain*. Oxford: Blackwell, 1979.

Coates, Ken, and Tony Topham. *Trade Unions in Britain*. Nottingham: Spokesman, 1980.

Coote, Anna, and Beatrix Campbell. *Sweet Freedom: The Struggle for Women's Liberation*. London: Pan Books, 1982.

Coote, Anna, Peter Kellner and Jane Stageman. *Hear This, Brother: Women Workers and Union Power*. London: New Statesman, 1981.

Drake, Barbara. *Women in Trade Unions*. London: Labour Research Department, 1920.

Eaton, Jack, and Colin Gill. *The Trade Union Directory: A Guide to All TUC Unions*, London: Pluto Press, 1981.

Equal Opportunities Commission. Annual reports. Manchester: EOC.

———. *A Guidance of Job Evaluation Schemes Free of Sex Bias*. Manchester: EOC, 1980.

————. *Health and Safety Legislation: Should We Distinguish Between Men and Women?* Manchester: EOC, 1979.

————. "I want a Baby . . . but what About My Job?" Manchester: EOC, 1979.

————. "I Want To Work, but What About the Kids?" Manchester: EOC. 1978.

Hakim, Catherine. "Job Segregation: Trends in the 1970's." *Employment Gazett* (1981): 521–29.

Hamilton, Mary A. *Mary Macarthur*. London: Leonard Parsons, 1925.

Hunt, Judith, and Shelley Adams. *Women, Work and Trade Union Organisation*. London: Workers' Educational Association, 1980.

Labour Research Department. *Women's Rights at Work*. London: LRD Publications, 1979.

Lewenhak, Sheila. *Women and Trade Unions: An Outline History of Women in the British Trade Union Movement*. New York: St. Martin's, 1977.

Mackie, Lindsay, and Polly Pattullo. *Women at Work*. London: Tavistock, 1977.

Moss, Peter, and Nickie Fonda, eds. *Work and the Family*. London: Temple Smith, 1980.

National and Local Government Officers Association. *Equal Rights Working Party Reports*. London: NALGO, 1975.

Pinchbeck, Ivy. *Women Workers and the Industrial Revolution, 1750–1850*. 1930; reprint ed., London: Cass, 1969.

Ratner, Ronnie Steinberg, ed. *Equal Employment Policy for Women: Strategies for Implementation in the United States, Canada, and Western Europe*. Philadelphia: Temple University Press, 1980.

Sedley, A., *Part-Time Workers Need Full-Time Rights*. London: National Council for Civil Liberties, 1980.

Sloane, Peter J., ed., *Women and Low Pay*. London: Macmillan, 1980.

Snell, Mandy. "The Equal Pay and Sex Discrimination Acts: Their Impact in the Workplace." *Feminist Review* 1 (1979): 37–57.

Solden, Norbert C. *Women in British Trade Unionism, 1874–1976*. Totowa, N.J.: Bowman and Littlefield, 1978.

Trades Union Congress. *A Charter for the Under-Fives*. London: TUC, 1978.

————. *Charter of Aims for Women at Work*. London: TUC, 1977.

————. *A Charter of Equality for Women Within Trade Unions*. London: TUC, 1979.

————. Reports of annual conferences. London: TUC.

————. Reports of the annual conferences of trade unions catering for women workers. London: TUC.

————. *Women in the Trade Union Movement*. London: TUC, 1955.

Wainwright, David. *Discrimination in Employment*. London: Associated Business Press, 1979.

7 IRELAND

Deborah Schuster King

The status of women in unions in the Republic of Ireland at the beginning of the 1980s has been determined by a curious mixture of circumstances, some that have fostered militancy, others that have impeded change. Ireland has a long history of organization among women workers, and in recent years female union membership has increased rapidly. In the 1970s the percentage of the female labor force that is organized grew from 40 to 63 percent, and the 63 percent of organized women constitute 32 percent of all trade union members, giving Ireland one of the highest rates of trade union organization among women in the world.[1]

The high percentage of organized women, as well as the dramatic overall increase in union membership in the seventies, has resulted in vanguard demands by Irish women for increased power within the trade union movement. For in spite of their relatively high organization rate, few women have achieved leadership positions. This circumstance, which has begun to receive serious attention from various trade union bodies, now appears likely to stimulate Irish unions to establish positive structures and programs to facilitate participation by women.

External influences, the result of Ireland's entry into the European Economic Community (EEC) and contacts with other European trade unions, have been significant factors in raising the consciousness of both men and women on working women's issues. Legislation on equal pay and equal opportunity probably would not have been enacted in the seventies were such laws not mandated by EEC directives. As a result of the legislation, however, Irish unions have already negotiated and litigated a large number of claims for equal pay for work of equal value, at a time when in other countries, such as the United States, the issue is just beginning to be recognized.

Against these positive factors must be weighed the strong influence of the Catholic church and the long-standing high level of unemployment in Ireland. Both church teachings and job scarcity have served to keep married women out of the workplace and to perpetuate the view that work and work-related activities are essentially a male preserve. In general, the economic and social climates in Ireland are less favorable to the advancement of women than are those of most of the other countries discussed in this volume. Rights that have long been established elsewhere, such as guaranteed maternity leaves, have only recently been won in Ireland. Demands for flexible hours, parental leaves, and other conditions that would facilitate shared parenthood have as yet received little attention.

WOMEN IN IRISH UNIONS

The substantial increase in the number of organized women workers over the last ten years is attributable to several factors, including growth in sectors of the Irish economy that employ large numbers of women and an increase in militancy and union consciousness among clerical and other white-collar workers. Previously unorganized clerical and technical employees in companies with unionized blue-collar workers, as well as those employed in such white-collar industries as insurance, have joined unions in large numbers during the past decade.

Despite this growth and the increased attention to women's issues that accompanied it, the status of Irish women workers within their unions and at work has not yet begun to reflect their strength (see Table 7-1). There is only

TABLE 7-1
Women's Positions in Ten Irish Unions, 1979

Union	No. on Executive	No. of Women on Executive	Women as % of Executive	Women as % of Membership
ASTI	15	3	20	59
ATGWU	24	1	4	20
CPSSA	14	4	29	75
FWUI	15	0	0	33
INTO	11	2	18	70
ITGWU	18	0	0	33
IUDWC	18	4	22	62
LGPSU	13	4	31	50
POWU	13	2	15	39
TUI	11	2	18	42
Total	140	34		

Source: "Trade Union Survey, 1979: Women in Trade Unions (Dublin: Irish Congress of Trade Unions Research Service, 1979).

one woman on the Executive Council of the Irish Congress of Trade Unions (ICTU), the national trade union confederation that represents all but a handful of small unions. (This woman was elected in 1980 and was the first woman to serve on the Executive Council in over ten years.) A survey published by the ICTU in 1979[2] revealed that only 47 out of the 600 delegates who attended the confederation's annual policy-making conference were women. Similarly, fewer than 10 percent of the participants who contributed to the debate were women. The survey indicated that women were also woefully underrepresented on working committees of the ICTU, many of which include members co-opted from affiliated unions; only four committees of the congress included women.

Women blue-collar and service workers appear to have made the least progress in increasing their representation on union decision-making bodies. For example, blue-collar women are a substantial proportion of the 33 percent female membership of the two largest unions in Ireland, the Irish Transport and General Workers Union (ITGWU) and the Federated Workers Union of Ireland (FWUI). Women employed in garment, tobacco, food, electronics, and textile firms and in hotels and restaurants are members of these unions. Despite the large number of women members, until 1982 there were no women on the executive council of either organization, and the two women who finally succeeded in gaining seats in that year were both white-collar workers.

In the white-collar and public sector unions, women are better represented, although in no case does the percentage of female executive council members approach the percentage of female union members. In the seven major public and white-collar unions, the female members accounted for in 1982 ranged from 39 to 75 percent of the membership, while the percentage of women on the executive councils ranged from 15 to 36 percent.

The situation with regard to full-time union positions has improved somewhat in the recent past, but again the number of women in such posts is in no way representative of their numbers in the ranks. The 63 percent of women workers who are trade union members are concentrated overwhelmingly in twelve of the fifteen biggest unions, in which they account for 40 percent of the membership. These unions represent 88 percent of all women workers, but of their 213 full-time officers in 1982, only thirteen were women (up from six in 1979).

While some progress has been made by white-collar workers through local bargaining on such issues as child care leaves or flexible hours, most manufacturing and service workers have not negotiated these rights. Progress on training and promotions for women into higher-paid supervisory or managerial positions or into jobs traditionally held by men has been minimal in both blue- and white-collar sectors.

OBSTACLES TO EQUALITY

A major obstacle to women's attempts to achieve full equality has been and is the existence of substantial unemployment. While accurate statistics on the extent of Irish unemployment over the years are not available (because of a lack of information on labor force participation, as well as the fact that emigration dramatically reduced the number of unemployed during certain periods), there is no doubt that Ireland has long had a severe unemployment problem in comparison with other countries.[3]

It has been widely recognized that at times of job scarcity, support for the employment of women—particularly married women—diminishes. According to a report published by the EEC on the subject: "Although the national economic situation and trends determine the structure and climate within which both men and women seek and find work, at a time of growing unemployment and underemployment, women are seen as a threat to men, and it is very difficult to ensure their right to work on a footing of equality."[4] High unemployment and massive emigration throughout the twenieth century have affected Irish attitudes. There has been general opposition even to allowing single women access to better-paid jobs, which, it is felt, are needed by married men with dependents, and married women who work have been accused of lacking a social conscience. Brother Vivian Cassells, a vocational guidance counselor, in 1975 castigated married women for working "though they realise that by so doing they are depriving many young people from starting their careers."[5]

The negative attitudes created by economic conditions have been reinforced by Catholic teachings that advocate women's devotion to home and family, rather than to work and union activity. Both these factors limited the participation in the workforce of married women, so that Irish women workers are predominantly young and single and view work as an interim occupation between school and marriage.

Government policies instituted in the 1930s and 1940s reflected both church teachings and a desire to minimize pressure for jobs. The Irish Constitution of 1937 expresses the view, in Article 41.2, that the workplace is not really the domain of women:

> In particular, the state recognizes that by her life within the home, woman gives to the State a support without which the common good cannot be achieved.
>
> The State shall, therefore, endeavor to ensure that mothers shall not be obliged by economic necessity to engage in labour to the neglect of their duties in the home.

The legal prohibition of the sale of contraceptives (modified in 1980) has resulted in large families, further reducing the possibility that married

women will look for work outside the home. Because divorce is also prohibited, Ireland has not experienced the phenomenon that has occurred
elsewhere of large numbers of divorced women with children entering the
workforce.

In the 1930s the government adopted a "marriage bar" in the civil
service, requiring women to resign upon marriage. This practice was followed throughout Irish industry as well as the government until the 1970s
and had an extremely negative effect on efforts to extend training and
promotion for women generally. All women were viewed as potential brides
who would be short-term employees. Still another government-imposed
deterrent was a tax system that disproportionately taxed the earnings of
married women.

The report of the Brennan Commission, established to investigate and
make recommendations on employment policies in the civil service in the
1930s, illustrates the prevailing attitudes toward women. With regard to
equal pay, the report stated: "In those cases in the Civil Service where men
and women may be employed indifferently we find special reason for sup-
posing that on the whole when all relevant aspects are taken into account the
woman does not give as good a return of work as a man."[6] The report also
expressed grave doubts about training women for responsible positions
because they might marry and leave the civil service.

THE IRISH WOMEN WORKERS UNION

As a result of all these conditions, until recently little progress
has been made by unions on women's issues, although women have been
active in them since the early 1900s. One of the few unions in Europe
specifically founded to organize women workers, the Irish Women Workers
Union (IWWU) has been operating in Dublin since its founding by the great
labor leader, Jim Larkin, and his sister, Delia, in 1911. The IWWU was
formed to "improve the wages and conditions of the women workers of
Ireland and to help the men workers to raise the whole status of labor and
industry."[7] It was a general workers' union, organizing mostly among the
unskilled in a number of trades and industries, beginning with laundry
workers, but recruiting more skilled workers where it could, including
nurses in mental hospitals.

The union's early years were marked by its participation in the great
lockout strike waged by Dublin workers in 1913 over the issue of union
recognition. Although this struggle was lost, the IWWU's active role served
to bring women into the labor movement, and within a few years the union
succeeded in gaining bargaining rights with many employers. The new union
was caught up in the three great struggles then moving and shaking Ireland:
the nationalist struggle against British rule, which reached a tragic climax in

the 1916 Easter Rising; the struggle for women's suffrage, and the industrial struggle. There were strong ties between the IWWU and the middle-class and aristocratic feminists who staffed soup kitchens in the 1913 strikers, and many of the early women trade union leaders were suffragettes or activists in the nationalist movement. They were able and effective leaders who forcefully voiced the concerns of women workers on issues like equal pay as early as 1917.[8] Many feminist leaders lent their support to the IWWU's effort to organize laundry and printing trades workers in the 1920s and 1930s.

IWWU laundry workers in 1932 obtained a forty-seven-hour week, a week's holiday with pay, and fixed overtime rates—considerable gains for a depressed group in a generally backward economy and society. Another depressed group was that of the rosary bead workers, many of them homeworkers. After a strike in 1940, the IWWU obtained a requirement for the registry of homeworkers and inspection of their conditions to control sweatshop competition and give some protection to the workers. In 1945 a three-month strike of laundry workers won a precedent-setting two weeks of paid holidays.

These successes and the growing number of women in factory employment led other unions to develop an interest in organizing women. During the 1930s women's membership in unions as a whole rose from perhaps 20,000 at the beginning of the decade to 35,000 at its end. Growth continued during the war years, until a total of 55,000 women union members was reached in 1950. As the general unions organizing both men and women, however, greatly increased their membership, that of the IWWU began to decline, so that from the 1960s onward the union has had a diminishing influence in the Irish labor movement.

Generally respected by male trade unionists, leaders of the IWWU were elected to serve as presidents of the ICTU on three occasions. However, the IWWU and other unions with large female memberships frequently had to fight against the implementation of such restrictive policies as excluding women from certain civil service categories or married women from the teaching profession; consequently, they had little time or strength to struggle for new advances. They never succeeded in securing a commitment to the principle of equal pay, and blatant discrimination—such as the granting of smaller across-the-board increases to women—was common as late as the 1960s and even into the early 1970s.

The one area in which pre-1960 trade union women can perhaps be faulted was the failure to recognize the implications for single women in the perpetuation of discrimination against married women, particularly in measures that limited the access of married women to employment. The overwhelming majority of trade union women were single, and many were affected by the prevailing views of the time. For many years the IWWU continued to debate the pros and cons of married women's working. In 1932

IWWU's president, Louie Bennett, in her address to the Irish Trade Union Congress, declared that "the modern tendency to draw women into industry . . . has not raised their status as workers nor their wage standards. It is a menace to family life and in so far as it has blocked the employment of men it has intensified poverty among the working class."[9]

The history of the IWWU, however, showed that unskilled women workers could be organized and that they and other women were capable of long strikes. They were too patient most of the time, but at times they surmounted old habits of subordination in a generally authoritarian society.

CHANGING CONDITIONS: THE SIXTIES

It was not until the 1960s that attitudes toward the employment of women began to change. The change was brought about by a number of factors, the most important of which were a softening of church policy and a more favorable economic climate.

In the 1960s new economic policies encouraged industrialization by providing grants and tax shelters to foreign companies that commenced operations in Ireland. These policies spurred the Irish economy, created jobs, and eased unemployment somewhat. Irish people came to be more optimistic about the future now that they could expect to find work in Ireland rather than having to go abroad.

An unexpected result of this economic program was an increase in the proportion of organized women workers. Although the government's grant policy favored companies that would provide employment for male workers, a large number of female-intensive industries found the schemes attractive and opened factories in Ireland. While the relative proportion of male and female workers in the labor force remained constant, the rise in industrial employment for women (as opposed to such work as domestic service, formerly a large source of female jobs) increased their level of unionization. One condition of government grants is that companies must agree to recognize a union, and most firms even before opening sign union contracts that more or less guarantee existing industry conditions and payscales. Another growth area in the sixties was the public sector, which is highly organized and is also a large employer of women.

Of perhaps equal importance were Vatican II and the ecumenical spirit that led to a questioning of traditional views, including those about the role of women in society. The first agitation for the legalization of birth control began about this time. The advent of television also brought Irish people into contact with different life styles and contributed to their adoption. Finally, increased militancy and activity on the part of women resulted in the establishment of a Women's Advisory Committee to the ICTU in 1962. As the result of a convention resolution proposed and seconded by women delegates, the committee was appointed "for the purpose of furthering trade union organization among women workers generally and of acting as an advisory committee to the Executive Council on economic, industrial and social matters of special concern to women workers."[10]

It is therefore not surprising that the 1960s saw the first movement toward narrowing the gap between the wages of male and female workers. In the mid-sixties women trade unionists began vigorously protesting against the practice of granting lower annual wage increases to women. As a result, in 1969 women actually secured a higher percentage increase under most collective bargaining agreements than did men.[11] By the early seventies the public sector had adopted the practice of granting equal increases.

A factor that appears to have facilitated the movement toward equal pay was the increasing centralization of collective bargaining in Ireland after World War II. As industrial and national patterns began to develop and agreements were discussed at conferences involving many unions, equal pay could be debated in the context of a particular round of negotiations, rather than in the abstract, as it had been earlier. As a result, by 1971 the average wage of female workers—53 percent of the male rate for several decades— had risen to 59 percent.[12]

WOMEN IN THE LABOR FORCE IN THE EARLY 1970S

Despite these advances, an analysis of labor force data for the late sixties and early seventies highlights the second-class status of women in employment. Only 34.4 percent of women of working age were in the labor force, one of the lowest rates in Europe.[13] The situation was especially severe for married women, who comprised only 3 percent of the total labor force, and for women residing in rural areas, where unemployment was very high for both women and men. Married women in particular were affected by the scarcity of part-time jobs and the lack of child care facilities. Women who looked for work were confined to a narrow range of jobs within a relatively small number of industries. In 1971 over four-fifths of working women were in eleven broad occupational groups.[14] The largest group was clerks and typists, who accounted for one in four women at work. Of those women working in the manufacturing sector, 47 percent were in the textile, clothing, or footwear industries and a further 20 percent were employed in the food, drink, and tobacco trades. Ninety-one percent of the women classified as professional and technical employees were nurses, nuns, or teachers. Within both industries and occupations, women were generally employed at the lowest levels; very few filled managerial or technical positions. Women were excluded in practice from entering apprenticeship programs in traditional male trades, even when such programs were government-sponsored.

The Commission on the Status of Women

Pressure from women trade unionists in the 1960s led the ICTU to request the Department of Labour to set up a committee to consider the problems of working women. The commission that resulted was set up in 1970 to investigate the position of women in Irish society and make recommendations for change. It included respected academics, trade unionists, business leaders, and heads of women's organizations. Its credibility was high, and its findings carried considerable weight with policy-makers as well as the general public. The report it produced, a comprehensive, 277-page analysis, included sections on employment, social welfare, taxation, education, politics, and the home. While the general tone was moderate, the report advocated reform in virtually every area of Irish life. With regard to employment, it recommended the implementation of equal pay by 1977, the elimination of the marriage bar, the provision of twelve weeks' maternity leave, and the establishment of machinery to prevent sex-discrimination in employment and to facilitate the entry of women into apprenticeship programs.[15] Published in 1972, the report and its recommendations were the subject of widespread media coverage and had a significant impact on Irish attitudes.

Women trade unionists used the recommendations to pressure their own unions to take specific action toward equality, and in fact the report became in effect a bottom-line trade union position. After its publication it was difficult for any union leader publicly to advocate anything less than the report recommended. Throughout the seventies the recommendations were used by the unions in lobbying for legislation and in their negotiations.

External Influences

Events outside Ireland also influenced Irish attitudes. Women as individuals and in their organizations were strongly affected by the ideas and struggles of women in other countries. They closely followed the literature, subscribed to European and American publications, and participated in international meetings. "Women's Liberation" became the subject of television debates, sometimes with leaders of the women's movement from other countries participating. International Women's Year provided additional impetus for organizations and the media to focus attention on women. Research projects were undertaken and special seminars held on equality for women. Conferences often featured speakers from outside Ireland. The information they imparted about moves toward equality in their countries encouraged Irish women in their efforts.

Events around International Women's Year also led to increased cooperation between traditional women's organizations and trade union women and raised their consciousness of the link between equality at work and equality in other areas of life. The interest of women's groups in work-related issues increased accordingly.

Women trade union leaders were particularly aware of events in Britain and, to a lesser degree, the United States and looked to both countries for specific ideas and strategies. Irish unions learned a great deal from Britain about the tactics employers were using to avoid suits under the British equal pay laws (such as segregating women in specific jobs and low grades and using job evaluation systems to legitimize sex discrimination). They attempted, with some degree of success, to prevent employers in Ireland from taking similar actions and fought to secure provisions in Irish legislation that had worked well in Britain.

Irish women were also influenced by the efforts of some British unions to increase the participation of their female members. Discussions about such practices as reserving seats on the executive councils of trade union bodies frequently referred to the special conferences held by the British Trades Union Congress (TUC) on issues of particular concern to women workers and to the British policy of electing a certain number of women representatives to the TUC executive. In the late seventies, the similar policy of the National Union of Public Employees (NUPE) in Britain was often cited as an example Irish unions might follow. There was general agreement among active women trade unionists that the WAC's range of activity was too narrow and that they needed an organization that could pursue a more aggressive policy on women's issues. The committee could not take a public stand on any issues, as its role was simply to advise the ICTU executive. Moreover, participation in WAC activities was restricted, as only women appointed by their unions could attend WAC meetings or seminars. Unions tended to appoint the same people each year, overlooking many concerned women.

The formation in the United States in 1974 of the Coalition of Labor Union Women (CLUW) provided Irish women trade unionists with another strategy: an organization outside the official trade union structure that might supplement some of WAC's activities and surmount some of its restrictions. CLUW offers a support network to women in their work within their own unions. Its goals are to encourage American unions to (1) organize the unorganized; (2) promote affirmative action in the workplace; (3) work for legislation of benefit to working women; and (4) increase the participation of women in unions. The inspiration of CLUW was one factor leading to the creation of the Trade Union Women's Forum (TUWF), an Irish organization with a similar structure and goals.

The demands of British and American women for equality in the workplace as well as in the trade union movement also influenced the program of Irish women. For example, the Working Women's Charter prepared by two women activists in the ITGWU and adopted from a charter that appeared in 1975 in a British women's liberation magazine.

Of great importance in the 1970s, in both influencing attitudes and creating pressure for change, was Ireland's entry into the EEC. Agitation for equal treatment for women at work—and in particular for married women and women with children—was considerably greater in the other EEC member states than in Ireland. Major EEC directives on economic and social policy in the seventies dealt with equality for women workers, both married and single, including equal pay and equal access to training and employment.

In the early 1970s the Irish female labor force was still largely composed of young, single women. According to the 1971 census, over 65 percent of women workers were under twenty-nine years of age. The percentage of married women working—13.5 percent—was lower than in any other EEC country. In six of the nine member states, married women accounted for over 50 percent of the female labor force.[16] Since a condition of EEC membership is the agreement to abide by its directives, Ireland was compelled to adopt some policies far in advance of any that would have resulted solely from internal pressures.

Effects of the Recession

A downturn in the Irish economy in the seventies made Ireland's membership in the EEC particularly significant. With the return of high unemployment and inflation, domestic support for equality, which had been growing slowly since the sixties, began to falter. In addition, by the seventies the traditional outlet for the unemployed—emigration to England or America—had begun to close down. New U.S. immigration laws severely limited the number of Irish immigrants, and few job opportunities existed in Britain. Competition for jobs among recent high school and college graduates was intense, with hundreds and sometimes thousands of people applying for a single job.

As a result there was a resurgence of opposition to women's entry into nontraditional jobs and to equal treatment for married women. For example, support for women's employment in the traditional male crafts was official ICTU policy, But when AnCo, the state-sponsored training authority, established a committee to study female apprenticeships in 1975, the union delegate to the committee stated that his union would picket AnCo headquarters if a single woman was apprenticed in its trade! Other trade officials were in full support of such company policies as cutting the seniority of women upon marriage or requiring married women to be first laid off regardless of seniority. A study I conducted in 1975 showed that both shop stewards and rank-and-file industrial workers agreed that married women's rights should be limited.[17]

In light of such attitudes, it is extremely unlikely that legislation requiring equal treatment or equal pay for workers regardless of sex or marital status would have been enacted in the seventies had it not been for the EEC. In accordance with EEC directives, however, the Employment Equality Act went into effect in 1977, forcing employers to abolish discriminatory seniority and hiring systems and drop the marriage bar, among other changes. The act also established the Employment Equality Agency to monitor the equal pay and equal opportunity legislation and to promote public understanding of and compliance with its principles.

EEC membership did not, however, eliminate the need for activism on the part of trade union women. Legislation for full equal pay was due to take effect on December 31, 1975, the date required by an EEC directive. Advocates of equal pay, including trade unionists and women's groups, had assumed that the government would fulfill its obligations and were therefore caught by surprise when the government announced that it would seek an EEC derogation to allow Ireland to postpone the implementation of the act until December 31, 1977.

An organization calling itself the Ad Hoc Committee for the Promotion of Equal Pay, made up of women trade unionists, members of women's organizations, and other supporters, quickly mobilized. Within ten days they collected over thirty-six thousand signatures and called an emergency protest meeting demanding that the government honor its commitment.

The government continued to pursue a derogation, but in the end the EEC denied its request. The government now turned to subverting the requirement, using a subterfuge to withhold equal pay from many civil service workers. In the civil service, women and single men were on a lower pay scale than married men. Although the government had in the past agreed that equal pay meant moving all workers to the married men's scale, it now created two scales—one for single and one for married workers. Since the marriage bar had only recently been lifted, most women civil servants were single and therefore received no increase in pay. Eventually a campaign by the civil service unions in behalf of equal pay for these workers was successful.

WOMEN ORGANIZE

The attempt to postpone equal pay emphasized the tenuous nature of many of the gains women had made, but it also dramatized the fact that there were many women who were not being activated by their own unions or the WAC. The TUWF, founded in 1976 by a core group of women from the Ad Hoc Committee for Promotion of Equal Pay, now expanded to include fifteen women (many of them former or present members of the WAC) from nine unions. The organizers of the Forum intended to provide information and encouragement to women workers to increase their activity. The organization runs meetings, supplies speakers to women's groups, the media, and local union meetings, and publishes articles and booklets on issues of concern to trade union women.

One of the Forum's first projects was a widely circulated booklet called "Make Sure You Get Equal Pay." It clearly and simply outlined the provisions of the act and warned of ways employers might try to circumvent the law. The booklet was particularly important because the Irish legislation contains a provision for equal pay entitlement in cases where "work of equal value" is being performed, a new concept that needed emphasis and explanation. It includes a "Think Equal" section designed to encourage women to challenge traditional concepts of job worth and to demystify the legislation for workers and trade union staff. In another TUWF project using new ways to reach people on women's issues, Forum members worked with a Dublin theater group to write a play about equal pay. The result was a comedy with songs and music depicting scenes from office and factory life. It ran for several weeks at a Dublin theater, with a number of special performances at other sites.

Despite the success of its projects, Forum members were dissatisfied with their inability to attract rank-and-file women industrial and service workers to their events, although the Forum developed some following among clerical workers. Most people who attend its programs were shop stewards, activists, or union staff members. Opening lines of communications with women workers was difficult. All trade union staff members and most shop stewards, particularly in the blue-collar sector, were men. The Forum had few ties with these officials, and the layoffs and plant closings of the seventies had led many of them to believe that advances for women could be achieved only at the expense of men. Consequently, the TUWF decided in the beginning of 1977 to initiate projects involving male staff and shop stewards that would promote a dialogue between men and women trade unionists on women's issues.

The Forum's efforts began with a request to the Dublin Council of Trade Unions (a regional affiliate of unions associated with the ICTU) to co-sponsor a full-day program on women workers and the recession. The council agreed, and invitations to send representatives went to all area unions, including the craft unions. Earlier seminars on women's issues had been attended almost exclusively by women. Now twenty-one unions participated, and plumbers, carpenters, and electricians interacted with sewing machine operators, secretaries, and teachers. It was a first in Irish trade union history, a conference at which men and women workers dealt with the problems of women workers as an issue of mutual concern.

A change in the role of the WAC was also in progress. In the seventies the WAC began significantly to influence ICTU positions on women's issues and to become increasingly militant and independent. It advanced positions on equal pay and equal opportunity bills that then became the official Congress position. In 1978 the WAC publicly announced its support for the Contraception Action Programme (CAP), a campaign aimed at legalizing birth control in Ireland, even though the ICTU viewed the WAC as an internal committee that was not empowered to take public stands on issues. The ICTU executive objected to the WAC's stand as both a breach of former practice and an endorsement of a "non–trade union issue," but when the WAC stood firm, citing the demand for freely available contraceptives in the Working Women's Charter as their authority for endorsing the campaign without prior Executive Council approval, the executive did not force a confrontation on the issue.

In 1979 the WAC again flexed its muscles, this time in a seminar described in the *Irish Times* as "completely different from any that had gone before."[18] Many participants were newly organized workers and blue-collar women who had become active in the unions in the pursuit of equal pay. They were new to WAC activity and were generally younger than those who had attended earlier seminars. The keynote speaker proposed that the WAC be upgraded and given resources, staff, and the means to reach individual women at their places of work. Bursting the old barriers of "education only," WAC delegates decided to vote on a course of action to guide the ICTU and its affiliates in encouraging women's participation in union affairs. They adopted a resolution calling for a working party of the WAC to draw up a program of action on equal pay, trade union education for women, and a revision of union structures and administration to encourage women's participation, and to report on this program to the ICTU executive. They also voted to hold another seminar in six months to hear a report on the working party's recommendations and the executive's response.

New demands addressed to the national unions included the appointment of equality officers and the adoption of policies of "positive discrimination through providing reserved seats for women on policy and decision-making bodies." Almost immediately several unions began seriously to consider establishing women's officers or women's divisions.

Informal networks established through the WAC and TUWF meetings came to be a standard means of communicating information and rallying support among women. One result was a campaign to secure the appointment of a leading woman trade unionist as the first chairperson of the

Employment Equality Agency in anticipation of the Minister of Labour's probable selection of a chair who would not agressively pursue the implementation of the new equal rights legislation. The success of this effort greatly increased the likelihood that the legislation would make an important difference in the conditions of women workers.

These informal networks included, among other groups of professionals, women in the media. News articles exposed discriminatory conditions and practices, generated support for strikes of women workers, and became a valuable source of information about upcoming meetings, demonstrations, and projects.

Women trade union staff members, though few in number, significantly contributed to the unions' growing response to the needs of women workers. Research workers at the ITGWU initiated projects of special concern to women, analyzing discriminatory aspects of pension plans and publicizing newly negotiated contract clauses on maternity leave. The ITGWU developed courses on equal pay and equal opportunity, held throughout Ireland, which were widely attended by shop stewards as well as rank-and-file members. The ICTU also ran courses on equal pay and opportunity as well as initiating an innovative training program that combined personal development and trade union issues. Participants were released from work with pay to attend both the ITGWU and ICTU programs.

NATIONAL BARGAINING AND WOMEN'S ISSUES

These developments regarding women workers' rights occurred simultaneously with some dramatic changes in Irish labor relations. Traditionally, Irish unions have insisted on "voluntarism" and have opposed government interference in matters that could be the subject of collective bargaining or trade union action.[19] Collective bargaining agreements are not held to be legally binding contracts, and in the private sector there is no provision for final and binding arbitration of grievances.[20] The Labour Court, established in 1946 to promote industrial harmony, serves as mediator but not as arbitrator in disputes over either rights or interests. Its recommendations can be rejected by either party.

The 1970s saw the development of a new type of bargaining, as well as the introduction of legislation governing a wide range of workplace issues. Under the pressure of a government threat to impose wage controls, unions agreed to exercise wage restraint through the mechanism of "National Agreements" to be negotiated by the ICTU and the Federated Union of Employers (FUE).

The climate in the seventies demanded that unions give more than lip service to sex equality. However, an analysis of the way women's issues were handled under National Agreements reveals less than a full commitment on the part of the leadership to women's rights. Beginning in 1972 National Agreements provided for percentage increases designed eventually to close the gap between men's and women's rates for the same or broadly similar jobs. In disputes over equal pay—unlike other cases—the agreements required binding determination to be made by an equal pay commissioner attached to the Labour Court. The intent appears to have been to discourage equal pay strikes while preserving the strike weapon for other issues.

In 1975, although full equal pay had not been achieved, the National Agreement made no mention of the subject, presumably because equal pay legislation had just been enacted. The wisdom of the traditional trade union reliance on bargaining in wage matters was demonstrated when the government announced its intention to delay the enforcement of the very legislation it had just adopted: had an equal pay provision been in the 1975 National Agreement, the government's action could have had no effect. The unions' reliance on legislation rather than collective bargaining on this crucial issue suggests that it was not a major objective, an interpretation further supported by the fact that trade union criticisms of the inadequacy of the law were not followed by efforts to negotiate the indicated improvements.

Other women's issues not dealt with in EEC directives—such as prohibiting discrimination because of pregnancy or the introduction of adequate maternity leaves—were also not addressed in national bargaining in the seventies. In response to WAC pressure, the ICTU supported maternity leave legislation, and a law on the subject was adopted in 1981. Similarly, unions did not support proposals to modify the punitive tax on the earnings of married women until 1980.

There are several reasons why the Irish trade unions, like most others, have failed on the whole to promote women's interests at the bargaining table. A substantial minority of women workers are not union members. Of the 63 percent of Irish working women who are union members, few participate in union life or exercise their potential power. A study conducted in 1977 by the ITGWU found that women and young men see the union as dominated by older men who fail to share or understand their problems.[21] Women's short-term view of work life further affects their attitudes toward union activity. In a survey conducted by the author in 1976, only one of approximately seventy-five women queried stated that she expected to continue work after having children. Although white-collar women largely share these views, more of them than blue-collar women have been influenced by the women's liberation movement and have some plans to return to work when their children are older. Other studies show that a return to work is closely associated with higher levels of education.[22]

The pattern of Ireland's industrial relations in the seventies has also contributed to apathy. National Agreements have removed collective bargaining from the workplace and deprived many new members and particularly women of the opportunity to participate in or learn from the process. They have excluded rank-and-file workers even from the process of drawing up proposals for bargaining. As participants in or close observers of local bargaining, they could have gained some understanding of power relationships, organizational techniques, and communication skills—all essential tools for union activists. Instead, one or two officials, invariably chosen from among the men, represent each national union in negotiations. The large numbers of women who joined unions mainly because they worked in factories where membership was a condition of employment have never experienced the union as a vehicle of change. Many are even unaware that wage increases gained under the National Agreement result from collective bargaining.

White-collar workers have had rather more activist experience. In the private sector many have organized the staffs of their own companies and thus come into the union as a result of a struggle with their employers, an experience that has given them some understanding of their potential power. The government's attempts to sidestep its equal pay obligations have increased the union consciousness of many women in the public service. Not surprisingly, the longest strike for equal pay in the seventies was conducted by several thousand women telephone operators in the state-run company.

PROSPECTS FOR CHANGE

Substantial progress has been made on a number of fronts since the WAC seminar in 1979. In 1982 the ICTU adopted a far-ranging policy document recommending concrete programs for trade union action on women's rights at the workplace and within the trade union movement. It discusses the need for a two-pronged approach to equality issues through legislation and collective bargaining. Recommended legislation actions include strengthening the Employment Equality Act, the extension of rights under the 1981 maternity leave legislation, and the establishment of flexible hours.

The section of the report on collective bargaining is particularly comprehensive and detailed. It suggests that affiliated unions negotiate "equality agreements" with each employer, including the "procedure and practices to be introduced to implement this policy." The agreements are to cover the employer's policies on recruitment, promotions, training, equal pay, maternity and paternity leaves, child care facilities, and any other local issues; a mechanism to monitor progress is also recommended. The report suggests that the government set an example for private sector firms by agreeing to establish such provisions in key government services and urges the public sector unions to begin work on this project.

The document discusses in depth women's participation within the trade union movement. Many suggestions to increase participation are suggested, ranging from initiating organizing campaigns in unorganzied companies to establishing an annual women's conference in the ICTU and strengthening the role of the WAC. The appointment of a full-time equality officer to work with the WAC and the women's conference is also recommended. The report advises affiliated unions to establish similar structures and suggests that a specific block of time be devoted at the annual conference of each union to the progress that has been made in women's rights at work and within the union in the past year. A number of suggestions are also offered to facilitate women's participation on the local level, including negotiating time off with pay to attend union meetings and training programs and providing child care at meetings.

While the document does not recommend that the ICTU or affiliated unions establish reserved seats on executive councils for women, it does suggest that the issue of equal representation be seriously considered, particularly by unions with large female memberships. Both the ITGWU and the FWUI have also issued policy documents endorsing similar plans.

OBSTACLES IN THE EIGHTIES

While these developments are encouraging and indicate that progress for women workers is likely to continue to the eighties, such progress will require continued pressure from women trade unionists and their allies. Many of the strategies discussed in the ICTU document are contrary to the traditional functioning of unions. Bargaining for and enforcing equality agreements will require union leaders to confront the prejudices of male members, who are likely to object to preferential treatment for women. In the past, Irish unions, in taking public stands on social issues, have not tried to bring their members into agreement and so have avoided dealing with members' apathy or hostility on such issues.[23] Increasing participation by women will also require more meetings, more activity, and more involvement by all members. A thorough democratization of the trade union movement may not be welcomed by those trade union leaders who are happy with the status quo.

The socioeconomic climate in the eighties may also make rapid progress difficult. History shows that the progress of Irish women toward equality has been strongly influenced by the state of the economy, demographic factors, and church policy. Trends at the beginning of the decade suggest unfavorable developments in all these areas. Statements by the pope, for example, indicate that church policy on birth control will not change soon. The baby boom of the sixties, the result of favorable economic conditions and a decline in emigration, now means a large increase in the labor force not matched by increases in job openings. The rising level of youth unemployment can only mean renewed pressure against programs for women, and especially married women.

Irish women anticipate a difficult struggle. To carry it through, trade union women are seeking alliances with other women's groups and looking to the Employment Equality Agency and supporters in the media. Above all, they continue to agitate among both unionized and nonunion women.

GLOSSARY

AnCo	Irish Training Authority
ASTI	Association of Secondary Teachers of Ireland
ATGWU	Amalgamated Transport and General Workers Union
CAP	Contraceptive Action Programme
CLUW	Coalition of Labor Union Women (United States)
CPSSA	Civil and Public Services' Staff Association
EEC	European Economic Community
FUE	Federated Union of Employers
FWUI	Federated Workers Union of Ireland
ICTU	Irish Congress of Trade Unions
INTO	Irish National Teachers Organizations
ITGWU	Irish Transport and General Workers Union
IUDWC	Irish Union of Distributive Workers and Clerks
IWWU	Irish Women Workers Union
LGPSU	Local Government and Public Services Union
NUPE	National Union of Public Employees (Great Britain)
POWU	Post Office Workers Union
TUC	Trade Union Congress (Great Britain)
TUI	Teachers Union of Ireland
TUWF	Trade Union Women's Forum
WAC	Women's Advisory Committee

NOTES

1. "Trade Union Survey, 1979: Women in Trade Unions" (Dublin: Irish Congress of Trade Unions Research Service, 1979).

2. Ibid.

3. Adrian Sinfield, *The Longterm Unemployed* (Paris: Organisation for Economic Cooperation and Development, 1968). OECD and International Labour Organisation statistics on unemployment in Ireland are undifferentiated as to men's and women's absolute and proportional amounts and rates. For the decade of the 1970s, they show a sudden rise in 1975/76, which had not fully receded to 1974 levels by 1980 (ILO Yearbook of Labor Statistics [Geneva: ILO, 1980]):

No. of Unemployed

Year	Total	Mfg.	Service	Commercial	Total as % of Labor Force
1970	41,600	12,100	6,900	5,800	7.2
1972	48,200	15,200	8,000	6,500	8.1
1974	48,100	16,000	8,300	6,500	7.9
1976	83,500	30,000	12,900	10,500	12.3
1978	74,700	25,200	13,400	9,400	10.7
1979	66,400	21,800	12,900	8,300	9.3

4. "Memorandum: Communication of the Commission to the Council on Equality of Treatment Between Men and Women Workers" (Brussels: Commission of the European Communities, 1975).

5. Christina Murphy, "The Married Woman's Right to Work," *Irish Times* (Dublin), April 30, 1976.

6. Mary E. Daly, "Women, Work and Trade Unionism," in *Women in Irish Society: The Historical Dimension*, Margaret MacCurtain and Donncha Ó Corráin ed. (Dublin: Arlen House, 1978), p. 76.

7. Ibid.

8. Ibid.

9. Ibid.

10. Ibid., p. 78.

11. Ibid., p. 79.

12. Ibid.

13. Lucy McCaffrey, *Women and Work in Ireland: A Compilation of Statistics* (Dublin: AnCo—The Industrial Training Authority, 1979), p. 9.

14. *Census of Population of Ireland, 1971* (Dublin: Stationary Office, 1975).

15. *Report of the Commission on the Status of Women, 1972* (Dublin: Stationery Office 1972).

16. McCaffrey, *Women and Work*, p. 12.

17. Deborah King, *Attitudes to Women at Work with Particular Reference to Attitudes Toward Married Women* (Dublin: AnCo—The Industrial Training Authority, 1976).

18. Mary Maher, "Every Third 'Working Man' Is a 'Woman,'" *Irish Times* (Dublin), September 21, 1979.

19. George F. Daly, *Industrial Relations: Comparative Aspects, with Particular Reference to Ireland* (Cork: Mercier Press, 1968).

20. Ibid., p. 305.

21. Anne Speed, *Some Thoughts on the Organisation of Women and Youth in the Irish Transport and General Workers Union* (Dublin: ITGWU, 1977).

22. Brendan Walsh, "Women and Employment in Ireland: Results of a National Survey," Paper no. 69 (Dublin: Economic and Social Research Institute, 1973).

23. Brian Hillery, Aiden Kelly, and Arthur March, *Trade Union Organisation in Ireland*, Study no. 11 (Dublin: Irish Productivity Centre, 1975), pp. 177–78.

BIBLIOGRAPHY

Chubb, Basil. *The Government and Politics of Ireland*. 2d ed. Stanford, Cal.: Stanford University Press, 1982.
Daly, George F. *Industrial Relations: Comparative Aspects, with Particular Reference to Ireland*. Cork: Mercier Press, 1968.
Daly, Mary E. "Women, Work and Trade Unionism." In *Women in Irish Society: The Historical Dimension*, edited by Margaret MacCurtain and Donncha Ó Corráin. Dublin: Arlen House, 1978; Westport, Conn.: Greenwood Press, 1979.
Fine-Davis, Margret. "Attitudes Toward the Status of Women: Implications for Equal Employment Opportunity." Report to the Department of Labour. Dublin: Department of Labour, 1977.
Hillery, Brian, Aiden Kelly, and Arthur Marsh. *Trade Union Organisation in Ireland*. Study no. 11. Dublin: Irish Productivity Center, 1975.
King, Deborah. *Attitudes to Women at Work with Particular Reference to Attitudes Toward Married Women*. Dublin: AnCo—The Industrial Training Authority, 1976.
Maher, Mary. "Every Third 'Working Man' Is a 'Woman.'" *Irish Times* (Dublin), September 21, 1979.
McCaffrey, Lucy. *Women and Work in Ireland: A Compilation of Statistics*. Dublin: AnCo—The Industrial Training Authority, 1979.
McCarthy, Eunice. "Women and Work in Ireland: The Present and Preparing for the Future." In *Women in Irish Society: The Historical Dimension*, edited by Margaret MacCurtain and Donncha Ó Corráin. Dublin: Arlen House, 1978; Westport, Conn.: Greenwood Press, 1979.
MacCurtain, Margaret. "Women the Vote and Revolution." In *Women in Irish Society: The Historical Dimension*, edited by Margaret MacCurtain and Donncha Ó Corráin. Dublin: Arlen House, 1978; Westport, Conn.: Greenwood Press, 1979.
MacCurtain, Margaret, and Donncha Ó Corráin, ed. *Women in Irish Society: The Historical Dimension*. Dublin: Arlen House, 1978; Westport, Conn.: Greenwood Press, 1979.
"Memorandum: Communication of the Commission to the Council of Equality on Treatment Between Men and Women Workers." Brussels: Commission of the European Communities, 1975.
Murphy, Christina. "The Married Woman's Right to Work." *Irish Times* (Dublin), April 30, 1976.
Porter, Mary Cornelia, and Corey Venning. "Catholicism and Women's role in Italy and Ireland." In *Women in the World*, edited by Lynne B. Iglitzin and Ruth Ross. Santa Barbara, Cal.: Clio Books, 1976.
Report of the Commission on the Status of Women, 1972. Dublin: Stationery Office, 1972.

Speed, Anne. *Some Thoughts on the Organisation of Women and Youth in the Irish Transport and General Workers Union.* Dublin: ITGWU, 1977.

"Trade Union Survey, 1979: Women in Trade Unions." Dublin: Irish Congress of Trade Unions Research Service, 1979.

Walsh, Brendan. "Women and Employment in Ireland: Results of a National Survey." Paper no. 69 Dublin: Economic and Social Research Institute, 1973.

"Women in Ireland." *Administration* (Institute of Public Administration of Ireland) 23, no. 1 (Spring 1975).

8   ITALY

Bianca Beccalli

A mobilization of working women with strong feminist over-
tones developed in Italy in the mid-1970s, awakening in the trade union
movement an interest in the "woman question" that had not been felt for
some years. For an earlier explicit interest in women's issues in Italian trade
unions, we have to go back to the fifties or to the turn of the century.

I shall start off my analysis of women in Italian trade unions with a short
description of the basic structural trends in women's employment. At the
beginning of Italian industrialization, soon after the formation of the new
Italian nation in 1861, women (and children) made up the great majority of
the wage earners, as in other industrializing societies. In the following
decades women's employment declined. Peculiar to the Italian case was a
slow, steady decline in female employment throughout the twentieth century, until the trend was reversed in the 1970s. Until the 1950s another
important structural feature peculiar to Italy was the large agrarian sector,
which employed many women and provided the basis for a strong, organized
movement of agricultural workers. This movement was very influential in
shaping the relationship between women and trade unions. As this paper
focuses on the seventies and eighties, however, I shall not go into a historical
reconstruction of women's struggles to influence the policies and strategies
of the agricultural labor movement.

The tradition of political unionism, so prominent in Italy in some
decades, will be examined against actual union policies. How far did the
apparent openness of Italian unions result in actual gains for working
women? What accounted for this political tradition? How far does it affect
the current development of the trade union movement in Italy? How is it

---

This paper is a result of a period of comparative studies on women and unions in
Italy and in the United States that was made possible by a grant from the German
Marshall Fund. The analysis of women's wages and employment was done jointly
with Paolo Santi.

influenced by such developments as the shrinking of the traditional industrial base for unionism, significant changes in the composition of the labor force, and the increasing importance of campaigns on issues outside the economic sphere?

I shall also examine the variety of actions women have taken in confronting these issues, which in turn raise some general questions about goals and means. Should women struggle for equality—for access to the male world of work and power—or for a radical reorganization of that world? Is equality a necessary step toward change, or does it work against change? Must women's participation in social struggles and union activities always take distinctive forms—as it has in the past—outside the norms and procedures of negotiation and representation? How can this pattern of participation be reconciled with the need for sustained and efficient action? These problems, which are the general problems of women's politics, have arisen throughout the history of working women.

STRUCTURAL TRENDS AND POLITICAL TRADITIONS

Trends in Women's Employment

Industrialization began considerably later in Italy than in other developed countries. In 1901 the labor force amounted to 17.4 million, of whom 62 percent were in agriculture and 23 percent in industry. At least 6.0 million wage earners worked on the land. By comparison, only 2.6 million were in industrial occupations, with roughly 1.4 million in other categories.

The proportion of women active in the labor force had already started to decline in the last decades of the nineteenth century. At the beginning of the twentieth century, the proportion of women wage earners was about as high in industry (35 percent) as in agriculture (40 percent); in other sectors, with the exception of elementary education, it was minimal. Thirty-two percent of all women were active in the labor market (or 41 percent if one considers only the population over ten years old). These figures are not much different from those given for other European countries. The proportion of women active in the labor force, however, continued to decline, although the number of women actually working was probably at least 10 percent higher than census figures suggest: in 1911, the official figure was 29 percent; in 1921, 27 percent; in 1931, 24 percent; in 1951, 20 percent. Women tended to leave the labor force after marriage or the birth of their first child, creating a different age structure among working women, from that found in other industrialized societies. The reasons for this phenomenon were many: the persistence of a culture that denied work outside agriculture or the family home to married women; structural changes that brought about a reduction in employment in the sectors in which women workers were most concentrated; a high level of unemployment and hence a plentiful supply of cheap male labor; and the slow growth of new female occupations.[1]

The women working in the primary labor market were for the most part young, and they therefore experienced double discrimination in regard to wages. At the beginning of the century, female day-laborers in the agrarian sector earned only about 55 percent of the wage of their male co-workers; the wages of women employed in industry ranged from 35 to 50 percent of those men earned. The differential in the agrarian sector increased between the last decades of the nineteenth century and the years just after the First World War; then, as a result of successful strikes, the wages of women day-laborers increased more rapidly than those of the men. In industry wage differentials between the sexes narrowed during the First World War but widened almost immediately afterward. During the Fascist period women working on the land earned 55 to 60 percent of male earnings, while blue-collar women earned 45 to 50 percent of male wages. In this period, especially in the second half of the 1930s and during the Second World War, women's employment in the service sector and the public sector increased. In the latter the principle of equal pay was officially endorsed, but numerous laws in fact prevented women from occupying the higher posts in the bureaucracy. Finally, a large number of women continued to work part time, in cottage industry, or as domestic servants—in other words, in the secondary labor market, where the wage levels were considerably below those in the primary market.

The late seventies and early eighties witnessed a great change in women's participation in the labor market. A much discussed peculiarity of the Italian labor market—the low and falling participation rate of women—began to change in the early seventies, and in 1981 the rate stood at 26 percent, still much lower than that of other industrialized countries, but definitely increasing. Of the total increase in employment between 1972 and 1981 (1,757,000 workers), women accounted for 1,348,000, more than three-quarters. (Female unemployment also increased strikingly, from 9.6 percent in 1974 to 14.4 percent in 1981, as against a male unemployment rate of 5.4 percent in 1981.) The biggest increases in employment occurred among women of child bearing age, between twenty and forty-four years, whose participation rates had been the lowest in international comparisons. Women not only returned to work after age thirty-five but stayed in their jobs in the younger and most fertile age cohorts.

Can we apply the usual demand-and-supply scheme to explain this increase? We will have no difficulties with the demand side: much of the increase of employment in the seventies was concentrated in the tertiary sector, public and private, where women were already overrepresented. In industry, the increase largely occurred in the small business sector, where again, women's participation rates have always been high.

The driving forces on the side of supply are more interesting and complex. Two trends in particular are relevant: the increase in education and the decline in the birthrate. Education expanded rapidly in this period, particularly for women, who accounted for 43 percent of those receiving high school diplomas or university degrees in 1970 and 45 percent of those graduating in 1980. Even more impressive are the demographic data: in the baby-boom triennium of 1960–62, the fertility rate per thousand women of childbearing age was 68.0; it was almost twenty points lower (48.8) in the 1979–81 triennium, with the Italian population now stationary. The trend was particularly strong in the second half of the seventies. The decline in fertility rates was most marked in the most fertile age cohorts (twenty-one to twenty-nine), and it was strongest in the most urbanized and industrialized areas of the country.

Developments in collective consciousness and behavior in the seventies paralleled and magnified the influence of these structural factors. The referendum on divorce and the laws on abortion and equal opportunity represent milestones in the social emancipation of women. The first two reforms were passionately fought for in the political arena, and women's vote in the abortion referendum surprised everyone, becoming a symbol of the modernization of Italian society.

The Political Tradition of Italian Unionism

Events at the turn of the century shaped the Italian labor movement and the position of women in it. Notwithstanding the changes that took place later in Italian society, including the dramatic interruption of Fascism, there remain some remarkable continuities with the basic pattern established in the early period. Because Italy has not had socialist and feminist historians to recover the experience of women in the labor movement,[2] I can here only sketch that pattern.

Despite the structural weakness of the working class in Italy, the Italian labor movement was a crucial actor on the social and political scene; indeed, the presence of the emerging socialist movement set the terms of social and political conflict throughout the period. There was a close connection—even overlap—between "economic" and "political" struggles. Popular protest was often the result of trade union action, and the emerging trade unions were constantly involved in struggles to legitimate their existence.

The backwardness of political democracy, for its part, likewise shaped the political character of the early Italian unions. Trade unions faced the problem of organizing a heterogeneous and mostly new working class.

Peculiar to Italy was the lack of intermediate strata between the small number of highly skilled workers, organized in "leagues" with a long craft tradition, and the wide mass of young unskilled workers, whose employment was unstable. The few old craft workers were rapidly overwhelmed by the process of industrialization, and no sector of the new work force was strong enough to establish a unified union organization. Craft unionism was quickly wiped out. The process of building wider trade unions concentrated on two basic structures: in the early 1890s most of the "Chambers of Labor," and between 1901 and 1905 most of the national industrial unions, were formed. Both tended to be open to the lower strata of workers, to engage in struggles for general goals, and to be highly political. Their internal features reflected the general politicization that connected trade union action with the socialist movement outside.

The Chambers of Labor were a peculiar type of trade union.[3] Territorially organized, they grouped together workers of different sectors and occupations. They were based on the old craft leagues, but organized the unskilled and the unemployed as well as skilled workers. Their functions included collective bargaining and representing workers' interests on issues ranging from control over hiring practices to social and political reforms.[4] Labor activists of this period considered the Chambers primitive, compared with the more mature craft and industrial organizations of other countries, and expected them to give way to more specialized organizations. In fact, the Chambers of Labor have lasted up to the present and have helped to maintain the political character of Italian unionism.

Women's role in the Chambers of Labor has not been studied, but they were welcome in principle as part of the unstable proletariat that the Chambers of Labor aimed to organize. The Chambers were formally in favor of equal pay,[5] and women's commissions were established in several. Moreover, several programs involved not only workers, but the community at large, including women.[6]

As far as we can surmise from the available data, the relationship between the industrial unions and women was somewhat more contradictory. The resistance to women's presence in both employment and the unions may have been stronger here, although the situation differed from one union to the next. Three unions will serve as examples. At one extreme was the typographical union, rooted in the old craft traditions, which maintained control over apprenticeship. This union admitted women, who were in any case a small minority, but barred them from access to the higher skills.[7] The clothing and textile union placed no direct restrictions on women, who were the great majority of workers in the sector and were quite militant, but it was dominated by males—about 90 percent of the union membership—and shaped by male culture and organizing methods.[8] One of the roots of the union's weakness was the difficulty of connecting the remarkable militancy of its base to a solid organization.[9]

The agricultural workers' union, for a long time the largest in Italy, was at the opposite extreme from the typographical union: it had no previous craft tradition, and its structure and policy were nonhierarchical. The struggles of agricultural workers were intense, sometimes involving a whole territory and spreading from workplace to community. The organization was necessarily decentralized, and there was a high degree of membership participation. Women took part in both the struggles and the organization, as the available membership figures indicate.[10] These characteristics of the *braccianti* (branch) struggles and organization lasted into the 1950s, and we can see their general influence on Italian unionism long after the *braccianti* ceased to be the most important sector of organized workers.

The history of all three unions reveals a discrepancy between working women's militancy and their representation in leadership positions, although the degree of underrepresentation varied from one union to the next. It is revealing that women leaders in the early socialist movement were called "fuggenti meteore"—"streaking comets." The clothing and textile union leadership, as we have seen, was overwhelmingly male even at the shopfloor level, where older male skilled or craft workers directed the young unskilled women.[11] There were no women delegates at the first congress of this federation, held in Pisa in 1903.[12] On the other hand, there are records of many women leaders at various levels in the agricultural laborers' union. The most striking fact is that a woman, Argentina Altobelli, led the national union, the powerful "Federterra," from 1905 onward. A few Chambers of Labor in agricultural areas also had women leaders. Several, including Altobelli herself,[13] did not come from the ranks but were middle-class socialists.

The Italian labor movement's openness to outside intellectuals, which has had consequences for the relationship between feminism and unionism, is a distinctive characteristic of the movement: Michels considered it a key to understanding its political and "moral" character, as compared with the German and other European cases.[14] The structural weakness of the Italian industrial working class and the importance of agriculture together provided a setting for the development of a socialism with a much more heterogeneous class composition than was found elsewhere in Europe, and the fragmented and heterogeneous nature of the movement reinforced its "moral," political character.

Feminism and Socialism in the Italian Unions

The recruitment of leaders from the outside—not necessarily from the upper class—has remained a characteristic of the Italian labor movement[15] and has helped to guarantee continuing openness to feminism. Feminist ideas and initiatives developed in Italy in the last decades of the nineteenth century. In other countries the distinction between feminism within and feminism outside the labor movement often developed into open conflict. In the Italian case, however, there was no marked separation between the two, in part perhaps because the social bases of the two positions were not so well defined or far apart. The labor movement in fact attracted many actual and potential feminists. A new stratum of educated women had developed by the end of the nineteenth century, one consequence of the establishment of the state educational system in the new Italian nation. Some of these women—for example, "le maestrine socialiste," the socialist elementary school teachers—were recruited into the labor movement, and some became union organizers. Such women were aware of the new feminist ideas that spread throughout Europe at the end of the century, and they helped to bring a new sensitivity to feminism into the labor movement.

The political history of feminism and socialism in Italy would doubtless make more sense if both social processes were better understood in detail. The research available presents a tale of differences and contrasts, but not of separation. Anna Maria Mozzoni and Anna Kuliscioff, the two leading figures of, respectively, "bourgeois" and socialist feminism, provide good examples of this contrast and its limits. Mozzoni came from a liberal democratic background and moved toward socialism, considering the socialist movement and socialist women to be crucial in the battle for women's emancipation. But she felt that emancipation should not be postponed or subordinated to the goal of socialism: women of all social classes should undertake their own struggles for the right to work, civil and political rights, and changes in culture and mores. Women's emancipation and socialism had a different relationship in Kuliscioff's writings: she believed that feminism had to be not only closely connected with socialism, but dependent on it. Only working-class and socialist women could wage the struggle necessary to remove women's oppression, and this struggle could develop only within the general framework of a socialist transformation. These differences emerged clearly in the campaigns for women's suffrage and protective laws for working women.

In 1902 a protective law in behalf of working women limited the use of child labor, banned female labor in underground jobs, introduced some protections for women working night shifts, and, principally, made it illegal for women to work in the first four weeks after childbirth. Similar legislation had been enacted before this in other European countries. Compared with the Socialist party's proposal, the law was narrow and weak,[16] but both pointed in the same general direction. Women in the unions and the Socialist party supported the campaign for protective legislation.[17] The feminists outside the labor movement, on the contrary, opposed protective legislation for women on the ground that it would reinforce their traditional, inferior position. The debate between the feminists and the socialist women on this point marked the maximum difference between the two positions: Mozzoni and Kuliscioff faced each other in a well-known exchange of polemical writings in the socialist newspaper *L'Avanti!* in 1898.

The difference between the two positions was less marked on the suffrage issue. Both feminist and socialist women supported the inclusion of women in the battle for universal adult suffrage. The Socialist party, however, was divided, and those in favor of demanding suffrage for males only prevailed, despite the internal pressures of Kuliscioff and others.

Women and the Unions under Fascism

The mobilization for World War I drew women in great numbers into the workforce, as it did in other countries, but they were expelled soon afterward. In the years of social struggles and political turmoil that followed the war, the woman question disappeared as a specific issue. The Fascist regime directed new attention—of a somewhat ominous sort—to women. Women's reproductive role was an important theme in Fascist ideology, and the regime's demographic policies, based on the goal of expanding the Italian race, encouraged and protected maternity while discouraging women from working. Neither the demographic policies nor the campaigns to expel women from the workplace had a great impact, except in areas like public administration, where women were formally barred from employment. Altogether, long-term trends seemed to resist the state's policies.

WOMEN AND THE UNIONS FROM WORLD WAR II
TO THE SEVENTIES

The Tradition of Class Unionism

Trade unions were reconstructed in Italy after World War II as highly centralized and political organizations. Throughout the fifties and sixties, they were weak at the workplace and divided along political lines. Their political character was in one sense stronger than it had been in the pre-Fascist period, since the unions re-emerged at the end of the war through a specifically political process: the working-class mobilization against the Fascist regime and the German occupation produced a powerful network of political militants, mainly Communists, in the factories, and this became the new network of union activists. The political alignment of the militants preceded and supported their union involvement.

Political initiatives under the control of the parties also accounted for the organization of the unions outside the workplace. The territorially based "horizontal" structures, like the Chambers of Labor locally and the General Confederation nationally, preceded the "vertical," industry-based structures, and in the early years after the war the territorially based organizations were more important. The leaders in the new structures were recruited from among the political organizers, and for some time there was a considerable overlap and turnover between party and union leadership, some of which still remains. Given the close interdependence of unions and parties, conflicts in the political arena were immediately echoed in the unions. The biggest national confederation, the Confederazione Generale Italiana del Lavoro (General Confederation of Italian Labor—CGIL), which was dominated by the Communist party but was initially built with a broad alliance of all the anti-Fascist parties including the Christian Democrats, split in 1948 when the Catholic minority set up a separate national confederation, the Confederazione Italiana Sindicati Lavoratori (Confederation of Italian Trade Unions—national confederation, the CISL). Later a smaller Social Democratic confederation, the Unione Italiane Lavoratori (Union of Italian Workers—UIL), was formed.

The politicization of Italian unionism did not stem, however, only from its relationship with the political parties as defined by political events at the end of the war.[18] To some extent it was also a response to the problems unions had faced in Italy from their formation at the end of the nineteenth century. Although Italian society had developed over the intervening half-century, the industrial working class was still a small sector within a very heterogeneous population; while politically militant, it was economically weak. A broad definition of the role of trade unions prevailed. According to the CGIL unions were to be "class unions" with a distinct ideology, policy, and form of organization, as opposed to "business unions" or "association unions."[19] They were to be oriented toward the defense of class interests as opposed to the immediate interests of their members, who should act as political subjects, not economic ones. Politicization thus has a distinct trade union dimension, reinforced by the unions' connection with the political parties, but not entirely dependent on it. Such continuities with the pre-Fascist period deserve further exploration.

Women and Class Unionism

The unions were more open to women and women's issues in this period than before. Two general aspects of class unionism as practiced by the mainstream trade union movement—that is, the CGIL (socialist and communist component)—are especially relevant to the relationship between unions and women.[20] The first is the unions' concern for progressive legislation and interest in including social issues—not only economic ones—in collective bargaining. The second is their concern for the weaker components of the labor force, which have often had priority within official bargaining and organizing policies. Both aspects suggest a potential for a progressive policy toward women, whose problems as workers, are heavily influenced by social and cultural conditions outside the workplace and who are typically a weak part of the workforce.

Progressive union policies were supported, and to some extent maintained, by organizations specifically concerned with union women. A national "women's commission" was established by the CGIL as early as 1945, and in the following years women's commissions were formed in all the big Chambers of Labor and in many unions. These were subsidiary organizations, without autonomous power within the unions, charged with the tasks of educating, coordinating, and mobilizing women unionists and putting proposals from women before the union leadership. Within these limits they had for years an important role in setting union policy on issues of protection and equality, the two themes of the unions' approach to social legislation.

As in other countries, during the fifties there was a gradual shift in emphasis toward equality, at least in the limited sense of equal pay for equal work.[21] Equality for women—their right to vote, to work, to equal treatment in the workplace—was a goal of all the left-wing parties and of the rebuilt CGIL.[22] The left, however, also emphasized the "essential functions of the family" as women's privileged arena and likewise the need for Communist and Socialist women to work together with Catholic women's groups to modernize the family and improve women's conditions. This background helps to explain the "compromise" that the left and the conservative Catholic forces reached on Article 37 of the constitution, which sanctions equality between men and women in regard to the right to work and wages but also states that the conditions of work for women should not endanger their "essential family and maternal roles." The article's ambiguity reflects the divergence of views between the two political forces and is the basis for continuing debates on the interpretation of the law, which in fact remains largely unimplemented.

Because of the weakness and ambiguity of the law, for example, for years the courts permitted differences in wages for men and women doing the same jobs, since they interpreted "equal work" as "equal performance." Thus, even the basic goal of equal pay had to be picked up years later in collective bargaining. The assertion of women's right to work effected some changes in the formal structure of discrimination in a few of the higher professions, particularly those from which Fascists had barred women, although it was not until 1963 that the law opened to women the higher positions in public administration. Women's right to work was likewise supported by the maternity law of 1950, which made it illegal to fire women who were pregnant or had a child less than a year old, and by the 1963 law that made it illegal to fire women for one year after they were married, a common practice until the 1960s and one sanctioned by labor contracts. Many other mechanisms of discrimination were not tackled until the late seventies, when the problem of equality was raised again with the passage of an equal opportunity law.

More than equality, however, protection for working women was the priority in the unions' social policies after the end of the war. In 1946, before the first collective agreements for the main industrial categories were signed, an overall national agreement between the CGIL and the top employers' federation on the protection of pregnant workers provided for a period of compulsory leave, three months before and six weeks after child-birth, with benefits set at two-thirds of the worker's wage. One year later the level of benefits was brought up to 70 percent of wages for clothing and textile workers.

The CGIL proposed a law for the protection of working mothers that was adopted by the women members of parliament from the left-wing parties, led by the Communist Teresa Noce, national secretary of the clothing and textile workers' union. The proposal called "progetto Noce," was supported by a two-year mass campaign in which the textile union and Communist women were particularly active.[23] The law that was eventually passed in 1950, though different from the one originally proposed, was judged at the time to be one of the best laws for the protection of maternity in capitalist countries.[24] It provided for compulsory leave from work for three months before childbirth and eight weeks afterward and for breaks for breastfeeding during working hours for the first year of the child's life in special nurseries to be set up by the employers. It also increased the benefits during the period of maternity leave to 80 percent of the wage and made it illegal to fire women during pregnancy and for a year after childbirth.

After the passage of the maternity law the unions' goal for women became the achievement of equal pay through collective bargaining. Equal pay was a main theme of the first national conference for working women, held in 1954 after long preparation and a remarkable mobilization.[25] Partly as a result, the Italian government was an early ratifier of the International Labour Organisation's convention on equal pay, but the actual impact of the ratification was nil, since it did not include an implementation statute.

Attempts to deal with the problem of unequal pay continued through the fifties, with many local and national meetings and conferences and repeated efforts to include the issue in collective bargaining. Unions produced documentary evidence on wage discrimination in the workplace and denounced the harsh conditions of women workers. All these initiatives were slow to bear fruit, partly because the unions were weak in these years, and it was not until 1961 that the unions achieved a national agreement on equal pay.

Other collective bargaining agreements, however, were important for women as a weak group in the workforce. After World War II and until the early sixties class unionism in Italy meant that unions considered the interests of such underprivileged groups as the unemployed and those working in small shops and in the underdeveloped areas of the country. Collective bargaining was supposed to benefit all the workers of a given category, not just union members. In fact priority in collective bargaining demands until the late fifties was given to such issues as employment and minimum wages. The bargaining strength of the unions based in the large factories of the North was used to enhance the interests of wider strata of workers and the power of the trade union movement as a political actor.

Internal and external forces eventually caused a departure from universalistic class unionism in the late fifties and early sixties. Before we consider these forces, however, let us examine the policies the unions deployed and their effects on the condition of women. Little research has been done in this area, but the following section tentatively considers the consistencies and inconsistencies of class unionism with respect to women and evaluates the impact of the unions' policies.

Ideology Put To the Test: Collective Bargaining after World War II

I shall compare the unions' practices with their ideology in two areas: women's employment and wages. In the first area the policy was relatively clear. A series of agreements between the CGIL and Confindustria, the association of employers, which tried to reconcile two contradictory objectives: to allow firms that had been involved in production for the war effort to lay off some of their excess workers and to find jobs for veterans, especially ex-prisoners and ex-partisans, returning to civilian life. In the end, women paid the price for these agreements. Italian unionism has never acknowledged the principle of seniority, and the agreements allowed layoffs among workers who had entered the factories after the outbreak of the war or "who had in their families other wage earners." In both cases it was women in particular who suffered. In many firms even the workers' own plant-level organizations called for the dismissal of women workers, although in others workers fought successfully to maintain job levels.

Union policy on pay differentials was more complicated. Although the unions did not actively pursue the goal of equal pay, they aggressively defended the lowest-paid workers, winning for them between 1945 and 1947 greater raises proportionately than the better-paid workers received and thus narrowing considerably wage differentials by sex. This advance did not challenge the assignment of women to separate classes from male workers or their exclusion from the highest wage levels.[26] Nevertheless, wage differentials between male and female workers with the same level of skill were reduced in this period from 50 to 30 percent for adult women.

Cost-of-living bonuses, introduced in 1945, were another matter. The bonuses were tied to fluctuations in the price index and were intended to defend workers' buying power, heavily depressed during the war years. These raises were not calculated as a fixed proportion of wages but were given at a flat rate; women workers over twenty received 13 percent less than male workers of the same age.[27]

Discrimination in basic wage rates was generally accepted, but discrimination in the cost-of-living bonuses provoked strong protests. In Turin women went on strike, with the support of the leadership of the UDI and against the wishes of the unions' leadership, and succeeded in gaining equal cost-of-living raises. The struggle spread to Milan and forced the national leadership of the CGIL to intervene—to restore the differential. Two years later the general secretary of the textile workers' union, Teresa Noce, again raised the issue of parity during a bargaining session. The employers resisted strongly, and when the matter came to a head, the general secretary of the CGIL, a Communist, decided to accept the status quo.

Inflation remained high between 1945 and 1947, and increases in wages came largely from the bonuses tied to the cost-of-living index. Since the bonus differential was less than that prevailing in basic wage rates, the general wage differential was therefore reduced. In 1938 a skilled adult woman worker in the engineering industry earned 54 percent of what a comparably skilled male earned; at the beginning of 1946, 77 percent; in June 1947, 80 percent. Although the average differentials were larger because female workers tended to be younger than the male working population, the general rise since the Fascist period was considerable.

This narrowing of sex differentials was more the result of egalitarian policies based on class solidarity than of policies designed to increase women's wages. Later efforts to achieve equal pay for women brought male and female wages still closer together. The national agreement on equal pay for manual workers in industry, which was signed in 1960 after years of campaigning and negotiation, abolished the separate scale of skill levels for women and gave them significant pay raises. In 1962 an agreement on equal pay for nonmanual employees was signed, and the following year a similar agreement covered nonindustrial sectors. On average, differentials between men and women covered by wage contracts were reduced by 12 to 15 percent in the early sixties.

The 1960 equal pay agreement was considered a landmark in union policy, and, indeed, formally it was. In practice, however, the principle of equality was blunted by the operation of a number of other factors. To begin with, the unions also adopted a policy of seeking higher pay raises for semiskilled workers, who were overwhelmingly male. The intent was not to slight women, but that was the effect. Second, market factors limited the impact of union policies on equal pay; for instance, some bonuses and raises over and above the contractual rates were given by employers only to men.

Thus, although the average contractual wage for a woman in the clothing industry was in 1966 only 9 percent less than that of a male worker, the difference in earnings was more than 22 percent.

Working-class Militancy and Trade Union Renewal

At the end of the 1960s and in the early 1970s, a wave of working-class struggles changed the structure of Italian trade unionism and had a profound impact on Italian society and politics. The strike rate was the highest among the Western countries (if one excludes the isolated peak of the French May), and so was the increase in unionization: 60 percent between 1968 and 1978, bringing the overall rate up to 46 percent. This wave of militancy was the result of both changes in the composition of the Italian labor force and such wider social and political trends as the student movement. Trade unions were ready to play a leading role within the new wave, even at the expense of undergoing a radical renewal.

The changes in the Italian working class had begun during the fifties with the massive migration from the South to the North, from the economically backward areas of the country to the more industrialized ones,[28] of a new generation of young, unskilled workers. Although new to both industry and the unions, they were seeking representation. They were the new collective actor in the cycle of strikes in Italian industry. The unions, which had previously organized mainly the skilled sectors of the working class, were weak and did not have much to lose. They too were looking for representation and for new power, wherever it might appear.

When the wave of strikes began, the unions therefore tried to assume the leadership. The price was a radical change in their organizational structure and policies. The workers were internal immigrants, in contrast to the guest workers of other European countries, and thus difficult to ignore. Through their numbers, they markedly influenced union policies. Changes in trade union policy included a new emphasis on equality (a solidaristic wage policy, with flat-rate wage increases, and a reduction in the range of the skill categories were both introduced in 1969) and on the hierarchical organization of work, the division of tasks on the shop floor, and problems of health and safety. Basic changes in trade union structure were also instituted. A new emphasis was put on union democracy: the workplace meetings were given formal power, and a new workplace structure—the shop stewards' council—became the basic unit of trade union organization. The influence of the students' movement was evident in both the form and the content of the unions' political action: against authority and the division of labor; for equality; for direct action and participatory democracy. The influence was not only cultural; interactions between workers and students (and, later, the New Left) took place at the factory gates, in the streets, in meetings, and in various organizations. As we will see below, however, women were marginal to this process of renewal.

By the mid-1970s the extraordinary workers' mobilization was over. The unions had become strong. The traditional characteristics of Italian unionism—centralization, politicization, weakness—had changed: the unions had achieved a high degree of control over the workforce; they were strong at the workplace level vis-à-vis the employer and at the national level vis-à-vis the state. The institutionalization of this new strength set off a different mechanism, producing a renewed centralization in place of participatory democracy and more influence for the political parties in place of union autonomy. At the rank-and-file level, the commitment to unity and equality were gone, and the fragmentation of old and new interests and demands pushed the unions more and more into the role of mediators. A policy of compromise at the factory level developed at the same time that the "historical compromise" of the Communist party more and more influenced trade union politics at the national level.[29]

Yet the mobilization had some lasting effects. First, the power and privileges of the older, skilled workers had been shaken, and women, as a new and weak component of the workforce, did not have to face a powerful structure of interests based on craft and seniority in the unions. Second, an extensive network of activists had been created during the years of extraordinary collective enthusiasm. Radical trade union politics had become a crucial part of their lives. Within this group of activists, trade union feminism would develop.

THE FEMINIST MOBILIZATION
INSIDE THE UNIONS

Women were involved in this process of mobilization and yet were marginal to it. The few quantitative data available on women's participation in unions in Italy illustrate this pattern of participation and exclusion.[30]

Most sources agree on two basic facts: First, women's membership in unions is roughly proportional to their participation in the workforce, though there are variations in some sectors. CGIL research shows that women made up 29.3 percent of its membership in 1977, when they were 30.2 percent of the workforce. Comparable figures can be obtained from the data bank of the Federazione Lavoratori Metalmeccanic (the Federation of Metal Workers and Machinists—FLM) for 1980, which gives a regional unionization rate of 56 percent for women in the three main confederations. This is only slightly less than the male unionization rate of 62 percent.

Second, despite this high unionization rate, representation in union hierarchies goes down as one goes up the bureaucratic ladder. The number of
women delegates as a percentage of the female workforce is 1.9 percent
according to the FLM data bank, whereas the figure for men is 3.2 percent,
and similar data can be derived from CGIL research. And if one excludes
the unions' technical and secretarial personnel (overwhelmingly female),
women almost disappear: they are 6 percent of full-time officials in the
CGIL and 1 percent of the national leadership of all unions.[31]

The present state of research on women in trade unions makes some
data difficult to interpret. Among unpaid officials, and even among full-time
paid ones, women tend to be younger than men: recent recruitment probably played a role in this, but one should also take into account the tendency
of women in the older age cohorts to drop out of the workforce. Women
officials are also, on average, more highly educated than male ones.

The recruitment of women in the seventies was exceptional; it probably
more than equaled the recruitment of men. We do not know how much this
influx altered the previous sex composition of the unionized workforce or
the union leadership, but it was in absolute terms remarkable. Compared
with that of other industrial countries, the rate of female unionization in
Italy is high, and the "cooling off" through which women are discouraged
from seeking leadership roles operates on top of a high level of rank-and-file
participation.

Women were an important component of the unskilled workforce that
formed the backbone of the new movement, and they also made up a large
proportion of the office workers in industry who in these years organized
and struck for the first time. They were visible in strikes and demonstrations
and mass assemblies, but they rarely had leadership positions or took the
floor in meetings. As long as the wave of collective enthusiasm lasted and the
new trade union identity was being built, women's marginality was not even
perceived. It was only in the mid-seventies that this situation changed.

Around 1975 the first "collectives" of women trade unionists were
formed. The original initiatives were taken at the local level: in Milan and
Turin first, then in Genoa, Padua, and Rome, groups of trade union women
organized to discuss their problems in the big factories or the union headquarters. Who were these women? Who took the initiative? What were the
problems they discussed? What kind of action did they take?

The "New Feminism" and the Unions

The initiative to form working women's collectives was usually taken by
women who belonged to or had been influenced by the New Left or the "new
feminism," or both. Often they were union officers or rank-and-file mili-

tants; sometimes they were students or young teachers "external" to the labor movement. In either case, aligning themselves with working women was their way to combine a socialist with a feminist orientation.[32]

The new feminism developed in the first half of the seventies, when the first wave of middle-class feminism began to influence the second wave of working-class feminism, both indirectly, through the movement's high visibility, and directly, through feminist militants who brought the message into trade union circles. A parallel with the student movement can be discovered in the formation of the two waves of feminism. The hard core of the feminist movement of the early seventies was made up of students who had participated in the 1968 movement. The larger themes of 1968 were to become central to the feminist movement as well: critiques of the division of labor and authority in society and the family and of the "cultural production" of society.[33] These themes were in fact soon abandoned by the emerging New Left; when the students' mobilization of 1968 gave way to the workers' struggles of 1969, the student militants shifted their interest to the factories. In the face of an exceptionally militant working class, the students singled out and exalted classical "Marxist-Leninist" theories of strategy and organization from among the movement's broad array of critical ideas. Several organizations grew out of this process, differing in the details of their ideologies but similar in their organizational structure, in the style of their militancy, and in the marginal position offered to women. Women realized their marginality only when a creeping crisis developed in these small organizations, which combined extremely high levels of participation and total sacrifice of personal life with short-term revolutionary expectations. Even before the official failure of the New Left project in the political elections of 1976, collective critiques had begun to appear in 1973 and 1974, accompanied by individual withdrawals. Feminism was the most important of the critiques, combining a stress on radical ideological and organizational innovation with a return to some of the original ideas of 1968.

The first collectives developed in the areas of greatest working-class militancy—the industrial unions, especially the engineering unions—not the traditionally female sectors of the economy, such as clothing and textiles, where unions were not particularly militant, or in the areas where women were newly employed, such as services, which were marginal to the struggles of the early seventies.

Groups of women began to meet in some of the large plants in the North and in several of the big cities. The women involved had participated intensively in union work and in the political struggles of the preceding years, and their discussions were in the beginning often addressed precisely to this experience: what did it mean to be women and at the same time union militants?

Much of the language and many of the techniques used by these groups were borrowed from the new feminism, and the style of discussion was similar to that of consciousness-raising sessions. The basic rule was separatism—a real break with the tradition of working-class organizations. The discussion would usually start with the personal problems of the participants and then go on to deal with the recent failures or present shortcomings of political movements. The small group developed an analysis of the daily lives of the participants, focusing particularly on the frustrations encountered in the search for a new identity through collective political experience. Trade unions were criticized in terms of their own explicit values. For example, the unions had through the years of militancy and organizational upheaval emphasized equality, but hierarchy and an unequal division of labor were the reality women faced as union activists. Feminism provided the instrument for analyzing personal power relations in the daily life of work and politics, disguised as they were by ideology, and demonstrating the reproduction of patriarchy in the unions and the workplace.

The prevalent style of union militancy was "masculine"—a model with which women could identify only at great cost. In their collective discussions the women expressed the uneasiness and weariness that they had hidden for years as they tried to imitate this male model in order to escape their marginal role—to "count." Their practical, affective orientation found no place except at the margins of union activities. If women did not want to deny "their emotional side, their orientation towards satisfying needs, their desire for tenderness," they could "keep others company; cheer them up or soothe their spirits; chant slogans at the head of a march, pass out leaflets, or smile at passersby to gather support; arrange the chairs and keep the papers in order; or generally supply social services."[34] If they wanted to count, they had to deny their deep inclinations. Marginal but integrated, or "mutilated" in order to count. "There are very few possibilities of extracting a viable individual life out of these crushing alternatives. A few can manage, and they are extraordinary women, who maintain a fragile and wearying equilibrium with great intensity and an uncommon humanity." The internal conflict of the women militants—which they called *lazerazione*, or "laceration"—was at the center of impassioned debates: union politics could not be changed if women ignored this conflict or put it aside. How could one build mass participation on a "laceration"?

According to the militants' analysis, the difference between men and women should not be denied but, on the contrary, recognized and built upon. Picking up on the message of the new feminism, they saw women not only as victims of discrimination, but also the embodiment of an alternative approach to life and politics. Consequently, they concluded that women should not demand a bigger share of the pie; rather, they should develop their alternative approach. "Equality of opportunity" for women was dismissed as a goal; the solution, instead, was to change the rules of the game for both men and women. Although the protest against discrimination had been important in bringing these women's collectives into existence, now their answer to the problem of inequality within the labor movement was not more participation or more "opportunities," but a new collective experience in which the goal of change in personal relationships would not be deferred and means as well as ends would be emphasized. The result of this analysis was that women confronted the unions with a request for autonomy.

The Success of Feminist Unionism

In the confrontation between feminists and the unions in the late seventies, the women won their basic demand for an autonomous network of women inside the unions. Only self-analysis and the experience of an autonomous, decentralized, nonbureaucratic structure, they insisted, would allow the growth of a movement of working women capable of bringing about real change.

Initially, the demand met considerable resistance. Union leaders, especially Communists, considered separatism a threat to working-class unity and feared that the loose and informal character of the women's organization would make central control of class unity difficult. The new movement's ideas were equally disturbing; the radical critique of gender roles challenged—in different ways—both the Catholic and the Communist unions. The Communists had always intended gradually to "modernize" the family, but never to question it. They were cautious in raising sexual and family issues, so as not to upset their delicate relationship with the Catholic world, and suspicious of radical feminism, which they thought of, correctly, as connected with the New Left.

Between 1975 and 1978 the network of women's collectives spread rapidly. Coordinating committees were formed at the local and national levels, starting in 1977 with a national coordinating committee of women shop stewards in the engineering union. The rise and growth of the movement became generally visible in that year when women workers by the thousands marched in separate sections of national union demonstrations. The left wing of the unions directly supported the growth and legitimation of the women's groups.[35] By the end of 1978, the new role of women in the unions was recognized, and the unions opened a debate—still going on—on the precise forms the autonomous women's structures should take. Feminist ideas—the critique of the family and gender roles, the emphasis on sexuality and emotion—were officially accepted into trade unions discourse. A few years earlier this would have been unthinkable. The recognition of women moved from the area of innovative union militancy to that of organization. In the most recent stage of this process, the CGIL in 1981 decided to convene a national conference of women shop stewards and union representatives, the first CGIL women's conference since the equal pay agreement was signed and the women's commissions in the unions were dissolved twenty years earlier. Addressing the over two thousand enthusiastic participants, the Communist head of the CGIL and general secretary of the federation of Italian unions, Luciano Lama, acknowledged the importance of sexual politics above and beyond the struggle for equality and against economic exploitation.

The network now includes small firms and small cities and to some extent the South, but its spread has followed the pattern of militant unionism. Participants continue to be mainly rank-and-file activists, white-collar employees rather than manual workers, young union officials, and politicized intellectuals and housewives outside the unions. The presence of "outsiders," important in the initial phase, later became still more important, thanks in particular to the unions' educational program under the "150 hours" agreement, an adult education program that developed roughly parallel with feminist unionism and considerably influenced it.

The program, a typical product of the new unionism of the early seventies, was the fruit of a 1972 collective bargaining agreement that allowed workers to use up to 150 hours of their paid working time to participate in courses in the public education system. Up to 2 percent of the workforce in a productive unit could leave the job in order to take courses. The courses were not intended to benefit the workers individually—the hours could not be used, for instance, for vocational training—but to encourage the development of a new collective consciousness. There was massive participation in this educational experience. The teachers were, at least in the cities of the North, largely drawn from among the militant students of the late sixties, and the program was at first a national experiment in political education.[36] Official estimates suggest that in Milan over fifty thousand workers took courses between 1972 and 1982.

The released-time courses had a special importance for women. In the mid-seventies courses for women only treated various aspects of women's condition: the history and sociology of the family, health and sexuality, work, and politics. They were taught by women (often by feminists) and attended by housewives and students as well as union members. The courses were based largely on self-analysis, although they included contributions by experts, and the general approach was exactly the opposite of the "training for leadership" that dominates trade union women's education in other advanced capitalist countries.[37] These courses were not designed to make it easier for women to enter the male world by giving them the general knowledge, the technical expertise, and the assertiveness they lacked;

rather, they were meant to strengthen women through knowledge of and pride in their difference.[38] The first five years of the 150-hours program roughly coincides with the development of feminism in the unions. The courses often led to the formation of women's groups and so helped support the network of trade union feminism.

Initially the new feminism in the unions focused less on pursuing specific external goals than on winning recognition and building a new collective identity. Along with the 150-hours courses, public agitation for abortion rights and other issues and the consciousness-raising activities of the women's collectives were significant as both means and context, producing a remarkable and successful cultural growth. A number of factors help account for the success of the movement. The trade unions, particularly their left wing, were open to influences from outside the labor movement, and many working women and union activists were exposed to the ideas of the New Left and the feminist movement. Later, when the cycle of working-class militancy and trade union renewal was over and the process of bureaucratization and detachment of the leaders from the rank and file had begun, feminism provided women militants with a theoretical basis for collective reaction.

Problems of Feminist Unionism

Women had won the right to tackle their own problems with their own tactics, outside the normal channels of union activity. This victory had, however, another side to it: namely, the normal processes of union decision making remained intact. At the end of the seventies, women had no more influence than before on union politics or policies, even those pertaining specifically to women. The greater cultural sensitivity of the unions toward women's concerns did not reflect a change in practice. Women had gained a space for themselves within the unions, but they remained confined within that space. The larger goal—rising from a recognition of women's difference—of producing changes in union politics and society at large remained blocked.

The basic dilemma of feminist strategy is whether to give priority to equality or to demands based on the differences between the sexes. Consider two issues that have divided the movement in Italy: work schedules and nontraditional jobs.

The question of part-time work has been particularly divisive.[39] Feminists and the union left generally agree on the desirability of reducing working hours of both women and men, but not on the desirability of allowing part-time contracts. The more "emancipatory" or "equality-minded" component of the feminist movement opposes part-time work, since it tends to confirm women's inferiority and ghettoization; the more "difference-minded" component favors part-time work, on the grounds that it allows women to satisfy their needs for both income and time with children. The controversy has produced a change in the usual pattern of alliances between feminists and trade union leaders: the left-wing leaders, who have in the past defended the "heretical" experiments of the feminists, oppose part-time work as a concession to the employers, while the moderate leaders support it as part of a more flexible trade union policy. (This position is also consistent with a conservative view of women's role in society.) The debate has become confusing, and the movement seems to be stuck. In 1979 some important women's coordinating committees came out against part-time work, reflecting their general left-wing allegiance. Later, both feminists and union leaders changed their positions as a result of the economic crisis. Provisions for part-time contracts have actually been introduced in the main national collective agreements, under certain conditions: the choice of part-time work must be voluntary and revocable; part-time jobs must provide all the rights and benefits of full-time contracts; and such work must not be reserved exclusively for women. There have also been attempts to regulate part-time contracts by law. But these developments have been neither controlled nor directly influenced by the debates and the efforts of the trade union feminists.

A similar difficulty has emerged with regard to the problems of women in nontraditional jobs. At the end of 1977, an equal opportunity law was passed in compliance with the recommendations of the European Economic Community and without lobbying by the left-wing parties, the unions, or the women's movement.[40] The law opened to women jobs that had been segregated on gender lines; it canceled many of the protective regulations governing women's work, and it made discrimination against women in hiring illegal. Because the law delegated some aspects of its implementation to collective bargaining, the unions and the feminists in the unions were forced to take a stand on it. The unions were favorable in principle to hiring women for nontraditional jobs, but were not ready to spend much energy to implement the law, which would have required them to establish and support lines of action against discrimination that the law did not explicitly provide. The feminists, for their part, were divided on the prospect of an "equality" that was full of disadvantages. Because the law tackles discrimination only in the hiring process and does not provide for new professional training for women or for mechanisms to reform career patterns, "equality" meant in most cases only access to low-level jobs. Left-wing union ideology suggests that women should enter the nontraditional jobs, including the heavy and dangerous ones, and thus bring about changes in the workplace that will be useful to men and women; this they describe as using women's unique abilities on behalf of general change. But this view is overly optimistic: the chances of changing the workplace in the short run are small, and in most cases women must take the job as it is or leave it. Hence, working women face a basic dilemma: does equality come first, even when it means additional burdens for women? Why should women struggle to get into heavy, dirty, and risky jobs? Why should they push to work night shifts, which ideally should be abolished for men too? Is this the best way to use women's "unique abilities," or should women try to preserve their protected status? As a result of these uncertainties, the feminist impact on union policy toward the equal opportunity law has been modest and limited to a few individual cases.

The conflict between women's special needs and equality partly explains the impasse the movement now faces. Other conflicts concern the means of political action and the movement's structure. The women of the movement chose to organize themselves separately and in a different way: to reject the division of labor, hierarchy and delegation, negotiation and compromise that characterize normal union politics. They chose likewise not to seek more power under the existing power relationships, but rather to develop a movement in which women could put into practice new forms of social relations. A "movement style" organization obviously runs many risks: for example, ineffectiveness due to the failure to bring its influence to bear at opportune moments through the right channels[41] and declining participation due to the difficulty of maintaining a balance between the personal and the political. There are likewise the problems of representing large groups without formal mechanisms of representation, and hence the risk of a growing gap between the movement and those it represents. Italian trade union feminism experienced this whole array of problems.

By 1980 the movement had started to decline, and the previous mixture of collective and conflictual action and the development in small groups of an alternative style of interpersonal relationships had disappeared. Some of the women who had discovered through the movement their needs and the legitimacy of such needs in the face of self-sacrifice, instrumentalism, mediation, and goal deferment required by trade union organization left the public arena altogether.[42] They often moved to a radical redefinition of their lives through divorce, different work, or different social relations.[43] At the opposite pole from this retreat, however, new initiatives for equality and power for women are emerging. Trade union activists who are pursuing these initiatives are not "speaking for themselves" on the basis of their own needs, as their predecessors did. Instead, they tend to address a wider constituency of working women, and hence the problems of representation and effectiveness—in both the trade union and the workplace—are crucial.

CHALLENGES FOR THE EIGHTIES

In conclusion, two aspects of the structural changes in the relationships between women and work deserve special mention. First, the increased participation of women in the labor market does not imply a decline in the sexual segregation of the workforce.[44] Politics and legislation have not contributed much to counteract the market forces maintaining sexual segregation. The Italian women's movement was not strongly or single-mindedly oriented toward equal opportunity, and although the equal opportunity law of 1977 opened to women some previously segregated jobs, it lacked clear rules for implementation, monitoring, and enforcement.

Second, the social basis of the unions is changing very fast. A new population of women workers, with new demands for representation, confronts the unions in the 1980s. They are different from the working women of the mid-seventies, when union feminism developed. They often work in nonindustrial, nonmanual jobs or nontraditional industrial jobs. They are more likely to be mothers with young children, and they are usually better educated. They are different culturally: their political socialization was not shaped by direct contact with the big post-1969 wave of union militancy, and their female identity was not defined through direct contact with the new feminism as a political movement, although they have been indirectly influenced by the movement's fallout, its social diffusion, and its reinterpretation through the media.

Feminists in the unions face a difficult challenge in the 1980s, as they confront these structural and institutional changes as well as a bad economic climate. There is, first, the danger that the collective identity that was formed through the movement in the late seventies could become a mere subculture. If it is to be the basis for further political action, some fundamental readjustments to the new population of working women will be necessary; union feminists cannot just speak for themselves, as they did in the first years of the movement. The difficulties involved in defining goals and choosing means bulk large in the face of the new, wider constituency.

On the other hand, this new constituency offers opportunities to the trade unions and feminism. Although working women in the eighties have advanced some way on the road to emancipation, a large, diffuse demand for equality and promotion remains untapped and still seeks representation. The economic crisis has deepened this demand, since the defense of women's jobs and general prospects at work has become a major test of equal treatment. And aside from the demand for equality, there are remnants of the discontents and impulses for change that the movement expressed in its early years, sentiments that likewise remain to be tapped.

Given the pool of unmet, unrepresented demands, radical innovation through trade union feminism remains a live possibility. Between the retreat of trade union feminism into a marginal subculture and the simple economic defense of women's sectional interests, there is still room to maneuver. What happens to this possibility will depend considerably on the receptivity of the unions themselves. Unions everywhere face serious challenges that the economic crisis only exacerbates. The shrinking of the traditional industrial base for unionism, the end of "affluence," changes in the composition of the labor force, all affect the future of industrial unionism. The trade union (and academic) response to these problems, in Italy as elsewhere, has focused on "mastering the crisis," generally on the terrain of relations between unions and the state. Possibilities for mobilization and the representation of interests outside the economic sphere have not received the same attention.[45]

In the face of similar difficulties, the unions of some countries have poor prospects of altering their organizational policies or their priorities in collective bargaining. The Italian case, however, seems rather hopeful when compared with such relatively consolidated and rigid systems as that of the United States. Italian trade unionism has maintained its tradition of political openness—a tradition that may well aid its adjustment to changing conditions and changing needs. Partly because of its late development, the Italian trade union movement, may now be in a more favorable position to work out modern union policies, including ways to respond to new demands from women. The story of feminism and the Italian unions is not at all closed.

GLOSSARY

CGIL	Confederazione Generale Italiana del Lavoro: General Confederation of Italian Labor
CISL	Confederazione Italiana Sindicati Lavoratori: Confederation of Italian Trade Unions
FLM	Federazione Lavoratori Metalmeccanic: Federation of Metal Workers and Machinists
UDI	Unione Donne Italiane: Union of Italian Women
UIL	Unione Italiane Lavoratori: Union of Italian Workers

NOTES

1. These trends are evident in the official statistics, which document only the primary labor market. If one adds the secondary labor market, the picture of women's participation changes considerably. It is impossible to measure the extent of the secondary market, but Italian historians and economists have long appreciated its significance and have judged it considerably more important in Italy than in other industrial societies.

2. The almost total absence of studies in the field of working women's history is in itself an interesting phenomenon, which is paralleled in the sociology and history of the post–World War II labor movement. Besides showing the specific lack of sensitivity to these problems on the part of Italian scholars, it reflects the general underdevelopment of social history and of women's studies in Italy.

3. The Chambers of Labor were modeled on the French Bourses du Travail, which Italian socialists (in particular, Gnocchi Viani of Milan) had encountered on the occasion of the "Universal Exposition" in Paris in 1889.

4. In the debate over the Chambers' role that developed in socialist circles in Italy at this time, their social and political functions were underlined, as was their "autonomy" from the Socialist party: the Chambers were to develop a "proletarian policy," as distinct from a "socialist policy." "Bebbono le Camere del Lavoro diventare socialiste?" ["Should the Chambers of Labor Call Themselves Socialist?], *Critica Sociale*, 1 December 1901.

5. The statute of the Chamber of Labor of Milan in 1891 affirmed women's right to work and the principle of equal pay for equal work.

6. Such campaigns included the 1900 struggle in Milan for school lunches and citywide general strikes.

7. In Milan women were admitted to the ranks of compositors, apparently the only women in Europe who were. In the frequent periods of economic crisis and high unemployment, the union encouraged the entry of women into apprenticeships precisely because they could not reach the higher positions and hence did not threaten the trade hierarchy; in boom periods female employment fell.

8. The intense anticlericalism of hardcore male union members did not help in organizing this young and precarious female workforce, and this was one of the few areas in which Catholic influence and organization developed among the workers. There were even attempts to develop some all-female organizations outside the trade union structure, a rare phenomenon in Italy.

9. Union policy in at least one area widened the gap between base and union. In 1904 the national union changed the union dues from a percentage of the wage to a fixed amount, discouraging the membership of unskilled labor.

10. Women's unionization was somewhat higher in the agricultural sector than the national average. In some areas with strong *braccianti* (branch) organizations, such as Emilia, women accounted for one-third of the union membership, close to the level of their presence in the workforce.

11. This was the case, for instance, with the struggles in the Biella area: in 1889 the strike of mill girls working as machine-weavers was led by the older craft workers' league, which was made up of skilled hand-loom weavers. A similar situation developed in the 1904 strikes in Biella, the first important test for the new industrial federation.

12. Giuliano Procacci, *La lotta di classe in Italia agli inizi del secolo ventesimo* (Rome: Editori Riuniti, 1970), p. 42.

13. She had received a university education and was the wife of a well-known novelist of the time.

14. See Roberto Michels, *Il proletariato e la borghesia nel movimento socialista italiano* (Turin: Bocca, 1908). Michels notes that class distinctions had traditionally been less marked in Italy than in other societies, as evidenced by the low degree of segregation in public places and leisure associations.

15. The phenomenon probably has to do both with the openness and the needs of the labor movement and with the "supply" of these potential organizers. For an analysis of the development of Italian higher education and of intellectual unemployment over the last century, see Marzio Barbagli, *Disoccupazione intellettuale e sistema scolastico in Italia (1859–1973)* (Bologna: Il Mulino, 1974).

16. The law applied only to industrial workshops over a certain size; it did not provide any wage for maternity leave; and it countenanced all sorts of exceptions. For a detailed analysis of the law and the evolution of Italian legislation on women's work over the last century, see M. V. Ballestrero, *Dalla tutela alla parità* (Bologna: Il Mulino, 1979).

17. Anna Kuliscioff was a principal supporter of the campaign for protective legislation; she did not believe that the law would operate to expel women from the labor force, and she was well aware of the inhuman exploitation and working conditions to which women were subjected. Party and union organizers doubtless had an interest in defending women workers, but other interests and ideologies deeply rooted in the labor movement were definitely not in favor of women's emancipation. Male workers sometimes openly expressed the wish to reduce competition from female labor, and diffused in many areas of the socialist movement, and fed by a positivist ideology, was an ideological strain maintaining women's biological inferiority and essentially reproductive role.

18. For a more detailed discussion of the complex relationship between the different characteristics of political unionism see B. Beccalli-Salvati, "The Rebirth of Italian Trade Unionism, 1942–54," in *The Rebirth of Italy*, S. J. Woolf (London: Longmans, 1972).

19. For a comparative discussion of class unions and association unions, see A. Pizzorno, *I soggetti del pluralismo* (Bologna: Il Mulino, 1980).

20. For the sake of brevity, I here oversimplify a complex historical picture and gloss over the Catholic component of the Italian labor movement, the CISL.

21. Alice Cook in her Introduction identifies the phases of unions' policies toward women: periods of total exclusion of women from the unions, followed by periods combining a moderate interest in both equality and protection. The latter periods benefited the male labor force as well as working women, since women's conditions of work—wages, hours, etc.—were no longer so poor as to endanger men's wages and standards of work. See Alice Cook "Women and Trade Unions," paper presented to the World Congress of Sociology, Uppsala, 1978.

22. Early in 1945, before the end of the war, the congress of the CGIL in the part of Italy liberated from the Germans voted in favor of women's suffrage and equal treatment for working women. The latter was better defined at the first National Congress of the CGIL in 1947, which passed the "Mozione delle lavoratrici italiane," a kind of charter for Italian working women, stating the principles of equal right to work for all men and women, equal pay, equal access to all occupations, and equal entitlement to pensions and other social benefits. Women's suffrage was granted in 1946.

23. The communist women were part of a women's mass organization, the Unione Donne Italiano (Union of Italian Women—UDI), which was formally independent of political parties and included women without party affiliation. The great majority of members were, however, members of the Communist party, and the party had a strong influence on the organization, approaching total control in certain periods. On the UDI's history, see G. Ascoli, "L'UDI tra emancipazione e liberazione (1943–1964)" in AAVV, *La questione femminile in Italia del 1900 ad oggi* (Milan: F. Angeli, 1977).

24. For an analysis of the law, see its background, its strengths and flaws and

the further improvements in it in the following years, see Ballestrero, *Dalla tutela alla parità*.

25. Official records note over 20,000 mass meetings held in the factories before the conference and over 1,000 delegates gathered in Rome for the conference itself.

26. Highly skilled workers in the textile industries were the only exception to this rule.

27. For women between eighteen and twenty, the difference was 22 percent; for those between sixteen and eighteen, 16 percent; only for those under sixteen were the cost-of-living raises equal for both sexes. The differences in both wage rates and cost-of-living raises varied from one region to another.

28. It is estimated that between 1951 and 1971 upwards of 5 million people left less developed agrarian areas for the industrial centers.

29. See P. Lange, G. Ross, and M. Vannicelli, *Unions, Change and Crisis: French and Italian Union Strategy and the Political Economy, 1945–1980* (London: Allen and Unwin, 1982).

30. National statistics on union membership with a breakdown by sex are still unavailable. Only in the last few years have attempts been made to gather the relevant information, and these are limited either to a single union confederation or to a single region. The research of E. Biagioni, S. Palmieri, and T. Pipan, *Indagine sul sindacata* (Rome: ESI, 1980), is the best source for the CGIL. The unpublished data bank of the Federazione Lavoratori Metalmeccanic (Federation of Metal Workers and Machinists—FLM) of Lombardy gives detailed data for that region for all three main confederations, but is limited to the engineering sector. Useful information can also be gathered from *Rassegna Sindacale*, no. 5 (1979), a special issue.

31. For the CGIL, see Biagioni, Palmieri, and Pipan, *Indagine sul Sindacato*, p. 277, table 4. Even this figure overstates the decisional power of women inside the CGIL, since full-time women officials tend to be more numerous in collegial bodies (6.5 percent) than in positions with executive authority (4.3 percent). See M. D'Amato, "Il lavoro della donna: movimento sindacale e partecipazione femminile," *Sociologia del Lavoro*, no. 3 (1978).

32. For a description of the combination of influences out of which Italian trade union feminism developed, the best source is a book by two participants: Flora Bocchio and Antonia Torchi, *L'acqua in gabbia* (Milan: La Salamandra, 1979). A review of the book and some excerpts from it were published in *Feminist Review* (Spring 1981).

33. On the influence of 1968 on feminism, see M. L. Boccia, "Per corsi del femminismo," *Critica Marxista*, no. 3 (1980).

34. The quotations in this paragraph come from Bocchio and Torchi, *L'acqua in gabbia*, p. 99 (my translation).

35. By "left wing" I refer generally to the industrial categories, especially the metal workers, where the left-wing CISL is particularly powerful and where the new militant unionism took root and often had the support of a majority of union members.

36. The picture in the early eighties is somewhat different. Participation in the courses has declined, and their character has changed as a result of the economic crisis and different union priorities.

37. See Barbara Wertheimer, ed., *Labor Education for Women Workers* (Philadelphia: Temple University Press, 1981), especially the chapter by Alice H. Cook and Robert Till-Retz, "Labor Education and Women Workers: An International Comparison."

38. See Laura Balbo, "Women's Access to Intellectual Work," *Signs* 6 (1981): 763–70, which underlines the value of these courses in helping women to develop intellectual and cultural activities.

39. See Intercategoriale Donne di Torino (Interunion Women's Committee of Turin), *La spina all' occhiello* (Turin: Musolino, 1979), and Bocchio and Torchi, *L'acqua in gabbia*.

40. The minister of Labor at the time was a Christian Democrat, not particularly favorable to the unions or women's work. There are curious parallels between the passage of this law and the passage in 1964 of Title VII of the Civil Rights Act in the United States. For an analysis of the background to the law and international comparisons, see T. Treu, *Lavoro femminile e uguaglianza* (Bari: DeDonato, 1977).

41. One such failure concerned the demand for forty hours of parental leave. This demand was one of the few put forward by union feminists that embodied their goal of promoting general change through attention to women's special needs. The women's coordinating committees asked that forty hours of paid leave from work be granted every year to parents, either mothers or fathers, to take care of children under ten. This would not only meet an immediate need of working women, but also (at least with paid leave) challenge the division of roles in the family. Nurturance, the feminists claimed, is a basic and fulfilling human experience of which men are deprived. In 1979 the demand was included in some important local and national union platforms, but in the first round of bargaining it was dropped everywhere. The representatives of the feminists were too weak to defend it against other priorities: weak in relation to their own social base, since the demand had been put forward more by activists than by the rank and file, and in relation to union leadership, to whom they appeared only as isolated individuals.

42. An extreme case, and a symbolic one, is that of Flora Bocchio. A trade union officer since the mid-sixties, and the central figure of trade union feminism in Milan, she left office, wrote a book, went to live in the countryside, and later became a filmmaker for Italian television.

43. Research on the life histories of working women who attended 150-hours courses shows that the courses—that is, the contact with trade union feminism—have been instrumental in triggering widespread and deep changes. See G. Chiaretti and M. Piazza, "Donne delle 150 ore," research report, Regione Lombardia (Assessorato alla Cultura) (Milano, 1982).

44. The continuing segregation is well documented in census data, which show clearly not only that women are underrepresented in the highest skill categories, but that the ratio between their participation at the highest levels of the hierarchy and their overall participation decreased between 1951 and 1971 as a result both of a decrease in this ratio in all sectors and the fact that the sectors in which the ratio was the highest have been decreasing in weight in Italian manufacturing industry. See G. Geroldi, "Il tasso di partecipazione femminile nelle industrie manifatturiere," mimeographed, 1983.

45. See V. Rieser, "Il sindacato di frone ai mutamenti nella composizione di classe," *Inchiesta*, no. 56 (1982), and P. Santi, "Il Piano del Lavoro nella politica della CGIL: 1949–1952," in *Il Piano del Lavoro della CGIL*, ed. F. Vianello (Milan: Feltrinelli, 1978).

BIBLIOGRAPHY

Ascoli, G. "L'UDI tra emancipazione e liberazione (1943–1964)." In AAVV, *La questione femminile in Italia del 1900 ad oggi*. Milan: F. Angeli, 1977.

Balbo, L., *Stato di famiglia*. Milan: Etas Libri, 1976.

———. "Women's Access to Intellectual Work." *Signs* 6 (1981): 763–70.

Ballestrero, M. V. *Dalla tutela alla parità: la legislazione italiana sul lavoro delle donne*. Bologna: Il Mulino, 1979.

Barbagli, M. *Disoccupazione intellettuale e sistema scolastico in Italia*, (1859–1973). Bologna: Il Mulino, 1974.

Beccalli, B. "Protesta giovanile e opposizione politica." *Quaderni Piacentini*, no. 64 (1977).

Beccalli-Salvati, B. "The Rebirth of Italian Trade Unionism, 1943–54." In *The Rebirth of Italy, 1943–59*, ed. S. J. Woolf. London: Longmans, 1972. (Revised and extended in Italian ed. Bari: Laterza, 1974.)

Bezza, E. "Contrattazione collettiva e Fiom durante la prima guerra mondiale." *Giornale di Diritto del Lavoro e di Relazione Industriali*, no. 15 (1982).

Biagioni, E., S. Palmieri, and T. Pipan. *Indagine sul sindacato*. Rome: E.S.I., 1980.

Bocchio, F., and A. Torchi. *L'acqua in gabbia: Voci di donne dentro il sindacato*. Milan: La Salamandra, 1979.

Boccia, M. L. "Percorsi del femminismo." *Critica Marxista*, no. 3 (1980).

Chiaretti G., and M. Piazza. "Donne della 150 ore." Research report, Regione Lombardia (Assessorato alla Cultura). Milan, 1982.

Cook, A. "Women and Trade Unions." Paper presented to the World Congress of Sociology, Uppsala, 1978.

D'Amato, M. "Il lavoro della donna: movimento sindacale e partecipazione femminile." *Sociologia del Lavoro*, no. 3 (1978).

Ergas, Y. "Femminismo e crisi di sistema: il percorso politico delle donne attraverso gli anni '70." *Rassegna Italiana di Sociologia*, no. 1 (1981).

Geroldi, G. "Il tasso di partecipazione femminile nelle industrie manifatturiere." Mimeographed, 1983.

Intercategoriale Donne di Torino (Interunion Women's Committee of Turin). *La spina all' occhiello*. Turin: Musolino, 1979.

Kul;scioff, A. *Proletariato femminile e partito socialista*. Milan: 1910.

Lange, P., G. Ross, and M. Vannicelli. *Unions, Change and Crisis: French and Italian Union Strategy and the Political Economy, 1945–1980*. London: Allen and Unwin, 1982.

Michels, R. *Il proletariato e la borghesia nel movimento socialista italiano*. Turin: Bocca, 1908.

————. *Storia critica del movimento socialista*. Florence: LaVoce, 1926.

Pierono Bortolotti, F. "Movimento femminista e movimento operaio: ap unti di storia." *Critica Marxista*, no. 5 (1978).

————. *Socialismo e questione femminile (1892–1922)*. Milan: Mazzotta, 1974.

Pizzorno, A. *I soggetti del pluralismo*. Bologna: Il Mulino, 1980.

Procacci, G. *La lotta di classe in Italia agli inizi del secolo ventesimo*. Rome: Editori Riuniti, 1970.

Regalia, I., M. Regini, and E. Reyneri. "Labour Conflicts and Industrial Relations in Italy." In *The Resurgence of Class Conflict in Europe since 1968*, ed. C. Crouch and A. Pizzorno. Vol. I. London: Macmillan, 1978.

Rieser, V. "Il sindacato di frone ai mutamenti nella composizione di classe." *Inchiesta*, no. 56 (1982).

Santi, P. "Sulla crisi del sindacato." *Quaderni Piacentini*, no. 4 (1982).

Treu, T. *Lavoro femminile e uguaglianza*. Bari: DeDonato, 1977.

Turati, F. "Bebbono le camere del lavoro diventare socialiste?" *Critica Sociale*, 1 December 1901.

Wertheimer, Barbara M. ed. *Labor Education for Women Workers*. Philadelphia: Temple University Press, 1981.

Zanuso, L. "La qualità della vita a Milano: un' indagine sulle famiglie milanesi— Prima analisi dei dati relativi alla condizione femminile." Research report, City of Milan. Milan, 1982.

9 JAPAN

Tadashi Hanami

In prewar Japan women's place was prescribed by their position in the traditional family system: the father or grandfather held the dominant position as head of family and the eldest brother occupied the second position, while all the women, including the mother, were subordinate. The Japanese social structure was based on this family system, with the emperor as head of the family-state. In general, women were second-class citizens without full legal and political rights, including the right to vote.

After the Second World War, the traditional system was challenged by the democratic values espoused by the Occupation and enthusiastically accepted by the Japanese people. The 1946 constitution reflected this change. It prohibited discrimination based on sex, race, creed, social status, or family origin and thus introduced equality between men and women as a basic legal principle.

This change in law had no great effect on social life. Indeed, the traditional male dominance in both family and society was not to be easily abolished. However, the new education system based on the democratic principles introduced by the Occupation contributed to a gradual change in attitudes toward women. The participation of women in social affairs and politics developed rapidly in this period. The women's groups that now emerged had their roots in the prewar suffragist associations and the organizations dedicated to the abolition of prostitution, but the introduction of universal suffrage in 1945 meant that Japanese feminists could turn their attention to other political programs beneficial to women. Their first victory was the abolition of legal prostitution in 1956. The Labor Ministry was reorganized so as to provide two divisions in the Women's and Minors' Bureau: a Women's Labor Branch to deal with the problems of women in the labor force, and a Women's Affairs Branch to deal with the question of women's general social status. Through these divisions the bureau developed a close working relationship with women's organizations, thus aiding women's causes not only in the field of labor but in society at large.

Women Workers

To a greater extent than in most industrial countries, women made up a substantial part of Japan's nonagricultural workforce in the prewar years. In 1875, 209,000 of a total of 588,000 nonagricultural workers were women; in 1905, 289,000 of 916,000; in 1920, 339,000 of 1,155,000. Thereafter their total labor force participation rate (LFPR) declined as men moved rapidly into the whole range of nonagricultural occupations, but by 1935, just before the Second World War, there were still 431,000 women (compared with 1,522,000 men) in the labor force outside agriculture.[1]

Table 9-1 shows that the LFPR of women (including agricultural employment) remained fairly constant at about 50 percent from 1925 to the early 1970s, when a gradual decline set in. However, in view of the relative stability of these rates through both prewar and postwar years, two factors should be considered. First, before the war well over 60 percent of women workers were in the agricultural sector; in the postwar period the agricultural labor force declined dramatically, so that today only slightly more than 10 percent of the total labor force is employed in agriculture. Second, the recent decline in the female LFPR reflects increased female participation in higher education and delayed entry into the labor force.

In the prewar period the agricultural sector comprised mainly independent and family workers who also served as a reserve army of labor for the

TABLE 9-1
Labor Force Participation Rates in Japan, by Sex,
in Percentages of the Population of Each Sex
(various years, 1920–1978)

Year	Total	Male	Female
1920	72.7	92.1	53.4
1930	69.8	90.5	49.0
1940	71.1	90.1	52.5
1950	65.5	83.2	49.3
1955	70.8	85.9	56.7
1960	69.2	84.8	54.5
1965	65.7	81.7	50.6
1970	65.4	81.8	49.9
1975	63.0	81.4	45.7
1976	63.0	81.2	45.8
1977	63.2	80.6	46.6
1978	63.4	80.5	47.4

Sources: 1920–1950—calculated from Bureau of Statistics, Prime Minister's Office, *Population of Japan* (Tokyo: Bureau of Statistics, 1975), p. 45; 1950–1978: Prime Minister's Office, *Labor Force Survey* (Tokyo: Prime Minister's Office, 1979).

industries in the cities. When business prospered and labor was in demand, they moved into the factories, only to return home when business needs diminished. The young rural women who were recruited into the cotton textile industry also worked for short periods in factory labor. Their wages supplemented the family income for a few years between school leaving and marriage. Thus, women workers in the prewar period were, for the most part, temporary migrants from the countryside.

The war changed this situation for a few years, as it did in many other countries. The shortage of young males in the labor force meant that women were recruited to work in the munitions industries and later in heavy steel, construction, and chemicals. Women made up only 13 percent of the workforce in the last three industries in 1941, the last war year for which official statistics are available, but this figure represented a fivefold increase between 1935 and 1941, a period when the number of men employed rose by 400 percent.

Despite the government's encouragement of women to work in heavy industry during the war, they continued to be treated as an auxiliary labor force. Government policy statements at the time specified that they were to be used only for "simple and easy work," for "light handwork calling for dexterity," and "as semiskilled or unskilled workers." Women worked for ten or twelve hours a day and invariably at lower wages than men received. As we shall see later, these male-female wage differentials continued to prevail long after the war.

The economic disaster that followed the Japanese defeat took a heavy toll among the female labor force. After the wartime increase, the number of women workers, which had stood at 3,875,146 in 1940, declined to 2,952,930 in 1947. This was a 23.8 percent decrease, as compared with a decrease of 13.6 percent among men. In the worst period of depression, 1949–1950, more women were dismissed than men: 350,000 as compared to 180,000. (The same trend is visible in the post–Korean War recession of 1952–1953.) With recovery, women returned to the labor force. From the immediate postwar economic recovery until the years of high economic growth in the 1960s and 1970s, the increase in the number of women in the metal, machinery, and chemical industries was remarkable, although textiles continued to be the main employer of women, accounting for 43 percent of all female industrial workers.

The Unionization of Women

The Yuaikai (Friendship Society), the first significant organization of workers in Japan, established a women's section in 1915 that gave women quasi-membership in the embryonic union. Yet in 1925, when women made up well over half the factory workers covered by the Factory Law (870,000 out of 1,400,000), only 7,000 women were affiliated with unions. This fact can be explained by the nature of their labor market function and experience: most were young; they moved back and forth between wage labor and agriculture; their total years of employment were few. In addition, they were part of the paternalistic family system in the feudal society that prevailed before the war.

After the war the psychological obstacles to organization disappeared with the emergence of democratic ideas and the legislation of equality between the sexes. The encouragement given to the unions by both the Allied Forces and the Japanese government also to some degree helped women to cast off their social inhibitions against union membership. The organization rate for women immediately after the war approached 50 percent. This rate, however, declined sharply by the mid-fifties and reached 30 percent during the 1960s. The decline in the organization rate for men was not nearly so sharp; nevertheless, the falloff in membership among both men and women reflected the widespread and growing apathy toward union organization that characterized the 1960s, as living standards rose following explosive economic growth. The sharper decline among women was due in part to a continuation of the prewar conditions characterizing their work life: the fact that most of them worked in small and marginal firms or family enterprises and their tendency to view work as temporary and premarital. Another important element was unquestionably the small amount of attention male union leaders were prepared to give to women's problems.

The negative attitude of trade unionists toward women is a continuing fact in Japan's labor history, though it was considerably more conspicuous in the prewar period in the communist-dominated unions than in the rather right-wing Sōdōmei (Japanese Confederation of Labor). As early as 1925, a serious dispute occurred in Hyogikai (Trade Union Council, a radical union federation that seceded from Sōdōmei in 1924) when a proposal was made to establish a women's section. The leaders opposed the move on the grounds that such a section would develop into an independent organization of women, resulting in a confrontation between men and women. At the same time, workers' political groups neglected women's interests and relegated women's groups to a subordinate role in the labor movement's political parties.

Women Unionists and the Women's Movement

Before the war the various nonlabor women's organizations included working women without being allied in any way to the workers' movement. Their aim was to activate women as citizens. They were concerned with such issues as prices for consumer goods, pollution, and prostitution, but were not much interested in programs for working women. For political reasons they maintained close working relations with some of the opposition labor parties, but they were unable to mobilize them effectively on women's issues.

After the war the situation improved when women who had established the League of Women Voters out of the old universal suffrage organization went on to work in behalf of women's interests generally. Other women's organizations concerned with consumers' and community interests also emerged, chief among them the Japan Housewives' Association and the National Federation of Women's Business and Professional Clubs. All of these worked independently of the political parties.

In contrast, the unions—and with them their women's sections—were seriously divided among ideological lines into separate federations, each with its own political party. Women workers in these male-dominated unions were unable to reach out effectively to the nonpartisan women's movement, nor were the nonpartisan groups able to reach out to the unions. Thus, both groups made slower progress than they might have toward building united support for women's rights.

Public Policies on the Status of Women

The postwar constitution provided complete equality under the law for men and women. It guaranteed freedom of speech, assembly, and association and freedom of thought and conscience; any group was free to organize in behalf of its own interests. It further guaranteed equal educational opportunity and stated that marriage was to be based only on the mutual consent of both parties and to be maintained by mutual cooperation, with equal rights for husband and wife. The Women's and Minors' Bureau in the Ministry of Labor, through its branches on Women at Work and Women's Affairs, had the responsibility of carrying out public policies aimed at achieving equality between the sexes. Thus, the main problems were not in the legal system or explicit public policy but rather in social customs and practices based on a paternalistic conception of women's role in society and work life. For example, women had equal opportunities in education, and beginning about 1960, more women than men were enrolled in institutions of higher education. Because of the widespread practice of using women only as auxiliary labor, however, women tended to enroll in such programs as the arts, which were not marketable professionally but which improved marriage prospects. Prevailing societal attitudes continued, despite the law, to postulate a traditional family in which the male had the dominant role. Yet all the while the number of working wives grew steadily, women worked more years than formerly, and patterns of family life responded to birth control and the modernization of housework.

A Labor Standards Law (LSL) was adopted in 1947 under Occupation influence. On the whole it reflected the norms then widely accepted in Western societies and promulgated by the International Labour Organisation (ILO) in a number of its conventions on health and welfare, hours and places of work, and maternity leaves and benefits. One article called for equal pay for equal work.

Thus, by the end of the 1960s, not only were the laws propitious, but favorable trends were developing in family life and gender relations and were to continue right through the next decade.

WORKING WOMEN IN THE SEVENTIES

Changes in Labor Force Participation

Between 1960 and 1978 the number of women in the labor force increased by 73 percent, from 7.3 million to 12.8 million, while men's LFPR rose only about 51.9 percent, as Table 9-2 makes clear. Women's share of the total labor force increased from 31 percent to more than 33 percent. Not only did the number of working women grow, but other demographic factors changed markedly. In 1962, for example, married women made up 33 percent of the female labor force; by 1974 this figure had risen to 50 percent, and in 1978 it stood at 55 percent. The percentage of unmarried women in the labor force declined from 55 percent in 1962 to 34 percent in 1978. No longer could it be said that women were a reserve army of labor who worked for only a few years before marriage.

Further evidence of this change in women's workforce attachment is visible in the statistics on the average age of working women. Between 1960 and 1978 it increased by almost eight years to 34.1, and the gap between the average ages of male and female workers narrowed from 5.5 years to 3.1 years during the same period. Women's average length of service in paid

TABLE 9-2

Number and Percentage of Employed Persons
in Japan, by Sex,
(various years, 1960–1978)

	No. of Workers (in thousands)		
Year	Male	Female	Women as % of Total
1960	16,320	7,380	31.1
1965	19,630	9,130	31.8
1970	22,190	10,960	33.2
1974	24,660	11,720	32.2
1978	25,190	12,800	33.7

Source: Prime Minister's Office, *Labor Force Survey* (1978).

employment has increased more than 50 percent, from 4.0 to 6.1 years, while the seniority of men has gone from an average of 7.8 to 11.1 years, an increase of a little more than 42 percent.[2]

Women's educational level rose rapidly in the period from 1960 to 1978, as the table recording the schooling of newly employed persons shows (Table 9-3). These figures also reflect the divergent choices of men and women entering institutions of higher education in response to management's continuing policy of employing women mainly at low-level jobs in segregated occupations. Direct evidence for this bias appeared in a 1977 Labor Ministry survey showing that well over half the companies questioned refused to employ women university graduates, the pool from which management candidates are selected.[3] Even when companies hire such women, they place them in low-level jobs without real possibility of promotion.

Part-Time Work

The number of part-time workers increased rapidly after 1975, from 735,000 to 1,146,600.[4] While women made up less than half the part-time workforce in 1960, their share of this sector increased rapidly from 1970

TABLE 9-3
Percentage of Newly Employed Persons in Japan
by Educational Level Attained
(various years, 1960–1978)

Year	Middle School	High School	College (2-year)	University (4-year)
Female				
1960	54.4	42.1	1.7	1.8
1965	43.2	50.8	3.5	2.5
1970	20.2	64.8	10.5	4.5
1975	9.2	64.0	18.3	8.5
1976	8.3	63.2	19.5	9.0
1977	7.1	63.3	20.2	9.4
1978	6.4	62.8	20.6	10.2
Male				
1960	46.2	41.0	0.9	11.8
1965	40.6	43.4	1.3	14.9
1970	19.8	56.0	1.7	22.5
1975	9.2	52.1	2.3	36.4
1976	8.3	51.8	2.2	37.7
1977	7.7	52.5	2.2	37.6
1978	7.2	52.2	2.0	38.6

onward until they represented two-thirds of the total in 1978. The proportion of part-timers in the total female labor force almost doubled from 1960 to 1978 (Table 9-4). The increases were mainly in the tertiary industries, including public service, sales, transportation, and communication.

Labor Market Segregation

Women in 1978 were mainly employed in three occupational areas: as clerical workers (32.0 percent), production (24.5 percent), and the service trades (13.4 percent). Notable, though not enormous, increases have taken place during the seventies in women's employment in the professional/ technical, clerical, and sales categories. The very low and generally stagnant proportion of women among managers suggests that most female professional/technical workers are in such low-level positions as nurses, teachers, and laboratory technicians. Thus, the high proportion of women in this category does not by any means indicate a leveling up of female labor across occupations. A survey of newly opened jobs for women during the period from 1963 to 1968 shows that a majority of them arose as a result of the mechanization, automation, or computerization of the work process and provided few, if any, opportunities for advancement.[5] Another survey more recently undertaken showed that only 3 percent of those participating in

TABLE 9-4
Workers Employed Less than Thirty-five Hours
Per Week in Japan, by Sex,
Excluding Agriculture (various years, 1960–1978)

	All Employees (in thousands)			Female Employees (in thousands)		
Year	No. of Employees	No. of Part-Timers	Part-Timers as % of Total	No. of Employees	No. of Part-Timers	Part-Timers as % of Total
1960	2,106	133	6.3	639	57	8.9
1965	2,713	178	6.6	851	82	9.6
1970	3,222	216	6.7	1,068	130	12.2
1971	3,332	238	7.1	1,089	143	13.1
1972	3,384	241	7.1	1,093	146	13.4
1973	3,529	279	7.9	1,159	170	14.7
1974	3,551	303	8.5	1,143	184	16.1
1975	3,550	353	9.9	1,137	198	17.4
1976	3,623	314	8.7	1,174	192	16.4
1977	3,682	321	8.7	1,221	203	16.6
1978	3,715	330	8.9	1,251	215	17.2

Source: Prime Minister's Office, *Labor Force Survey*.

company decision making were women.[6] More than half of the 1,340 enterprises responding had no women in positions of division head or higher.

The low status of women in employment is largely a result of management policies. The 1977 Labor Ministry Study showed that only 44.7 percent
of the 5,000 enterprises surveyed allowed the promotion of women to
managerial positions, while more than half absolutely denied such opportunities to them. Among those that nominally permitted promotion to
women, the usual practice was to set a low limit or quota for their entry into
such posts. Just over 40 percent of the enterprises allowed the promotion of
women up to the level of department head, but only 27.3 percent considered
promotions to a higher division level.

LABOR MARKET POLICIES AFFECTING WOMEN

The Unions

Most Japanese unions are organized at the level of the enterprise and
accept as members only regular employees of their company. This means
that both temporary and part-time workers are typically excluded. In the
1960–1978 period, the proportion of female temporary workers in employment increased from 8.0 to 12.0 percent, while males in this category
declined from 4.3 to 2.8 percent. The proportion of women employed on
daily contracts has held steady at something over 40 percent, while the figure
for men has declined from 4.0 to 2.8 percent.[7] Unions, concerned as they are
with the long-term regular male employee, tend to neglect the interests of
women and to sacrifice them during economic crises. Nevertheless, substantial numbers of women belong to unions, particularly in the sectors where
their employment rate is high: in retail and wholesale trade, finance and
banking, and public service. These occupations appear to lie, moreover, in
future growth areas in the service sector. Table 9-5 shows the 1978 union
organization rate within the major sectors of employment.

Since unions were first permitted to organize in 1948, the organization
rate for both men and women has been in steady decline. This trend has
continued right through the 1970s, as Table 9-6 makes clear.

Officially, of course, unions favor full employment policies. In recent
years, however, they have had to deal with severe layoffs, and in doing so
they rarely propose solutions that protect female union members. In negotiating or consulting on such matters, companies and unions generally adopt
one of two standards for selecting those who must be laid off. One is to select
employees whose performance is poor, a standard that might apply more to
men than to women; the other is to search out those workers whose personal
financial circumstances will presumably be least affected by dismissal. This
means, first, young, unmarried employees of both sexes, and, next, married
women whose husbands are wage earners, on the assumption that such

TABLE 9-5
Union Organization Rate in Japan, by Sex and
Employment Sector, 1978

Sector	% of Work Force Organized	Women as % of Union Membership	Women as % of Total Workforce
Total	32.6	27.4	100.00
Agriculture, forestry,		14.2	0.3
and fishing	22.0	4.7	0.0
Mining	45.3	6.3	0.1
Construction	16.9	14.4	2.9
Manufacturing	37.6	21.3	26.4
Wholesale/Retail	9.5	37.6	9.2
Finance, insurance,			
and real estate	63.3	18.7	0.1
Transportation and			
communication	64.4	9.8	6.0
Electricity, gas,			
and water supply	75.3	9.8	0.7
Private services	22.5	44.1	23.3
Public services	74.2	34.4	13.9
Miscellaneous	25.2	—	—

Source: Labor Ministry, *Basic Survey of Labor Unions* (Tokyo: Labor Ministry, 1978).

women are secondary breadwinners and hence that their income is dispensable.

Vocational Guidance and Training

Most vocational training in Japan happens on the job. Trainees are chosen by management in accordance with perceived company needs. Unions, therefore, do not consider training a matter for their concern. Since women are rarely selected for promotion, their training consists almost entirely of an introduction to their jobs immediately after they are hired. Their range of responsibility within their narrow assignments may be somewhat extended as years go by, and lateral transfers with minimal retraining may take place, but only as company needs dictate. The 1977 Labor Ministry study revealed that so far as training for upward mobility is concerned, fewer than 20 percent of the surveyed establishments gave the same training to both men and women, while about 13 percent gave women no training at all. Nearly one-third of those training women gave them different training than they did men.

TABLE 9-6
Changes in Numbers of Union Members and
Estimated Organization Rate by Sex in Japan
(various years, 1948–1980)

Year	Women (thousands)			Men (thousands)		
	No. Employed	No. of Union Members	Est.% Unionized	No. Employed	No. of Union Members	Est.% Unionized
1948	3,300	1,510	45.7	9,290	5,030	54.1
1951	3,620	1,350	37.4	9,740	4,330	44.5
1955	4,790	1,470	30.8	10,870	4,710	43.3
1959	7,160*	1,770	28.1	15,320*	5,310	37.3
1963	8,280	2,530	30.6	17,660	6,740	38.2
1967	10,430	2,890	27.7	20,560	7,580	36.9
1971	11,040	3,280	29.7	22,780	8,410	36.9
1975	11,900	3,450	29.0	24,790	9,020	36.4
1979	13,100	3,340	25.5	25,900	8,830	34.1
1980	13,740	3,380	24.6	26,380	8,860	33.6

*Because of a change in statistical methods, the number of employed persons and the organization rate for this year do not match.
Sources: Unpublished calculation by the Women's and Minors' Bureau of the Labor Ministry, 1981, based on Labor Ministry, *Basic Survey of Trade Unions* (1981), and Prime Minister's Office, *Labor Force Survey* (1980).

Public Policies on Equality

The legal framework governing labor market policy and practice is peculiar for each country. As we have seen, the Japanese constitution provides for equality under the law, regardless of race, creed, sex, social status, or family origin. The LSL calls for nondiscrimination on a number of these grounds, but refers to sex only in respect to wages. The reason for this differential legal construction is by no means clear, but a majority of legal theorists explain that the LSL excluded specific mention of equal treatment of men and women with respect to general working conditions because women already had specific protections not applying to men under other articles of this same law.

The government in its administration of the LSL tends to a broad construction, extending protection against sex discrimination as far as possible under the constitution. Court decisions for the most part support this view, holding any discrimination against women because of their sex to be unlawful because of the constitutional guarantee of sex equality. Discriminatory dismissal of women—because of age or marriage, for example—has been uniformly ruled unlawful.[8] In cases of dismissals after marriage, the courts also rely on Article 24 of the constitution, which guarantees freedom of marriage.

The protective articles of the LSL, as I have said, cover a number of working conditions. Presumably these were adopted to protect the health and safety of women workers as mothers. Their hours per week are limited; they may not engage in night work (exceptions are made for nurses and others whose night work is deemed necessary, but the number of night hours per month that may be worked is limited); they may not work below ground or above certain heights. A number of special provisions govern work during pregnancy and maternity, menstrual, and nursing leave, provisions that the unions very much favor and actively support. Recently the Labor Ministry's Advisory Council on the LSL has raised the suggestion that many of these provisions are out of date and no longer correspond to the nature of work and the working environment for women: the LSL was introduced more than thirty years ago, and there have been major changes in the conditions of working women since then.

In recent years the government has begun to emphasize the need for training to help certain categories of women find employment. Its program includes agencies that provide technical training for job-seekers and vocational guidance at public employment offices for part-time workers. Another program, directed to widows who must return to the labor force, provides benefits while they receive training at certain special agencies and public training centers and in addition gives grants to employers who hire widows or give them adjustment training.

The Government as Employer

Most government recruitment of employees is based on examinations which vary according to the qualifications required for the position. For general administrative categories, both national and local governments presumably observe strictly the principle of equal treatment in employment. Few women, however, take the examinations, especially for placement in the higher ranks. In 1978, when 246,285 people took examinations for national administrative offices, 34,525, or 14 percent, were women, and the majority of them were not seeking positions above the fifth of eight categories. Women in fact occupy fewer than one percent of the positions above the third category.

Women are not eligible to take examinations or to participate in training for certain categories of government jobs including some in the post office, tax office, immigration office, police force, prison system, and the emperor's palace guard. Women may not study at the Defense University or the Defense Medical School. The Agency for the Planning and Promotion of Women's Affairs in the Prime Minister's Office and the Women's and Minors' Bureau of the Labor Ministry have made some attempts to change government policy in these areas, but with limited success. In 1979 the government began to allow women to take the examinations to qualify as aviation control officers and to enter the Aviation Safety School and the Navigation Safety School.

More women are in local government offices. In 1978, 1.02 million women were employed in them, making up 33 percent of the total number of local government employees. Although this percentage is somewhat below the national women's LFPR, female employment in local government has risen rapidly since 1975, when only 590,000, or 28 percent of the employees, were women: the majority of these women are nurses or other health workers.[9]

Public Policies on Private Sector Employment

In spite of the recent government emphasis on the improvement of women's status, especially in employment, the record of the Women's and Minors' Bureau in the Labor Ministry has on the whole been less than satisfactory. The bureau's goals for women have been below what the courts have allowed. In 1965, for instance, the ministry officially declared that the early retirement system for women did not contradict any provisions of the LSL, even though the constitutional guarantee of equality made it undesirable. The following year a court issued the first judgment declaring the compulsory retirement of women at marriage illegal, and in 1967 a number of similar decisions rejected compulsory early retirement in any form. The Labor Ministry, however, did not follow these up with any official statement on discriminatory retirement systems. It seemed to find its justification in the fact that the LSL is not explicit about sex equality in employment beyond the requirement of equal pay for equal work, although it provides that work rules contradicting either the LSL itself or the law in general are null and void. The ministry seems to be trying to cope with these illegal practices by "administrative guidance" rather than by clearcut enforcement. The Prime Minister's office reported in 1978 that of the 17,100 large enterprises receiving administrative guidance that year, 6,300 had abolished discriminatory retirement systems.[10] Good, but not good enough.

The best that can be said is that the government is moving at a slow pace to enforce equality in employment. In June 1980 its reluctance to sign the United Nations Convention on the Elimination of All Forms of Discrimination Against Women, adopted by the General Assembly at the end of 1979, was reported. Among the reasons it gave was that the LSL only guaranteed equal treatment in respect to wages.[11]

The LSL Study Committee, advisory to the Labor Ministry, in 1978 proposed the introduction of new legislation to ensure equal treatment of men and women in employment and abolish most of the protective provisions for women now embodied in the law, keeping only a few statutes concerning maternity. The government, which in Japan is almost entirely responsible for bringing in bills, has continued to delay the drafting of appropriate legislation. The report of the advisory committee sparked considerable controversy in women's groups, some supporting, others attacking its recommendations. The unions are a major power on the side of those unwilling to see protective legislation abolished. Unquestionably, this division gives comfort to the reluctant bureaucrats who might otherwise find themselves under considerable pressure to draft legislation that would further diminish women's unequal status. What can occur when sufficient pressure is mounted is well illustrated by the eventual ratification of the UN convention referred to above, the result of strong pressure from women's organizations and considerable publicity in the national press, as well as the pressure generated by the mid-decade world meeting of women in Copenhagen. It remains to be seen how quickly implementing legislation will follow.

WOMEN IN THE UNIONS

Since Japanese unions include all the employees of a given employer, distinctions among them cannot be made according to the type of workers organized—manual, white-collar, professional, and so on. The main differences among unions are ideological. Neither their structure nor their political affiliations and commitments appear to make much difference in the way they deal with women: all support equality in theory but do little to realize it. The major differences among unions on this issue are between those with a high percentage of women members—unions in textiles and telecommunications are two outstanding examples—and those with a low female membership. The former deal to some extent with such issues as child care and maternity and nursing leaves. The latter typically do not raise these issues, and many write contracts perpetuating employers' traditional policies on early retirement for women.

Women's Needs and Demands

When women worked only for short periods in a kind of auxiliary workforce outside the unions' scope, their interest in union affairs was not very strong. But the longer women are employed, the more they put forward their own specific demands, particularly for equal treatment. Moreover, as they continue to work past marriage and childbirth, they develop an interest in protective measures, especially in relation to maternity.

To some extent unions have made efforts to integrate women into their activities. By and large, however, males continue to control union affairs and to regard women's needs as secondary, excusing this attitude by the low level of women's participation in the unions. And so history, tradition, excuse, and rationalization come full circle.

Women in Union Office

Women's participation in union office is very weak. Only one survey has been done of sufficient scale to say exactly what their level of participation is. In 1978 Zensendomei (Japan Federation of Textile Workers) surveyed 74 enterprise unions comprising over a thousand local unions.[12] Since the responses to the questions were prepared by leaders in the affiliated unions, they undoubtedly reflect predominantly male views. Although female membership in the federation is about 41.8 percent, the total number of female union officers was 61 out of a total of 840, or 7.2 percent. Only 25 of the 74 unions had one or more female officers, and these were more numerous at the plant level than at headquarters. Of the 7,726 plant officials, 1,649 (21.3 percent) were female. Few women held the three top positions at union headquarters—the president, vice-president, or secretary-general. Only in one case were both president and secretary female. No other union had any woman among its highest officers. Locally there were 104 vice-chairwomen, 21 female secretaries, and 1 female vice-secretary among more than a thousand unions.

Structural Adaptations: The Women's Divisions

Most unions have a women's division or a women's and youth division. The Zensendomei survey showed that 40.3 percent of their unions had established women's divisions and 26.4 percent had women's and minors' divisions. These were established originally to facilitate recreational and cultural activities to attract young men and women into the union. More recently they have broadened their scope and purpose to work at improving women's conditions and put forward demands for equal treatment in promotion, job assignment, and general working conditions, including workplace child care centers. Most strongly support the preservation and even the extension of protective laws.

The Zensendomei survey further showed that 27.4 percent of the unions had reserved seats for women in their executive bodies and some other specialized committees. About 11.0 percent had reserved seats for women at conventions. Another 9.6 percent allowed for the appointment of women as observers at conventions and executive meetings. Only 1.4 percent of local unions, however, had reserved seats for women in plant or workshop committees.

Programs to Improve Women's Participation

The Zensendomei survey endeavored to measure women's participation in union activities as compared with men's and received considerably lower estimates of female activity (Table 9-7). Respondents were asked to explain women's low participation rates and got such replies as the following: 41.1 percent said that women lacked commitment to work and were employed only for short periods; 20.0 percent believed that women were "self-centered" rather than socially or organizationally motivated; some stated that women feel "no need for a union." From unions whose female members were mostly married, the response was that "women have no time because of the demands of their home lives."

The survey further revealed that 63.0 percent of the unions encouraged women to participate in training courses, usually sponsored by the upper levels of the union's organization, and 42.5 percent have conducted special training courses for women as a first step toward preparing them for leadership. A good many of these unions further try to promote communication among women through special workshop meetings.

Child care for textile union meetings is for the most part provided through women's mutual self-help, and usually only when meetings are organized by and for women. Even these efforts occur on no very significant scale. (It is still rare for men to share household duties, child care, and education, and apparently no union has raised this issue or conducted a campaign to promote this solution to the problem of women's double burden.) Released time for education or trade union meetings is prohibitied by trade union law on the grounds that such grants of paid time off would represent financial assistance by employers to unions.

TABLE 9-7

Participation in Textile Union Activities in Japan,
by Sex and Marital Status, as Reported by Union Leaders

Sex and Marital Status	High (%)	Medium (%)	Low (%)
Male	25.4	69.4	4.2
Female			
Unmarried	11.1	75.0	13.9
Married	4.3	48.6	47.1

Source: Zensendomei, Present Situation and Problems of Participation of Female Members in Union Activities, 1978.

Female Staff in Unions

Only a few women hold staff positions in Japanese unions, and they are usually assigned to the women's divisions. The most important job that women perform in the unions is interpreting for international activities; the number of interpreters has been growing in recent years, particularly since the International Women's Year events of 1975. Although in a few cases worker representatives sit on company boards, it is not surprising, given the small number of women staff members, that so far no women are among them.

Collective Bargaining

Japanese unions annually enter into a coordinated action, called the "spring offensive," in which they carry out a schedule of demonstrations and negotiations mainly directed toward getting a uniform percentage increase in wages. Bargaining on the distribution of this increase and on working conditions takes place almost universally at the plant or enterprise level. To participate in these activities, women would have to be influential in the decision-making bodies of their enterprise unions, and as we have seen, this is not the case.

Occasionally union negotiators consult with the workers, although this practice has not been widely adopted. Theoretically, bargaining and consultation are quite distinct, but in practice they are often very similar.[13] On the whole, bargaining is more formal, and individual grievances are more apt to be handled by consultation than through formal procedures that may be backed up in the courts. Opportunities for advancing women's interests seem somewhat more favorable through the informal channels of consultation, but these are only exceptionally available. In a number of important instances in recent years, unions were so unenthusiastic about handling the women's grievances that the women have chosen to go to court. Most of the lawsuits involving dismissals upon marriage or to the imposition of early retirement were brought by the dismissed women themselves without help from their unions.[14] In most of these cases the unions have had contracts with management explicitly agreeing to women's early "retirement" (read "dismissal"), and they cannot support an anticontractual action. Suits over different wage rates for men and women fall into the same category. Unions, however, can and do have some influence on matters important to women. We turn now to some specific problems and their solutions.

Bargaining Outcomes

Although wage differentials between men and women have narrowed somewhat in recent years, women workers' average monthly earnings in

TABLE 9-8
Japanese Women's Monthly Earnings as a
Percentage of Men's in Enterprises
with More than Thirty Employees
(various years, 1960–1978)

Year	Earnings as % of Male Wage
1960	42.8
1965	47.8
1970	50.9
1974	53.9
1978	56.2

Source: Labor Ministry, *Monthly Labor Statistical Survey* (1979).

1978 were only 56.2 percent of male workers' (Table 9-8). Four factors contribute to this wide difference. First and most significant is the fact that women's work is mainly segregated and women are assigned to lower-status jobs that are mainly lower-paid than men's. Second, wage scales in Japan are largely determined by seniority, and women work fewer years than men. Third, women generally have attained lower levels of education than men before starting to work; fewer working women, for example, have attained the postsecondary level. Fourth, women on the average work fewer hours than men, a factor partly accounted for by the limitation on women's hours imposed by the LSL and partly by the considerable proportion of women working part time. In 1978 women worked an average of 165.1 hours per month, compared with 179.6 for men.

Managerial employment policies are the most decisive cause of unequal work opportunities for women and account for the radical job segregation between men and women. Japanese unions, however, organize only already employed people and do not enter into the hiring or job assignment processes.

Aside from some efforts to improve the laws on menstrual and maternity leave, unions have made no particular efforts in behalf of women's health and safety. The LSL provides for twelve weeks of maternity leave, six weeks before and six weeks after birth, not necessarily paid, and for two thirty-minute periods a day for nursing a baby up to the first birthday. These are minimum standards. The Ministry of Labor in a 1978 survey found that 14.5 percent of the surveyed enterprises allowed longer maternity leaves and 38.5 percent allowed leaves with some pay; 8.5 percent allowed for longer nursing periods than the minimum, and 41.7 percent paid women for this lost time.[15] The survey did not indicate whether it was union pressure, employer initiative, or joint agreement that created these favorable circumstances.

Although Japanese enterprises emphasize the provision of welfare facilities of all kinds—housing, vacation resorts, savings associations, recreation facilities, and so on—they have made no particular effort in either the private or the public sector to establish programs specifically for women beyond the nursing facilities required by law. Zensendomei is an exception in endeavoring to improve dormitory accommodations for women in the Osaka area and perhaps others and in instituting some educational and recreational activities in them. Other notable exceptions are certain joint union-management programs in the Telecommunications Corporation, a public enterprise.

I have noted above the union's failure to oppose management policies regarding layoffs and dismissals for working women. The fate of part-time workers is no better. Because most of them are hired technically as "temporary workers," they are outside the scope of the lifetime employment system and are often ineligible for union membership. In recent years, however, some unions of department store workers—a sector where female part-time employees constitute a majority of the workforce—have begun to treat them as permanent employees: within the system and hence subject to its biases and benefits.

POLITICAL ACTION

Women's issues receive more attention in the political arena than in collective bargaining. With the growing interest of women in politics and the increasing number of women voters, most of the parties have established women's sections. Three of these—the Socialist, the Social Democratic, and the Communist parties—are closely related to factions within the union movement. All of the parties, from the Liberal Democrats on the right through the Communists, in 1983 have put up women candidates, and there were twenty-five women in the Japanese parliament.[16]

Although the women's divisions of the unions were set up, as we have seen, to stimulate interest in union activities and immediate enterprise working conditions, they have taken a more political turn in response to the recent emphasis on women's status in public policy and the ideological orientation of each national center. They support women candidates, play an active role in the advisory committee to the Office of Women's Affairs in the Prime Minister's Office, and stand firmly for the defense of the protections offered in the LSL.

Earlier I noted that organizations in the women's movement are mainly nonpartisan and have found it somewhat difficult to achieve coalitions with women in the political parties and the unions. Recently, however, on certain issues of compelling interest to women, there has been considerable crossing of political lines.

ISSUES AND OUTCOMES IN THE 1980s

It might be useful to draw up a balance sheet to indicate where Japanese public policy stands now and where concerns will focus in the next few years.

Family Policies

Family policy is an area of great personal freedom in Japan. Birth control has for some time been widely advocated and a broad range of devices is generally available. Child allowances are generous, and tax exemptions include children under the age of twenty and those attending universities. Japanese women thus have the nominal freedom to continue their working life after marriage, if they wish and if jobs are available. Problems arise, however, for women who look for child care facilities, which are in very short supply. This scarcity, combined with the implicit prohibition under the lifetime employment system of extended leaves of absence, means that women face a critical decision about their future employment a few weeks after childbirth. Poor housing forces many women to work in order to improve family living conditions, but a decision to work sooner or later can come into conflict with the hope of having a child.

Labor Market Issues

The attention of union women now centers on those sectors where women find the greatest opportunities for employment, and these are the growing information industries, particularly the electronics-related ones. Within these areas women's higher educational levels and tendency to stay longer in the labor market raise hopes for promotion and higher status.

The question of equal pay will continue to be troublesome so long as the market for men's and women's work is almost totally segregated, for the Japanese are still concerned with the rather literal concept of equal pay for equal work and have not yet considered "comparable worth." Improving women's wages at the bottom of the scale through the legislation of national minimum wages is not on the agenda. To the extent that minimum wages exist, they are regional and industrial and have only limited effects on standardizing general wage levels, particularly for women.

Change in a Male-Dominated Society

The notion that men and women should have different statuses is deeply rooted in Japanese society. Such a bias, often noted, is even reflected in the language, which differentiates women's roles and vocabularies from those of men. Even public institutions exhibit considerable insensitivity to the differential treatment of the sexes, as is evident, for example, in school curricula that require "homemaking" of girls while offering "handicraft" to boys. But criticism of these matters is sporadic and has never commanded the audience that might become a movement for thoroughgoing social equality. The UN Women's Decade has had a remarkable impact on Japan, however, encouraging the government as well as private organizations and enterprises to think about a wide range of women's issues. While the broader issues of the decade, such as world peace, human rights, and international economic solidarity, have had little impact, the nascent women's movement, though not yet fully aroused to international issues, concentrates on a wide range of problems specific to Japan's women.

CONCLUSION

The role of women in the labor market has expanded remarkably since the end of the war, the result less of women's actions than of economic pressures during a period of rapid economic growth. Only after 1970 did women begin to make demands for equality and broader opportunities at work and in society generally. To the extent that the gains of these earlier years are the result of long-term economic developments, they are probably irreversible. But as economic changes have become regressive, women's advances too have become vulnerable. The "oil shock" of 1973 began the process of reversal.

Economic growth brought about changes not only in women's labor market role, but in their consciousness and social attitudes as well. Once they had experienced the effects of longer work lives and the broader social role that accompanied them, it was difficult to assign them the old roles in the workplace, family life, and society generally. The expected growth of the tertiary sector in the eighties, moreover, suggests a somewhat favorable future for women. It is not so much that the new industries in the tertiary sector will produce increased job opportunities as that they will completely change styles of working life. Labor will need more knowledge and higher skills; working schedules will feature shorter hours and work weeks; changes in career and workplace and continuing lifelong education and re-education will become standard. This expansion in workers' lives will certainly reduce the handicaps that characterize women's work now.

Shorter hours and work weeks, for example, will reduce the difference between full- and part-time workers. Lifetime employment will lose its central meaning as career changes become more common in Japanese society. Changes in family life will inevitably follow and further reduce women's handicaps, as frequent career changes and lifelong education reshape the role of men as the main breadwinners. And all these factors will necessarily affect recruitment policies and so lessen the discrimination against women.

On the other hand, the loose labor market that will characterize the 1980s will tend to encourage discrimination against women. The movement of the labor force from secondary to tertiary industry will unquestionably call forth a high turnover in employment; as a result some industries will decline quickly and new ones emerge. The international relocation of industries will also have an impact on the Japanese economy. These restructuring processes will produce frictions in the labor market, which women will be readily sacrificed to reduce. Women certainly cannot rely on being favored by such economic prospects. A planned and conscious effort of considerable magnitude will be necessary if women are to find advantages in these economic shifts.

Are women prepared for an undertaking of these dimensions? The influence of women in the unions is minimal; their political position, while improving, is not strong; the various women's groups are divided over matters as central as protective legislation. Yet the growth of the movement and the general public concern about equality have been remarkable, and they have been greatly aided by the activities and programs of the UN Women's Decade. Government policies and attitudes have changed markedly, especially since the establishment of the Special Agency for Planning and Promotion of Women's Issues in the Prime Minister's Office.

With all these changes, the role of the unions themselves must be reformed. Enterprise unions, characterized as they are by parochial interests and loyalties, will not be able to maintain themselves in the face of increased career mobility, industrial reorganization, rising living standards, diversification of workers' interests, and, especially, the organization of new white-collar industries. The unions will have to become concerned with human factors in working life, for their limited economic goals will not meet these pressures. Their targets must be more diverse and their structures more flexible if they are to deal with issues of community and society outside the workplace. Women's roles in these changed unions will be significant because the new issues are closer or identical to those that have been central to women all along.

Hyogikai	Trade Union Council
ILO	International Labour Organisation
LSL	Labor Standards Law
Sódómei	Japanese Confederation of Labor
Yuaikai	Friendship Society
Zensendomei	Japan Federation of Textile Workers

NOTES

1. M. Unemura, "Changes in Employment by Industrial Sectors, 1880–1940," *Keizai Kenkyu* 24, no. (April 1973): 107–16.

2. Labor Ministry, *Basic Survey of Wage Structure* (Tokyo: Labor Ministry, 1978).

3. According to this survey only a little over 20 percent of the enterprises covered had an explicit policy of employing university graduates of both sexes; nearly 30 percent had a policy of employing only male university graduates. Labor Ministry, *Survey of Employment of Women Workers* (Tokyo: Labor Ministry, 1977).

4. Part-time work has been variously defined. This figure refers to workers whose hours are shorter than those of normal workers. Table 9–4 refers to workers whose work week averages less than thirty-five hours.

5. Association for Employment Promotion, *Trends in the Female Labor Force and Jobs Newly Opened for Women, 1963–1968* (Tokyo: 1969).

6. Prime Minister's Office, *Report of the Survey on Women's Participation in Decision Making* (Tokyo: Prime Minister's Office, 1979). "Employees participating in decision making" are defined as those who are division heads or of higher rank.

7. Permanent workers are those employed for indefinite periods; temporary workers are those who are employed on contract for a specified period, usually from one to six months, but whose contracts are frequently renewed; daily workers are those employed from day to day.

8. For a full discussion of these types of dismissal, see Alice H. Cook and Hiroko Hayashi, *Working Women in Japan; Discrimination, Resistance and Reform* (Ithaca, N.Y.: New York State School of Industrial and Labor Relations, Cornell University, 1980).

9. Prime Minister's Office, *Present Status of and Policies for Women*, 1980, p. 149.

10. Ibid., p. 188.

11. Ibid.

12. Zensendomei, *Present Situation and Problems of Participation of Female Members in Union Activities* (1978).

13. For more details on bargaining, see Tadashi Hanami, *Labor Relations in Japan Today* (Tokyo: Kodansha International, 1979), and *Labour Law and Industrial Relations in Japan* (Deventer, the Netherlands; Kluver, 1979).

14. See Cook and Hayashi, *Working Women in Japan*.

15. Prime Minister's Office, *Present Status of and Policies for Women*, 1980, pp. 230, 231.

16. In the Upper House there are 252 seats; the Diet has 511 members.

BIBLIOGRAPHY

Akamatsu, Ryōko, ed. *Joshi rōdō hanrei* (Cases on Female Labor) Tokyo: Gakuyō Shobo, 1976.

―――. *Nihon fujin mondai shiryō shūsei* (Collection of Documents on the Problems of Japanese Women). Tokyo: Domes Publishing, 1978.

Cook, Alice, and Hiroko Hayashi. *Working Women in Japan: Discrimination, Resistance and Reform*. Ithaca, N.Y.: New York State School of Industrial and Labor Relations, Cornell University, 1980.

Hanami, Tadashi. "Protection or Equality?" *Japan Labor Bulletin* 18, no. 12 (December 1979).

―――. "Women Workers and Retirement After Marriage." *Japan Labor Bulletin* 8, no. 5 (May 1969).

Herold, Renate. *Die Blume am Arbeitsplatz: Japans Frauen im Beruf* (The Flower in the Workplace: Japan's Women at Work). Tübingen and Basel: Horst Erdmann Verlag, 1980.

Institute for Japan Studies. *Die Japanerin in Vergangenheit und Gegenwart* (The Japanese Woman, Past and Present). Vienna: University of Vienna, 1981.

Moriyama, Mayumi. *Kakukoku hosei ni miru shokuba no danjo byōdō* (Equality Between Men and Women in the Workshop as Revealed in the Legislation of Several Countries). Tokyo: Tokyo Nunoi Publishing, 1979.

Ohba, Ayako. *Kawariyuku fujin rōdō* (Changing Woman's Labor). Toyokeizai Shimpō, 1965.

Ohba, Ayako, and S. Ujihara, eds. *Fujin rōdō* (Woman's Labor). Tokyo: Aki Publishing, 1969.

Ohkōchi, K. and S. Isoda, eds. *Fujin rōdō* (Woman's Labor). Tokyo: Kōbundo, 1956.

Sano, Yōko. *Joshi rōdō no keizaigaku* (Economics of Female Labor). Tokyo: Nihon Rōdō Kyokai, 1947.

Sanpei, Takako. *Hataraku josei no rekishi* (History of Working Women). Tokyo: Rihon Hyornsha, 1956.

Shakai Seisaku Gakkuai (Association of Social Policy). *Fujin rōdō* (Woman's Labor). Tokyo: Yūhikaku, 1961.

Shimazu, Chitose. *Fujin rōdōsha* (Women Workers). Tokyo: Yuwanami Publishing, 1953.

―――, Fujin to rodō (Women and Labor) Tokyo, Shinnihon Publishing, 1970.

―――, Gōrika to fujin rōdōsha (Rationalization and Women Workers) Tokyo, Rōdōjumposha, 1965.

Shiozawa, Miyoko. *Kekkon taishoku go no watashitachi* (After Retirement at Marriage). Tokyo: Iwanami Publishing, 1971.

Takahashi, Nobuko. "Women's Wages in Japan and the Question of Equal Pay." *International Labour Review* 3, no. 1 (January 1975).

Takenaka, E., and T. Nishiguchi. *Onna no shigoto, onna no shokuba* (Women's Work and Work place). Tokyo: Sanichi Publishing, 1962.

10   Norway

Harriet Holter and
Bjørg Aase Sørensen

Democracy in Norway has developed with the breakthrough of one new political group after another.[1] Women workers, who have long fought for their rights in a society that has used and abused their work, are the latest such group. Their history, by and large still unwritten, is filled with open questions and striking contradictions that are yet to be explored in systematic research.[2]

One such contribution is that between those Norwegian women who accept secondary and passive roles and those who struggled militantly to achieve gains for women.[3] While male resistance was often strong, not all women avoided confrontations. Norwegian women virtually took the vote in 1905 by organizing an unofficial referendum among themselves.[4] Women were an important part of the resistance movement during the German occupation (1940–45). Women's groups also contributed significantly to the debate about Norwegian membership in the European Common Market. (Norway decided by referendum not to become a member.) In the 1980s women and women's groups led the work movement for nuclear disarmament and global peace. Women in the political parties, unions, and women's organizations have also been a major force in the establishment of a broad social policy that is usually seen as the core of social democracy in the Scandinavian welfare states.[5]

A second tension in Norwegian women's history comes from their dual commitment to the labor movement and to women's concerns. Working-class women, waged and unwaged, joined the labor movement that gained a foothold in Norway in the last part of the eighteenth century, by its emphasis on social change, full employment, and economic security. We still do not know how much of the early movement's social policy was created by women unionists, but we do know that female members frequently had goals of their own, visions for the future of the working class that were not always shared by men.[6] While male unionists may have thought socialism would automatically liberate women, women's groups within the labor

239

movement often voiced women's immediate demands, such as suffrage, and noted that the labor parties might have to rely on the votes of working-class women to build safe majorities. Yet their commitment to a strong labor movement moderated their militancy on feminist issues.

A third contradiction can be seen in male responses to women's rights activism: frequent opposition, but occasional support and cooperation. The principle of sex equality arose in Norway over stubborn opposition,[7] and though women have won legal equality in most areas, resistance remains. Sex discrimination is deeply embedded in traditional customs and habits and is often unspoken and unrecognized. Yet at some critical points, males, especially union leaders, have turned out to be women's allies.

As we analyze the past and current situations of Norwegian women, several other conflicting tendencies emerge: determination among women to fight combined with obedient membership in political organizations; advances in legal rights accompanied by an apparent hesitancy to use them.[8]

THE DEVELOPMENT OF THE LABOR MOVEMENT

Between 1848 and 1851 a socialist couple, Marcus and Josephine Thrane, achieved an economic and political organization of workers and farmers unique in European history in the preindustrial phase.[9] They established almost three hundred associations of sawmill workers, miners, craftsmen, smallholders, and farm and forestry workers with a membership perhaps as high as thirty thousand. (Norway then had a total population of 1.4 million.) Although the old craft system was losing its importance and new factories were developing along with a different kind of labor relations, there were probably no more than thirteen thousand industrial workers at the time. In 1851 Thrane was jailed, and his imprisonment broke him and the movement. But this "thranitter" movement, espousing equal rights, universal suffrage, and the need to take economic and political action to free the poor and oppressed, influenced a whole generation.

The industrialization process developed rapidly after 1870, especially around the turn of the century, when new technology harnessed waterpower to produce cheap electrical energy. As in many other countries, industrial work was probably a female province in the beginning; and men entered industry when the old craft system broke down. Norwegian historians maintain that the first women to be employed in industry found work in textile, tobacco, and food-processing factories.[10] International research now questions the labeling of branches as traditionally men's or women's and explains the drop in the number of women working in Norwegian industry in the period from 1900–1915 as the result of male workers' pushing the women out. (The traditional explanation points to structural changes in industry, most importantly the rise of the wood, pulp, paper, and chemical industries, which all favored male employment.) Women and children were paid special, low rates; up to World War I, women received at most 40 or 50 percent of men's wages for the same work, and they were sometimes working with hazardous materials. Yet with industrialization came a new wave of socialist and trade union organizing that eventually eroded vital parts of the old social system in Norway.[11]

Unions and Party

In the 1870s workers formed the first unions of typographers, tailors, bakers, saddlers, and other craftsmen, sensing the power inherent in the employers' need of their skills. The Labor party was founded in 1887 and the Federation of Labor (Lansorganisasjonen i Norge—LO) in 1899. A year later the employers responded by organizing the Federation of Employers (Norsk Arbeidsgiverforening—NAF). In the years after 1870 the patterns of organization among women workers varied: some established independent unions; others joined unions that organized workers of both sexes.

At times sharp antagonism marked men's and women's relation in the workplace.[12] The tailors, for example, established separate unions for women as a means of controlling them. In the typographical trade in Oslo, women organized their own unions against their male colleagues.[13] There were female workers' initiatives in this period that gained substantial support from male union leaders, who were impressed by the women's determination and willingness to fight. The Labor leader Carl Jeppesen, for example, publicly supported the Female Tobacco Workers' Union during its strike for equal pay in 1899. Jeppesen wrote then: "Two-thirds of the cigar workers are women, and of course the workers demand the same pay for men and women who do the same kind of work."[14]

A turning point for women came in 1889 when the newly formed Labor party came to the support of 300 striking female matchworkers. This strike was remarkable in many ways. The women, disfigured by phosphorus, went out into the streets displaying their anger and suffering, for the danger to the workers of exposure to chemical materials was as important an issue as their low wages. The women won support not just from the labor movement, but from several liberal and humanitarian groups as well. By raising the question whether employers had the right to profit at the expense of workers' health, and by calling public attention to the particular exploitation of women workers, the matchworkers' strike attacked assumptions underlying the industrial order. Although they themselves gained nothing directly from their action, their strike had wide effects.

Between 1889 and 1901, as the labor movement was recovering from the depression, twenty women's unions were formed. These unions became strongholds of social and political consciousness.[15] From the beginning their ties with the Labor party were strong. Organized women were an integral part of the general socialist movement, and their struggles for suffrage (gained in 1913) and equal pay were conducted in a class-conscious, if male-dominated, political environment. The party's official position was that male and female workers were entitled to its undifferentiated support, and it included a women's branch among its special groups. The women's branch enjoyed great autonomy, but women's questions, when not understood as matters of general social policy, were not a central issue at the time.

During the first two decades of the century, the LO grew despite defeats in several sectors and became more radical. Although internal struggles over the form of organization threatened the union, the centralist tendency won out, and the confederation came to exercise power and control over its affiliates. National legislation regulating labor disputes gave it considerable authority. Central strike funds were established, and in response the employers too centralized their organization.

The close connection between the Labor party and the unions, as well as the division of labor between them, has been a significant factor in the development of women workers' strategies. The unions assumed the task of improving wages and working conditions and left to the party most issues of political principle and ideology, including many feminist issues. In consequence, over several decades the party was one of the few channels for realizing women's programs. Some issues, however, fell by the wayside. Between 1910 and 1920 women conducted wildcat strikes against the unequal pay rates called for in the first nationwide agreements between employers and unions, while male union organizers attempted to enforce them.[16] The party evidently regarded it as more important to push for general wage increases in the hope that the male breadwinner could support the whole family.

In 1927, at the start of the Great Depression, which began early in Norway, the party joined with unions in insisting that women should leave paid work when they married so as to give their jobs to men. Since only about two thousand married women were in the paid labor market in Norway at that time, the rule was largely symbolic. Women union leaders protested against it, and working-class women remembered this break in solidarity even after the rule was abolished in 1935 and later outlawed by the Supreme Court.[17]

Postwar Development

The German occupation of 1940–1945 put an end to normal political work and internal struggles within Norway, and for some years after the war there was a general political truce to allow the rebuilding of the country. Women sought to cooperate across party lines, the effort breaking down only over the abortion issue.[18] With a few interruptions the Labor party has been in power in Norway since the late 1940s and has had the opportunity to pursue its social policies.

Social democratic welfare policy holds the government responsible for economic growth, full employment, and the elimination of gross social inequalities. The dominant idea is to correct the unfortunate consequences of the operation of a capitalist economy without changing the economic system or its structure of ownership. The policy finds expression in an extensive social security apparatus operated by control measures built to respond to the functioning of a number of economic variables. Over several decades the policy has helped women to move from private, unpaid domestic tasks to paid service jobs organized by the state and community. Moreover, attempts to democratize educational policy have had less than the intended effect on working-class participation in education, but they have contributed to a rapid rise in women's educational levels.

In the early postwar period, the party pushed to improve working-class housing and provide support for mothers in the postpartum weeks, two programs of particular relevance to women. And in 1946 a general child allowance became an integral part of the social security system. The government placed new building blocks into the foundation of the welfare state during the fifties.[19] In this decade socialist as well as nonsocialist women's organizations insisted that labor organizations support women's rights even as their workforce participation declined. Marriages were comparatively stable, contributing to a baby boom.

The social sciences also contributed to the discussion of women's problems and status in the fifties. They introduced into Norway and other countries the concept of "sex roles," opening up to scientific study women's long-neglected part in society and focusing attention on the need for changes in men's, as well as women's, roles.[20]

The sixties brought changes in industrial structure, technology, and economic development. Increased mobility and urbanization radically influenced women's lives. The cost of living rose, and as it became increasingly difficult for a single breadwinner to provide for a family, more and more married women sought work, often part-time, outside the home. There was a general demand for labor in the Norwegian economy. Divorce rates increased, family ties tended to loosen, and the woman who remained at home became more isolated. The availability of contraceptives made family planning and lower birthrates possible. For all these reasons the number of married women working outside the home increased markedly, and many of these women joined the unions.

By the end of the sixties, Norwegian women had officially gained a gender-neutral set of laws calling for equal political rights, employment opportunities, equal wages, and, in marriage equal rights and responsibilities for both. Reality, however, fell short of these laws, even for professional women, and women with fewer personal and social resources had even less opportunity to profit from such laws. This disparity between norm and reality frustrated women and became a matter of concern to Norwegian policy-makers. A tripartite Council on Equal Pay, with representatives of labor, management, and government was established in 1959, the first of its kind in the Western world. In 1961 the LO and the employers' federation, the NAF, agreed to phase out women's wage scales by 1967.

The political parties soon began to include specific and positive demands for women's rights in their programs. The family was seen as a "vulnerable institution" requiring a "policy of social security and welfare programs." Not least important was initiating the transfer of responsibility for the aging, with a system of old-age pensions and provisions for institutional care outside the family. The extension of health care services to the whole population was equally significant. Such programs, whatever their other purposes, lessened—though they did not eliminate—some of the burden on women in the home and encouraged them to take up paid employment.

Entry into the labor market was not in itself enough to improve women's circumstances. When work was low-paid, low-status, monotonous, and unhealthy, a working woman's situation had not improved, especially when she continued to bear the burden of running the household alone. The fact that women's educational level was simultaneously rising did not encourage docile acceptance of the gap between official policies and reality. It was in part this disparity that brought about the explosive outburst of feminism in Norway at the end of the 1960s. The new movement, stimulated by a sociopolitical consciousness that was international in scope, was also part of the general antiauthoritarian revolt of the decade. We will turn later to its effect on working-class women and their union activities.

THE LABOR MARKET

Labor Force Participation

Until the late 1960s, Norwegian women had a lower labor force participation rate than women in most Western countries (see Table 10-1). The proportion of married women working outside their homes was particularly low. Change began to occur in the 1960s and in the 1970s women's participation rate almost doubled, while men's continued to decline. The greater demand for women's labor coincided with a rising level of education for both men and women, lower ages at marriage, and a decline in family size. It is important to note, however, that the increase in women's rates is largely due to an increase in their part-time work. Married women with part-time jobs

TABLE 10-1
Women as a Percentage of the Labor Force in Norway
(various years 1875–1978)

1875	1900	1930	1950	1960	1970	1975	1980
29.1	26.7	27.0	24.0	23.0	29.0	37.8	40.0

Sources: Population censuses, 1875–1980; Central Bureau of Statistics.

are the new feature of the labor market but an investigation in the late seventies indicated that many married women seeking employment could not find suitable work,[21] while others who found jobs could not accept them because they lacked child care facilities.

Norway has developed public child care more slowly than other Scandinavian countries, with the result that demand far exceeds supply. In 1978 the highest municipal rate of coverage for children 0–7 years old was 35 percent placement. It is generally accepted that day care is a government responsibility, and official bodies finally began developing plans for full coverage in 1981. Until that is achieved, many working women must continue to organize their own child care.[22] They seek part-time work, shift work, and work outside normal hours (often under unpleasant conditions) and at the same time devise all kinds of private child care arrangements, sometimes even enlisting the child's father as caretaker.[23]

Labor Market Segregation

Men and women work in different and unequal labor markets. A recent national study on the standards of living in Norway demonstrates the effects of this segregated labor market.[24] Women get less on-the-job training than men because they constitute a labor reserve that can be called into the market when there are too many jobs for men to fill or men refuse the offered conditions; they can be dispensed with when work is scarce. The study further notes that because women prefer to work shorter hours, particularly if child care is not available, they are less acceptable for jobs on which the employer wants full control of overtime work. Since these conditions prevail in manufacturing, women prefer to work in the service trades, and they tend to work in smaller enterprises, where conditions are poorer and less stable than in the large firms.

The same study examined men's and women's exposure to varying environmental factors at work. It revealed that women have less freedom and discretion in their jobs, but men, who occupy most of the higher supervisory positions, suffer more from physical and psychosocial strains.[25]

The fact that women are socialized to accept what is allotted them without complaint, while men demonstrate their masculinity by being critical of conditions, may explain some of these differences.

The most important occupations for women, according to the 1970 census, were in clerical work, the services, retail sales, industry, the paraprofessions, and communications. The predominantly male occupations, on the other hand, were in industry, management, the professions, farming, and forestry. When men and women work in the same sector, their occupations and statuses are strikingly different. Among 285 professions and occupations in Norway, women have no or minuscule presence in 70 and represent 10 percent or less of the employees in 156 more, whereas men are found in almost all occupational categories. Women have only a small share of the better jobs. Private industry typically places them in jobs that carry little responsibility and only need easily replaceable workers. In the top and middle management, women are rare and their presence actually diminished over the twenty-one years between 1953, when 2.5 percent of managers were women, and 1974, when 1.3 percent were. In 1956, 5.7 percent of foremen were women; in 1974, only 1.8 percent were.[26] Public administration is somewhat less segregated. The number of women in influential positions in this area has been increasing over the last decade, partly as a result of special recruitment programs.

Employers in the public and private sectors are required to end labor market segregation. Educational and vocational counseling seeks to make it clear to girls and young women that nontraditional vocations are open to them. An official ruling forbids advertising specifically for either men or women. A public official called the Equality Ombud is charged with the investigation and settlement of charges of discrimination. The law on sex equality was strengthened in 1979, and reports show that labor market cases are among those most frequently brought to the Ombud.

Since 1973 the government has required that organizations (such as trade unions) entitled to nominate citizens to public boards and commissions propose lists with as many female as male names. The appointing authorities make their selections from these lists with the aim of achieving a fair representation of both sexes.[27] As a result, by the second half of 1980, 31 percent of members on all government boards and committees were women. There have been significant attempts to introduce quota arrangements in favor of women in education and work life. Quotas were proposed for higher-level appointments in the public services in a recent government plan, which also suggested that government subsidies to new industrial establishments be made contingent on the firms' offering jobs to women. This proposal was, however, withdrawn by the conservative government that came to power in 1981.

A recent report on women entering male-dominated trades and industries concludes: "At the very least, women have shown that they can do men's work."[28] Yet with one notable exception, unions took no initiative in bringing women into these trades. Their attitudes vary from passive good will through indifference to reluctance and outright opposition. The decision to employ women is often taken over the unions' heads—by the personnel office for instance—and there is still resistance to having women competitors in the male work environment.

Feminists, seeing government and union organizations' responses to labor market segregation as slow and halfhearted at best, call for the implementation of one or more of the following strategies:

1. a new labor market policy of genuine equality of opportunity, including outreach to women, multiple training opportunities, and inducements to public and private employers to take affirmative action to hire, train, and promote women;
2. immediate and expanded programs of child care by municipalities, where the responsibility for child care rests;
3. persuading firms and public agencies that employ women to provide child care; and
4. pressuring trade unions to exert their influence for all of these strategies.

Wages

Wages are a key indicator of the general discrimination against women in society and in the workforce. Married women now stay longer in the workforce than formerly, but married and single women alike suffer from the general belief that women are not really committed to a career and therefore are not worth training or promoting. Women's low wages, which reflect this lack of training and opportunity, may lead to lower aspirations and thus help to ensure the fulfillment of such expectations.

Open discrimination in pay for the same work is rare nowadays. Rather, hidden discrimination is the rule. It occurs, for example, when jobs with similar tasks have different titles. When separate schedules for men's and women's wages were abolished, it was with the understanding that wages would thereafter be based on the job and not the sex of the worker. Job evaluation is the usual method for arriving at a reassessment of women's wages, but it is a complicated tool that depends on evaluations made by engineers or committees. While intended to be neutral, these evaluations often prove rather subjective, and "work of equal value" has turned out to be a difficult concept to apply.

During the 1950s women's industrial wages declined as a percentage of men's. They stood at 67 percent of the male rate at the end of that decade. In the 1960s and the first half of the 1970s, they rose to 78 percent of men's wages, but this trend leveled off in the second half of the 1970s with the recession in the industrial branches producing for the domestic market.

In white-collar employment, Norway has reduced the gap between women's and men's salaries more than most other countries, even other Scandinavian countries. A 1975 survey of nine occupations in which women predominate showed their monthly salaries ranging from a low of 79 percent of men's salaries (for archivists) to a high of 90 percent (for electronic computer operators).[29]

Part-Time Work

Part-time work is mainly, though not exclusively, women's domain. In 1975 every fourth employed person was a part-timer, and 87 percent of part-timers were women. These proportions show no sign of abatement. Moreover, according to a 1978 poll, a large proportion of the unemployed women seeking work would like to have part-time jobs. Yet part-time work in its present form contributes to job segregation and to women's lower wages.

Part-time work raises questions of policy for unions, industry, government, and women themselves.[30] Employers frequently find higher productivity and lower absenteeism among part-timers than among full-timers. Few tensions and conflicts develop when part-timers and full-timers work together in low-ranked jobs and clerical work, but difficulties are more apt to arise in factories and in highly skilled jobs. In recent years both government and management have come to agree that part-time work should be encouraged. Not so the trade unions.

The LO sees government and private employers as encouraging part-time work in order to decrease the number of reported unemployed and to support a marginal labor force held in reserve. Moreoever, the unions may well see such marginal workers as a threat to traditional worker solidarity. Only 31 percent of part-time employees are union members, exactly half the rate in 1978 for full-timers. The relatively few male part-timers have an even lower rate of organization than the women. This lower propensity to organize is not accounted for by age, education, job experience, size of workplace, or branch of industry, so studies of the unionization of part-time workers are now focusing on differences in family situation, informal groupings and networks on the job, and the characteristics of various unions.[31] Union attitudes toward part-timers might be changed by redefining solidarity; and part-timers attitudes toward unions might be changed if unions bargained for them.

Unions in fact vary considerably in attitudes and practices with respect to part-timers. The Clerical and Retail Employees' Union has recently come to accept part-timers and works consistently to improve their conditions. At the other extreme, the Typographers' Union is adamant in its insistence that all employees are to be treated formally alike in every respect, even when the resulting differences in the reality of conditions undermine solidarity between part-time and full-time employees in a trade or a workplace.

Solutions may need to wait upon a more equal mixing of workers in part-time employment. When more men accept part-time work, it will almost certainly be upgraded. And if men's part-time work gives them more time to participate in domestic chores, the arrangement will have a doubly beneficial effect in diminishing the sex segregation of the labor market.

WOMEN IN THE UNIONS

Union Centralization

LO has long been among the most powerful organizations in Norway. Like other centers of power, LO is a male-dominated organization, and women who wish to rise in positions of power meet strong resistance. Yet social equality requires that women share positions of power. If it is true, as we optimistically believe, that women in the LO are on a slow march to sharing power, it is important that this bastion not be the last they enter as equals.

Women's presence in the unions was recognized as early as 1940 with the establishment of a special LO women's committee made up of women members of the boards of national unions. By 1950 a woman had been added to the LO secretariat to head the work of this committee, although she became entitled to a voice and vote only in 1961. Until 1981 this office provided the only two secretariat positions filled by women.

What are the causes and effects of male dominance within the union movement? The pronounced centralization of the LO, says a recent study, "means that the national perspectives of the top leaders are brought to bear on local or industry-specific issues that union members confront. In effect these leaders' perspectives permeate the union movement."[32] The LO's centralization is particularly evident in negotiations for wages and working conditions. The concentration of power in the national federation has inevitably reduced rank-and-file participation in a major union function, collective bargaining, and it has produced a specialized bureaucracy where mastery of bargaining issues and tactics depends on union training. Women's access to training and to elected or appointed office at these upper levels has been limited by their family responsibilities and by male resistance to their participation.

The national unions are as centralized as the LO. Their executive committees, each in its own right an effective center of power, are elected every four or five years at national conventions, and a third to a half of these officers become full-time union officials. Women appear only sparsely at this level, even in the so-called women's unions. The disparity between proportions of women in the membership compared to the actual number of women executive committees of most unions with many women members is shown in Table 10-2. In the local unions, women's position is probably somewhat better, but we have no recent data on female leadership there. In 1965, however, when about 20 percent of the total membership of LO unions was female, only about 10 percent of local board members were women. Every observation of unions finds the same pyramid of women's participation that occurs in other social spheres: they constitute a considerable part of the rank and file, but the higher one goes in the organization, the fewer are the women.

The close ties between the LO and the Labor party have resulted in an integrated career ladder that limits women's access to power. There is no

TABLE 10-2
Women in Union Membership and on National Executive Committees
in Norway, 1971

Union	% of Women Members	No. of Women on Executive Committee	No. of Members Executive Committee
Hotel and Restaurant	78	2	7
Garment and Tailoring	72	2	13
Clerical and Retail	65	5	12
Municipal Employees	58	3	17
State Civil Service	46	4	9
Food	40	2	11
Postal	36	1	11
Social Workers	32	3	7
Printing	26	0	13
Telegraph	23	3	8
Musicians	21	1	10
General Workers	18	1	11
Goldsmiths	16	0	6
Chemical	16	1	17
Seafarers	15	1	7
Paper and Pulp	10	2	21
Metal	9	1	15

Source: Interview by Bjørg Aase Sørensen with LO official, 1978.

collective affiliation between national unions and the party, but many locals are affiliated to it. Formal dual affiliation is in fact less important than the tight network of male bonds between the two structures. To aspire to a union career, a woman must normally be active in the party as well and have been elected to an unpaid position in her local or in an interunion district council. Such positions lead to attendance at LO schools for training in union operations and at conferences and negotiations where experience is gained and abilities are tested. All this requires that a person be the mistress of her own time outside work. Women with family responsibilities some- times manage to take part in local study and training activities, but they find it almost impossible to get away from home for the advanced courses, which run a full week or longer.

Women's Union Participation

By 1980 LO had a membership of 742,000 in a labor force of 1,679,000, and 32.7 percent of its members were women. This proportion has increased steadily since 1950, as Table 10-3 showed. Unions outside the LO represent large groups of women in the professions and semiprofessions, including teachers and nurses. Such unions had 219,000 members in 1978, including 113,000 women; the increase in women's membership lately has been higher than the increase in men's. These unions pursue a somewhat different political course from that of the LO unions. Some, like the Women's Telecommunication Union, a purely women's association, have been very outspoken on feminist issues; others have a lower profile in this respect.

In the postwar period LO membership has been declining in compari- son with that of the unaffiliated unions. The total number of organized employees in Norway has, however, kept approximately constant since the 1950s. The organization rate in 1980 was 64 percent for men and 50 percent for women.

TABLE 10-3
Proportion of Women in the LO and in the Labor Force
(various years, 1950–1980)

	1950	1960	1970	1975	1980
Women as % of LO members	17.7	18.0	23.2	26.6	32.7
Women as % of all employees	24.0	23.0	29.0	37.8	40.0

Source: Jan Erik Karlsen, *Hva skjer i fagbevegelsen?* (What Goes On in the Labor Movement?) (Oslo: 1977).

During the period between 1956 and 1975, women made up about 71 percent of all new recruits to the unions, while men's organization rate was falling. Yet the steadily rising proportion of women in the LO has still not reached the proportion of women in the labor force. And although women represent the growth factor in union membership, they have not presented the unions with any strong demands in return for their affiliation.

The majority of women's sectors are weakly unionized, in contrast, for example, to the metal workers, where union membership is about 97 percent and a worker who does not join the union within three months of employment will feel the strong disapproval of his fellow workers. By contrast, in the retail and clerical fields, social pressure against joining the union is such that workers who sign up can be the objects of ostracism or other negative sanctions from fellow workers. Recently, women in the retail trades have also experienced employers' sanctions for their union activities.

Men's role as breadwinners, their lifelong commitment to paid work, and the hierarchical structure of work organizations have all shaped the unions. Male workers' problems are at the core also of those informal collectivities that develop in most workplaces as bases for union activity, for the unions are to some degree formal expressions of the informal relations among workers. The rules and practices that have grown up on the job have protected males' workplace solidarity and therefore have been reflected in union policy and practice. Their rejection of individual solutions and their reliance on "the common rule" is often at variance with women's needs to adjust to both domestic tasks and job requirements.

Women traditionally have developed different and more varied kinds of collectivities than have male workers. These typically are built on a personal kind of fellowship that provides mutual support but has only limited potential for defense and almost none for offense, even in behalf of vital interests. Women do not share the average man's sense of security on the job. Many recognize that they are part of a reserve army of labor and that their domestic obligations push them into unstable work relations. Even when they form, as they sometimes do, strong, union-oriented groups, these may appear weak or even untrustworthy to their male colleagues. However, according to the sociologist Marit Hoel, women are the new carriers of solidarity, and they form strong collectivities in some industries.

Again and again, women have had the experience of being hostages within the labor movement. When women delegates to the national conventions of the Clerical and Retail Workers' Union in the 1970s attempted to organize a women's caucus, they were accused of being "fractionalists," breakers of labor solidarity, because their demands were not those of men. Women's special issues are often manipulated off the agendas of union meetings and negotiating committees. Welcomed as rank-and-file members, women are resisted as "influentials."

Women deal with their exclusion in various ways. One is to deny that work and the union are relevant to their lives and to participate in both at a minimum level. Another is to question the legitimacy of all organizations, whether union or management, that insist upon the literal and mechanical enforcement of rules that in fact, though not in form, penalize women. More and more women reject an "education" that brings them into the male world and its norms. With the rise of the new feminist movement and the general activism of the late sixties, however, many younger women devoted themselves to opening and widening channels for women's exercise of power within the unions. A young female workforce within a plant or office can produce and follow through with a tougher program than many older women have ever achieved.

Independent organizing has produced some good results. When the Oslo Trade Union Council abolished its women's committee in 1977, some women unionists established their own organization outside the union structure, the Oslo Working Women's Association. Though independent, it is not considered divisive. It works to increase women's influence and cooperation within the unions and has succeeded in organizing a number of joint efforts of union women, especially in connection with the national congresses of the LO.

Collective Bargaining

Norwegian workers had an early tradition of direct action for better wages and working conditions. Some women launched strikes, and others were involved in most of the major conflicts. Beginning with the painful matchworkers' strike of 1889, women's strikes, whether legal or illegal, were desperate reactions to their own weak positions. Although the right of workers to organize was generally recognized by 1914, the system whereby men defended their rights was long of doubtful value to women because of their lack of power and access to leadership.

Following the strike wave of 1931, and in the face of massive unemployment, a Labor government came into office in 1935 (though it was without a majority in parliament until 1945). The new political climate and the development of an elaborate system of collective bargaining, labor law, and welfare legislation effectively curbed most tendencies to direct action for some decades. On the industrial scene, the new situation was summed up in a Basic Agreement, often called the charter of labor in Norway, that was first signed by the LO and the NAF in 1935. Still in effect after periodic revisions by the two federations, it automatically forms part of every collective agreement between them. Both parties, of course, "mutually recognize the employers' and the workers' freedom of organization." During the life of a collective agreement, however, no work stoppages or lockouts may take place; these are lawful only between agreements. Grievance procedures are established and disputes on rights under collective agreements are settled by the Labor Court. The agreement now includes guidelines for cooperation and planning at the workplace level and defines the rights of shop stewards and union members.

Although the most significant bargaining is conducted nationally between the LO and the NAF, or between employers and employees of each branch, two important kinds of wage negotiations go on at the workplace: negotiations over additions to the general raise achieved in central negotiations and merit raises for individual workers. These local negotiations take place every six months or every year, according to custom and practice in the plants.

Some union programs have resulted in decided improvements for women, particularly in industry. One scheme to improve the lot of women, particularly the majority in low-wage work, is the "low-wage fund." In 1980 the unions won a low-wage fund as part of the overall wage contract between the federations of the unions and the employers. For some groups of women this had an immediately favorable effect on wages, although a side effect of the program was a transfer of money to companies owned by multinationals. The low-wage fund is Norway's attempt to achieve a solidary wage. It is financed partly by the workers and partly by the low-paying industries and is based on the difference between the male workers' wages in each branch and the average wage in all the branches of an industry. An earlier scheme to improve women's wages brought them from 78 percent of the industrial average in 1971 to 84 percent in 1978. Such programs minimize the effects of discriminatory practices arising in part from women's original lower base pay and in part from the sexist biases of job evaluation.

Would women do better under less centralized bargaining? Do their demands have a higher priority in local bargaining than in LO or national union strategy? Perhaps women in the higher-paid occupations would gain, but most women are in the lower-paid occupations and industries. In Norway, unlike Sweden, it is questionable whether wage gains for the highly paid have pulled up the wages of the low-paid. The concepts underlying wage policies may be more important than the degree of centralization. In any case, the Swedish solidary wage for manual workers is the result of a bargaining system even more centralized than the Norwegian one.

If women were to participate significantly in bargaining committees, they might at least keep women's issues on bargaining agendas. How to get them onto the committees is the urgent question. Some change is coming from outside the unions: the 1977 Workers' Protection and Working Environment Act requires that workers elect rank-and-file safety stewards, and many women have come forward for these posts, especially in trades where women predominate. Such women learn by doing; they acquire competence in these jobs. They see the union from the inside, observing how shop stewards and other worker representatives do their jobs and learning how to meet management face to face and defend their fellow workers' rights. A report in the metal industry states that for these very reasons women see the function as important, although they also have seen how little importance management attaches to it.

Women's Organizations and Politics

Women's organizations, formerly not a strong political force in Norway, have recently increased their influence. Although these organizations represent a wide range of views, in the 1970s they were able to collaborate quite successfully on a number of issues. The new feminist movement has probably been the most important influence in securing collaboration and in supporting new demands and attitudes among union women.

Working-class women on the whole participate less than working-class men and middle-class women in organizational life, whether in unions, political parties, or elsewhere. The very structure of organization and political activity constitutes a barrier for women with limited education and traditional sex role training. Working women in all organizations in fact find more effective channels of political action in the working-class parties than in the unions, which prefer to have the parties and the government deal with women's nonwage issues by legislation rather than deal with them themselves through collective bargaining.

Within the labor movement, women have traditionally maintained national and international networks linking women in various working-class parties. Recently, women in the Labor party have turned with renewed interest to their women's secretariat and its local affiliates, and the secretariat has broadened its agenda to include matters of general interest to women. The smaller labor parties are also deeply involved in feminist issues. The numerically insignificant Marxist-Leninist party is influential in the largest feminist organization in Norway, mobilizing a number of young working-class women in its ranks.

Government Policy

Norwegian government ideology has for a long time officially supported sex equality. By the beginning of the seventies, a stronger policy on equality was being developed. The Equal Status Council and its secretariat, which took over the functions of the Council on Equal Pay, were established in 1977. An Equal Status Act, effective in 1979, covers hiring, promotion, dismissal, and affirmative action; it instituted the office of the Equality Ombud and an appeals board to handle complaints of discrimination, though it has serious limitations in that it is not applicable in private life—for instance, in the family. The Family Affairs and Equal Status Department in the Ministry of Consumer Affairs and Government Administration also considers equality issues and has the responsibility for developing and monitoring the government's equality policy.

Measures to facilitate women's employment include attention to public care, education, and job improvements called for in the Workers' Protection and Working Environment Act. Such legislation is based on the premise that women's paid work will be the foundation for a stronger position within the family.

This active public policy on equality, in addition to the benefits it has brought to women as individuals, has given women's organizations a new significance. It has also brought sharply to the fore tactical and strategic differences among organizations. The more radical feminists keep their distance from a policy that they consider a compromise on women's rights; others—perhaps most women—believe that sex discrimination can best be corrected by gradual reforms in the patriarchal system.

Issues and Outcomes

In view of the many barriers that women face, their achievements are more remarkable than their failures. Some postwar improvements in women's status have unquestionably been the result of a general rise in the standard of living of a modern industrial society: mechanization of housework and a higher level of education, for example. Some developments, notably women's improved control of their own fertility, are the fruits of technology. Other changes, however, are largely the result of women's efforts: the right to abortion, increased participation in politics, improvements in women's relative wages, more public concern for child care facilities, and more and better health services for women and children. Equal wages are, however, still to be achieved and still a major demand of union women.

The issues of main concern to working women have shifted during the postwar period. In the full-employment economy of Norway (there was 2 percent unemployment at the end of 1981), the emphasis on the right to work has shifted to the right to paid work near one's home. Instead of attracting people to where work is available, national policy now encourages employers to move where people are. Women's organizations and the trade unions are demanding more rapid realization of the program for day care centers and creches.

Protective legislation was long an issue dividing not only bourgeois and working-class women, but also working-class women among themselves. Such laws weaken women's ability to compete equally with men for jobs, training, and pay. Norway at present limits protection to conditions related to maternity. Recent legislation grants women working in the private sector twelve weeks of partly paid maternity leave; women in public administration have won leave at full pay. Men may take two weeks' unpaid paternity leave. The LO takes the position that both men and women must be protected from exposure to toxic substances.

Feminists and trade union women now demand shorter hours for all workers, not just for women and the parents of small children. "A six-hour day for all" became a central demand for unions and parties in 1982, and the LO has put this topic on its discussion agenda. The LO has also demanded a fifth week of paid annual vacation, but this demand does not by any means serve parents' needs for shorter daily hours. Most important perhaps are union women's attempts to introduce "equality agreements" in individual firms, where women and the local unions can monitor them. This move was first made by women in the Union of Government Employees.

There is a women's opposition in the trade union movement in Norway today. Not all union women participate in or agree with the demands of the opposition, but it seems to be gaining support over time. Its most important goals are the abolition of male domination in the unions and the achievement of equal pay and truly equal working conditions, a six-hour working day for all, paid leaves for parents in certain cases, and equality agreements in all firms.

In the unions' long fight for the rights of the working class, they have claimed the same rights for women as for men and made the same demands upon the men and women in their ranks. This they have seen as equal treatment for the two sexes. But the circumstances of most women are not the same as those of most men. Unequal circumstances mean that the same demands have profoundly different impacts upon the sexes. In effect, such demands put pressure on most women to change their behavior so that they can become full members of the work group, the union, and the labor movement as a whole, for a "full member" is defined in terms of male behavior. Women's inferior status in the workplace and the home means that demands that are, on the surface, equal are actually a form of discrimination that perpetuates old inequalities.

Had the unions reformed their own structures to reconcile the differences between formal and real equality of rights and demands, they might have led other social and political organizations toward the goals of sex equality. Initiatives from within the LO could still tip the scales in behalf of working women. Instead, while guarding their self-determination in their

own limited sphere, the unions have left the formulation and implementation of programs for basic equality to the Labor party and Labor governments.

GLOSSARY

LO   Landsorganisasjonen Norge: Norwegian Federation of Labor
NAF   Norsk Arbeidsgiverforening: National Federation of Employers

NOTES

This chapter deals with unions historically linked to the labor movement; thus,
we do not discuss the employee groups that have never been linked to the LO.

The authors want to express their gratitude to Val Lorwin, Alice Cook, Gerry
Hunnius, and Donald Van Houten for valuable comments and suggestions for
improvement.

1. This is a major argument in the works of a Norwegian historian of the
working class, Halvdan Koht.

2. Several books and booklets published in connection with jubilees of unions
and local union branches are important sources for this history. The labor movement
keeps certain records in the Arbeiderbevegelsens Arkiv (Labor Movement Ar-
chives) in its headquarters at Youngstorvet in Oslo. Much of the material has been
only partially studied.

3. These latter women include writers like Camilla Collett, feminist politicians
like Aasta Hansteen, the abortion-rights advocate Katti Anker Møller, and the first
inspector of women's working conditions, Betzy Kjelsberg.

4. This period is discussed in the notes made by Betzy Kjelsberg for a planned
autobiography. This material can be studied in the Handskriftsamlingen (manuscript
collection) in the University Library in Oslo.

5. New research, much of it by women, has taken up the question of women's
influence on the formulation of the social policy orientation of social democratic
ideology. Sørensen finds evidence for such influence in material from local industrial
communities. Marit Hoel holds that the whole labor movement has been instilled
with new social values by women and women's groups; see "Kvinneperspektiv på
arbeidersolidariteten" (A Women's Perspective on Working Class Solidarity), in
Kvinneforskning: Bidrag til samfunnsteori, ed. Haukaa, Hoel, and Haavind
(Women's Research: Contributions to Social Theory) (Oslo: 1982).

6. It is sometimes claimed that women tend to be more "altruistic" in their
goals. See chapters by Hildur Ve, Hjørdis Kaul, and Bjørg Aase Sørensen, *Kvinner i
fellesskap* (Women Together), ed. Harriet Holter (Oslo: 1982).

7. For a history of the first period of female activism, see Anna Caspari
Agerholt, *Den norske kvinnebevegelsens historie* (The History of the Norwegian
Women's Movement) (Oslo: 1937; reprint ed., 1973). More recent developments are
analyzed in Harriet Holter and Runa Haukaa, "Kvinnekår og kvinnefrigjøring"
(Women's Situation and Women's Liberation), in *Norges kulturhistorie* (History of
Norwegian Culture), vol. 8 (Oslo: 1981). The new women's movement in Norway is

described by Runa Haukaa in *Bak slagordene* (Behind the Slogans) (Oslo: 1982). See also Ida Blom and Gro Hagemen, *Kvinner selv* (Women by Themselves) (Oslo: Aschehoug, 1977).

8. This topic is discussed in several Norwegian works published in the 1970s. See, for instance, Harriet Holter, *Sex Roles and Social Structure* (Oslo: 1970); Berge, Kalleberg, and Leira, eds., *I kvinners bilde* (In Women's Image) (Oslo: 1977); Berit Aas, "A Five Dimensional Model of Change: Contradictions and Feminist Consciousness," *Women's Studies International Quarterly* 4 (1981); and Berit Aas, and Glenn Wilson, *The Great Sex Debate: Are We Equal?* (London: 1983).

9. On this chapter in Norwegian history see, for example, Frances Sejersted *"Den vanskelige frihet," 1814–1850* ("The Difficult Freedom," 1814–1850) (1978). A more detailed discussion is found in Pryser, *Thranerørsla i norske bygder* (The Thrane Movement in Norwegian Communities) (1977).

10. Egil Ertrevag, "Kvinner i industrien i Norge, 1870–1915" (Women in Norwegian Industry, 1870–1915), in *Wages and Conditions of Working Women in the Nordic Countries, 1850–1914*, ed. G. A. Blom (Trondheim; 1976).

11. Edvard Bull and Knut Mykland, eds., *The Norwegian History*, vols. 13 and 14 (Oslo: Capppelen, 1978–1980).

12. See Blom and Hageman, *Kvinner selv*.

13. Recorded in Bjørg Aase Sørensen, "Arbeidskvinner og verdighet" (Working Women and Dignity), in Berg, Berge, Kalleberg, and Leira, *I kvinners bilde*.

14. This material is found in the Arbeiderbevegelsens Archiv in Oslo. Our translations.

15. Memoirs and biographies of local unions leaders and leaders of women's party branches contain valuable material about women's activities in unions. Research based on oral histories may provide new understanding.

16. See, for instance, Bjørg Aase Sørensen, *Levevei og arbeidstakerresurser* (Life Styles and Resources of Workers) (Oslo: Aidok, 1981).

17. See F. Romcke, *De arbeiderfiendtlige lover* (Anti-Labor Legislation) (Oslo: 1937).

18. The abortion issue caused important debates among Norwegian women of several generations in the twenties, shortly after World War II, and again in the seventies. A law permitting abortions on demand was passed in 1979.

19. Harriet Holter, and Hildur Ve Henriksen, "Social Policy and the Family in Norway," in *Sex Roles and Social Policy*, ed. Jean Lipman-Blumen and Jesse Bernard (London and Beverly Hills, Ca.: Sage, 1979).

20. See Holter, *Sex Roles and Social Structure*, and "Sex Roles and Social Change," *Acta Sociologica* 4, 1970.

21. NOU, *Arbeid for kvinner* (Work for Women), Norwegian Official Investigations, no. 6 (1978).

22. See, for instance, "Everyday Care: Women's Self-Organized Ways of Providing Help, in Paid and Unpaid Care," Worknote no. 5 (Oslo: Norwegian Council for Science and the Humanities Secretariat for Women's Research, 1979).

23. See Annemor Kalleberg, *Foreldre på skift* (Parenting on Shift) (Oslo: Institute for Social Research, 1980).

24. NOU *Levekårsundersøkelsen* (The Standard of Living Study) (Oslo: Oslo University Press, 1976).

25. Ibid.

26. Data presented by the Council on Equality, 1978.

27. Women's access to the public sphere has recently been studied; see Helga Hernes, *Staten: kvinner ingen adgang* (The State: No Admission for Women) (Oslo: Oslo University Press, 1982).

28. See Synnøve Aga, "To Skritt fram og ett tilbake" (Two Steps Forward and One Back), in *Marked for arbeid* (Market for Work), ed. Ted Hanisch, Helge Halvorsen, and Gunvor Strømsheim (Oslo: Oslo University Press, 1980).

29. Published in the periodical *Økonomisk Rapport* 7, 1976. Women in Norwegian industry are paid according to piecework systems that have been eliminated for most male workers. See Ståle Seierstad and Bjørg Aase Sørensen with Øyvind Ryste, *Arbeidsmiljø og lønnssystem* (Work Environment and Wage System) (Oslo: Arbeidsforksningsinstituttene, 1979).

30. B. Ingebrigtsen, "Fagorganisering blant deltidsarbeidende kvinner" (The Degree of Unionization Among Part-Timers), mimeographed. (Oslo, 1980); Jorun Berg Slagnes, *Deltidsarbeid og samhold* (Part-Time Work and Solidarity), in *Kvinner i fellesskap* (Women Together), ed. Harriet Holter (Oslo: Oslo University Press, 1982).

31. Berg Slagnes, *Deltidsarbeid*.

32. John Highley, G. Lowell Filed, and Knut Grøholt, *Elite Structure and Ideology* (Oslo: Oslo University Press and New York: Columbia University Press, 1976).

BIBLIOGRAPHY

Berg, Anne Marie. "Union Growth, Feminist Issues." Mimeographed. Oslo: Institute for Social Research, 1981.

Bull, Edvard. *The Norwegian Trade Union Movement*. Brussels: International Confederation of Free Trade Unions, 1956.

Galenson, Walter. *Labor in Norway*. Cambridge: Harvard University Press, 1949.

Means, Ingunn Norderval. "Norway: Integrating Public Policy and Women." In *Integrating the Neglected Majority*, edited by Patricia A. Kyle. Brunswick, Ohio: King's Court Communications, 1976.

Strømberg, Erling. *The Role of Women's Organizations in Norway*. Oslo: Equal Status Council, 1980.

11 SWEDEN

Gunnar Qvist, Joan Acker, and Val R. Lorwin

Sweden has gone farther than any other industrial capitalist society in removing barriers to equality between the sexes in working life. Yet Swedish women are still far from equality in practice, as distinguished from formal equality of rights. They have lower wages and salaries than men, and their work has less autonomy and prestige; their job opportunities are more restricted, and they have far less power in the trade unions. After looking briefly at the early unions and the Social Democratic party (SAP) and at the trade union scene today, we shall consider the positive changes of the postwar years, some of the gaps between promise and performance, and, finally, the question of whether Sweden has already approached the limits of the advances that can be made toward equality through broad social policy, labor market action, collective bargaining, and internal trade union action in an environment of public commitment to equality.

UNIONS AND THE SOCIAL DEMOCRATIC PARTY: THE EARLY HISTORY

The history of the legal emancipation of Swedish women is part of the history of the dismantling of the old agrarian society and the transition to a modern industrialized one. Changes in the law were aimed at removing obstacles to the utilization of women in a changing workforce, rather than at giving them equality with men. By the mid-nineteenth century, as the guild system was being abolished, women were freed from the requirement to get official permission to seek employment. But although married women gained the right to dispose of their own earned incomes in 1874, they continued until 1920 to need their husbands' consent before they could enter into paid employment.

From the 1860s onward, Swedish society offered employment opportunities for women in schools, hospitals, the railways, the postal, telephone, and telegraph services, and other forms of public and private administration. Many upper- and middle-class women obtained employment and economic independence within these fields, but they also experienced sex discrimination in pay, promotion, and influence. Some of these women eventually organized collectively to improve their conditions. In 1884 the Fredrika Bremer Society, Sweden's first feminist organization, was founded. It is alive and well and still an important force in the fight for women's rights. By the turn of the century, women had created national trade unions for nurses, female schoolteachers, women employed in the postal and telecommunications services, and women with an academic education.

Some of these female trade unions gradually amalgamated with their male counterparts, and these larger units formed the basis for the new white-collar confederations created during the 1930s and 1940s: the TCO (Tjänstemannens centralorganisation—the Swedish Central Organization of Salaried Employees) and the SACO (Sveriges akademikers centralorganisation—the Swedish Confederation of Professional Associations). Many, however, remained purely female until the 1960s, when they disappeared in the wave of consolidation and rationalization in the union movement. The amalgamation of once-female unions with male unions and their participation in new confederations led to greater influence for the unions but also to growing male influence over the problems that concerned women.

The history of female manual workers was different. Between 1870 and 1900 a number of trade unions for female workers were established, but as a rule they were absorbed after a few years by the corresponding unions for men. Toward the end of the nineteenth century, several nationwide unions were formed, and these created a central confederation, the Landsorganisation i Sverige (Swedish Confederation of Labor—LO) in 1898. In spite of LO women's efforts to win greater equality at work, equal pay, and greater representation in the trade unions, and in spite of the passage by the LO of a resolution for equal pay in 1909, little was accomplished to benefit female manual workers. Collective agreements accepted the existing division of labor and the accompanying disadvantages for women, including special lower pay scales. Women received only half the strike pay and sickness or unemployment benefits of men.

The LO had been formed under strong, but not exclusive, socialist influence. In the early days the roles of unions and party were blurred and overlapping. The Social Democratic party (Socialdemokratiska arbeitarparti—SAP), founded in 1889, operated to some extent as a trade union confederation until the beginning of this century. After 1900 it was left to local, not national, unions to decide whether to affiliate with the party. Many did, and in other ways the party and the LO earned the popular description "two branches of the same tree" by a close collaboration that has lasted to the present day.

LO and party leaders generally agreed in placing their main emphasis on class, not gender, issues and on the interests of working-class men. They were the bearers of the revolution according to Marxist doctrine, and although there was not much Marxism or revolutionary zeal in the pragmatic Swedish labor movement after the first decade of the twentieth century, issues of women's equality remained of secondary importance. In addition, the bourgeois composition of feminist associations caused labor leaders to see the contemporary women's movement as a threat to working-class solidarity. Women, especially in the LO and the SAP, hesitated to identify themselves as feminists lest they be called "separatists," and remnants of these assumptions persisted into the last quarter of the twentieth century.[1] In the 1930s, however, progressive women and members of the women's section of the SAP, such as Alva Myrdal, were driving forces behind the new family and gender policies of the nation. The most important of these were financial support for mothers and children, a more humane abortion law, free access to contraceptives, and more open sex education. All were essential steps on the road to the equality of the sexes.

WOMEN'S STRUCTURES IN UNIONS

By 1945 women's labor force participation had begun to increase and their membership in trade unions to rise. The work of women activists in the trade unions had its first significant postwar success in 1947, when the LO formed a Women's Council with its own staff person. In 1948 the LO initiated its first educational and training courses especially for women, with enthusiastic response. Training included instruction and practice in public speaking and conducting meetings.

The founding of the central LO Women's Council was followed by the establishment of women's committees in the LO district organizations. At the same time, spurred by postwar economic expansion, the LO and the Swedish Employers' Federation (Svenska arbetsgivareföringen—SAF) were beginning to work together on the recruitment of women into the paid labor force. Labor shortages aided the efforts of women trade unionists and others to improve the situation of working women.

In 1948 the LO and the SAF established a joint committee to investigate women's pay. An LO-SAF Joint Women's Labor Council, inaugurated in 1951, supported a variety of measures to encourage women to enter the labor force: higher wages, part-time jobs, the provision of day care, and education for more efficient housework. Although in fact little was accomplished in the 1950s to improve wages and working conditions for women, the basis for later measures was being laid, and more and more women were taking up paid work.

At this time labor shortages were common to almost all developed

European nations. Other nations' factories, mines, and low-paid service industries hired southern Europeans, North Africans, Yugoslavs, Turks, and Greeks, as did Sweden for a time. Sweden also hired many Finns. In the 1960s Sweden turned instead to its own women. Why did it go counter to the momentarily easier choice of other European industrial nations? For one thing, it appeared to be less expensive to induce Swedish women to enter or re-enter the labor market in a greater variety of occupations than before than to continue assimilating masses of immigrants. The cost of immigrant labor was calculated not, as in some other nations, in terms of accommodations (often miserable) for male workers who usually left their families in their homelands, but in terms of an infrastructure of housing, health services, schools, vocational training, and language instruction well beyond what most countries supplied to those euphemistically called "guest workers."

Another, nonpecuniary element also entered into the analysis. As the LO put it, "the appearance of a foreign worker proletariat . . . would create a fertile soil for the growth of anti-immigrant feeling, which would hit the migrants in particular, but would also hamper the whole process of development toward a society based on equality and solidarity." Since employers would hire the "young, fit, and experienced" among migrant workers, said the LO, their continued recruitment in large numbers would create great difficulties for marginal groups among both Swedes and migrants already in the country: older men, the disabled, and women. It would "slow down the trend toward greater equality for women in the labor market . . . which is taking place too slowly in any case."[2]

This increasing emphasis on recruiting Swedish women into the labor force, although not in the first instance entirely motivated by the goal of greater equality between the sexes, called for policies that made for greater equality by diminishing women's "double burden." By the 1960s a high proportion of married women were working for pay, many of them at part-time jobs, and over a third of the mothers with children under seven were in the labor force.

As women's labor force participation increased, mounting concern over women's problems was expressed in the trade unions. The TCO, with a large female membership, followed the example of the LO and in 1962 established a council on women's problems. In 1967 it joined the LO-SAF Joint Female Labor Council.

THE SEX ROLE DEBATE

In the 1960s the debate on women's status took on a new form that became known as the "sex role debate." Previously, policies supporting women's entry or re-entry into the labor market had been justified on the

TABLE 11-1
Labor Force Participation Rates in Sweden,
by Sex, Marital Status, and Maternity
as Percentages of the Population of Each Group Aged 16–74
(various years, 1940–1980)

Year	Men	Women	Married Women	Women with a Child 0–6 Years Old
1940			15.4	
1950			25.1	
1960			41.1	
1965	83.9	48.7	43.9	36.8
1970	80.6	52.8	51.5	49.7
1975	80.0	59.2	59.3	60.8
1980	78.4	64.6	66.2	68.5
				(1978)

Sources: National Statistical Board of Sweden—(SCB), "AKU årsmedeltal" (Yearly Averages of Labor Force Participation), Historisk Statistik for Sverige I Befolkning 1720–1967 (Stockholm: 1969), p. 83; and Namden för jämställdhet i arbeitslivet—(JA SAF/PTK), Siffror om män och kvinnor (Men and Women, Key figures) (Stockholm: Tryck Kugel Tryckeri Aktiebolag, 1979), pp. 135 and 139.

grounds of women's "freedom of choice."[3] But now, this was seen as only a conditional freedom—conditional on women's continuing to carry almost the entire burden of housework and child care. Informal groups of intellectuals, political activists, trade union staff, government personnel, and journalists, particularly in the SAP and the Liberal parties, affirmed that equality required a revolution in men's roles in addition to that taking place in women's roles.[4]

The prerequisites for equality were formulated in a report, Towards Equality,[5] presented to the Social Democratic party in 1969 by Alva Myrdal for a SAP working group. The vague wording of the SAP Manifesto of 1960—"Women shall have fully equal status with men in regard to education, work, and advancement"—was given concrete meaning in the 1969 report, adopted as the SAP program for women:

- the goal is a society where "rights, obligations and work are no longer allocated according to sex";
- "a prerequisite for equality between men and women is that they have equal status in working life";
- "sex discrimination in recruitment, promotion, and wages must be eliminated";
- "the economic independence of married partners is a basic condition for equality";

- "the family with two wage earners should become the standard model in the planning of long-range changes in the social insurance system";
- "the tax system should be the same for everyone regardless of sex, civil status, or form of cohabitation";
- "the right to paid leave from work after the birth of a child should be shared between the parents," since they should share the supervision and upbringing of the child; and, finally,
- "the struggle for equality should guide national planning."

This policy reflects an emerging consensus during the 1960s that men would have to assume equal responsibility for the home and child care if women were to have equal opportunity in the world of work. Men too were deprived and disadvantaged by their avoidance of home and parenting responsibilities. Men too had to strive for equality. The new goal was emerging of the couple as "two equal parents, two breadwinners, two citizens, and two individuals in leisure activities."[6] The trade unions concluded that the approach to equality should no longer focus only on women. Both the LO (in 1967) and the TCO (in 1970) dissolved their women's councils and replaced them with family councils. Since then, most questions about women's status have been subsumed under family policy in both confederations. Public policy of the 1960s also emphasized the family. In 1969 sex role equality was specified as an educational goal in a new curriculum for the national system of elementary schools. While this was a substantial advance, there was no comparable attack on the sex segregation of the labor force at this time.

As the decade ended, the labor force participation of women was rising rapidly (Table 11-1), and the composition of the female labor force had changed—now most women workers were married, and a larger proportion of them had young children. But this labor force was still largely segregated by sex, as was much of the expanded employment in the public service sector, especially part-time work within that sector. Yet Sweden entered the 1970s with a broad commitment by the trade unions, the government, and even the employer associations to end sex discrimination. The numbers of women in the trade unions were increasing rapidly, and more women were speaking out on women's issues.

THE UNION SCENE TODAY

By 1980 the LO represented over two million workers; the TCO, over one million; and the SACO/SR about two hundred thousand. The large, independent white-collar federation is a distinguishing feature of the Swedish labor scene. The LO and the TCO, and, to a lesser extent, the

SACO/SR (Statstjänstemännens Riksförbund) have played major roles in shaping policy on sex equality as well as other social issues.

The percentage of the Swedish workforce that is organized is probably the highest of any country, about 90 percent in all. Some 70 percent of working women are organized, the highest proportion in any country except, perhaps, Finland. Unions that are centralized but generally democratic (by any realistic current standards) speak for a large proportion of the population in a society where group interests are widely organized and recognized in public policy formulation and implementation.

During most of the postwar era, collective bargaining in both the private and public sectors has been highly centralized. This is especially true for manual workers in the private sector. Corresponding to union centralization has been the employers' organization of the SAF in the private sector and of central bargaining agencies for the national government, local government, county government, and government-owned industrial enterprises. Agreements between national union confederations and private and public employer organizations have initiated many social changes, including basic changes in the division of national income between workers and other social groups and within the working class. These agreements have sometimes paved the way for national legislation; on the other hand, government has entrusted many labor market functions to industrywide bargaining between unions and employers and to a third, final stage of bargaining by local unions and local establishments or enterprises. Centralization is thus not stifling, especially in a country whose population is only a little over eight million.

There have been considerable political resources available to organized labor, especially the LO. Like other Western Europeans, Swedes use the term "labor movement" to mean the main body of organized manual workers, in this case the LO and the political party with which it is closely associated, the SAP. The party and the LO are linked by history, ideology, joint working groups and informal cooperation, overlapping leadership, and the collective affiliation of a sizable proportion of LO members to the party. Swedes do not speak of the TCO or the SACO/SR as "organized labor" or "the labor movement" (though we shall do so in this paper); instead, they refer to them as "associations" or "federations." Swedes base this distinction in part on the TCO's and the SACO's lack of connection with a political party, as contrasted with the LO-SAP linkage. The TCO and the SACO are politically neutral, and "their neutrality is respected by all parties, while at the same time the two organizations do not hesitate to articulate the interests of their members even on highly controversial issues."[7]

Union leaders, especially those of the LO, have often been members of the Riksdag, the Swedish parliament. The labor confederations, moreover, are normally active in the long, careful process of preparation for important legislation in which the major interest groups are represented according to the rather unique Swedish blend of parliamentary decision making, interest group consultation, and bureaucratic power. They are represented not only on the committees that formulate the bases for Riksdag decisions, but also on the boards that administer the policies emerging from those decisions. Among the boards most important for women's status and activities are those for labor market policy, education, health and social affairs, and social insurance.

WAGE SOLIDARITY AND THE ACTIVE LABOR MARKET POLICY

In the 1960s Sweden pioneered in a remarkable combination of economic rationalization and egalitarian wage planning, of which women were among the chief beneficiaries. What became known internationally as Sweden's active labor market policy came at the initiative of the LO and the Social Democratic government, with major programs formulated and implemented in great part by the private sector "labor market partners"—the LO, the TCO, and the SAF.

The active labor market policy combined the imperative of full employment with that of increased productivity through such positive measures as improved vocational training and retraining and the more efficient matching of labor supply and demand through a vigorous public employment service. Higher wage levels, especially among the hitherto low-paid, would force weak companies to rationalize or go under, thus concentrating resources in companies fit to survive. Low wages for women had to go, as a matter of social justice and because they subsidized inefficient firms and inefficient sectors of the economy at the expenses of Sweden's productivity, its ability to compete in international markets, and its standard of living.

A government commission on low incomes reported two-thirds of the "extremely low-paid" and four-fifths of the low-paid over twenty-five years of age were women.[8] The Swedish response combined a many-faceted labor market policy with a continuing union drive to level wages upward, both between the sexes and among industries. Rationalization would cause some temporary unemployment, but here there intervened an efficient employment service, large-scale training and retraining efforts, and (as a last resort) a safety net of unemployment compensation, moving allowances, and public works jobs.

The first and simplest step toward equality of wages was to eliminate unequal pay for equal work, the lower pay scales for women that were then characteristic of almost all industrial societies. A national agreement between the LO and the SAF phased out all the women's pay scales by 1965. Thereafter, collective agreements made no mention of the sex of wage earners, and the LO treated women's wages as part of the general problem of low pay and rationalization. In raising the wage levels in low-paid industries as a whole, the LO's policy of wage solidarity also helped women, since many of the worst-paid industries—notably textiles and distribution—employed high percentages of women.

In round after round of annual or biennial national agreements, beginning in the 1960s and continuing through the difficult years of the late 1970s and early 1980s, the LO obtained various forms of wage increases favoring the low-paid job categories, mostly women, and the low-paid industries. The solidary wage policy was successful in raising low wages. The wage gap between the low-paid industries and the high-paid was steadily narrowed, and the wage gap between men and women in the LO-SAF bargaining area—that is, manual workers in the manufacturing sector—was narrowed from 30 percent in 1959 to only 7 percent in 1981.

The solidary wage policy was dependent upon the willingness of those in the higher wage brackets and the better-paying industries, almost all of them men, to forego some of the raises that they might otherwise have received in a period of economic expansion, labor shortages, union strength, and Social Democratic political power. And essential to that willingness was the centralized bargaining of the LO and the SAF: competitive bargaining by the component unions of the confederation would have made a solidary wage policy impossible. Peak-level bargaining was still implemented by national agreements industry by industry and by plant- or enterprise-level bargaining, where the normal self-interest of the more skilled and better-paid workers led them to seek concessions from management. But such gains were offset at the LO-SAF level (at the LO's insistence) by special funds increasing the low-paid workers' wages.

Men's acceptance of these restrictions on their ability to use their economic strength to get as much as possible for themselves owed much to the practice of union consultations with membership and to the widespread and deeply rooted system of workers' education. LO-SAP educational programs inculcated the ideology of egalitarianism characteristic of the Scandinavian democracies.

EQUAL RIGHTS IN THE 1970S

In 1972 an Advisory Council on Equality Between Men and Women was established in the office of the prime minister. Composed of members of his party, it had direct access to those in power. On equality issues, moreover, the nonsocialist parties did not generally oppose the Social Democrats. The Advisory Council took employment and education to be the two fields calling most urgently for action, and it was instrumental in the enactment of a series of measures in the 1970s that caused people—at least outside Sweden—to speak of that country as a model in the effort to diminish inequalities due to sex.

These measures supported working women both in the family and in the workplace. Day care for the children of working parents was one of its most obvious concerns. Although public financing of day care began as early as the 1940s, the level of such support had remained very low up to the mid-1960s. In the 1970s the national government accelerated its subsidies to municipal day care and established goals for substantially increasing the proportion of children under the age of seven (the age for starting school) who would receive such care, both in day care centers and (in smaller numbers) in family day care arrangements in people's homes.

Generous parental leaves and job protection for parents who take these leaves also support and encourage women workers. Since 1974 fathers as well as mothers have qualified for parental leave. This was a powerful innovation, though it is still mostly women who take advantage of these provisions. By 1982 parents could share nine months of leave at full pay and three additional months at a uniform per diem rate after the birth of each child or the adoption of a young child. These social security benefits are paid by the state. In addition, either parent may take paid time off to care for a sick child, up to a maximum of sixty days a year for a child up to twelve years of age. A parent may shorten his or her working day to six hours, and receive six hours' pay, until the child is eight years old. In the late 1970s about 12 percent of new fathers took some parental leave, though they took off less time than mothers did. White-collar unions did more to encourage fathers to take leave than did manual workers' unions.

Since 1971 the incomes of wife and husband have been taxed separately. Because the Swedish income tax is progressive, with high marginal rates, the net increase in a couple's income is higher if the person with the lower income increases his or her hours of work. This new tax policy contributed to equality by removing the financial penalty that the old system of joint taxation placed on women who entered the labor market or acquired new skills that brought pay raises.

A considerable variety of labor market measures sought to help women take up, or return to, paid work, to encourage employers to hire women for nontraditional jobs, to prepare women better for traditional women's jobs, and to prepare women and men for jobs traditionally held only by one sex or the other. Companies receiving regional development subsidies that created new jobs had to attempt to hire a balanced workforce—at least 40 percent of each sex—for the new jobs. Employers received subsidies for training women and men for jobs previously held only by the other sex. A number of projects gave women support for undertaking previously all-male jobs. For a time quotas restricted the number of women in training for nursing and child care work to encourage men to take up these occupations. However, the results of many of these programs in the private sector were disappointing. For example, in four years of subsidies to 287 firms to hire women for male-dominated occupations, only 1,125 women were hired,[9] less than one-tenth of one percent of the female labor force.

The powerful Labor Market Board, on which the trade unions had a majority of members, changed its early view of its role as chiefly to provide jobs for those without them; it now attempted instead "within the framework of the need for labor power in society, to give each who can and wants to work the effective support to realize his [sic] free choice of employment."[10]

The national government promulgated an Equality Ordinance in 1976 and an Equality Circular in 1977 that required government authorities to draw up plans to recruit and nominate women for traditionally male jobs, and vice versa, and to institute personnel training and redesign jobs to promote equality. Efforts were made to obtain equal representation of the sexes on public bodies, and the national government sponsored information and recruitment drives to persuade members of the underrepresented sex to apply for positions dominated by the other sex.

Equality Agreements in the Private Sector

The unions, especially the LO, had been the initiating agents of, or had at least actively supported, legislative and administrative efforts related to income tax reform, day care, parental leave, and labor market measures to reduce sex segregation. But on issues of labor relations, such as wages, hiring, and promotion, the unions opposed legislation and insisted that such matters were best settled by collective bargaining. Where wages and salaries were concerned, they could point to the nearly universal union membership and to agreements with public and private employers. But they could not claim to have pre-empted the field of equal opportunity by union action and collective agreements.

Some women's organizations and the conservative parties had proposed equal opportunity legislation, but it was not until a conservative government came into power in 1976 that it became a serious possibility. At that time the trade unions in the private sector were not working with management on women's issues; the joint union-management council on women's problems had been abolished in the early 1970s. However, as the probability increased that a law on equality would be passed, the trade unions began talks with private sector management on the problem. An equality agreement between the SAF and the PTK (Privattjänstemanna Kartellan—the bargaining cartel of TCO unions in the private white-collar sector) was signed in 1977 and was soon followed by an equality agreement between the LO and the SAF. Both of these were "frame" agreements, to be followed by implementing agreements at the plant or local level.

The LO-SAF agreement provided for equal pay for equal work, equal opportunity for employment, training, and meaningful work, and equal ability to combine job and family life. The responsibility to develop positive measures at the plant level, including equitable policies of recruitment and training and the removal of obstacles to the achievement of equality, rested with management. Cases of discrimination were to go for settlement to the tripartite Labor Court.

The PTK-SAF agreement specified equality in recruitment, training, and promotion. It called for equal pay for work of equal value, not just equal pay for equal work (as in the LO-SAF agreement), and it established a joint SAF-PTK Committee for Equality at Work with responsibility for positive action to end discrimination. This committee was instructed to propose corrective measures, obtain information, give guidance to companies at the local level, and initiate and monitor pilot projects. In disputes not settled through negotiation, the committee would act as arbitrator. Disputes could be taken to the committee by the employer, the union, or the individual employee or would-be employee.

In the three years between the signing of the agreements in 1977 and mid-1980, when another procedure for handling grievances went into effect under the new equality law, no cases went to the Labor Court under the LO-SAF agreement. One case of discrimination went to the PTK-SAF committee for arbitration. Although the absence of cases might mean that no problems existed or that they were satisfactorily handled at lower levels, the early enforcement of the new law, discussed below, suggests otherwise.

Little progress has been made on voluntary action to reduce sex discrimination. The primary form of positive action has been the establishment of "equality groups," voluntary discussion groups, usually sponsored by the employer, sometimes by the union. A few experimental programs have been undertaken, but the results have been minimal.

The Act on Equality Between Women and Men at Work

In 1976 the Equality Ordinance for employees in the public sector came into force. In 1979 parliament approved the Act on Equality Between Women and Men at Work, covering both the public and the private sectors, which took effect in 1980. It prohibits job discrimination on the basis of sex and mandates positive action to achieve equality. However, an agreement between the labor market parties supersedes the act insofar as positive action is concerned. Employers are to initiate such action; trade unions do not have explicit responsibility for equality work except in their capacity as employers. Finally, the act provides for the appointment of a full-time Equal

Opportunities Ombudsman with the responsibility for enforcing the law, and an Equal Opportunities Commission. The first ombudsman appointed was an experienced woman judge. Complaints may be brought directly to the ombudsman by an individual. The ombudsman then confers with the management and union involved and asks the union to negotiate a settlement. If no settlement is reached, the union or the ombudsman may take the case to the Labor Court.

In the first one and a half years of the law's existence—up to December 1981—146 complaints of sex discrimination had reached the ombudsman's office.[11] The ombudsman was asked to intervene to force positive action to alter discriminatory practices in another 87 cases. Carrying out her responsibility to initiate the process of setting legal precedents, she took three cases to the Labor Court. The first to be decided involved the choice of a young man in preference to an older woman for a job in a municipality. The principle was won for the woman: she had superior qualifications, and the failure to hire her was ruled to be sex discrimination. The municipality had to pay a fine, but the man kept the job.

The law has no teeth. It provides for compensation to aggrieved individuals for loss and moral injury due to discrimination and for fines when employers fail to comply with obligations for positive measures. However, there is no requirement that the party found to have suffered discrimination be given the job, promotion, or raise, or that employers institute plans for ending discrimination by a certain time. Where there is a previously existing collective agreement on positive measures, as noted above, that agreement takes precedence. Failures to act in accordance with such agreements are to be dealt with through the use of the sanctions specified in the agreement, but there is no record of any union's attempting to do this.

Labor Legislation

Swedish labor had until the 1970s insisted on the primacy of collective bargaining in labor relations. Then, finding that employers' resistance to union demands was stiffening while the emphasis on productivity was permitting them to go far toward dehumanizing the work environment, labor, and especially the LO, pushed through a series of major legislative measures enlarging the rights of unions and the protections of workers. Unions in all sectors supported this legislation, unlike that on sex equality, and two of the three nonsocialist parties supported the Social Democrats in putting through the labor laws of 1973–1976 at a time when parliament was evenly divided between the socialist and nonsocialist groups.

The new laws protected the job security of employees, safeguarded shop stewards in the performance of their functions, provided for employee representation on company boards, provided for worker participation in decisions about all aspects of work, and greatly strengthened the law on health and safety at work and the rights of workers and their representatives in determining changes in their work environment. We shall refer to this law by its Swedish initials, MBL (Medbestämmandelagen) for brevity's sake and because there is no agreement on the English translation of its title.

All these laws, of course, affect women workers as well as men. The increase in the number of union representatives, such as health and safety delegates, and the expanded training for them mean that an increasing number of women are getting education and experience in union functions. This process is most evident in workplaces with high proportions of women employees. The MBL also creates the possibility of much more active involvement of the unions with equality issues. The employer is required to negotiate with the union on almost every impending change. The union may initiate negotiations on any matter affecting employees, including, for example, the establishment of affirmative action programs. The MBL has apparently not been used yet to promote sex equality: a recent search failed to locate even one example of union utilization of the MBL for negotiations on affirmative action.[12] Women union activists recognize the potential for change in the MBL and other laws, but they often find equality issues so low on the list of union demands that they are never reached or, if reached, are bargained away for traditional demands that male negotiators see as more important.

LABOR MARKET SEGREGATION

A higher proportion of women work for pay in Sweden than in almost any other industrial capitalist country. By 1980, 64.6 percent of women between the ages of sixteen and seventy-four were in the labor force, and they constituted 45 percent of Swedish workers. The labor force participation of women in the prime working ages was even higher: for example, over 84 percent of women between the ages of thirty-five and forty-four were in the labor force in 1980.[13] These figures may, however, be somewhat inflated because they include the large number of employed women with young children who are on leave at any given time.

Women continue to work in a much more limited number of occupations than men. Sweden's is, in fact one of the most sex-segregated labor forces in Europe.[14] That segregation limits the occupational choices of women, threatens their job security, and is largely responsible for the gap between their earnings and men's. Despite the reform of the school curriculum to eliminate sex typing, girls and boys both make almost the same occupational choices as they did before the reform.

The simplest and most accessible measure of sex segregation by occupations is probably that recently developed by the Organisation for Economic

Cooperation and Development (OECD). It measures the difference between the female share of a particular occupation and the female share of the total labor force.[15] The statistical measure does not necessarily indicate distance from the goal of desegregation; for example, if the female share of the total labor force is 36 percent, that does not mean that the goal must be 36 percent of women in coal mining or 64 percent of men in child care. Changes in the index do, however, indicate progress toward a goal, and while the index for Sweden stood at 51.6 in 1970, it had gone down only to 50.4 by 1977. Moreover, the slight decline in segregation between 1970 and 1977 is probably more the result of men's entering female-dominated occupations than of women's entering male-dominated ones. The increase in the latter phenomenon that has occurred may be due to a drop in male employment in those occupations, rather than a real increase in female employment.[16]

PART-TIME WORK

The sex segregation of the labor force has another dimension in industrial societies: many women hold part-time jobs, while almost all men hold full-time ones. In the last twenty years, the greatest increases in the labor force have resulted from women moving into part-time jobs from unpaid work at home.[17] Moreover, only a minority of women work full time all year round. For example, in the two-year period between 1978 and 1980, about 23 percent of Swedish women were employed continuously at full-time jobs, about 16 percent were out of the paid labor force entirely, and the balance was divided between those who worked steadily at part-time jobs and those who moved in and out of the labor market or moved between part-time and full-time jobs.

Part-time work, defined in the statistics as anything under thirty-five hours a week, accounts for about one-fifth of the jobs in the Swedish economy. While a slight increase in the number of men working part time has taken place because of inducements to early retirement, part-time work remains essentially women's work. Forty-five percent of employed women (and only 5 percent of men) work part time. Some women, especially those with young children or other heavy family responsibilities, prefer part-time work. For many, it is a transition between childbirth leave and a return to full-time work. Others would prefer full-time work but find that only part-time is available.

There have been lively arguments over the consequences of part-time work for women's chances of independence and for the trade union movement and over the extent to which women want it or take it for lack of alternatives. Most trade unions dislike part-time work because part-timers have a limited commitment to their jobs and therefore to the union and because the unions feel that part-timers' lower expectations are a threat to their hard-won labor standards. Feminist opponents of part-time work argue that only full-time earners can be equal to their spouses and that the acceptance of part-time work locks women into the responsibility for family work and the double burden that is almost as heavy in Sweden as elsewhere.

A few trade unions, notably in local government and distribution, have made a concerted effort to organize part-time workers, and despite the union movement's general reservations, it has obtained for most Swedish part-timers the protection of social insurance and other fringe benefits. While this coverage has raised the cost to employers of hiring part-timers, it has not as yet arrested the trend toward their increased employment.

Although great progress has been made in equalizing earnings in manufacturing, most Swedish women do not work in this sector, and the wage gap in the rest of the full-time labor force is much higher. In the private sector female white-collar workers earned about 77 percent as much as men in 1974.[18] In 1980 all full-time, year-round women workers earned, on the average, 78 percent of the earnings of all full-time, year-round male workers.[19] But because 45 percent of women workers were employed part time in that year, women took home about one-third, while men took home two-thirds, of all Swedish salaries and wages.[20]

EFFECTS OF THE RECESSION

Sex segregation's implications for unemployment are only beginning to emerge. Women workers are heavily concentrated in the social and health services in local communities. A high proportion of these jobs are part-time. Government at all levels is dealing with current economic difficulties partly through curtailing these services or not expanding them as rapidly as had been planned, and it is the part-time workers who are being laid off first. If the economic difficulties continue, services may be further curtailed to free resources for investment in new industries that produce for export. This, of course, would further reduce women's employment opportunities. Another possibility is that as traditional male jobs decline, equality will more and more come to mean that men move into traditionally female work areas. Although total Swedish unemployment is still relatively low by international standards (a little over 3 percent in 1982), it has been rising rapidly among young workers seeking their first jobs. Young women, more than young men, have difficulty finding jobs, and some are turning to early motherhood as an alternative. This trend could lead to a new group of women with few skills and little work experience who may yet have to work for a living.

Recession has impeded progress toward the goal of state-supported day care for all children of working parents. By 1979 only about 17.5 percent of children under the age of seven were in day care centers, and another 11.8

percent were in family day homes supported by municipalities. At the same time, over 65 percent of the mothers with children under seven were in the labor force. Lack of sufficient and easily accessible day care is one reason so many Swedish women work part time. It is common for parents to put their children on a day care center waiting list as soon as they are born and even then to have to wait two or three years for a place.

WOMEN'S ROLES IN THE UNIONS

By now it has become routine for trade union bodies in most countries to deplore the low level of participation and office holding by women. The LO has made a number of surveys of the extent of their participation from the workplace to the top levels and has published the results. It has even had the grace recently to say that it found those levels "frighteningly low."[21]

Although women's participation has probably increased in recent years at the workplace and local levels, it remains very low at levels that require absence from home for officers' training and participation in decision-making bodies. The LO has made serious efforts to decentralize some of its advanced training for union representatives, so that people with family responsibilities can take the courses that qualify them for union office without leaving home.

Although women constituted 41 percent of the LO's 1981 membership, there were no women on the national executive board, and women were underrepresented in other executive and legislative bodies and collective bargaining commissions of the confederation and national unions, including those with majorities of women members, as Table 11-2 shows. The picture

TABLE 11-2

Women as Percentage of Members and Elected Officials
in Swedish Trade Union Confederations, 1971, 1977, and 1980

	LO			TCO			SACO/SR	
	1971	1977	1980	1971	1977	1980	1971	1977
Members	30	36	40	43	46	57	31	32
Convention delegates	13	18	25 (1981)	16 (1970)	20	32	16 (1974)	24
General council	3	9	NA	16	16	NA	10	15
Executive board	0	0	0	20	20	23	12	20
National union presidents	0	0	0	9	8	NA	10	8

NA = not available
Sources: JA SAF/PTK, *Siffror om män och kvinnor*, p. 267; 1980 data from the TCO and the LO; SACO/SR data not available.

was better in the TCO, where in 1980 women made up 57 percent of the membership and 23 percent of the national executive board.

In some other countries women's underrepresentation in trade union life is paralleled in political life. In Sweden, as in other Scandinavian countries, women have a much less inadequate representation in political life. Their share of the total representation in parliament has gone up, without interruption, from 5.3 percent in 1945 to 27.8 percent in 1980. On county councils, their representation has increased steadily from 15.2 percent in 1970 to 31.1 percent in 1979; on municipal councils, from 14.0 percent in 1971 to 29.8 percent in 1980. The nonsocialist coalition cabinet formed after the 1979 election had five women among its twenty-one members.[22] Although more women everywhere with resources of time, information, and money are interested in political careers than in trade union careers, the contrast between Swedish women's recognition in unions and in political parties is striking.

Some trade unionists argue that equality demands that women and men in the unions be treated alike; others argue that while people in like circumstances should be treated alike, equality demands that those in unlike circumstances be treated differently. The LO and TCO women's councils and committees were abolished in favor of family councils in the name of equality and in the interest of stimulating men to take more active roles in the family. Many women have concluded that the change was a mistake. In a number of unions, especially white-collar unions, women's committees have been formed, some of which include male members. Some unions have again established training courses especially for women, and many have established equality study groups.

There are other indications that the unions are increasing their attention to women and to equality issues, even though women have barely penetrated the higher levels of decision making and collective bargaining. The LO and the TCO have full-time staff members at the confederation level working to promote equality, as do some of the national unions. One of these is the metal workers' union (Metallindustriarbetareförbundet) long the largest, most powerful, and probably most male-dominated union in the LO.

The municipal workers' union (Kommunalarbetarförbundet) has become the largest union in the LO. Eighty percent of its members are women, but the presidency and many other offices are still held by men. This union has developed successful educational and training programs for its members, mostly low-waged blue-collar workers, many of them part-timers. Programs worked out in collective bargaining with hospital authorities and other employers have created advancement opportunities for workers in routine jobs and career ladders by which semiprofessionals have qualified for professional posts. Even for members in the humblest jobs, such as cleaning women, union programs achieved through collective bargaining have added elements of special training (for example, instruction in the chemical properties of work materials) and of discretion in the organization of their customary tasks.

The food workers' union (Livsmedelsarbetareförbundet) in 1980 asked the Swedish Center for Working Life (Arbetslivscentrum) to do a study of equality issues in its industry. The study, focusing on seven typical factories, showed clear patterns of segregation of women in the most undesirable jobs with the poorest working conditions. Although male union leaders may have already recognized that women did the least desirable work, they had felt little pressure to alter the situation.[23] Following the presentation of the research report, however, the union instituted training in equality work for its officials.

THE LIMITS OF THE POSSIBLE?

Has Sweden gone as far as it is possible to go toward the equality of the sexes in a democratic industrial capitalist state? Why has it not gone farther?

Some of the conditions that made possible the pioneering changes between the mid-1950s and the late 1970s have disappeared or been seriously weakened. The once strong economy is now in the process of transformation under the most difficult and unpredictable conditions of international competition and national capital formation. Even so, Sweden is still, at least for the present, able to sustain most of its network of welfare institutions and labor market measures. The ideology of equality is still strong among its dominant trade union groups and the SAP. On sex equality, the Liberal and Center parties generally concur with the SAP, and only the Conservatives exhibit some traditional attitudes. The government bureaucracy continues to be open to measures to promote sex equality, and the nation remains committed to it. But formal equality has not yet been translated into practice in working life, education, or the family.

The occupational patterns of women's increased participation in the paid labor force helped to preserve the old sex segregation, while the rapid expansion of the state-supported service sector provided the greatest number of job opportunities for new entrants into the labor force. Despite some attempts to bring more men into this field, a highly sex-segregated labor market was perpetuated. The entry of women into these jobs, on either a full-time or a part-time basis, did not upset old sex roles: mother worked a few hours or even all day in a woman's job, while father remained the main breadwinner. Family patterns of authority and the allocation of tasks in the home continued to conflict with the schools' efforts to introduce the child to a world of sex equality.

The schools themselves conveyed contradictory messages about sex equality: elementary and secondary curricula designed to eliminate sex typing in studies, play, vocational orientation, and occupational choice were presented by a sex-segregated teaching staff. Nursery and elementary school teachers are almost all women, in spite of efforts to induce men to enter such work. At the higher levels of the educational pyramid, sex segregation continues, but in the opposite direction. The faculties of the institutions of higher education that give teachers their basic training are overwhelmingly male. Moreover, the new scholarship on women is only beginning to appear at the university level; little of this knowledge or perspective has been integrated into courses.[24] Research on women is still sparse, though increasing; women's studies are still peripheral, and most male faculty members know little of them. The reform of school curricula is also impeded by old-fashioned vocational counselors and by the more traditional media, the teenage and women's magazines.

The unions continue to argue that sex discrimination and affirmative action should be handled by negotiations between unions and employers, even though in the 1970s they promoted a spate of labor laws that rendered obsolete much of their old emphasis on collective bargaining to settle all labor relations questions. Sweden has therefore never had a strong, national affirmative action program, and a person who suffered discrimination in employment opportunity had no clear recourse until the equality act of 1980. This reluctance to act on equal opportunity was in sharp contrast to the unions' strong positive action on other major women's issues. But none of these other issues, not even the closing of the wage gap among manual workers, involved the lessening of male power in the workplace or the recognition that certain forms of conflict—over affirmative action, for example—may be part of the price of social progress.

In a comparison of social welfare policy formation in Britain and Sweden, Hugh Heclo has suggested that British politicians start from the assumption of divergent interests, whereas Swedish politicians start from the assumption that they need more information.[25] All recognized groups share in the amassing of such information. The Swedish process has on the whole been very successful, but its success depends partly on the muting and obscuring of conflict. In that process, women and other members of the weaker groups in society have gained much. At other times, they may lose. Perhaps the gains that they have made by law and by collective bargaining have for now reached a maximum, but women might make further gains by directly confronting the issue of men's power in civic, working, and home life.

Many women are reluctant to challenge men's power. One form of reluctance is particular to trade union and socialist women: the fear, especially among blue-collar unionists, that united action by women across class lines may be destructive of the class solidarity between working-class women and men. This idea is clear in the report on equality and solidarity presented to the LO convention of 1981, which states that "class differences are greater than differences between the sexes."[26] There has been no autonomous or semiautonomous women's movement within the trade unions, despite the existence of some spontaneous groups here and there; nor have independent women's groups come together in a militant mass movement.

Perhaps the reform impulse in this area has dissipated among the groups that were its chief bearers. The trade unions have taken on many new tasks to which they have given higher priority: the containment of unemployment, the maintenance of workers' incomes in the face of a shaken international economy, and a long debate over wage earners' investment funds. There has certainly been far less reforming zeal for sex equality among employers, with whom much of the responsibility for achieving it lies.

Many of the issues that have helped to raise the consciousness of both women and men about male power in other countries are only beginning to be faced in Sweden. Sexual harassment on the job, wife beating, and rape are among those issues. A recent report on prostitution, analyzing the institution in terms of male domination and female oppression, has generated controversy that may be fruitful. Some thoughtful Swedes see these problems as more widespread than Sweden's reputation as a rational, nonviolent, and egalitarian society suggests. Just as the problems of work life have a powerful influence on family life, so these general problems of male power and male violence cannot help but extend into the workplace.

Also to be considered are the unanticipated regressive consequences of some progressive measures. Parents may take long leaves to care for children and work shorter days in a child's early years. But both custom and economics have, so far, impelled women to use these options much more than men. Some employers are therefore reluctant to hire young women, who are perceived as likely to exercise the right to long or frequent leaves.[27] This perception tends to preserve traditional family roles and may have adverse effects on women's opportunities for training and promotion and even employment.

An evaluation of Swedish progress must take time into account. Generations have lived under patriarchy; efforts to emancipate women are, in comparison, brand new. Some of these efforts, fortunately, have shown results almost at once: wage policies favoring the lower-paid, for example. Others will begin to show results only after a generation or two or three because they call for changes in mentality and in the most intimate relationships, those of the couple and of parents and their children. The reform of the Swedish public school curriculum is only a single generation old. Parental leave goes back to 1974, and the national equal employment law and the major national collective agreements on equal opportunity in the labor market are of the late 1970s.

If our evaluation repeats the truism that social change takes time, it does so not to condone the failure of those with responsibility to act, but to stress the effort required of the observer to comprehend the forces of conservation and regression as well as the forces of change. There are different time frames for actors and observers. Impatience with inequality and injustice is a virtue in the actors, but patience and a long time frame are requirements for the sympathetic observer's study of the obstacles, as well as the ways and means, to progress. Sweden has not attained the limits of the possible, but it has shown that those limits may be pushed out much farther than they have been in almost any country outside Scandinavia.

GLOSSARY

LO	Landsorganisationen i Sverige: Swedish Confederation of Labor
MBL	Medbestämmandelagen: Act on Employee Participation in Decision Making
OECD	Organisation for Economic Cooperation and Development
PTK	Privattjänstemannakartellan: Bargaining cartel of TCO and other unions in the private sector
Riksdag	Parliament
SACO/SR	Sveriges akademikers centralorganisationen Statstjänstemännen-srikfskörbund: Swedish Confederation of Professional Associations
SAF	Svenska arbetsgivareföreningen: Swedish Employers' Federation
SAP	Socialdemokratiska arbetarparti: Social Democratic Labor Party
TCO	Tjänstemännens centralorganisation: Swedish Central Organization of Salaried Employees

NOTES

1. Gunnar Qvist, "Policy Towards Women and the Women's Struggle in Sweden." *Scandinavian Journal of History* 5 (1980): 51–74.

2. Landsorganisationen i Sverige, *Report on Labor Market Policy* (Stockholm: LO, 1975), p. 103.

3. Annika Baude, "Public Policy and Changing Family Patterns in Sweden, 1930–1977" in *Sex Roles and Social Policy*, ed. Jean Lipman-Blumen and Jessie Bernard (London and Beverly Hills: Sage, 1979).

4. Edmund Dahlström, ed., *The Changing Roles of Men and Women* (London: Duckworth, 1967).

5. *Towards Equality: The Alva Myrdal Report to the Social Democratic Party* (Stockholm: Prisma, 1971).

6. Rita Liljeström, et al., *Roles in Transition* (Stockholm: Council on Equality Between Men and Women, 1978), p. 28.

7. Nils Elvander, "In Search of New Relationships: Parties, Unions, and Salaried Employees' Associations in Sweden," *Industrial and Labor Relations Review* 28 (October 1974): 68.

8. SOU (Statens Offentliga Utredningar) 1971, vol. 39. *Den svenska köpkraftsfördelningen 1967: Låginkomstutredningen.* (The Swedish Purchasing Power Distribution: Low Income Investigation.)

9. Nämden för jämställdhet i arbetslivet (SAF/PTK), *Siffror om män och kvinnor* (Men and Women, Key Figures) (Stockholm: Tryck Kugel Tryckeri Aktiebolag, 1979).

10. Cited by Hugh Heclo, *Modern Social Policies in Britain and Sweden* (New Haven: Yale University Press, 1974), p. 139.

11. Anita Dahlberg, working paper, Arbetslivscentrum, Stockholm, March 1982.

12. Joan Acker, unpublished research on the relationships between the MBL and sex equality measures, 1981.

13. Lillemore Gladh and Siv Gustafsson, *Labor Market Policy Related to Women and Employment in Sweden* (Stockholm: Arbetslivscentrum, 1981), p. 4.

14. Organisation for Economic Cooperation and Development, *Women and Employment: Policies for Equal Opportunities* (Paris: OECD, 1980).

15. Ibid., pp. 44–46.

16. Gladh and Gustafsson, *Labor Market Policy*, p. 19.

17. Marianne Pettersson, *Deltids Arbetet i Sverige: Tabellbilaga Appendix*, (Part-time Work in Sweden: Statistical Appendix) (Stockholm: Arbetslivscentrum, 1981), table 1.

18. Ibid., p. 12.

19. Landsorganisationen i Sverige, *Equality and Solidarity* (Stockholm: LO, 1981).

20. Gladh and Gustafsson, *Labor Market Policy*, p. 1.

21. Landsorganisationen i Sverige, *Kvinnor i facket: undersökning om kvinno representation inom fackförenings rörelsen, 1977* (Women in Unions: Examination of Women's Representation in the Trade Union Movement, 1977) (Stockholm: LO, 1978, and *LO News*, no. 2 [1978]: 10–11).

22. Maud Eduards, "Sweden," in *The Politics of the Second Electorate: Women and Public Participation*, ed. Joni Lovenduski and Jill Hills (London: Routledge and Kegan Paul, 1981), pp. 216–18.

23. Annika Baude (director of the study), personal communication, 1981.

24. Birgitta Wistrand, *Swedish Women on the Move* (Stockholm: Swedish Institute, 1981), p. 49.

25. Heclo, *Modern Social Politics*, pp. 304–22.

26. Landsorganisationen i Sverige, *Equality and Solidarity*, p. 147.

27. Karin Widerberg, Institute of the Sociology of Law, University of Lund, personal communication, 1982.

BIBLIOGRAPHY

Baude, Annika. "Public Policy and Changing Family Patterns in Sweden, 1930–1977." In *Sex Roles and Social Policy*, ed. Jean Lipman-Blumen and Jessie Bernard. London and Beverly Hills: Sage, 1979.

Castles, Francis G. *The Social Democratic Image of Society*. London: Routledge and Kegan Paul, 1978.

Dahlström, Edmund. *The Changing Roles of Men and Women*. London: Duckworth, 1967.

Edgren, Gösta, Karl-Olof Faxén, and Clas-Erik Odhner. *Wage Information and the Economy*. London: Allen and Unwin, 1973.

Eduards, Maud. "Sweden." In *The Politics of the Second Electorate: Women and Public Participation*, ed. Joni Lovenduski and Jill Hills. London: Routledge and Kegan Paul, 1981.

Elvander, Nils. "In Search of New Relationships: Parties, Unions, and Salaried Employees' Associations in Sweden." *Industrial and Labor Relations Review* 28 (October 1974).

Forsebäck, Lennart. *Industrial Relations and Employment in Sweden*. Uppsala: Almqvist and Wiksell, 1980.

Gladh, Lillemore, and Siv Gustafsson. *Labor Market Policy Related to Women and Employment in Sweden*. Stockholm: Arbetslivscentrum, 1981.

Heclo, Hugh. *Modern Social Politics in Britain and Sweden*. New Haven: Yale University Press, 1974.

Kyle, Gunhild. *Gästarbeterska i manssamhället* (Guestworkers in Male Society). Stockholm: Liber Forlag, 1979.

Landsorganisationen i Sverige. *Jämställdhet och Solidaritet* (Equality and Solidarity). Stockholm: LO, 1981.

Landsorganisationen i Sverige. *Report on Labor Market Policy*. Stockholm: LO, 1975.

Liljeström, Rita, et al. *Roles in Transition*. Stockholm: Council on Equality between Men and Women, 1978.

Meidner, Rudolf. *Co-ordination and Solidarity: An Approach to Wages Policy*. Stockholm: LO and Prisma, 1974.

Mellström, Gunilla F., and Mariann Sterner. *Improving Working Conditions and Advancement Opportunities of Women*. Gothenberg: University of Gothenberg, 1980.

Nämden for jämställdhet i arbetslivet-SAF/PTK. *Siffror om män och kvinnor* (Men and Women, Key Figures). Stockholm: Tryck Kugel Tryckeri Aktiebolag, 1979.

Öhmann, Berndt. *LO and Labour Market Policy since the Second World War*. Stockholm: Prisma and LO, 1974.

Organisation for Economic Cooperation and Development. *Women and Employment: Policies for Equal Opportunities*. Paris: OECD, 1980.

Pettersson, Marianne. *Deltids Arbetet i Sverige* (Part-time Work in Sweden). Stockholm: Arbetslivscentrum, 1981.

Qvist, Gunnar. "Policy Towards Women and the Women's Struggle in Sweden." *Scandinavian Journal of History* 5 (1980): 51–74.

————. *Statistik och Politik: Landsorganisationen och Kvinnorana på Arbetsmark-naden* (Statistics and Politics: The Swedish Confederation of Labor and Women in the Labor Market). Stockholm: Prisma and LO, 1974.

Rollén, Berit. "Equality between Men and Women in the Labor Market: The Swedish National Labor Market Board." In *Equal Employment Policy for Women*, ed. Ronnie Steinberg Ratner. Philadelphia: Temple University Press, 1980.

Sandberg, Elisabet. *Equality Is the Goal: A Swedish Report for International Women's Year, 1975*. Stockholm: Advisory Council to the Prime Minister on Equality between Men and Women, 1975.

Scott, Hilda. *Sweden's "Right to be Human," Sex-Role Equality: The Goal and the Reality*. Armonk, N.Y.: M. E. Sharpe, 1982.

SOU (Statens Offentliga Utredningar) 1971, vol. 39. *Den svenska köpkraftsfördel-ningen 1967*: Låginkomstutredningen (The Swedish Purchasing Power Dis-tribution: Low Income Investigation).

Stephens, John D. "Impasse and Breakthrough in Sweden." *Dissent* (Summer 1981): 308–18.

Towards Equality: The Alva Myrdal Report to the Social Democratic Party. Stock-holm: Prisma, 1971.

Wistrand, Birgitta. *Swedish Women on the Move*. Stockholm: Swedish Institute, 1981.

12 THE UNITED STATES OF AMERICA

Barbara Mayer Wertheimer

Out of the total range of human possibilities, the activities most highly valued in any particular culture will tend to be enclosed within the domain of the dominant group; less valued functions are relegated to the subordinates. . . . Dominants are usually convinced that the way things are is right and good, not only for them but especially for the subordinates. All morality confirms this view, and all social structure sustains it.—Jean Baker Miller[1]

HISTORY REVISITED

The development of the United States cast women in a more central economic role than history books have ever recorded. Their role differs from that of women in the other industrialized countries described in this volume, beginning as it did with the settling of a sparsely inhabited new land where life was primitive and its main goal was survival.

Early labor in the colonies was compulsory; society could not afford nonworking members. In New England men or women who did not work could be jailed, although the town would more likely find employment for them under the supervision of a spinner, weaver, shoemaker, or housewife. When necessary, the colonies set quotas on work to be produced in the home: in Massachusetts around 1680, each family with a spinner had to produce three pounds of linen, cotton, or wool a week for thirty weeks out of the year. The shortage of labor resulted in wages considerably higher than those in Europe, and although the colonies tried to set wage limits, the principle of supply and demand operated to keep them high. Nonetheless, women in the mid-eighteenth century received for their work one-third less than the lowest-paid unskilled free white male and one-fifth less than hired-out male slaves.

Because white women in the colonies were in short supply and high demand, they had more freedom than their European counterparts and could enjoy an economic partnership with men. Women produced almost everything the family wore, ate, or used. In addition, they assisted husbands, sons, and brothers in their trades, took over when the men were away hunting or fighting, and carried on the family business when they were widowed. Following the Revolution, however, when English common law was enforced more uniformly than it had been in the colonial period, married women almost everywhere lost the right to make contracts and own businesses; even the clothes they wore might legally belong to their husbands. This would not change until the mid-nineteenth century, when married women's property acts were introduced in a number of states.

By the end of the eighteenth century, the stage was set for the rise of the factory system, which drew women away from the home to become the country's first industrial workers. First, there was the demand for finished products to take west as new lands opened and transportation improved. Second, there was the invention of the necessary machinery—the cotton gin, spinning jenny, and weaving looms, with ample waterpower to run them—to combine with available credit and capital. Finally, the War of 1812 brought with it an embargo on goods from Britain. By 1820, some 12,000 workers had found employment in the mills; by 1830, 55,000 had, of whom 39,000 were women. The fourth national census (1820) reported women employed in over a hundred industrial occupations.[2] Millowners, to reassure powerful agricultural interests that they would not take men off the land or keep them from settling the West, recruited young farm women, well educated for the time and thus easy to train, who were eager to earn money in something other than domestic employment (the major occupation for women outside their own homes). Employers also believed that they were hiring docile workers. But within a decade these women were protesting against wage cuts and the speed-ups. By the 1840s they had organized a major association of women millworkers in Lowell, Massachusetts, with branches in other New England mill towns. They aimed at legislative reform and a ten-hour day at a time when women were still denied the vote.

It was extraordinary that women workers were organizing at all. During the eighteenth century, unions emerged in the skilled trades as artisans resisted the encroaching technology that was steadily diminishing their crafts. As the country moved through the nineteenth century, workers attempted to organize against brutal, unsafe factory conditions, long hours, and low pay. Skilled workers in a plant often had little interest in organizing the unskilled men and even less interest in women. Women's organizing had to be done on their own, and unions of women workers were mainly local ones, for women were isolated from women in other cities and towns. Their small groups lacked the funds, experience, or support to sustain their strike efforts. Millowners blacklisted strike leaders throughout New England from future employment and evicted them from their boardinghouses, and they got no help from men's unions, who saw women as a source of competitive cheap labor. During the final quarter of the century, these unions began to lobby for protective laws for women in an effort to eliminate female competition altogether.

Although domestic work would remain the main source of employment for women into the twentieth century, the last half of the nineteenth century saw "women's work" in industry become indelibly marked as such. The Civil War (1861–1865) brought women into government employment for the first time as clerks, at half the salaries of men. Nursing became a profession for women. With the sewing machine and the ready-made clothing industry came tenement sweatshops employing women and children.[3] Retail stores began to hire women as clerks, and male telephone switchboard operators were replaced by women. With the invention of the typewriter in the 1870s, office work too began its conversion to a female profession: in 1870 only 3.3 percent of office workers were women; by 1900 women made up 75.7 percent of all stenographers and typists.[4]

Throughout the nineteenth century, female millworkers, shoe workers, collar starchers, stitchers and sewers, compositors, retail clerks, and others tried, with very limited success and against overwhelming odds, to organize. Although the American Federation of Labor (AFL), founded in 1886, chartered some local women's unions, trade unions of skilled workers did not admit them.

Then, on a raw November day in 1909, 20,000 New York garment workers, almost all of them women, left their factory lofts and began a strike that was to last thirteen weeks. Known as the "Uprising of the 20,000," it laid a firm foundation for the International Ladies' Garment Workers Union (ILGWU), founded in 1900 and still the major labor organization in the women's garment industry. Only a few months later, a similar eruption in Chicago, begun with a walkout by women in the men's clothing industry over a wage cut, set in place the other U.S. garment union, the Amalgamated Clothing Workers of America (later, the ACTWU). Although women's efforts created these unions, whose membership continues to be 75–80 percent female, the key leadership always has been made up of men. This is true of the U.S. labor movement in general, whether the unions are new or old, whether women compose a majority or a minority of the members.

As the country moved into the twentieth century, women's role in the home changed forever from one of production to one of maintenance. The continuing invention of labor-saving devices for the home, often viewed as freeing women for the labor force, at the same time served to reduce the status of the housewife as the need for her specific skills to produce goods in the home was eliminated. By 1900 two out of every five Americans lived in cities. Providing an unending source of cheap labor and markets for ready-made goods and services, immigrants swelled the population, 20 million coming between 1880 and 1915. With urbanization, the birthrate began to drop and the school-leaving age to rise. In 1910, 25 percent of boys aged ten to fifteen and 12 percent of girls that age were employed; by 1930, these figures had dropped to 6 percent of boys and 3 percent of girls in that age group.[5]

World War I marked the entrance of large numbers of women into heavy industry. Their wartime contribution was so substantial that it led President Woodrow Wilson to give strong support to the federal suffrage amendment, and in 1920 women voted in their first national election. Union membership rose during the war, from 8 percent of the labor force to a high of more than 5 million, or 20 percent, by 1920. At this high point, however, unions numbered only 365,000 women among their members, and that number fell to 260,000 by 1927,[6] not surprising in a decade in which a "Bolshevik scare" and a public antiunion reaction combined with corporate paternalism to head off unionization. In the same period (1917–1927), the number of women over fifteen in the workforce rose 27.4 percent, from 8.3 million to 10.6 million. Of these, married women increased their number from 1.9 to 3.1 million, a 28.9 percent increase.[7] As economic conditions worsened for industrial workers during the 1920s, married women began to replace the children, now in the classroom, as the family's secondary wage earners.

When Franklin D. Roosevelt took office as president in 1933, one in every four American workers was unemployed; millions more worked less than a full week at reduced wages. Workers earned as little as five cents an hour, and many were paid not in money, but in scrip. Now, for the first time in U.S. history, the federal government began to assume responsibility for the well-being of its citizens. In the first two Roosevelt administrations, Congress passed more welfare legislation than in the preceding 140 years. The government established old age and survivors' insurance and a federal minimum wage and maximum hours law. It provided for the workers' right to organize unions of their own choosing and to bargain collectively. These laws, sought by reformers for decades, began with the National Recovery Act (NRA) of 1933, which recognized the right to organize. The National Labor Relations Act (NLRA) was passed in 1935 after the demise of the NRA and became a Magna Charta for labor. With it came the birth of a long-term, successful industrial union movement: the Committee for Industrial Organization, later the Congress of Industrial Organizations (CIO). The old AFL and the new CIO both increased their membership rapidly as workers rushed to join unions. Whereas barely 3 million workers were union or employee association members in 1933, 8 million were by 1938.

Women workers (especially married women) and minorities were the particular victims of discrimination during the Depression, not only in private industry, but also in the government's employment and recovery programs, which failed to include many of the 3.5 million women out of work. Under the NRA in 1933 and 1934, 465 codes establishing minimum rates of pay were adopted by employers' and trade associations, sometimes in consultation with unions, and 25 percent of these set lower wages for women than for men. Public assistance, established at this same time, was limited to family men, and jobs programs introduced at the same time were not open to women with employable husbands.[8] Black women suffered even more discrimination, as the "white only" advertisements for jobs illustrated all too well. It was in this period, however, that industrial union organization began to include women as well as men. Women themselves staged sitdown and other strikes for union recognition. They entered the new industrial unions on a more nearly equal footing with men, but, as noted above, they rarely held key leadership posts.

By 1940 the country was retooling to supply military equipment to its allies, and the workforce included 14 million women. At the height of the war, in July 1944, that number had increased to 20.6 million, including 1.5 million black women, many of them in industrial jobs for the first time. Over half the increase in the wartime female labor force was among women between the ages of twenty-four and sixty-five, most of them married.[9] At the war's end employers expected these women to leave their jobs to make room for the returning soldiers; in some plants, in fact, women had had to promise to do so at the time they were hired. Between 3 and 4 million women were laid off from their defense industry jobs, but many returned not to their kitchens, but to the lower-paying jobs they had held before the war: to offices, restaurants, and household work. In the immediate postwar period, overall employment rose, and by 1950 as many women were again in the labor force as during the war. The participation of married women continued to grow, and it has not stopped yet. In 1940 only one-third of all working women were married; by 1960 three-fourths were.[10]

Eli Ginzberg and Hyman Berman, looking at the years from 1940 to 1960, see the longest unbroken economic expansion in America's history.[11] Women's incomes were needed to put husbands or children through school. Postwar expectations of the "good life" collided with the rising costs of consumer goods that had been unavailable during the war. Both business and service industries expanded steadily to meet the demand for housing and equipment whose purchase had been postponed not only by the war, but by the Depression that preceded it. The postwar baby boom added to this demand for goods.

Labor unions had won such fringe benefits as employer-paid vacations and holidays and some medical coverage in wartime negotiations when wage restrictions were in effect, and these benefits spurred the growth of the service sector. As jobs opened, women were there to fill them, reinforcing occupational segregation. Millions of women also entered the labor force as part-time workers.

Whether women's jobs were full-time or part-time, almost invariably they paid less than work done by men. This happened in part because women interrupted their work to bear and rear children and therefore had difficulty building seniority, lost out on promotions, were the first candidates for layoffs. Moreover, they entered the job market at the least skilled levels. Protective labor laws limited their employment opportunities; craft unions did not admit them to membership, thus effectively barring them from apprenticeship programs and most of the skilled trades; employers hired them almost exclusively for "women's jobs." Furthermore, most women worked in sectors of the economy that were not yet unionized. Nor was the post–World War II period one in which union organization flourished. The passage in 1947 of the Taft-Hartley Act, designed to limit and regulate labor unions, underscored a decline in the labor's influence and public image.

The Civil Rights Movement of the sixties riveted the country's attention on the inequities suffered by minorities in employment, housing, voting rights, public transportation, and access to public education. As Congress enacted laws to deal with these issues, women benefited in two critical areas. The Equal Pay Act (1963) was intended to equalize pay for equal or substantially equal work in the same plant or office. It was the first federal law that demanded a comparison of the actual content of jobs performed, rather than job titles or even job classifications, both of which had often been used to conceal lower pay rates for women. A year later women found themselves included in Title VII of the Civil Rights Act of 1964, which barred discrimination in employment and was administered by the Equal Employment Opportunity Commission (EEOC). There followed presidential executive orders covering federal employees in a similar way. The basic laws were now on the books to enable women to gain equality in the workplace. Labor's support had been a critical factor in their passage.

During the remainder of the sixties, most of the discrimination cases brought before the EEOC involved male minority workers. In the seventies, however, more and more women workers brought their cases to the commission. The women's movement, emerging out of the experience of the Civil Rights Movement, began to reach union and other working women.

CURRENT PROBLEMS OF WOMEN IN THE LABOR FORCE

In 1979 the number of women in the labor force was 44 million, and it was officially predicted in 1980 that this figure would rise to 47 million by 1985 and to 51 million by 1990, even with low general economic growth.[12]

The most startling increase has been in the labor force participation of married women, 55.4 percent of whom were employed in 1978. Of employed married women with children under six, 43 percent were working in 1978, as compared to 30 percent in 1970 and only 12 percent in 1950. Of all married women with children six to seventeen, close to 60 percent were working or seeking work in 1979, up from 28 percent in 1950.[13] The Department of Labor reported in March 1979 that three out of five families including a married couple had at least two wage earners. During the seventies employed women who were the sole support of their families rose to a record number: 8.5 million, or one out of every seven family heads.

Most women work for economic reasons. This is underscored by the fact that women constitute three out of every ten multiple job holders, twice as many as a decade earlier—658,000 in 1969, compared with 1.4 million in 1979—although the number of men holding two jobs has remained constant at 3.3 million.

Part-Time Work

Companies of all kinds are turning more and more to a part-time work force. These workers present a special problem for unions. They are hard to organize and just as hard to involve in the mainstream of union activity: many have only a short-term commitment to their jobs, and not a few are students or older workers supplementing retirement pay. It is also hard to get pro-rated benefits for them. Some unions, notably the unions of retail workers, have been successful at doing all three, and part-timers play an important and active role in these organizations.

Occupational Distribution

Where do women work? The occupational segregation begun in the nineteenth century continues. Close to 80 percent of all women are clustered in about 20 of the 420 occupational classifications listed by the Department of Labor. About 73 percent are in sales, clerical, service, and operative jobs (Table 12-1). These areas of women's employment include major growth sectors of the economy—all predominantly white-collar and clerical occupations that provide entry-level, semiskilled jobs. Recent projections of employment to the year 1985, issued by the Department of Labor, indicate that jobs in the areas employing the most women show the highest projected rate of employment growth.[14]

Three out of every five new workers in the seventies were women—12 million women to 8 million men. They have entered not only the traditional women's jobs, but also many nontraditional fields, such as coal mining, carpentry, and plumbing, though at a considerably lower rate. Only 2

TABLE 12-1

Occupational Distribution of Employed Women
in the United States
(various years, 1950–1978)

Occupation	1950*	1960	1970	1978	1981†
Professional-technical	12.5	12.4	14.5	15.6	17.4
Managerial-administrative					
(except farm)	4.4	5.0	4.5	6.1	7.5
Sales	8.7	7.7	7.0	6.9	6.9
Clerical	27.8	30.3	34.5	34.6	35.6
Craft	1.5	1.0	1.1	1.8	1.9
Operatives (incl. transport)	19.6	15.2	14.5	11.8	10.6
Nonfarm laborers	0.8	0.4	0.5	1.3	—
Service (except private					
household)	12.4	14.8	16.5	17.7	17.4
Private household	8.7	8.9	5.1	2.9	2.4
Farm	3.6	4.4	1.8	1.3	—

*For 1950, data are for women fourteen and over; for later years, data are for women sixteen and over.

†Because the 1981 data are somewhat differently assembled by categories, it is not possible to report two small occupational groups.

Source: For the years 1950–1978—Bureau of Labor Statistics, "Women in the Labor Force: Some New Data Series," no. 575 Report (Washington, D.C.: Government Printing Office, 1979); for 1981—Bureau of Labor Statistics, "The Female-Male Earnings Gap: A Review Employment and Earnings Issues," Report no. 673 (Washington, D.C.: Government Printing Office, 1982), p. 8.

percent of all skilled trades apprentices and 10 percent of skilled workers are women.[15]

The Department of Labor's goal for women employed by federal contractors in the construction trades was set at 6.9 percent by April 1981.[16] The U.S. Commission on Civil Rights reports that between 1960 and 1970 the number of women in the skilled trades rose from 277,000 to 495,000, an 80 percent increase.[17] Whether this rate will continue under the relaxed affirmative action guidelines promulgated by the administration that took office in 1981 is doubtful.

Wages

Not only do women tend to be clustered in lower-paid jobs, but even within highly paid groups, they are concentrated at the low-paid, low-status end of the scale. This holds for sales, medicine, the law, teaching, nursing,

TABLE 12-2
Distribution of Wage and Salary Income
in the United States in Percentages of Workers
of Each Sex at Each Income Level, 1980

Annual Pay ($)	Female	Male
8,000	80	20
9,000	65	35
10,000	60	40
11,000	58	42
12,000	40	60
13,000	34	66
14,000	20	80
15,000 and over	5	95

Source: American Federation of State, County and Municipal Workers, "Pay Equity, A Union Issue for the 1980s" (Washington, D.C.: AFSCME, 1980), p. 9.

librarianship, and technical occupations. This effect can be seen in Table 12-2.

It is useful as well to compare the median weekly earnings of full-time male and female wage and salary workers over a decade (Table 12-3). Such a comparison demonstrates that although wages and salaries have risen steadily between 1967 and 1978, the wage gap between men and women remains constant.

TABLE 12-3
Median Annual Earnings of Year-Round
Full-Time Workers Fourteen and Over
in the United States, by Sex, 1960–1981

Year*	Annual Earnings ($)		Women's earnings as % of men's
	Women	Men	
1960	3,293	5,417	60.8
1963	3,561	5,978	59.6
1966	3,973	6,848	58.0
1969	4,977	8,227	60.5
1972	5,903	10,202	57.9
1975	7,504	12,758	58.8
1978	9,350	15,730	59.4
1981	12,001	20,260	59.2

*Data for 1960–1966 are for wage and salary workers only and excluded self-employed workers. Data for 1979–1981 are for persons fifteen years of age and over.
Source: Bureau of Labor Statistics, "The Female-Male Earnings Gap," p. 9.

Unemployment

The unemployment rate for women since 1950 has been consistently higher than that for men. In 1979 they were 43.0 percent of the labor force but 50.3 percent of the unemployed.[18] Even though, as noted above, the expanding employment sectors are those offering jobs primarily to women, there are still too few jobs for the number of women seeking work. Many traditionally female jobs in labor-intensive industries have been eliminated as plants close down, move out of the country, or relocate in rural, low-wage areas of the Sunbelt.

Minority women carry a double burden. Unemployment has always affected minority workers more than white and minority women more than minority men. Table 12-4 shows these unemployment rates for 1979.

The median income of black families is 60 percent of that of white families, and they are four times as likely to be living in poverty. In addition, women head 34 percent of all minority families, compared to 11 percent of white families. Almost half (49 percent) of minority families headed by women live on less than poverty incomes. (In 1980 the federal poverty guideline for a family of four was $7,450.) Hispanic women are disproportionately represented as operatives in the garment and similar industries, which are particularly subject to seasonal as well as cyclical unemployment and have the lowest figure growth prospects.

However, the 5 million black women workers have made a number of economic gains over the past decade. They have achieved virtual parity in earnings with white women, although not with black men. The percentage of black women in private household, service, and farm jobs dropped from 62 percent of all employed black women in 1964 to 45 percent by 1970, and it has continued to fall. Almost one-third of all black women now hold

TABLE 12-4

Unemployment Rates in the United States,
by Sex and Race, in Percentages
of Each Group Unemployed, 1979

Adults	%	Teenagers	%
White men	3.6	White men	13.9
White women	5.0	White women	13.0
Hispanic men	5.7	Hispanic men	17.4
Hispanic women	8.9	Hispanic women	21.3
Black men	9.1	Black men	34.0
Black women	10.8	Black women	39.2

Source: U.S. Department of Labor, Women's Bureau, "Twenty Facts on Women Workers" (Washington, D.C.: Government Printing Office, 1980).

white-collar jobs. In 1979 Hispanic women still trailed all other women in earnings: an average of $7,414 a year, compared with $8,566.[19]

We now turn to the relationship of these women to the American labor movement. How has women's role in the unions changed to reflect their new numbers? Are the occupational areas where women work—most of them traditionally nonunion—becoming organized?

WOMEN AND THE LABOR MOVEMENT

The proportion of organized workers in the labor force has been shrinking, a reflection of the impact of technology on the labor force and the decline of the blue-collar sector. White-collar and service workers now outnumber blue-collar workers almost two to one; there are more than 62 million persons in the former sectors and only 32 million in the latter.[20] The expansion of services, including state and local government services, is rooted both in population growth and an aging population's need for services. It reflects, too, the rise in individual and family incomes and a concomitant demand for services and consumer goods.

What about union membership, always in the past strongest among blue-collar workers? Although it has continued to increase over the past twenty years—there are now 24.3 million workers in unions and employee associations—the percentage of union members among wage and salaried workers is virtually the same as it was two decades ago. Yet union members earn more and have more substantial fringe benefits than nonunion workers. Union women earn an average of $2,000 a year more than unorganized women, with differentials ranging from 5 percent in transportation to 38 percent in service jobs. In 1977, 33 percent of nonunion workers earned less than $150 a week, compared with only 11 percent of those with a union contract.[21]

To what degree has unionization taken place within the major employment sectors? Blue-collar workers are 40 percent organized, compared with 17 percent for white-collar and service workers. However, white-collar workers, many of them in the public sector, now make up more than one in four (28 percent) of all union members, in contrast to one in eight as recently as 1960. One of the most extensively organized segments of the labor force is made up of professionals (salaried, nonmanagerial workers)—teachers, nurses, doctors, social workers, civil service employees, entertainers, journalists, and so on—who now number 6 million of the 24.3 million organized workers.[22]

Since 1956 there has been a decrease of more than 8 percent in blue-collar unionization, reflecting the slowed growth in that sector as well as labor's declining public image. The rise of 13 percent in the level of organization among white-collar and service workers is unsatisfactory in view of the overall 37 percent growth in employment in these sectors and points to the need for intense organizing efforts if the labor movement is to keep pace with employment growth.

Black and other minority workers are a higher proportion of organized labor (14.2 percent) than of the labor force (11.6 percent). Thirty-three percent of black workers and 29 percent of Hispanic workers are covered by union contracts, compared with only 26 percent of white workers.

Today, women are found in more unions than ever before. They make up at least half of the membership in thirty-nine national unions and associations, while the number of unions with no women members is down from thirty-nine in 1972 to eighteen in 1978.[23] Nevertheless, the clustering of women in sex-stereotyped jobs is paralleled by the concentration of two of every five women union members into just seven unions and major associations (Table 12-5).

The rapid growth during the seventies of unions in the public sector has brought hundreds of thousands of women into the labor movement, many for the first time. The four largest public sector unions have high proportions of women members: the National Education Association (NEA), the American Federation of State, County and Municipal Employees (AFSCME), the American Federation of Teachers (AFT), and the American Federation of Government Employees (AFGE). Upwards of 40 percent of all public workers in federal, state, and municipal employment belong to labor unions or associations. Women in the public sector are

TABLE 12-5
Women Members in Selected U.S. Unions
and Associations, 1979

Organization	Members	Women Members
UAW	1,534,425	164,937
ANA	187,000	181,390
CWA	508,063	259,112
ILGWU	348,380	278,704
AFT	500,000	300,000
IBEW	1,011,726	303,518
ACTWU	526,000	330,660
AFSCME	1,020,000	408,000
UFCWU	1,235,500	480,105

Source: Adapted from U.S. Department of Labor, Bureau of Labor Statistics, "Directory of National Unions and Employee Associations, 1979" (Washington, D.C.: Government Printing Office, 1980).

responsible, in the main, for the increase in the number of women unionists from 2.9 million to 6.9 million between 1954 and 1978.[24]

How have unions responded to their increasing numbers of women members? Have they integrated them into union structures and shared leadership responsibilities? A. H. Raskin, the dean of labor journalists, believes that "in organizing and advancement of standing, unions will do more for women than for men in the next decade."[25] Nonetheless, though women make up 28.1 percent of all members of labor unions and employee associations, in not one do they hold any of the top offices and at best they make up a small minority of the key executive board members.

In 1978 women held 31 out of 655 top elected or appointed offices in AFL-CIO affiliates and 109 of the 662 similar positions in unaffiliated unions and employee associations. They constituted 7.2 percent of national executive board members in national unions affiliated to the AFL-CIO, where they make up 24.2 percent of the total membership, and 35.3 percent of the executive board in employee associations, where they are 60.3 percent of the membership.[26]

Labor unions are overwhelmingly national in structure (some that include Canadian members operate as international unions), with regional and local unions serving as the main links to rank-and-file members. Policy is set nationally by an executive board (predominantly male) and carried out by the organization's key elected officers (male). No figures are available on how many women hold local union posts across the country. On the local and regional levels, however, unions with large numbers of women members are more than likely to have women staff representatives handling grievances, conducting educational programs, and organizing. Where the local union is predominantly female, so, usually, are the rank-and-file leaders. Where elected officers of local unions hold full-time, paid positions off the shop floor, they tend to be male, especially in the mass production industries, where men predominate in the workforce. Women are more likely to hold offices that are volunteer and unpaid. Elections for paid officerships are highly contested, require elaborate campaigns, and take both time and political experience. Research suggests that workers in high-status jobs (more often men) are more likely to hold union office than workers in low-status jobs (more often women).[27] Moreover, a man interested in union office learns political and administrative skills as a young union member during the very years when women tend to be home, bearing and raising children. When women re-enter the workforce, they find themselves at a disadvantage, not only because of the double burden of job and home, but because they lack the experience and organizing skills, and often the self-confidence, to try for leadership posts. In effect, women who seek to play an active leadership role in their unions must often accept what Kathleen Newland calls the "triple day" to combine workplace, home, and union career.

Some of the younger union leaders find the low participation rates among their women members a source of embarrassment. Attitudes have begun to change. Some unions are beginning to sponsor labor education that helps women members to bridge their experiential gap and to encourage their increased involvement and participation in union affairs. Several national unions have moved to increase the number of women on their national boards and staffs. To no small degree this is a consequence of the new militancy of women in the rank-and-file, such as those in the ILGWU and the American Postal Workers Union (APWU), who have introduced resolutions on affirmative action from the floor at their union conventions and organized to ensure their adoption. It also shows the impact of a new national organization, the Coalition of Labor Union Women (CLUW), which works within union structures to effect change.

The Coalition of Labor Union Women

Founded in 1974 at a convention that brought together 3,200 union women from almost every state, many paying their own way, CLUW adopted four goals: to move women up on the job and in the union; to achieve the passage of legislation to improve the status and condition of working women; to engage in political action and support more women for public office; and to organize unorganized women workers.[28]

In 1983 over seventy-two chapters of CLUW operated in cities across the country, providing a network of union women that cuts across union and association lines. Participation affords union women practical experience in running for office, lobbying, and developing strategy. Behind the organization of CLUW is a group of experienced, dedicated women union leaders and staff who saw that the time was ripe for mobilizing union women's growing strength, and helping women advance in their own unions. The spirit of change was in the air. The women's movement was beginning to reach union women, who had come to realize that they needed a way to exert more pressure on the power structure of their unions and to become part of that structure.

CLUW has been able to channel the energies and actions of its members by operating within established union structures. Its structure parallels that of a large national union. At the top is a representative governing board to which elected CLUW officers are responsible. Carefully outlined procedures govern its chapter activities. In this way CLUW seeks to influence the policies of both national unions and the AFL-CIO on women's issues and concerns. Some of the areas in which it has heightened union consciousness include the need for pay equity (that is, equal pay for work of comparable worth), paid maternity leave, improved health and safety for all workers without penalizing women of childbearing age, and passage of an Equal Rights Amendment (ERA) to the Constitution. To remedy the dearth of women in union leadership posts, CLUW has applied pressure from the top while developing the ability of its members, as active participants in their own unions, to apply pressure from below.

CLUW has chalked up a number of successes. Its president and officers have achieved national reputations. Through CLUW, union women for the first time worked with other women's groups to promote the ERA; similar cooperation is given credit for the passage of the pregnancy disability amendment to Title VII of the Civil Rights Act. (This law forbids the exemption of disability related to pregnancy and childbirth from employee insurance programs, requiring that pregnancy be treated like any other disability.) CLUW seeks adequate funding for training programs for unemployed women and for women moving into apprenticeships and skilled jobs. In January 1980 CLUW and the Industrial Union Department (IUD) of the AFL-CIO jointly sponsored the first of several national conferences on organizing the unorganized, where IUD staff members were joined by delegates from every CLUW chapter. Elmer Chatak, secretary-treasurer of the IUD, underscored the purpose of the conference: "Our presence here today attests to the fact that things have changed, and it is an iron-clad necessity that unions get involved in the spirit of that change."[29] At the conference the IUD committed itself to employing and training more women as organizers.

Women in Union Leadership

Further evidence that change is in the air came when two women were appointed to key posts on the AFL-CIO staff and in 1980 Joyce Miller, president of CLUW and a vice-president of the ACTWU, became the first woman to sit on the AFL-CIO executive council. CLUW members, found in nearly every union that includes women, provided a widely based constituency that could not be denied. At the 1981 AFL-CIO convention the next year, a second woman, Barbara Hutchinson of AFGE, was elected to the executive council.

This rising consciousness is in part accounted for by the increasing interest in education programs for union women. These are sponsored by university and college labor education centers as well as by unions themselves. In the United States close to fifty universities and colleges, most of them state-supported institutions, offer labor education at modest cost to union members. In 1972 the New York State School of Industrial and Labor Relations of Cornell University became the first such institution to establish college credit, as well as noncredit, education and leadership training programs especially for trade union women. The program begun that year has grown into the Institute for Women and Work, offering labor studies, leadership training, and career development courses for union and other working women throughout New York State. It has a library and materials center on working women and publishes books, course outlines, and monographs. Women and men who conduct such programs have formed their own network, the Standing Committee on Programs for Union Women, within the University and College Labor Education Association. Conferences, seminars, and residential schools for union women now offer to train future leaders for the changes in focus and direction that the movement needs to consider as white-collar, professional, and semiprofessional workers move into the ascendancy among the ranks of organized labor.

Increasingly, national unions are establishing departments of women's affairs or activities (a few unions have had such departments for twenty years or more). They aim through conferences and publications to develop women staff members, encourage the establishment of women's committees in local unions, and train women to move into local bargaining and grievance committees.

Several unions have pioneered in bringing to the forefront issues of concern to women. The Legal Department of the International Union of Electrical, Radio and Machine Workers (IUE) has filed court cases on pregnancy disability, wage discrimination, and race and sex discrimination in hiring and upgrading. The Communications Workers of America (CWA) in recent contract negotiations has won higher increases for lower-paid workers (mostly women) and a reduction in the number of job classifications so as to reduce some wide pay inequities. It has also waged a nationwide campaign on the issue of job pressures and stress. The 1980 contract between the AFGE, Local 12, and the U.S. Department of Labor permits the use of paid vacation time for pregnancy or child care, by male or female workers, as well as leave without pay for up to two years; flexible work schedules for a minimum of 60 percent of employees; longer career ladders to allow at least 10 percent of all openings to be filled by internal upward mobility; guarantees of an environment free of sexual harassment; and the right of parties to the agreement to bargain over the impact of new technology, with necessary training for affected workers. The contract states that "the parties agree to the principle of equal pay for substantially equal work"—a small beginning in the fight for pay equity.[30]

Other unions, among them the Service Employees International Union (SEIU), are active in recruiting and training women staff members. Ten years ago this union of 600,000 members had just 70 women national and local organizers out of a total staff of 650. Recently its staff numbered 300 women out of a total of 750. Early in 1981 SEIU joined with Working

Women, the National Association of Office Workers, to launch a clerical division, District 925. The head of Working Women was named acting president of District 925, and another leader of Working Women, Jackie Russ, became its executive director. The incorporation of this major unit into its structure was the first stage in SEIU's effort to use the expertise of Working Women's skilled staff and the resources of its thirteen chapters across the country to organize white-collar workers. Such efforts may well make the 1980s the decade in which America's white-collar workers more fully organize into unions.

The decade will see labor education programs for women focus more attention on contract language to overcome discrimination and win equality in the workplace. Such programs already are sponsored by a number of university labor education programs, by several unions, and by CLUW. Title VII of the Civil Rights Act has made unions as responsible as employers for discriminatory practices in plants, shops, or offices under contract, and unless unions are able to show good faith efforts to combat such practices, they too can be sued by affected workers. Union contract clauses that guarantee workplace equality are not only legal requirements; they assume even greater importance in the face of reduced federal efforts to enforce employment equality.

ISSUES FOR THE 1980s

Issues that concern union women in the 1980s also are issues for union men. Both men and women are parents, and the issue of adequate child care is as important to fathers as to mothers. A record 65 percent of women aged twenty-five to thirty-four—the years when children are born and nurtured—were working or looking for work in 1980.[31] These women workers are coming to expect partnership in marriage and a recognition of their rights when and if they become solely responsible for their families' support.

The foremost concern is the economy, which now presents workers, both women and men, with the combined burdens of inflation and unemployment. The administration's retreat in enforcement of the equal employment opportunity program underscores the fact that in a recession women are the first victims. Official resistance to social change runs strong, as is evident in the defeat of the ERA and the neglect of, and even outright opposition to, women's employment rights, the provision of child care and other social benefits, and the right to choice on when or whether to bear children. Federal budget cuts are deepest for the beneficiaries least able to mobilize powerful lobbies to fight them: the elderly poor, poor women, and children. These cuts in benefits and services—the latter provided mainly by women workers—increase female unemployment and make it harder to endure. The backlash threatens most of the gains women made in the sixties and seventies. Economic equality seems more elusive than ever.

A second force exerting pressures on women and minority workers is the technological revolution. Computer output has increased ten thousand times in the past fifteen years, replacing higher-cost human power with microprocessors, discs, tapes, and chips. The office of tomorrow could be paperless and virtually self-conducting. A marked alteration in the nature of white-collar employment inevitably follows. Within ten years the United States computer industry is predicted to become the largest in the world, exceeding automobiles and oil.[32] Will women readily gain access to the skilled jobs in the manufacture and maintenance of this equipment? New kinds of training must be available to women and minorities if they are not to be slotted into jobs that will shortly be ghettos.

The dehumanization that computer technology introduces to the workplace through worker isolation and what some writers have called "the black lung of the technical classes"[33]—that is, stress—will be a challenge to labor organizations as well as to management. It is possible that these issues and such others as retraining, job security, and the creative use of leisure will produce new labor union militancy in this sector of the labor force.

The shorter work week is a key issue in this recession, as was the 40-hour week in the depression of the 1930s. For close to half a century, there has been no major work week reduction, except in a few areas such as the garment and construction industries, and in offices, where a work week of 35.0 to 37.5 hours with paid lunch and coffee breaks has gradually become the norm. To be sure, longer paid vacations and an increase in the number of paid holidays have created a shorter work year. But gains in productivity through the introduction of new technologies must be shared with the workers, particularly as employment opportunities decrease and population continues to grow. In view of the burden most women carry at home, the benefits to them of a shorter work week are unarguable.

As more women enter the labor force in the 1980s, they will exert pressure on the market for a greater share of the good jobs. Statistics on college and graduate school attendance confirm this speculation. In 1978 college enrollments totaled 9.18 million. Men's enrollment had increased 16 percent over 1970 figures, but women's was up 56 percent. In 1980, for the first time, half of those enrolled in four-year postsecondary institutions were women. On the graduate level, women's increase was 103 percent, men's only 21 percent, above 1970. Women between twenty-five and thirty-four increased their enrollment 187 percent, compared to a 48 percent rise for men of the same age. Of all those over thirty-five who are back in school, women outnumber men two to one.[34] The motivation of women must be high. Although working women tend to earn less than men and large numbers of them are the sole support of their families, thousands are nevertheless assuming tuition and related costs (often including costs of child care) to continue their education.

This back-to-school movement among working adults, combined with the fact that professional and technical workers now form a higher proportion of labor union and association membership than ever before, should lead these organizations to put considerable emphasis on such benefits as tuition reimbursement and paid released time for retraining and study. In the United States, unlike many European countries, hourly and lower-level salaried workers do not receive paid released time either for union training or for job or career-related study. Unions may soon negotiate for the funneling of some of the savings from new technology into paid released time for study.

A fifth issue, child care, cannot be handled effectively by collective bargaining alone. The achievement of comprehensive child care, available to all families desiring it and in the variety of forms required to meet varying family needs, means gaining government support for a broad social policy laid down in statute and implemented with substantial financing. Unions will have to join with many other interest groups to work out the details of such a program and to campaign for its adoption. The need is intense. Today more than 8 million children are candidates for preschool child care with fewer than 1.5 million places available.

The issues go beyond child care. They include leaves for both parents in the first months or early years of a child's life, the possibility of shared jobs, variable working hours for men as well as women, and recognition that child care is a parental, and not just a maternal, concern. Support for programs to promote maternal and child health is a related question. Paid maternity leave, provided for in practically every other industrialized country, is not yet under serious consideration in the United States.

Other health issues make up their own pressing agenda for working men and women. The need for a system of comprehensive health insurance heads the list, as medical costs for individuals and families rise astronomically while spouses and children are only partially covered, if at all, under the available private plans. The enforcement of job health and safety standards all too often penalizes women of childbearing age and older women.

Pensions for women, because of their low wages and relatively short working life, are rarely adequate. Only 20 percent of women workers have pensions in addition to social security, which is not calculated to provide fully for the support of retired people and is in any case also linked to lifetime earnings.

An environment free of sexual harassment has recently surfaced as a demand. The EEOC has written definitive guidelines banning it in the workplace, and hearing officers and judges are administering severe penalties where it has occurred. Some unions have begun to make it a grievable offense and to deal with it promptly when it arises.

The most immediate and at the same time long-range issue of the eighties is pay equity: the question of how to deal with systemic wage discrimination rooted in the low value society attaches to the work women do. Since for the foreseeable future women will continue to work in segregated jobs where direct comparison with men's work and wages is impossible, the need in the United States, as in almost every country, is for reevaluation of women's work.

IUE, AFSCME and other unions in the private and public sectors are among the groups supporting the concept of pay equity. In November 1979 the AFL-CIO Constitutional Convention passed a resolution that read in part: "the AFL-CIO [will] treat job inequities resulting from sex and race discrimination like all other inequities which must be corrected, and urge its affiliates to adopt the concept of equal pay for work of comparable value in organizing and in negotiating collective agreements."[36]

In June 1981 the Supreme Court decided that women who are paid less than men may sue their employers, even if their jobs are not substantially like those performed by the men. The case in question involved jail matrons in Oregon whose jobs, when evaluated along with those of male jailers, were set at 90 percent of the worth of the men's but who were nevertheless paid 75 percent of the male rate. They sued their employer, the county. The Supreme Court, in remanding the case for reconsideration to the District Court, instructed it to take a "broad approach to the definition of equal employment opportunity . . . essential to overcoming and undoing the effect of discrimination."[37]

Just a month later the first strike over the issue of pay equity for women took place in San Jose, California, and was won by AFSCME Local 101. The two-year contract that resulted called for management to put up $1.5 million to help correct pay inequities. The mayor of San Jose, Janet Gray Hayes, said of the agreement that ended the nine-day strike: "This is a first giant step toward fairness in the workplace for women within the severe budget constraints of the city."[38] Several other unions are pursuing the issue of pay equity through collective bargaining, efforts at legislative remedy, and litigation.

As jobs are revalued upward, women's work status will rise. They can be expected to have heightened self-esteem, which will be reflected in many cases in their realization of their leadership potential in their unions and communities. They can also expect a more equitable relationship with their spouses as they make an increased economic contribution at home. Moreover, as women's jobs pay more, more men can be expected to enter them. A period of adjustment and accommodation must follow, as both men and women choose from a wide range of occupations.

The new and growing unity among women in the labor movement offers hope that they will be able to deal with these critical issues successfully. The sense of unity and mutual acceptance has been strengthened by the entry of black and Hispanic women into unions at a greater rate than their proportion in the labor force, and their movement into union and CLUW leadership roles locally and regionally.

As a result of women's growing assertiveness, unions in many cases have taken initiatives not only on the equal pay issue, but in opening up job opportunities. Unions have encouraged women to apply for apprenticeships and training programs; they have ensured job posting so that women and minorities can apply for more advantageous positions; they have bargained for plantwide seniority so that, at least in some cases, women and minorities who do move into more skilled jobs are not laid off first when layoffs take place. Unions can be in a position to eliminate discriminatory wage rates and promotion systems.

Women need to do more than develop solidarity among themselves; they must reach the men in their organizations and present women's needs in human terms to forge unity. Simone Veil, then president of the European Parliament, puts it this way:

> We have to be concerned about the backlash. Men worry and complain that we will take away their jobs, that we will make a recession worse. The system, the concept itself, must be changed so that a woman's job is seen as important as a man's. Legislated equality must broaden to become mental equality. It is an enormous thought, and it is up to each woman to change the minds of the men in her life.[39]

To win this status and influence, women must seek and achieve decision-making offices that provide them with power in their unions. They must force male unionists and legislators to deal with their problems. Only then can they win equity on the job and services for family members of every age.

GLOSSARY

ACTWU	Amalgamated Clothing and Textile Workers of America
AFL	American Federation of Labor
AFL-CIO	American Federation of Labor and Congress of Industrial Organizations
AFGE	American Federation of Government Employees
AFSCME	American Federation of State, County and Municipal Employees
AFT	American Federation of Teachers
ANA	American Nursing Association
APWU	American Postal Workers Union
CIO	Committee for Industrial Organization (later Congress of Industrial Organizations)

CLUW	Coalition of Labor Union Women
CWA	Communications Workers of America
EEOC	Equal Employment Opportunity Commission
Employee Associations	Nonunion associations formed by many white-collar and professional workers, mainly to lobby for or against legislation affecting their wages or professional status. As unions, particularly in the government field, have grown in the last decade, associations in self-defense have turned to collective bargaining but remained unaffiliated to the AFL-CIO. Examples are the ANA, the NEA and state Civil Service Employees Associations.
ERA	Equal Rights Amendment
IBEW	International Brotherhood of Electrical Workers
ILGWU	International Ladies' Garment Workers' Union
IUD	Industrial Union Department of the AFL-CIO
IUE	International Union of Electric, Radio and Machine Workers
NEA	National Education Association
NLRA	National Labor Relations Act (1935)
NRA	National Recovery Act (1933)
SEIU	Service Employees International Union
Taft Hartley Act	A 1947 amendment to the NLRA limiting union activities in several ways.
UAW	United Automobile Aircraft and Agricultural Implement Workers Union, which only in 1982 rejoined the AFL-CIO.
UFCWU	United Food and Commercial Workers Union

NOTES

1. Jean Baker Miller, *Toward a New Psychology for Women* (Boston: Beacon Press, 1976), pp. 6, 7.

2. Gerda Lerner, *The Woman in American History* (Menlo Park, Cal.: Addison-Wesley, 1971), p. 50.

3. Barbara Mayer Wertheimer, *We Were There: The Story of Working Women in America* (New York: Pantheon, 1977), p. 155.

4. Ibid., p. 159.

5. Irving Bernstein, *The Lean Years: A History of the American Workers, 1920–1933* (Boston: Houghton Mifflin, 1960), pp. 55–56.

6. Eli Ginzberg and Hyman Berman, *The American Worker in the Twentieth Century* (Glencoe, Ill.: Free Press, 1963), pp. 149–51.

7. Bernstein, *The Lean Years*, pp. 55–56.

8. Lois Scharf, *To Work and to Wed: Female Employment, Feminism and the Great Depression* (Westport, Conn.: Greenwood Press, 1980), pp. 112, 123.

9. Janet Hooks, *Women's Occupations Through Seven Decades*, Bulletin no. 218 (Washington, D.C.: U.S. Department of Labor, The Women's Bureau, 1947), p. 1.

10. Ginzberg and Berman, *The American Worker*, pp. 266–68.

11. Ibid., p. 268.

12. U.S. Department of Labor and Department of Health and Human Services, *Employment and Training Report of the President* (Washington, D.C.: Government Printing Office, 1980), p. 342.

13. *U.S. News and World Report*, June 16, 1980, p. 58, citing U.S. Department of Labor, Women's Bureau, *Women Workers Today* (Washington, D.C.: Government Printing Office, 1979), p. 11.

14. *U.S. News and World Report*, October 11, 1978, p. 60.

15. Women's Bureau, *Women Workers Today*, p. 7.

16. U.S. Department of Labor, Women's Bureau, *The Employment of Women: General Diagnosis of Developments and Issues*, U.S. Report for OECD High Level Conference on the Employment of Women (Washington, D.C.: Government Printing Office, 1980), pp. 5, 20.

17. U.S. Commission on Civil Rights, *Women Still in Poverty* Clearinghouse Publication no. 60 (Washington, D.C.: 1979), p. 22.

18. Women's Bureau, *The Employment of Women*, p. 19.

19. "Hispanic Workforce: Growth and Inequality," *American Federationist*, Washington, D.C., AFL-CIO (April 1979): 8.

20. U.S. Department of Labor, Bureau of Labor Statistics, *Employment and Training Report of the President* (Washington, D.C.: Government Printing Office, 1979), p. 8.

21. U.S. Department of Labor, Bureau of Labor Statistics, "Earnings and Other Characteristics of Organized Workers, May 1977," Report no. 556 (Washington, D.C.: Government Printing Office, 1979), pp. 2–4.

22. Jerome M. Rosow, "Labor's Agenda for the 1980s," *Executive*, N.Y. Graduate School of Business and Public Administration, Cornell University, vol. 6, no. 2 (Spring 1980): 41.

23. U.S. Department of Labor, Bureau of Labor Statistics, "Directory of National Unions and Employee Associations, 1979," Bulletin no. 2079 (Washington, D.C.: Government Printing Office, 1980), pp. 93–94.

24. Martin Estey, "The State of the Unions," in *The Unions: Structure, Development, and Management*, 2d ed. (New York: Harcourt Brace Jovanovich, 1976), pp. 15, 16.

25. A. H. Raskin, remarks at the First Annual Seminar for the Labor Press, Cornell University, New York State School of Industrial and Labor Relations, Metropolitan District, New York City, June 19, 1980.

26. Bureau of Labor Statistics, "Directory of National Unions," pp. 63, 95–98.

27. Mimi Abramovitz, *Where Are the Women? A Study of Worker Underutilization of Tuition Refund Plans* (Ithaca, N.Y.: Institute for Education and Research on Women and Work, Cornell University, New York State School of Industrial and Labor Relations, 1977).

28. When considering this emphasis on organizing, it must be kept in mind that the United States is the only major industrial country where there is a concerted opposition to unionization on the part of corporations. For example, in 1974 unions brought 20,000 charges of unfair labor practices against companies under the NLRA (*New York Times*, November 15, 1979). One-half of these were for dismissal of workers for union activity. Over fifteen hundred consulting firms sell their services to

management for the specific purpose of defeating union organizing efforts. The movement of industry from the Northeast and the North Central states to the South and Southwest (states with a low-wage, nonunion labor supply and with "right to work" laws forbidding union security clauses in labor agreements) also helps to deter organization in the private sector. Public employers, while not embracing unionization, cannot move away from it. These factors in part explain why in the seventies public workers had more success in organizing than workers in the private sector.

29. *CLUW News* (March–April 1980): 1.

30. U.S. Department of Labor, Office of Information, "Noticias de la semana," May 19, 1980, n.p.

31. *Connections* 5, no. 4 (Spring 1981): 3.

32. Alvin Toffler, *The Third Wave* (New York: William Morrow, 1980). See particularly "Beyond Mass Production"; see also Working Women, National Association of Office Workers, "Race Against Time: Automation of the Office" (Cleveland: Working Women, 1980).

33. *New York Times*, August 16, 1981.

34. *New York Times*, November 13, 1979; and Anne McDougall Young, "Back to School at 35 and Over," *Monthly Labor Review* (October 1978).

35. Ronnie Steinberg Ratner, ed., *Equal Employment Policy for Women: Strategies for Implementation in the United States, Canada, and Western Europe* (Philadelphia: Temple University Press, 1980); Joy Ann Grune, ed., *Manual for Pay Equity: Raising Wages for Women's Work* (Washington, D.C.: Committee on Pay Equity, Conference on Alternative State and Local Policies, 1980); Harish C. Jain and Diane Carroll, eds., *Race and Sex Equality in the Workplace: A Challenge and an Opportunity* (Ottawa: Women's Bureau, Ministry of Labour, 1980).

36. AFL-CIO Constitutional Convention, "Resolution on Equal Pay for Work of Comparable Value," Washington, D.C., November 15–20, 1979.

37. National Commission on Working Women, "*Women at Work, News about the 80 Percent*" 2, no. 2 (June 1981): 1.

38. *New York Times*, July 15, 1981.

39. Simone Veil quoted by George Haddad-Garcia, "My Side," in *Working Woman* (July 1980): 80.

BIBLIOGRAPHY

Bernard, Jessie. *The Female World*. New York: Free Press, 1981.

Bohen, Halcyone H., and Anamaria Viveros-Long. *Balancing Jobs and Family Life: Do Flextime Work Schedules Help?* Philadelphia: Temple University Press, 1981.

Bureau of National Affairs Special Report. *The Comparable Worth Issue*. Washington, D.C.: Bureau of National Affairs, 1981.

Chafe, William. *The American Woman: Her Changing Social, Economic and Political Roles, 1920–1970*. New York: Oxford University Press, 1972.

Chapman, Jane Roberts, ed. *Economic Independence for Women: The Foundations of Equal Rights*. Beverly Hills, Cal.: Sage, 1976.

Committee on Labor and Human Resources, United States Senate. *Sex Discrimination in the Workplace*. An Examination of Issues Affecting Women in Our Nation's Labor Force. Hearings before the Committee on Labor and Human Resources, United States Senate, 97th Congress, January 28 and April 21, 1981. Washington, D.C.: Government Printing Office, 1981.

Cook, Alice H. *The Working Mother: A Survey of Problems and Programs in Nine Countries*. Ithaca, N.Y.: New York State School of Industrial and Labor Relations, Cornell University, 1978.

Cummings, Bernice, and Victoria Schuck, eds. *Women Organizing: An Anthology*. Metuchen, N.J.: Scarecrow Press, 1979.

Hooks, Janet. *Women's Occupations Through Seven Decades*. Bulletin no. 218. Washington, D.C.: Department of Labor, The Women's Bureau, 1947.

Jain, Harish C., and Diane Carroll, eds. *Race and Sex Equality in the Workplace: A Challenge and an Opportunity*. Ottawa: Women's Bureau, Ministry of Labour, 1980.

Kerber, Linda K., and Jane deHart Matthews, eds., *Women's America: Refocusing the Past*. New York: Oxford University Press, 1982.

Lerner, Gerda. *The Woman in American History*. Menlo Park, Cal.; Addison-Wesley, 1971.

———, ed. *Black Women in White America: A Documentary History*. New York: Vintage Books, 1973.

Miller, Jean Baker. *Toward a New Psychology of Women*. Boston, Beacon Press, 1976.

Palmer, Phyllis M., and Sharon Lee Grant, *The Status of Clerical Workers: A Summary Analysis of Research Findings and Trends*. Washington, D.C.: George Washington University Women's Studies Program, 1979.

Ratner, Ronnie Steinberg, ed. *Equal Employment Policy for Women: Strategies for Implementation in the United States, Canada, and Western Europe*. Philadelphia: Temple University Press, 1980.

Roby, Pamela. *Women in the Workplace: Proposals for Research and Policy Concerning the Conditions of Women in Industrial and Service Jobs*. Cambridge, Mass.: Schenkman, 1981.

Sexton, Patricia C. *The New Nightingales: Hospital Workers' Unions, New Women's Issues*. New York: Enquiry Press, 1981.

Smith, Ralph, ed. *The Subtle Revolution: Women at Work*. Washington, D.C.: Urban Institute, 1979.

Stellman, Jeanne. *Women's Work, Women's Health: Myths and Realities*. New York: Pantheon, 1977.

Wallace, Phyllis A. *Black Women in the Labor Force*. Cambridge: MIT Press, 1980.

———, ed. *Women in the Workplace*. Boston: Auburn House, 1982.

Walshok, Mary Lindenstein. *Blue Collar Women: Pioneers on the Male Frontier*. Garden City, N.Y.: Anchor Books, 1981.

Wertheimer, Barbara Mayer. *We Were There: The Story of Working Women in America*. New York: Pantheon, 1977.

Wertheimer, Barbara Mayer, and Anne H. Nelson. *Trade Union Women: A Study of Their Participation in New York City Locals*. New York: Praeger, 1975.

Women's Labor Project. *Bargaining for Equality: A Guide to Legal and Collective Bargaining Solutions for Workplace Problems That Particularly Affect Women.* San Francisco: National Lawyers Guild, 1980.

Yohalem, Alice M., ed. *Women Returning to Work: Policies and Programs in Five Countries* (Federal Republic of Germany, France, United Kingdom, Sweden, United States). Montclair, N.J.: Allanheld, Osmun, 1980.

13 CONCLUSION

Arlene Kaplan Daniels

The review this book offers of women's experience in the trade unions of many countries enables us to assess the progress of women in paid work in industrialized societies. That assessment can be be made in the context of the work that women have always been expected to do.

Today the relatively recent distinctions between women's paid and unpaid work take on new meaning simply because great numbers of women have entered the labor force. They take jobs outside the home because they need to earn money. They are the growing number of single heads of households, joined by married women whose husbands' single salaries can not maintain their dependents. As women enter the labor force, they become in fact double job holders, adding paid work to the job they cannot abandon in the unpaid labor force—work in the home.

The new and growing numbers of women in the workforce are both a challenge and a problem for every nation's unions. The numbers provide an opportunity to recruit new members—an important task, especially in countries like the United States, where unions have been losing members. But this opportunity is, at the same time, a challenge because the continuing disadvantaged position of working women, even in union-dominated occupations, is a visible reproach to the labor movement.

The worldwide tendency of authority systems to be male-dominated extends to unions and has predictable consequences in them as well as in the labor market. Unequal pay and unequal opportunity in both choice of occupations and training for them and women's typical assignment to all-female job ghettos where work is degraded and unhealthful—these are all matters that unions have only rarely recognized and dealt with.

At the same time the demands for equality generated in every country by the women's movement lead women to expect better working conditions, jobs, and equal opportunities. Moreover, their expectations are encouraged

312

by the growing widespread concern voiced by activists in every sphere of social life—including union leaders—about continuing inequities.

The first issue for every working woman is how to manage the double burden of home and paid work in the all too limited time available. The union, to be sure, is concerned with shorter working time, but its concern arises from a different source, and the solution it proposes—a shorter work week—does not meet women's need for a shorter work day. To meet the demands of their double burden, women take up part-time employment. But the cost of part-time work is very high: not only do women earn less money because they work fewer hours, but part-time work is more insecure, lacks many fringe benefits, is in itself poorly paid, and offers no training or promotional opportunities.

Social interventions to assist women could be a way out, but no country provides adequate child care facilities or care for the elderly, although some few recognize that they should. Each woman individually is left to work out these problems for herself.

When a woman tries to better her lot through collective action, she faces a second issue: union participation becomes a burden to be added to family and paid work. Even women who can overcome such barriers find that union activity is neither immediately accessible to them nor easy to manage. Moreover, the few women who are able to carry this triple burden very rarely rise to positions of power, even in those unions where women make up a substantial part of the membership. Attainment of equity in the workplace and in the union seems to require a critical mass of female—and feminist—leaders in unions who are committed to the struggle to attain equity.

UNIONS: PART OF THE SOLUTION OR PART OF THE PROBLEM?

Historically, unions have contributed to the problems facing women at work. They have allied themselves with employers in pushing women out of better-paying, skilled work, fearing competition for the relatively limited number of good jobs. They have, in their defense, espoused two principles: the protection of women (and earlier of children) from the rigors of factory work and the need to keep men's wages high enough to provide for their families. Other issues affecting women were demoted to a low place on all agendas. In consequence, trade union women activists turned to the women's movement for guidance and support.

They soon faced attacks for doing so from male unionists, who generally have rejected the relevance of outside opinions and the right of outsiders without union experience to speak on labor issues, even those mainly of interest to union women. Union women are thus at an impasse. They continue to publicize their complaints about the slowness of the progress toward equity within the unions, and union leaders are apt to be thin-skinned and defensive about these criticisms. For the most part these men lead traditional domestic lives where male authority is the rule, and they find the principles of sex equality difficult to integrate into union life.

For the future, union organization presents a mixture of discouraging and hopeful prospects for women. The tendency toward more and more centralization of bargaining takes major decision making beyond the reach of local workers. Women new to union participation fail to gain the experience that older workers acquired in the days of local bargaining. On the other hand, central union administrations tend to be more progressive and sympathetic to women's demands than are many provincial leaders. Women must therefore place their trust in distant leaders, even though it is clear that women themselves rarely rise so high in union hierarchies.

The quandary for activist women is further complicated by the contradictory effects of provision by unions of special structures and programs designed to assimilate women into their organizations. While the programs offer women encouragement and recognition, they tend also to isolate them from the mainstream of union activity where the men preside.

In many of the countries described in this book, unions tend to pass what they see as "women's issues" over to the political arm of the labor movement. When these issues affect working conditions, however, they jealously protect them as only treatable through collective bargaining. In doing so they have found themselves in open opposition to most nonlabor women's organizations.

Where then is the leverage for far-reaching change within the unions? Experience seems to demonstrate that existing social institutions rarely give women an equitable share in worker benefits as a simple matter of justice. Rather, women themselves have had to exert pressure to bring about changes in law and its enforcement. On the whole, women have been successful where they have developed political clout both within the unions and in building coalitions with women's and even men's organizations on the outside.

CHANGING SOCIETY TO CREATE EQUITY AT WORK

Unions do not differ markedly from other institutions in society. When only lip service or minor and token changes will serve, unions are generally supportive of women. When drastic, expensive changes are required to accommodate women's interests—as they are if we are to deal adequately with part-time work, full-time scheduling, child care, parental leaves, and vocational training to bring women into the skilled trades— unions all too often agree with employers that such aims are too visionary, costly, and impractical. The problems clearly extend beyond unions themselves: the inequities in society disadvantage women before they can reach the labor market and become union members.

When unions do take up women's issues, they tend to focus narrowly on sex equity in the workplace, leaving the broader social issues to public boards and legislative bodies. Nor do unions commonly step forward to force employers to observe existing laws and regulations that govern sex equity at work; unions are seldom zealous in enforcing such regulations within their own offices.

The difficulties in a reconstruction of accepted modes are, in fact, monumental. Can the needed changes come about short of drastic upheaval, even revolution? Current work arrangements are deeply embedded in modern systems of work, whether the society is capitalist or socialist. The normative order of the national economy assumes workers acting as individual units, appearing and disappearing at the beginning and end of each work day. This view acknowledges no social responsibility for getting the worker to work, beyond the motivation offered by salaries and fringe benefits. Only when women's labor has been desperately needed in war or other boom periods have countries introduced social policies like communal dining, child care, maternity leaves, and a choice of work schedules. None of these programs have been extended into periods of recession. Few have challenged the notion that work and production are the paramount, significant activity of society and that family takes second place.

Rethinking the relation of work to the family requires questioning this order of priorities. Could the comforts and advantages of civilization and technology continue if the primacy of the workplace over family life were seriously questioned? Today's social and political—and, yes, union—leaders find the situation, particularly in the more affluent societies, fairly satisfactory. And they may be right to assume that women can and will continue to shoulder, even with mutinous grumbling, double and triple burdens. But a different view can be developed upon reflecting on the information presented in this volume.

Women have made steady, if modest, gains through union activity. Women's groups within the unions have produced some improvements within the labor market as well as in union governance, especially through coalitions with nonunion feminists. Such coalitions provide the pressure to make political lobbying effective and to make union women too powerful for their (male) leaders to ignore. They attract public attention and develop public concern that union leaders must in the end consider.

The opportunity to share power may have to be wrested from the existing power structure in real battles—even, perhaps, the battles that are destined to be more bloody than parliamentary. Yet the history of the labor movement, which makes such ominous predictions credible, also presents some hopeful omens. Dishonest and incompetent union leaders and those coopted by employers into "sweetheart" contracts have frequently been tossed out by concerned, alert, and newly activated members. A new leadership springs up from those in the rank and file who have taken matters into their own hands. Such a pattern was clearly discernible in the United States during the recession of the 1930s. The economic troubles of the 1980s offer similar circumstances, and this time union women should be among the new leaders.

In the long run a less stressful and a more equitable environment must benefit men as well as women workers, as class interests override gender differences in the workplace. Both men and women can benefit from women's contributions to the structure of work and the organization of unions. Women bring the experience gained in mediating work for family and society, and they know what changes the workplace must adopt to accommodate this mediation more comfortably. Their experience in child rearing makes them more accepting of new, less hierarchical forms of organization that allow for the articulation of nonmajority views and experiences. Indeed, women's experience as relatively powerless beings in a gender-stratified society can provide a greater understanding of minorities' issues and contribute to their solution in integrative rather than hierarchical terms.

In the event that unions do accomplish some such transformation within their own organizations, we can look to them as agents of social change, a force that can transform other social institutions and not just themselves. We expect no more, and no less, from them.

CONTRIBUTORS

JOAN ACKER, associate professor of Sociology and director of the Center for the Sociological Study of Women at the University of Oregon, has published on the subjects of women and work, gender and class, and theoretical issues in the sociology of women. She spent most of 1981 as a visiting research scholar at the Swedish Working Life Institute (Arbetslivscentrum), Stockholm, where she studied sex equality and work democracy and consulted on research on women and sex equality.

BIANCA BECCALLI teaches labor sociology at the University of Milan. She has published extensively on the postwar Italian labor movement and most recently has conducted a study of the role of women in American and Italian trade unions. In 1979–1980 she had a German Marshall Fund Fellowship and spent a year at the Center for European Studies at Harvard.

SARAH BOSTON has held a variety of official positions in the Association of Cinematic, Television and Allied Technicians (ACTT) and since 1970 has worked as a freelance documentary film director for the British Broadcasting Corporation. Her publications include *Women Workers and the Trade Unions* (1980) and contributions, entitled "Equal Pay" and "Women's Work," to *Conditions of Illusion* (1974).

ALICE H. COOK, professor emerita of industrial and labor relations at Cornell University, has traveled widely to write on problems of working women in industrialized countries and is author, among other publications, of *The Working Mother: A Study of Problems and Programs in Nine Countries* (1978); *Working Women in Japan: Discrimination, Resistance and Reform*, with Hiroko Hayashi (1981); and "Women and Trade Unions" in the spring 1982 issue of *Equal Opportunity International* (London).

ARLENE KAPLAN DANIELS, Ph.D., University of California at Berkeley, is professor of sociology at Northwestern University and founded and then directed the Program on Women there from 1975 to 1980. She has coedited several collections, including *Hearth and Home: Images of Women in the Mass*

Media, with Gaye Tuchman and James Benét, and *Women and Work*, with Rachel Kahn-Hut and Richard Colvard, both published by Oxford University Press, and has a work on women as community volunteers forthcoming.

BRITA FOGED, Cand. Phil., Political Science, Aarhus University, 1976, has since 1977 been a researcher at the Aarhus Institute of History,working particularly on questions involving the labor market, trade unions, and women's role, with a special interest in part-time work. Her publications include "Kvindearbejde 1950–71" (1976); "HK's Kivindeopfattelse" in the *SFAH Yearbook* for 1978; and articles in *Kvinder i elektronikindustrien* (1976) and in *Deltid-Kvindetid* (1979).

ELINA HAAVIO-MANNILA received her doctorate in sociology at the University of Helsinki and is associate professor there. She has studied also at Northwestern University and the University of Minnesota in the United States. She has published many books and articles and is presently studying changes in the life patterns of families in Finland as a part of a European cross-national study, as well as writing a book on Scandinavian women in politics.

TADASHI HANAMI, Ph.D., Law School of Tokyo University, has been a visiting research scholar and professor at universities in West Germany, the United States, and Belgium. He is presently dean of the Law Faculty at Sophia University, Tokyo, a research officer in the Japan Institute of Labor, and a public commissioner on the Tokyo Metropolitan Labor Relations Commission. He has published many books and articles including "The Influence of ILO Standards on Law and Practice in Japan," *International Labour Review* (1981) and *Labor Law and Industrial Relations in Japan* (1979).

HARRIET HOLTER, professor of social psychology at the University of Oslo, also supervises research on women at the Norwegian Research Council. A member of the Royal Norwegian Academy of Science, she does research on industrial relations and work life with a recent emphasis on sex roles, the family, and social policy. Her main work in English is *Sex Roles and Social Structure* (1979). As chair of a group of young scholars doing research on women's relationships to each other, she published *Kvinner i fellesskap* (Women Together) in 1982.

DEBORAH SCHUSTER KING, B.S. in labor relations, Cornell University, has been a full-time trade unionist since 1964. She is currently Education and Research Director of District 1199, New England Health Care Employees Union. From 1973 to 1978 she lived in Ireland, where she worked as a labor educator with the Irish Transport and General Workers Union.

VAL R. LORWIN at his death in 1982 was emeritus professor of history, University of Oregon. He had been a journalist, a trade union activist, and a federal civil servant. He was the author of *The French Labor Movement* (1954), co-author and editor of *Labor and Working Conditions in Modern Europe* (1966), and author of "Trade Unions and Women: 'The Most Difficult Revolution,'" in B. E. Brown, ed., *Eurocommunism and Eurosocialism: The Left Confronts Modernity*" (1979).

MARGARET MARUANI, Ph.D., sociology, Institut d'Etudes Politiques, Paris, is presently assistant to the chair of the sociology of work department, Conservatoire National des Arts et Métiers, Paris. She has published *Les Syndicats à l'epreuve du féminisme* (Unions and the Challenge of Feminism), and *Le Temps des chemises: la grève qu'elles gardent au coeur* (The Time of the Shirts: The Strike That They Keep in Their Hearts).

ANNE OLSEN, Cand. Mag., Danish literature and history, 1974, has worked as a journalist since 1980. She has contributed to *Kvinder i elektronikindustrien* (1976) and is now employed by DM, an academic organization.

HELLE OTTE, Cand. Mag., history and art history, 1978, has since 1980 been associated with the Institute of Political Science, University of Aarhus. She is engaged in historical research on women's programs for equal pay as part of the women's liberation movement.

GUNNAR QVIST at his death in 1980 was professor at the University of Gothenburg, author of a number of works on the history of women in Sweden, and director of the university's research project on women in industrial society. He prepared the first draft of the chapter on Sweden in this volume. His death interrupted its completion.

BJØRG AASE SØRENSEN is a sociologist on the staff of the Norwegian Work Research Institute, a governmental agency devoted to change-oriented research on industrial democracy and work environment. She had a visiting fellowship at the University of Oregon in 1982.

BARBARA MAYER WERTHEIMER, who died just before publication of this volume, was professor of industrial and labor relations, Cornell University (New York City Extension Office), and director of the university's Institute on Women and Work. A long-time labor educator, she was the author of *We Were There: The Story of Working Women in America* (1977) and editor-author of *Labor Education for Women Workers* (1981). She was at work on the second volume of her narrative history of working women in the United States, *Our Century, Our Time: The Story of Working Women 1914 to the Present*.

INDEX

321